Self as Person in
Asian Theory and Practice

Self as Person in
Asian Theory and Practice

Edited by
Roger T. Ames
with
Wimal Dissanayake and **Thomas P. Kasulis**

STATE UNIVERSITY OF NEW YORK PRESS

The cover is a representation of an anonymous Ming dynasty (1368–1644) painting, *Former Confucian Worthies and Sages*, dating from c. 1460. It is a vertical scroll with ink and colors on silk, measuring 118 × 62 cm., and is reproduced here with the permission of Shanxi Provincial Museum. The assembly of scholars is a montage fusing remembered cultural heroes from the classics, representations of distinguished historical figures drawn from images available to the artist, and portraits of Ming dynasty contemporaries renowned for their literary and cultural contributions.

Published by
State University of New York Press, Albany

Printed in the United States of America

For information, address the State University of New York Press,
State University Plaza, Albany, NY 12246

Production by Ruth Fisher
Marketing by Theresa A. Swierzowski

Library of Congress Cataloging-in-Publication Data

Self as person in Asian theory and practice / edited by Roger T. Ames ;
    with Wimal Dissanayake and Thomas P. Kasulis.
        p.   cm.
    Includes index.
    ISBN 0-7914-1723-9 (alk. paper). — ISBN 0-7914-1724-7 (pbk. :
alk. paper)
    1. Self (Philosophy)—Asia. 2. Agent (Philosophy) I. Ames,
Roger T., 1947–   . II. Dissanayake, Wimal. III. Kasulis, Thomas
P., 1948–   .
B5015.S34S44   1994
126′.095—dc20   93-9297
                                                              CIP

10 9 8 7 6 5 4 3 2 1

Contents

Introduction

Roger T. Ames

Self as Person in Asian Theory and Practice is our sequel volume to *Self as Body in Asian Theory and Practice* (SUNY, 1992) and anticipates a third volume in the "self" series, *Self and Image in Asian Theory and Practice*, which is now in press. This present volume continues our cross-cultural and cross-disciplinary exploration of various notions of self that ground alternative cultural traditions.

This SUNY Press series of anthologies on self emerges out of a project initiated and organized at the East-West Center in Honolulu by Wimal Dissanayake, a research associate at the center. Over the past few years, relatively small seminars—approximately twenty scholars on each occasion—have been convened at the center to bring experts representing different cultures and different disciplinary perspectives into conversation. Most of the articles included here were selected from papers presented and discussed in this forum. A major criterion in the selection process was to find a balance between reflection on those specific practices that define cultural differences, and the application of emergent theories once shaped and abstracted as instruments of explanation for cultural practices.

The perhaps uncontroversial starting point of the investigation of self is that different cultural experiences have produced importantly different conceptions of self and that these different conceptions of self need to be factored into any responsible evaluation of contemporary issues and problems. To actively address seemingly global issues as diverse as the promotion of human rights or the resolution of sexism in ways that avoid the familiar though often inadvertent lapse into cultural chauvinism, alternative cultural perspectives that begin from differing conceptions of self and self-realization must be fully articulated and respected.

Although the recognition that alternative cultural experiences produce different notions of self and hence different expectations for self-fulfillment might be uncontroversial, the question of what value we give this difference still remains. A. N. Whitehead in *Modes of Thought* makes a distinction between "matters-of-fact" and "importance."[1] This distinction can be best understood by illustration. We might, for example, ask the question, Is formal logical reasoning a universal characteristic of high cultures? The answer is not simple. Cultures are rich and diverse, and where it is indisputably a *matter-of-fact* that in the later Mohist canons of the Chinese tradition, for example, we can find some commitment to formalized logic, we must ask the further question, What is the *importance* of formal logic to the development of the Chinese philosophic tradition as a whole? If the answer to this second question is that logic has had at best only an incidental influence on Chinese philosophy, it can change the value of the assertion that formal logic developed in China from a clear demonstration of universality to a demonstration that what we, as a tradition, have taken as a necessary condition for responsible philosophical evidence has had only passing notice in one of humanity's most developed cultures. In other words, the relative unimportance of logic for China, far from encouraging claims of sameness, underscores the radical degree of difference that obtains among cultural traditions. In this case, the exception proves the rule.

In exploring alternative conceptions of 'self', what value do we give to universal assumptions about 'humanity' that will guarantee at least the necessary minimum of cross-cultural respect and, with it, the very possibility of comparison; and what value do we give to radical claims about difference that will hold cultural reductionism at bay and preserve the richness and diversity of competing cultures? In recent times, among those of us who take it upon ourselves to investigate other peoples, there seem to be two very different temperaments and agendas. Some students of alternative cultures are inclined to believe that, when all is said and done, human beings are pretty much alike; others do not. Some believe that behind all of the divergences, there surely must be universal problems that transcend cultural differences; others believe that behind the more obvious and uninteresting physiological and other apparently acultural similarities—one head, two ears, and so on—there are profound and exotic differences that derive from culture-bound ways of thinking and living.[2] Some believe that failing to regard the commonality as most important is to deny the alternative cultures their humanity; others believe that to assert such an essential commonality is to deny alternative cultures their uniqueness. While the contributors to this volume certainly line up on both sides of the distinction between an emphasis on sameness and an emphasis on difference, those authors representing non-Western traditions would argue that a different degree of emphasis on sameness and difference is itself a distinguishing characteristic among cultures. At the same time, there has been a sea change occurring within the Western academy, beginning at its philosophic center, which has brought strident universalistic claims about methodologies and architectonic orders under careful scrutiny and revived an interest in the currents and swells of particular histories and cultures.

It is because this tension between sameness and difference remains unresolved among cultures and within the Western tradition itself that we have divided the editorial tasks in such a way as to allow for full diversity of opinion. Each of the three editors has different areas of cultural specialization—Wimal Dissanayake (South Asia), Thomas P. Kasulis (Japan), and Roger T. Ames (China)—and each has accepted responsibility for editing and introducing those chapters within his geographical region. This division of labor guarantees not only a plurality of cultural perspectives on broad themes but also a plurality of individual perspectives on the more specific issues rehearsed in a collection of very different essays. These introductions are a further opportunity to lift the architecture of each section to the surface and compare themes shared among the various authors.

Although all three editors have participated fully in the major editorial decisions resulting in the compilation of this anthology, it was decided that Ames would be first editor and would be responsible for the overall coherence of this effort. To this end, Ames has introduced the opening section that brings Western and the non-Western traditions into discussion. It is in the effort to contextualize the particular philosophical explorations that further opportunities for philosophizing emerge.

Mattison Mines's essay, "Conceptualizing the Person," is being reproduced by permission of the American Anthropological Association from *American Anthropologist* 90, no. 3 (1988).

NOTES

1. A. N. Whitehead, *Modes of Thought* (New York: Free Press, 1938): 1–19.

2. A. C. Graham makes this point in his review of Benjamin J. Schwartz's *The World of Thought in Ancient China* (Cambridge: Harvard University Press, 1985), *Times Literary Supplement*, July 18, 1986. Schwartz is a relatively clear and accomplished example of the former category.

PART ONE

A Basis for Engagement

INTRODUCTION TO PART ONE

Roger T. Ames

Robert C. Solomon, in the opening essay of this anthology, provides the reader with a necessary context for considering the concepts of 'self' and 'self-realization' in some of the non-Western traditions. He rehearses the history of personal identity as this cluster of problems has been framed within the Western philosophic dialectic, providing an overview of the various generations of formulation and response that the disparate notions of self have generated, from Descartes's "thinking substance" and the "transcendental ego" of German idealism to the "brain-in-the-vat" excursus of contemporary analytic philosophy. In sketching out the contribution of major European philosophers in the process through which theories of self have gradually taken on their conceptual shape and content, Solomon worries over the tension between acknowledging cultural specificity and the predilection of systematic philosophy to brandish universalistic claims.

Solomon is impatient with the irrelevancies of professional philosophy and its self-indulgent "puzzles"; at the same time he is anxious to underscore the centrality of questions concerning personal identity in every moment of ordinary life. What is at stake for most of the modern philosophers taken within the context of the Enlightenment project is nothing less than the defense of individual autonomy and moral responsibility.

Against the background of a historical introduction to the conceptual vocabulary and major themes of the anthology, Solomon dwells on several issues which have some promise for cross-cultural engagement. He emphasizes, for example, the irreducibly social aspect of self: Sartre's "Being-for-others" where self, dependent upon status, requires recognition. He then turns to the question of "character" as it is embedded in virtue ethics: How is character inscribed? Is personal identity reducible to a set of manifest character traits, and if so, what becomes of free will? What does it mean to be "in character" and "out of character"? Again, with death being a boundary condition of some sort on self, why is such disproportionate weight given to the way in which one exits this world in defining one's personal identity?

Using Nietzsche to challenge assumptions about the "unity of virtues," and by extension, the "unitary self" that must be addressed by virtue ethicists, Solomon anticipates both Amélie Rorty's contribution in setting a direction for contemporary Western philosophic reflection on personal identity, and several of the Asian traditions that are inclined toward a "field of selves" notion of self.

In service to the multicultural dimensions of this anthology, Solomon turns to the underlying assumption of most of our authors, namely, that the construction of 'self' is a cultural product. He sees the movement toward cultural and epochal specificity as a welcome opportunity for philosophic reflection, both enriching the Western discussion by importing alternative models of self, and, in the comparison, bringing the diverse Western conceptions into clearer focus. At the same time, there are power differentials that can have catastrophic effects on world cultures. In his discussion of the ongoing encounter and exchange between European civilization and the Maoris (and alternative examples to the Maori situation are legion), he identifies the problem of forced redefinition as an impoverishing consequence of these same bicultural interactions.

This volume properly continues with an essay by Amélie Oksenberg Rorty, a scholar who has been at the center of recent philosophical discussions on the self within the Western tradition and who has written extensively on this subject.[1] Rorty is a philosophical archaeologist, and her essay here, like most of her work, is deeply concerned with exposing the layers of philosophical history. Her commitment to the history of an idea makes two important contributions to our project. First, her historical excavation discloses the richness and radical diversity of particular strata within the Western philosophic dialectic and, in so doing, registers a caution to those comparativists who, with broad sweeps, would caricature Western philosophy by defining it too narrowly in service to superficial and facile comparisons with other cultures. Second, in pursuing her own philosophical credo— a sustained commitment to the primacy of the particular—Rorty sounds a warning against the familiar problem of equivocation— philosophers talking past one another because of uncritical assumptions about vocabulary and conceptual content. In tracing out careful distinctions among passions, emotions, and sentiments from Aristotle to Rousseau, Rorty seeks to describe dramatic shifts and transitions in what the West as a cultural tradition has meant by a conception of self—both individuated, autonomous self, and civil self. Rorty concludes, again as is signatory of her work, by pointing out directions for continued exploration. Rather than decrying the seeming failure of Rousseau and modern philosophy to resolve into unity the sorely divided and conflicted "autonomous citizen," which, against the best instincts of the tradition, philosophical reflection over time had inadvertently constructed, Rorty reflects on and celebrates this unresolved and unresolvable complexity as a defining condition of any robust conception of self. In her own words, "the truth of the matter is that we are multiple selves: we are wild animal creatures; we long for, and are committed to identifying ourselves with a universalized rational autonomy. And even in the best of politics, we are also social subjects defined by the particular affectional relations that carry the dialectics of power relations in their wake."[2]

John C. Maraldo, a comparative philosopher whose research has focused primarily on contemporary Japanese philosophy, provides a first link between Rorty's historical reflections on modern conceptions of self and notions of self predominating in non-Western cultures. The starting point for Maraldo's study is the claim by Shimazaki Tōson, an early twentieth-century Japanese novelist, that a reading of Rousseau was the occasion for him to discover a 'self', an entity of which he had previously been unaware. The question then, is, Does Tōson discover Rousseau's 'self'?

Maraldo, like Rorty, begins by distinguishing the objective and superordinate "self-conscious self" of Descartes and Locke from the subsequent and much more subjective "self-consciousness" of Rousseau. What still makes Rousseau's sense of self resolutely Western and modern, however, is that it assumes an inner, isolated interiority accessible only through one's own reflexive consciousness. In an effort to uncover the full historical and cultural texture of Tōson's newly discovered self, Maraldo then compares the notions of self and, by extension, self-revelation, found in Rousseau's *Confessions*, with the Confucian Arai Hakuseki's *Told Round a Brushwood Fire* (*Oritaku shiba no ki*). Ostensibly both works are autobiographical, but where the *Confessions* probes into "delicate matters" to reveal Rousseau's "secrets of the soul," *Told Round a Brushwood Fire* provides a more sociological account of Hakuseki's life almost entirely devoid of the details of a psychic interior. Personal meaning for Hakuseki is manifest in a person's interactions with others, not in the private self of introspection. Maraldo attributes these differences in autobiographical focus to a contrast between the strong influence the Reformation's exaltation of the individual's inner life had on Rousseau, and the social expectations placed on the individual that were expressed by Hakuseki's work.

But Hakuseki's assumptions about self constitutes only one model among many available within the Japanese tradition. To illustrate the plurality and range of such models, Maraldo selects Hakuin's personal story in *Wild Ivy* (*Itsumadegusa*) of his own impassioned development from a "fear-obsessed child to a fearless teacher." The story line of Hakuin's autobiographical *Wild Ivy*, reminiscent of Rousseau in its personal detail and emotion, is extended by reference to his subsequent works, illustrating both the role of practice and the open-endedness of the Zen conception of True Self. Like Rousseau, Hakuin expresses those inner feelings recollected from the critical periods of his life. The purpose of these recollections, however, is not the same as Rousseau's. Hakuin views those inner dynamics not as his true self but as turmoils through which he has had to pass in order to achieve enlightenment. For Hakuin the True Self is not an object for self-reflection but a process of expression.

The self that Tōson claims to have discovered is like Hakuin's in its search for inner freedom, like Hakuseki's in its desire for moral justification, and like Rousseau's in its expression of conscience. But in the end, as an ambivalent self narrated into existence through Tōson's particular writing, it contrasts with all three. Given the distinct models of self that are created through different narrative practices, autobiography must be considered a pluralistic genre.

Maraldo concludes his exploration with a tension between particular selves and universal paradigms of self: while self in any tradition is unquestionably shaped by historically and culturally conditioned life-activity, each of these thinkers, from East and West, is seeking to express a more universal model of what it is to be human, one that reaches beyond their own times and circumstances. For Maraldo, this universality is most fully revealed only when the self remains unabstracted and is articulated within its appropriate life practices.

NOTES

1. See, for example, Amélie Oksenberg Rorty, ed., *The Identities of Persons* (Berkeley and Los Angeles: University of California Press, 1976); Brian P. McLaughlin and Amélie Oksenberg Rorty, *Perspectives on Self-Deception* (Berkeley and Los Angeles: University of California Press, 1988); Amélie Oksenberg Rorty, *Mind in Action* (Boston: Beacon Press, 1988).

2. See below, p. 0000.

1

Recapturing Personal Identity

Robert C. Solomon

The problem of personal identity is one of those problems often believed to be universal and perennial in philosophy. Every human being has some conception of him- or herself, and that conception can be called into question. But in many of its currently most-argued versions the so-called problem of personal identity is actually quite localized and only a couple of hundred years old, a provincial upstart in the Hellenic-Judeo-Christian philosophical tradition. The problem is easily, if misleadingly, summarized: Who am I? The answer, of course, is, it depends who's asking. But this seemingly simple quest for reference and identification suggests a number of distinct and quite different questions, with different presuppositions and, accordingly, provoking very different cultural and conceptual responses.

Taken at face value, the question "Who am I?" would seem to be a request for a name, appropriate, perhaps, after an accident or a long, drugged sleep. The name in turn implies a history and a place in a social nexus. In moments of moral crisis, the same question can be a cry of despair or deep existential confusion: "Who am I?" asks, What am I now to do? My history and my social place and position have been called into question. What concerns me is not what I have been but what I should be. Such existential crises evoke the angst much celebrated by Kierkegaard, Heidegger, Sartre, and all of those millions of Ericsonian adolescents. On the other hand, the problem of personal identity might be taken more generally to mean, What is it to be a human being? The answer to this question is built into virtually every language, if not every philosophical tradition, oral and mythological as well as scientist and epistemological; and in most cultural contexts, not excluding Europe and North America, to be a human being means

7

to be a person much like us, where "much like us" refers in one instance to Aristotle's fellow male Athenian aristocrats, in another to Clifford Geertz's Javanese, in another to George Bush's faithful Republicans, and in still another to the Chinese. "Human being" is not a biological category. It is a clumsy and often oppressive political weapon.

Taken back to the level of the individual, the problem of personal identity might be, What is it to be a self? That question readily invites an ontological or phenomenological response, a discourse on the transcendental unity of consciousness or Cartesian introspection, but it should also suggest the urgency of a cross-cultural and comparative quest. Insofar as the self—and one's concept of self—is socially constructed, there is every reason (and now volumes of research) to suggest that different peoples have different self-conceptions. So asked, the question is thus incomplete. It should rather be formulated, What is it to be a self in Chinese society? What is it to be a self in Yoruba society? What is it to be a self in Kaluli society? What is it to be a self in *bourgeois* Parisian society? What is it to be a self in Utku society? But, again, the question, What is it to be a self in Chinese / Yoruba / Kaluli / French / Utku society? should not be assumed to be merely descriptive anthropology. It slips easily into the question, What is it to be a person?—an explicitly ethical notion. The debate over abortion and animal rights, for example, often turns on whether fetuses and some vertebrates (at least) are persons. The question of personhood accordingly commands considerable attention in cultures that have suffered a severe dislocation, for example, by way of colonialism or by recently breaking out of traditional feudal or other hierarchical caste systems. There the problem of personal identity becomes nothing less than the philosophical quest for legitimacy and dignity.

Back in the academy, however, the problem of personal identity has become primarily an ontological puzzle—What is it to remain "the same" person over time?—and, secondarily, the more particular empirical inquiry, What is it to be this particular human being who I am? The first of these is sometimes distinguished as the problem of self-identity (as opposed to the secondary question of personal identity), although the answer to the one question obviously serves to answer the other as well. The ontological puzzle, like most of the puzzles that have defined Anglo-American philosophy in the last half of this century, invites ingenious moves and countermoves and has proven to be remarkably intractable. Because it has turned out to be so difficult, it is therefore considered a serious philosophical question, and it is the ontological puzzle that is in vogue today. It is often coupled with the more general problem of identity: What is it for anything to be "the same" over time? And to test the limits of both our ordinary concept of identity and our extraordinary philosophical imaginations, the problem gets defined in terms of the darndest transformations, far stranger than any Hindu or Greek—or even Kafka—ever thought up. John Locke began the tradition, wondering off-handedly what one would say if one man's memories were transposed to another person's mind. But in the past few decades, Bernard Williams, among others, has enriched the example to extravagant dimensions. Theoretical questions on mind and brain transplants have become extremely popular with philosophers. A generic example: A's brain and consequently A's memory, personality, and sense of personal identity are put in B's body while B's brain and consequently B's memory, personality, and sense of personal identity are put in A's body. Such mind and body swaps are sometimes accompanied with tantalizing questions, for example, what would you say if confronted with an extremely painful operation, to be performed on one's body without anesthetic but while it is "occupied" by someone else?[1] One can imagine how imaginative such discussions can become, and some of the best and brightest philosophers in the Anglo-American tradition have lept into the ring.[2] By the 1980s, when, incidentally, the Greatest Country in the World was ruled by a man with no brain, the idea that A's brain and consequently A's memory, personality, and sense of personal identity might be fully functioning in B's body had become a philosophical (and science fiction) commonplace. Who, then, was whom? Philosophers were shocked and impressed when it was pointed out that our ordinary conception of a person was not really equipped to deal with such circumstances.[3]

In the explosion of multicultural concerns and tumult of self-identity that defines the beginning of the twenty-first century, however, one would think that such effete intellectual puzzles would give way to those problems of self and personal identity that are such fertile ground for cross-cultural and comparative philosophical investigation and understanding. Instead, there has continued to be an almost obsessive exclusion of any but the (presumably universal) ontological version of the problem in the mainstream philosophy journals, despite the fact that, according to one of the best and brightest, it has become "dessicated."[4] Philosophical problems don't die, of course, and they are rarely resolved. But they do get ever more tedious. The technical wizardry currently employed in solving the problem of self-identity is evidence not of progress but of advanced conceptual osteoporosis. But given the fact that the question of personal identity continues to be a subject that fascinates nonphilosophers and would also seem to provide the philosophical key to a worldwide philosophical interchange, we might well retrace our steps and ask how that question has become so uninteresting, a mere puzzle, a professional "brainteaser" (if that is an appropriate expression in this context).[5] What is it that nonphilosophers find so exciting? What, after all, is the question? How has the debate gotten so restricted? Indeed, even in France—only twenty-two miles removed from some Anglo-American academies—the concept of a singular self that is taken for granted in the current debates has been fragmented and buried along with "the author" and the illusion of "presence." What are we to make of the notion of a multiplicity of selves, of the notion of "no-self"? Indeed, what should we make of the thesis that in some societies, the self and personal identity have little or nothing to do with introspection and memories but everything to do with one's place in the family, the group, the community? But why should this inward-looking Cartesian paradigm of selfhood be taken as essential and presumed to be universal? Why should we expect that the concept of a person—or the criteria for "the same" person— should be the same for a Buddhist and a Muslim, a Hindu and a Taoist, a monk and a Wall Street broker? What are we to make of the mythological-tribal concept of personhood among the Yoruba?[6] How important is reflection in the conception of self? Is it essential? In Western philosophy, there is the facile fusion of self-reference, self-consciousness, thoughtful self-description, and personal reflection.[7] And, as in so many self-referential matters, provocative if not profound insights are sacrificed to the tantalizing temptations of the paradox. And where we once had what seemed to be a perennial problem, we now have an intellectual Rubik's Cube, a puzzle.

The Puzzle's Progress

The problem of self-identity, in its current incarnation, can be plausibly traced back to peculiar notions in Descartes (that one's identity is first of all that of a "thinking substance") and Locke (that one's personal identity is bound up with memory). The total extent of published discussion *in* both authors is considerably less than ten pages, but contemporary elaborations *of* their theses fill department libraries. The current argument is filtered through Hume, of course, who declared somewhat paradoxically that when he looked into himself there was no self to be found, complicating the picture further by casting his skeptical eye on the identity through time of even the most mundane objects. After Hume, both the notions of self and identity began a long swim in the murky waters of German idealism, where they gained transcendental and eventually absolute status ("Himself as everything! How can Mrs. Fichte stand it?"[8]) The current crop of philosophers have for the most part avoided those Gothic transformations and confined themselves to the tried and true puzzles raised by Descartes, Locke, and Hume. Perhaps this is a mistake. If nothing else, Kant, Fichte, Hegel, and Schopenhauer force us to reexamine the concept of 'personal identity' from a radically new perspective. Suppose the self is indeterminate and personal identity is not necessarily to be equated with the individual person. The seemingly obvious fact of our individual identity, which Descartes, Locke, Hume, and most contemporary theorists take for granted, is thrown to the wind in German philosophy. And once that becomes open to question, then the notion of personal identity does indeed become interesting.

The notions of the self and personal identity do not give rise to just those puzzles and paradoxes of which G. E. Moore complained, "I find that all of my problems come only from other philosophers." Every American teenager can provide a heartfelt if philosophically ill-informed survey of the problem. Every instance of ethnic strife both home and abroad raises the issue, and every criminal case more or less depends on it. Indeed, every intimate relationship calls personal identity into question, as do pregnancy, serious accidents, and illnesses; the loss of one's job; the death of a loved one; or that *eigentlich* experience that Heidegger called *"SeinzumTode."* Some philosophers might quickly object, "but those are not *peculiarly philosophical* problems of self-identity," to which there are a number of appropriate replies, foremost among them a shrug of the shoulders. If indeed we are going to put the question of personal identity back into a "broadly naturalistic conception of the world" and consider "the more interesting and specific conceptions that have guided practical life," these very real contexts are indeed properly (though not peculiarly) philosophical. Looking back to the "peculiarly philosophical" context in which the question(s) of self and personal identity arose, I think that a considerably broadened view of the problem is justified.

Descartes, Locke, and Hume, or at least Descartes and Locke, were not particularly fascinated by philosophical "puzzles," that is, brainteasers of a "peculiarly philosophical" kind. They raised them up in passing, but they had bigger quarry in mind. They were concerned with a defense of the very notion of reason (which in its ordinary meaning did not arouse any particular excitement about the distinction between empirical and more rationalist procedures).[9] They were anxious to defend the autonomy of the individual against the authorities that be. They were, in their different ways, exploring the realm of "subjectivity" and defending the claim that in personal thought and experience could be found genuine knowledge. Descartes and Locke were concerned to prove, yet once again, the existence of God. Locke and Hume intended to provide a comprehensive theory of human nature and establish the universality of man [*sic*]. Hume, of course, challenged the limits of reason far more vigorously than his two predecessors, but his skepticism can be understood only within the embrace of the Enlightenment project of which he was so much a part. Puzzles about self and personal identity were of interest only within the context of a general philosophy that placed great importance and perhaps impossible weight on the notion of individual autonomy. Even Hume seemed quite happy to forget his doubts about the self within a few pages of his paradoxical observation that he could not find one. Kant, who followed, resolved Hume's paradox by splitting the lingering Lockean distinction between personal ("empirical") and self (now "transcendental") identity.[10] But if we are not to be satisfied with puzzles, that does not mean that we should search for profundities either. However attractive the dark waters of German idealism may on occasion seem, this is not the place to scuba dive in the obscure.[11]

Instead, I want to outline four different—very ordinary but also important—philosophical concerns where the philosophical investigation of the self and personal identity is in order. No doubt there are puzzles to be found in all of them, which may serve as bait for philosophers who feel uncomfortable very far outside of the bounds of narrowly epistemic justification. Whether any of these questions are "peculiarly philosophical" is not my concern, except insofar as I would want to defend the interdisciplinary status and multicultural import of such questions as their virtue rather than their vice. The first question remains fairly conservative, well within the bounds of philosophical and political orthodoxy, and simply raises to a somewhat more abstract (but not nonempirical) level the "existential" questions that are involved in any "identity crisis," whether in the growing pains of adolescence or the *angst* of later life crises. To what extent, however, is this much celebrated *angst* the product of a uniquely Western view, the painful consequence of an excessive emphasis on individual autonomy? And to what extent—as evidenced by the Japanese enthusiasm for existentialist philosophy, for example—is it a question with larger and growing dimensions? The second follows quite naturally from the recently renewed interest in what has come to be called "virtue ethics," which, often using Aristotle (less often Nietzsche) as a guide, emphasizes considerations of "character" rather than moral or utilitarian rules or principles in ethics. Again, it is a question with clear multicultural implications. Confucius, most obviously, taught a vision of the good life that was throughly defined by considerations of good character and the virtues that make up good character. Less obviously, many tribal ethics place character at the center of their moral concerns. (The ancient inhabitants of the island of Maui used to throw the umbilical cords of their newborn infants into the crater of the then active volcano Haleakala, in order to ensure the honesty of their children.) The third question raises more radical issues about individuality and the social construction of the self. In current debates about multiculturalism and the welcome new interest in other cultures and traditions of thought—not just in philosophy but in literature and the social sciences—the idea of alternative conceptions of selfhood, as "interdependent" rather than "independent," have been much discussed.[12] It is most unfortunate that so few of our most prestigious philosophers and philosophy journals have joined in that discussion, rife as it is with conceptual confusions and inflammatory hyperbole.[13] Finally, I want to focus on the perhaps embarrassing matter of love, which since the *Symposium* has found an enormous philosophical audience but only an occasional philosopher. In particular, I want to raise some questions concerning what Amélie Rorty has called the "permeability" of love, the fact that in love one changes his or her conception of (his or her own) personal identity in response to the features of the beloved. Indeed, love is, I have suggested and will suggest here, just such a sense of "shared identity," as Plato's Aristophanes in his well-known allegory imagined so many years ago.

Personal Identity and the Existential Social Self

What is an "identity crisis"? It is not, to begin with, the obvious, the sudden realization that the body one inhabits is not one's own. To be sure, such scenarios, for instance in Kafka's classic *Metamorphosis* or in Justin Leiber's philosophically delectable novel *Beyond Rejection*, raise all sorts of tantalizing questions (particularly when the switch in question is trans-species or trans-sexual), but these questions are far less concerned with the general idea of identity than the details of coping. The question, who is Gregor Samsa? does not arise in its preeminently philosophical form. Gregor Samsa is the unfortunate narrator of the tale, the horribly transformed family member, the petty functionary who cannot figure out how he can possibly make it to the office today. The question of personal identity and the subdued horror, from start to finish, have to do with the concrete problems of one might continue to call the "empirical" self, not with the "transcendental" narrative frame. How does one turn one's enormous, inflexible body over?[14] How is one to think of oneself with ("in"?) a giant insect's body? How does one deal with the horrified screams and disgust of a dear sister? How can one deal with one's dysfunctional family, knowing that (through no fault of one's own)[15] one is responsible? What is one to do with long-habituated conceptions of oneself as a loyal, hard-working employee, a good provider and an innocuous, perfectly ordinary citizen?

An identity crisis is, unhelpfully, confusion about who one is. It is not, for the most part, self-contained. Waking up as a giant insect in a world all his own, Gregor might still have to cope with the problem of getting off of his back, but the fact that he has turned into an insect is no longer a source of embarrassment or an obstacle to social success. Indeed, it might never occur to him at all, for where would the concept "insect" come from? An adolescent is at "that awkward age" not so much because his or her body is out of control as because one's social position—no longer a child, incompetent as an adult—is intolerable. An identity crisis is a social crisis. That is why Jean-Paul Sartre, after three hundred pages on the complex dialectic between Being "in-itself" and "for itself," "facticity" and "transcendence," insists on introducing "Being-for-Others" as a "primordial" and "not derivative" category of Being.[16] In just plain English, what one *is* is a function of not only the facts about one and what one thinks of oneself but also what others think of one and what they make of those facts. Indeed, one can read the third part of *L'etre et le neant* as a systematic undoing of what has been going on in the previous two parts. The facts that constrain personal identity are neither given nor determined by the subject. They are a matter of social construal, dependent on the context as well as the (often malevolent) motives of others. (Thus Garcin, a character in Sartre's play *Huis clos*, try as he might to construe himself as a hero despite his final cowardly performance in front of the firing squad, finds himself ultimately the victim of his two eternal roommates, Estelle, who could not care less about his *ex post facto* identity crisis, and Inez, who despises him.)

This picture of mutually construed personhood is borrowed, of course, from Hegel (from whom some of the awkward Teutonic terminology is also taken). In his "master and slave" parable in the *Phenomenology*, Hegel suggests (the text is too understated to do more than "suggest") that personhood essentially depends on what he calls "recognition" by another. The suggestion yields two philosophical theses; one very general; one, which Hegel pursues, more particular. The general suggestion is that one would not be a self at all without mutual recognition, and this recognition obviously refers to oneself as publicly embodied (as opposed to the Cartesian model of introspective self-identification). The argument is rendered somewhat more complicated by virtue of the fact that Hegel refers to the individuals involved as "self-consciousnesses," indicating that they already have some sense of self-awareness,[17] but the primacy of recognition of *persons* (human beings) rather than the purely mental self is evident enough, as it would be many years later for P. F. Strawson and Mark Johnston.[18]

It is Hegel's second suggestion, however, that he actually follows up in the text and employs as the vehicle for several subsequent twists and turns of the dialectic. This second suggestion is that the self and self-consciousness are first of all a matter of *status*, and status can be obtained, again, only through mutual recognition. In the stripped-down world of the parable, the proto-persons engaged in mutual recognition have not much to rely on, since they are presumably without social rank, bank accounts, a wardrobe, good upbringing, philosophical wit, or any of the other pedestrian virtues by which we compare and measure ourselves. So, Hegel says, they fight, "to the death" if necessary, but, of course, the death of one would defeat the aim of the other, namely, to be recognized. Hegel then describes the curious inversion that confuses all questions of status and, consequently, compels both master and slave to more philosophical attempts at self-understanding.[19] But the general point is this: personal self-identity is not just the abstraction, 'self-consciousness'. It is concrete and it is social (even when it perversely rejects both the concrete and the social, as in the subsequent chapters on romanticism, "the Law of the Heart" and "the Way of the World"). Our identity is never just as a person, a human being, or an organism of a particular animal species; it is as a *particular* person, a particular social being with particular features, virtues and vices. In Mark Johnston's words, anything less is but "the dry articulation of a vague generality," or as Hegel would say, "an empty universal."

An identity crisis, then, is not just confusion about who one is. It is an inevitable result of our mutually construed personhood. If the identity of the self is always underdetermined, as Sartre argued, and if the determination of that identity always rests in part with the sometimes competitive and often noncooperative recognition of others, as both Hegel and Sartre (not to mention familiar experience) suggest, then personal identity proves to be a spectacularly dynamic conception, particularly prone to philosophical prompting. Hegel's grand conception of oneself as *Geist*, Sartre's harsh conception of consciousness as "for-itself" and inescapably responsible for the world it lives in have been powerful incentives for those struggling with an adequate conception of self (although the message is more likely engendered by AA or EST than by way of the original texts of a serious philosopher). So, too, one thinks of many serious philosophers, including not only Hegel and Sartre but also Hobbes and Rousseau and Hume (despite his "self" doubts) who have contributed to this literature of personal identity and changed the way we think of ourselves. For all of them, identity is not just a puzzle to be solved. It is our shared human existence that needs conceptual shaping.

Personal Identity and Virtue Ethics

Virtue ethics depends on the intelligibility of the concept of 'virtue', which in turn, as a "state of character," depends on the adequacy of some special but rarely spelled-out sense of "character." Too often, character is taken to be just a collection of more or less coherent traits, which in turn are analyzed as dispositions to act in certain ways. To be sure, such traits are by no means wooden, mere reactions that are oblivious to context and more or less "automatic." Indeed, one of the primary traits of character insisted upon by virtue ethicists ever since Aristotle is *judgment*, which means precisely this sensitivity to context such that courage, for example, manifests itself in very different actions when facing a hostile mob, on the one hand, or a malignant tumor, on the other. But the concept of character as a collection of more or less coherent traits is inadequate, particularly given some of the considerations concerning the mutual determination and indeterminacy of personal identity above. Is a person a collection of more-or-less coherent traits, or do these traits depend to a considerable extent on the construal of others? (What is charming in one society is repulsive in another. What is witty in the philosophy seminar may be tedious and tiresome in the kitchen.) Does a person's character determine his or her behavior, as many defenders of "compatibilism" in discussions of "the free-will problem" have suggested (including Hume), or do we need to make room for the spontaneous gesture, the unexpected "act of will," behavior "out of character" which may become, nevertheless, clearly and perhaps even paradigmatically the hallmark of a person's self-identity?[20]

This is not the place to take on the seemingly interminable problem of free will, but an expression often used by both compatibilists and virtue ethicists, that an act "flows from a person's character," is one worth critical scrutiny. To be sure, we usually understand exactly what that metaphor means. A person has been brought up to be generous. He or she frequently has generous thoughts. He or she tends to perform generous actions "spontaneously," without deliberation or hesitation. (Indeed, deliberation, while it may be a philosophical virtue, is almost always evidence that one may not have the virtue in question.) Generosity "flows" from one's character in the sense that one does what one is used to doing, what inclination dictates doing, what seems perfectly "natural" for that person in that situation. No "act of Will" is called for, no conscious "push" or nagging reminder. A person acting "in character" does exactly what we would expect him or her to do. So understood, a person's identity can readily be comprehended as a collection of traits, from which predictable actions flow as freely as rain from a darkened cloud.

It does not follow, however, that "flowing from" is a causal notion, or the manifestation of an inherent disposition, or indeed anything other than a metaphor suggesting "meeting (and not disturbing) our expectations." But what of those cases in which the action in question does not "flow" from but rather flatly contradicts the person's established character? It will not do to simply deny the possibility of such an action. The problem is to account for what appear to be such actions. But the question here is one not of free will but of personal identity. From that point of view, how do we construe such behavior? The answer, however, is not quickly forthcoming. Sometimes we celebrate it, change our opinion of the person, and, consequently, our praise (or blame) changes him or her as well. Sometimes we dismiss it as an aberration of some curiosity, perhaps, but of no importance to our estimation of character. Most of the time we decide simply to wait and see what follows. Which way we go has much to do with the importance of the action in question, the ordinariness of the circumstances, the power of our prior expectations, the role and status of the agent in our company, and whether we will have to rely on the same person in similar circumstances in the future. So, too, when an act has magnificent or devastating consequences, it is difficult to dismiss it as insignificant (regarding the character of the agent) no matter how hard it is to explain or incorporate into our prior picture of the person. If, on the other hand, we with equal uncertainty find ourselves needing a similarly dramatic response in the future, we may well be reticent about shifting our expectations and our judgment of the hero-of-the-day's character. We will celebrate the response but withhold our praise of his or her virtue.

In extreme situations, for instance, the circumstances of combat or life-and-death emergencies, people sometimes perform remarkable feats that could not possibly have been predicted on the basis of their more mundane, day-to-day behavior. Accordingly, such behavior may not be exactly "out of character," even though it goes against what we might well have expected. We have not yet had the opportunity to estimate their character in extreme situations. But this already raises a serious problem about the seemingly monolithic concept of character: character depends on context. If we can have different and divergent views of a person's character in "ordinary" life and in extreme situations, we should at least be suspicious that a person's character might vary from the classroom to the bedroom to the office and the frenzy of the streets. And do we want to say that these are merely different "aspects" of character? How does one individuate characters, and why should we suppose that they are, as in the orthodox notion of self-identity, distributed one to a customer? But if character is contextual and segregated into different aspects of a person, then haven't we lost much of what we wanted of character and personal identity too? "He's quite a character on the squash courts." Perhaps. But then it is hard to see how virtue ethics can provide much of an alternative to the option of evaluating a person's actions on the basis of consequences or conformity to rational principles.

What we have been describing, however, is *our* estimation of *another's* character; but personal identity, regardless of our philosophical approach or sympathies, is not primarily an other-regarding question. It is self-regarding, a matter (in part, at least) of self-estimation, a matter to be considered from the first person, not the second- or third-person standpoint. This point stands quite independently of the thesis that self-identity is a matter of mutual recognition (which is why both Hegel and Sartre insist that they are doing "phenomenology"). But this introduces a predictable twist into the relation of character to personal identity. Character, as usually understood, is a factual matter. Character is a question of what in fact a person will do in such-and-such situations, and presumably there is some fact about him or her—summarized as a "trait"—that explains why he or she will do it. There are the usual problems about the status and nature of dispositions and how they serve as explanations, of course, but they are not in question here. The problem is rather that self-identity is not simply the recognition of one's own character. Indeed, self-recognition may even go against the virtues that supposedly constitute one's character. This is why, for example, some virtue ethicists insist so strongly on the "spontaneous" and nondeliberative nature of virtuous action, not simply to underscore their insistence that an act must "flow" from a person's character, but to further insist that the virtue in question is a virtue precisely because it is not the product of thought and reflection. A person who thinks to himself, as he gives to charity, I am a generous person (not to mention, What a generous person I am) is *thereby* thought to be less generous. A person who primes herself for action with, "I've got to have courage" thereby shows herself to be less than courageous. Of course there are limits to this diminution of virtue, and only someone wholly steeped in what Hume called "the monkish virtues" would insist that such implicit self-praise or self-prompting undermines or erases the virtue in question (which raises special problems, well-recorded in the history of Christian psychology, about such self-conscious virtues as humility). But it is a plain fact that generous people often do not recognize their generosity and courageous people do not acknowledge their behavior as brave. Their sense of their own identity, then, is quite distinct from the attributions of character that are due them from others. But then, how are we to understand their virtues?

One way to put this question is to worry with Aristotle, one early great Western virtue ethicist, about the place of *pride* and *shame* in the list of virtues. Pride, in part, is the virtue of recognizing one's own virtues. Hume, following Aristotle, praises pride and condemns humility, accusing the latter of unavoidable hypocrisy. This may be too harsh, but it makes what I believe to be an important, if paradoxical, point about character. It is not enough to act virtuously, Aristotle tells us. One must comprehend one's actions as virtuous. A person trained to act in conformity with the requirements of virtue, as a dog might be trained to mimic human courtesies, would not thereby be virtuous, only well-behaved. But the matter of the relation between the exercise of the virtue and its self-recognition becomes rather delicate, all the more so as the "spontaneous" nature of the virtue is emphasized and pride (as a vice, not a virtue) is degraded. And yet, the comprehension of oneself as virtuous is part and parcel of personal identity; in fact, for many people, it is the most essential part of their personal identities, more important than competitive status and success. (In Hegel, this is where the competitive nature of the master-slave confrontation turns into *Sittlichkeit*, tragically exemplified in the sisterly virtues of Antigone.)[21]

A more complicated route to the same conclusion goes by way of Aristotle's somewhat uncomfortable examination of shame. Displaying his discomfort, he calls shame a "quasi-virtue." Shame itself is no virtue, of course, but rather it is the proper reaction to a lapse in virtue. But this is just the point. A person who feels no shame, is "shameless," cannot possibly be virtuous. Virtue is in part the self-consciousness of being virtuous, and the shameful recognition of lapses in virtue—or worse, one's lack of virtue—is an essential ingredient in good character. Shame, however, is a proof of good character only in very small doses. Pervasive shame, if warranted, means that one's character is deeply flawed. Pervasive shame, if unwarranted, is morbid and pathetic. Nevertheless, and in either case, pervasive shame is one of those emotions that does serve to constitute a more or less unified conception of personal identity based on character, albeit an unhappy one. One further problem, of course, is that both matters of shame and pride are particularly prone to the distortion of self-deception (a matter that seemed not to bother the Greeks but drove Christians like Augustine and Pascal to desperation).[22] What one conceives one's virtues to be and what they can justifiably be shown to be are notoriously out of harmony, and here we come back to a new set of variations on the complex of "existential" questions we considered before. To what extent can a person's self-identity be based on self-deception? To what extent is a person's character determined by his or her conception of (his or her own) personal identity? To what extent is a person's character not merely a matter of "fact" but rather a matter of social construal, in which the first-person account of one's own identity is but a single, occasionally over-powered voice in the crowd?

Here are two final considerations for the virtue ethics notion of character and its relation to the problem of personal identity. First, it has often been pointed out—particularly by Nietzsche—that the Aristotelean (and Platonic) ideal of the "unity of the virtues" is in fact most implausible. One virtue conflicts with another, and quite the contrary of mutual reinforcement one aspect of one's character undermines another.[23] But just as character can be split by opposing virtues, personal identity can be split by identifying with these opposing virtues and features of character. Why would philosophers assume that the self is coherent or "transparent" to itself? Indeed, the devoted practice of philosophy itself would seem to be a prime example of how one set of virtues can wreak havoc with another, more mundane set of virtues. (Those who do fail to perceive the usual social reception of a manner that insists on continous skepticism, careful and critical examination of every thesis no matter how casual, and the literal construal of even the most hackneyed idiom may miss this point.) It is not only the phenomenon of self-deception that prompts us to think of the self as far more labyrinthian than the Cartesian *cogito* would suggest.[24] It is also the familiar fact that we recognize in ourselves not just one identity but several, some of them conveniently sorted according to circumstance and social surroundings but others, particularly in a time of crisis, in full-blown confrontation. One does not need to invoke "split brain" phenomena or other extreme psychiatric disorders in order to raise fascinating philosophical questions about the fragmented and partially hidden self.[25]

The final complication to be raised here has to do with, appropriately, final moments. It is a question that has always perplexed me, how deathbed conversions, for example, or a horrible death, can undo the whole history of a person's life and set in stone, as it were, an identity that may not in any sense be deserved. At the risk of becoming tedious, we might use Sartre's Garcin as an example again. His final act of cowardice seems to utterly undermine his lifetime of heroic dedication, as Inez cruelly reminds him. Or, consider the final scene in Goethe's *Faust*, when at the last moment the philosophical protagonist renegs on his pact with Mephistopheles and has his little worm of a soul carried up to heaven by angels. Villains are saved by a final gesture of absolution, and good souls are condemned to purgatory because of the accident that they died a few moments too soon, out of reach of a priest or savior. So, too, a person with a long and happy life suffers enormously at the moment of death, through suffocation, strangulation, drowning, a bullet to the chest or abdomen, bleeding to death from an unseen wound, crushed by a heavy vehicle or decapitated in an accident. But rather than think of a long and happy life ended by a few moments of horror (and sometimes the most horrible experiences in fact involve virtually no pain at all), why do we tend to dwell on those moments of horror as now having somehow defined the person's life? Why should they define one's personal identity?

Now, to be sure, the problem here concerned is not, by its very nature, one of *self*-identity, since the person whose identity it is no longer exists. But it is by no means a leap of "unconstrained imaginative conceit" that we consider such a person, like Sartre's Garcin, to be sitting in some philosophical Hell or Heaven trying *ex post facto* get their sense of themselves in order. Or, if this stretches one's eschatological imagination too far, one can always imagine without theological presuppositions that, in one's final moments, one's entire life "flashes before one's eyes," not just by way of instant replay, but combined with a philosophical narrative and commentary with a final epitaph in mind. What then do we make of the question of personal identity? It is a sobering thought (so sobering, in fact, that Heidegger weaved his existential sense of "authenticity" around just such an experience). Granted, pain can be unbearable, and one wants nothing more fervently than it should go away, but death effectively answers that desire. Why should this in turn affect our sense of our own identity? Most of our final experiences will be anything but pleasant, but that they should inspire horror—distinct from the fear of dying itself, that is—and require some alteration in our very conception of ourselves remains something of a mystery. What warrants the emphasis on character in virtue ethics is indeed a strong sense of the importance of constancy and continuity as opposed to the merely momentary and accidental in the determination of desert, whether or not one also believes that one will, here or there, be rewarded. What motivates the search for self-identity, I suspect, is something very similar.

Personal Identity and Multiculturalism

It is now virtually a platitude in the social sciences (and a tiresome piece of political jargon) that the concept of self varies from culture to culture ("difference"). In a summary article that is receiving widespread attention in psychology and anthropology, Hazel Rose Markus and Shinobu Kitayama suggest that "divergent contruals of self, others and the interdependence of the two" suggest deep implications for the understanding of different cultures, their systems of knowledge, ways of behaving, and the relativity of emotions.[26] The authors limit themselves to a somewhat unspecified discussion of two different modes of self-construal, "Western" and "non-Western," exemplified, for example, by American and Asian societies, respectively. They refer to the essential difference between these two construal of selves as "independent" and "interdependent." Their discussion is on occasion conceptually confused and their analysis cries out for a sympathetic philosophical commentary, but what they say certainly does throw a dark shadow across the universal pretensions of the "so-called Western view of the individual as an independent, self-contained, autonomous entity who (a) comprises a unique configuration of internal attributes . . . and (b) behaves primarily as a consequence of these internal attributes."[27] Some of this description is admittedly exaggerated, overgeneralized, and metaphorical, but the assumption that the self of personal identity is and must be individuated according to either the contingent enclosure of the epidermis or, more in the tradition, the peculiar contents of a single "mind" (whether or not this needs to be explained as a transcendental unity) is and should be put open to question. Hegel defended the notion of the nonindividual self (or "Spirit") on more or less a priori grounds, taking his departure from Kant.[28] The self is, as the French anthropologist Mauss suggested in 1938, a "delicate cateory," subject to substantial variation.[29] Markus and Kitayama, referring to hundreds of other authors, provide an account based on empirical observation and experiment (for example, comparing ascriptions of attributes and character as opposed to evaluating actions only and comparing measures of self-esteem in different cultures).[30] Again, a sympathetic philosopher could do wonders with this material, but the point I want to make here is that the very conception of personal identity is now up for grabs. Not only do we have the opportunity (indeed the obligation) to examine "*all* [or at least some of] the more interesting and specific conceptions that have guided practical life,"[31] but we have an opportunity to do it in precisely that arena that some philosophers still refuse to acknowledge, namely, under the auspices of "alternative conceptual schemes."[32]

This is not the place to pursue the rich conceptual geography of alternative construals of the self and the person in any detail, but it seems to me that the "multicultural" question of personal identity is an exceedingly promising topic for philosophy as we approach the new millennium (itself an ethnocentric construal, of course). The distinction between "independent" and "interdependent" construals of self seems to me overly simpleminded and only clumsily applicable to the hardly homogeneous societies mentioned by Markus and Kitayama. The United States and Canada are, despite the prevalent themes of certain sorts of movies, not at all so obviously wedded to their own romantic conception of the individual, and the idea that all non-Western, non-individualistic societies can be understood together under a single rubric, "interdependent," flies in the face of so much of the rich anthropological evidence that Markus and Kitayama cite in their discussion. Nevertheless, philosophy coupled with anthropology, conceptual analysis combined with careful and detailed attention to the diversity of what gets said and thought and displayed in behavior around the world might produce the kind of cross-cultural dialogue and mutual understanding that, as of now, less fanatical multiculturalists just dreamily imagine.

I want to use as an example just one rather specific multicultural or, with a narrower focus that is no longer adequate, bicultural confrontation of considerable historical significance, at least to the people involved and arguably as a model for historically troubled cultural confrontations elsewhere as well. It is the confrontation between the more indigenous aboriginal Polynesians, the Maoris of New Zealand who arrived (and eliminated the then-indigenous people) somewhere before the end of the first millennium and the (for the most part British) settlers who arrived during the nineteenth century. The historical story is by no means pleasant, but it is considerably more edifying than many similar tales of arrival, conquest and "manifest destiny." Indeed, the Maoris and the "Pākehā" achieved such a mutually satisfying living arrangement that for a period of several decades New Zealand could present itself to the world—and entertain as its own self-identity—as a harmonious biracial culture. This illusion was shattered by a serious of events in the past few decades, and what in fact has been a long-standing confrontation on land rights and reparation for past abuses now continues in the courts.[33]

What is of particular philosophical interest and relevance in this confrontation is the mutual misunderstanding of two very different sets of conceptions of justice and responsibility, which rest on two very different sets of conceptions of self- and personal identity. Maori justice, and the device by which the nineteenth-century settlers "legally" deprived the Maori of their territories, depended on wholly joint identity with (not "ownership" of) their land.[34] So, too, the Maori sense of responsibility was entirely collective, not individual, resulting in considerable disharmony in the essentially "Western" New Zealand criminal courts.[35] But for our purposes here, the primary context of disagreement lies in the understanding of what it is to be a person, and there the Maori and Pākehā versions and variations provide us with an accessible, concrete, and fascinating example of two philosophically profound yet clearly different conceptual schemes.

It is often said that the Western conception of self is "individualistic," perhaps excessively so. But insofar as this refers only to the obvious, namely the physical discernibility of individual human beings and some rudimentary awareness that "I feel this and you don't" (and vice versa), it is hard to understand what all the fuss is about. How could people *not* be individualistic? But here Hegel and the German idealists (as well as Spinoza) give us an armchair-bound clue, the idea that what weight one gives to merely physical individuality and how one construes the peculiar notion of what philosophers call "privacy" or "privileged access" makes all the difference. Maoris, to be sure, have just as firm a grasp of their physical individuality and the privacy of their own pains as any individualistic *Übermensch*. But the significance of any meaningful action or experience can be properly described only in collective or we might say, "corporate" terms.[36] An offense perpetrated by any member of a group or family is rightly blamed on the whole of the group or family. An offense suffered by any member of a group or family is felt equally by the whole of the group or family and revenge *(utu)* might rightly be taken by any member of the offended group on any member of the offending group.[37] An individual is thus wholly caught up in kinship relations. Indeed, the death of an individual is in an important sense not death at all.[38] One's real self is the "kinship self," and the kinship self survives. The "Western" idea that the group exists to serve the interests of the member of the group would be considered utter and dangerous nonsense.[39]

Of course, in the two hundred years of their joint tenure of New Zealand, the two conceptions of self have become entangled, although the influence has been, as one would expect, rather one sided. Maoris have become more comfortable with the idea of individual choice, and, indeed, in a society where a large percentage of the population is of "mixed blood," being a Maori becomes itself a matter of choice and commitment.[40] But the ongoing philosophical dispute is a fascinating case study of the way that cross-cultural debates and disputes proceed and the cautious, incremental steps that are necessary to bring about

mutual understanding. To assume that what is involved in such understanding is simply the translation of one language into the other or the
acceptance by one or both parties of the conceptual scheme of the
other is to miss the point of the whole discussion. Personal identity is
not just the question of who one is (as an embodied being with
thoughts, feeling, and memories). It is a much larger question of who
we are—where the "we" refers to any number of groups of which we
are members and with which we identify—and the complex question of
how we identify with the group or the groups in question.

Personal Identity and Love

Love seems to be an awkward topic for philosophers, despite the enthusiasm displayed for both the sexual and nonsexual varieties by Plato
and Aristotle, respectively. But in such emotions there is much to be
learned, particularly on the subject of personal identity. In her essay
"The Historicity of Psychological Attitudes," Amélie Rorty begins,
"There is a set of psychological attitudes—love, joy, perhaps some
sorts of desire—that are individuated by the character of the subject,
the character of the object, and the relation between them."[41] Now I
am not so sure about joy, and desire is too mixed and exciting a bag
for me to get into here, but love surely is just of this kind. Erotic or
romantic love might seem to be the first—and in any case most
titillating—example of love, but Rorty perhaps wisely focuses her
attention on the love of friendship or friendship-love.[42] She does not
assume that the love is reciprocated or symmetrical. Indeed, it is important for the concept she calls 'permeability' that the sense of self it
embraces includes the other but is, nevertheless, a "psychological attitude," that is, a feature of the person who loves, rather than a relationship between the lover and the beloved, however one might hope
or expect that the one will accompany the other. The "object" of love,
however, must nevertheless be a person, not a thing, and not just one
or another aspect of a person.[43] To say that love is permeable is to say
that "the lover is affected, changed not only by loving but by the details of the character of the person loved."[44] Such changes in turn affect
the actions of the lover and become part of a whole "narrative history"
in which the all-too-often highlighted ephemera of love—the pangs,
stabs, twinges, and thrills—can be identified as "feelings of love" only
by virtue of their (small) place in this narrative history.[45] What concerns Rorty is the continuity or "constancy" of love, a question that
does not concern me here. But insofar as the concept of 'permeability'
seems to me to capture an essential feature of love (both erotic and

friendly) and this feature has essentially to do with self and personal identity, I want to explore that conception here, however briefly.[46]

Ever since Plato, philosophers who have been concerned to analyze the essential features of love have had what I call an "obsession" with the object. Against a background of misunderstandings in which emotions and their like were taken to be mere "feelings" or physiological disturbances, this point of view was quite healthy, one might even say therapeutic.[47] In 1963, Anthony Kenny summed up the not-so-new emphasis on the fact that emotions are necessarily directed toward objects—their "intentionality"—by distinguishing between two kinds of feelings, those with and those without objects.[48] Love (like virtually all emotions) was decidedly of the former variety. Before him, Brentano had argued a similar thesis, which was picked up by Freud, who initiated a particularly vulgar series of coinages, such as "the love object." But long before Freud, Plato had taken a similar route to understanding love when he had Socrates, in the *Symposium*, suggest (among other things) that love was a longing for beauty, or rather Beauty (the Form and not any particular instantiation).[49] But that focused all of the attention on the brilliance of the true object of love, which, not surprisingly, by the twelfth century turned out to be God. What got neglected, I would argue, is the importance of the subject and, as Rorty rightly insists, the relation between lover and beloved.

But this relation is not, I repeat, the relationship *between* the lover and the beloved so much as it is the relation *as perceived* by the lover, the "subject." And whatever else that perception might consist of (including the beauty and charms of the beloved), it includes perceiving/conceiving of one's self, one's identity, in terms that are dictated with, through, and/or by the beloved. In the case of an actual relationship, that is, where the two people in question are actually talking to, listening to, looking at, and otherwise communicating with each other, the sense in which their identities are mutually (re-)constituted is fairly obvious. He says to her, "I like your hair that way," and that becomes her preferred way of viewing herself. She says to him, "I don't know how you can stand to read Heidegger," and his interest, perhaps immediately, starts to flag. It is no deep philosophical insight, nor does it require a quasi-paranoid notion of "Being-for-Others," to recognize that we are affected, often deeply and permanently, by the opinions and judgments of others, especially if they are people we care about very much, whom we wish to please and whom we wish to think well of us. But this is not merely a consequence or effect of love, nor is it merely a symptom of that psychological attitude. It is part of what makes love *love*, as opposed to mere admiration, adoration, sexual or other acquisitive or self-interested desire, mutual enjoyment, companionship, or shared interests (including an interest in one another).

Where the permeability or shared identity of love becomes more complicated and phenomenologically interesting, however, is where it is unreciprocated, indeed, where the beloved may not even know of the existence, much less the *amour*, of the other. In such an instance, the dialogue exemplified above goes on, in effect, within the psyche of the lover, but the exchange is not all that different for that change of locale. Of course, unrequited love has its freedoms, not least is the ability to conjure up unrefuted flattery on the part of the beloved and a conception of oneself that is entirely to one's liking (and within one's control). Thus Stendhal defiantly stated his romantic preference for the superiority of unrequited love, and Goethe is said to have declared, in what must be one of his best lines (out of millions), "I love you, but what business is that of yours." But love, whether reciprocated or not, essentially involves taking the (real or imagined) preferences and judgments of the beloved "to heart" and remaking one's own sense of self in their image.

The picture is further complicated when we consider the historical-cultural variations and the various ontological presuppositions of love. If love is a sharing of selves, the culturally determined nature of the self is going to be an important determinant of love and its kinds. In other words, one can experience certain sorts of love only if one has a certain sort of self and a certain conception of his or her personal identity. Friendship, as described by Aristotle in the *Nicomachean Ethics*, does not involve the same concept of friendship that is available to us, although we are obviously capable of picking out the similarities and applying them to our own purposes. *Eros*, as described by the various speakers in the *Symposium*, is not the same as our conception of "romantic" love. Indeed, that conception took another two thousand years to develop, by way of dramatic changes in the relations and status of men and women, the concept of 'marriage', the concept of 'passion', and, most important for our purposes here, the concept of 'self- and personal identity'. I have often used the story told by Aristophanes in the *Symposium* to illustrate my thesis of "shared identity," but it is obvious to what extent that illustration is limited, not only by its fanciful nature, but also by the concept of 'identity' that it presupposes. We are not, as in the Aristophanes story, "two halves of an original whole." Love alone does not "complete" us. And with reference to the *Symposium* as a whole, we do not see ourselves as an integral part of a more or less harmonious *polis*. Quite the contrary, we (and the scope of this "we" would have to be very carefully circumscribed) see ourselves as individuals, more or less but contingently connected to others through bonds of kinship or affection.

Romantic love attempts to combine the individualistic, independent self and the interdependent, shared self in what would have to be a rather unstable, tentative fusion. This is, indeed, just the portrait of love (and much more) that we get out of some of the romantic philosophers of the last century or so; and it is quite specific, I would argue, to a certain kind of culture. But what this tentatively shared self amounts to, and in what sense we are "permeable" to the other is a subject that deserves careful but kindly attention, neither the tweezers of overly restricted conceptual analysis nor the usual rubber gloves and long tongs of psychology. What other conceptions of love there might be, particularly in cultures with a quite different and already interdependent conception of self, is an extremely important and by no means easy investigation. In some such societies (Maori, for example) there seems to be no special conception of love similar to that which we designate "romantic." And what seems to be true of this one very special emotion may be true as well of the entire range of our emotional life. If emotions are not merely intrusions into the self, barbarians of the Freudian "it" banging on the gates of the ego, then much of what we should say of the self must also be said of our passions. The self, as Hume suggested two centuries ago, may be constituted not in thought but in our passions, and the nature and structure of our passions in turn may involve nothing less than the nature and structure of our whole way of life.[50]

Conclusion

We do not need to strain our imaginations, our intuitions, or our now-and-future knowledge of neurology in order to find philosophical problems of self and personal identity that can occupy our best minds and begin a long and fruitful conversation. We do not need highly improbable, if not impossible, examples of confused personal identity, when our lives are so rich with confusions, confrontations, and questions that urgently demand discussion and attempts at mutual understanding, if not answers. Questions of self and personal identity now define the possible peace of the world, and mutual understanding is no longer an exotic exercise but a quotidian necessity. If a seemingly classic (but in fact fairly recent) philosophical puzzle has become "dessicated," then let's drop it and turn to something more promising. And when the subject is the self as person, we do not have to look very far.

NOTES

1. For example, see Bernard Williams, "The Self and the Future," *The Philosophical Review* 79, no. 2 (1970).

2. Williams, "Self and the Future." Cf. David Wiggins, "Personal Identity" in his *Sameness and Substance* (New York: Oxford University Press, 1980); Peter van Inwagen, *Material Beings* (Ithaca: Cornell University Press, 1987); Sydney Shoemaker, *Self-Knowledge and Self-Identity* (Ithaca: Cornell University Press, 1963) and "Persons and their Pasts," *American Philosophical Quarterly* 7, No. 4 (1970); David Lewis, "Survival and Identity," in *The Identities of Persons*, ed., Amélie Rorty (Berkeley and Los Angeles: University of California Press, 1976); and Bernard Williams, "Bodily Continuity and Personal Identity: A Reply," in his *Problems of the Self* (New York: Cambridge University Press, 1973); Derek Parfit, *Reasons and Persons* (New York: Oxford University Press, 1984). Mark Johnston, "Human Beings," *Journal of Philosophy* 84, no. 2 (1987). And, of course, Steve Martin and Lilly Tomlin in *All of Me.*

3. Parfit, *Reasons and Persons*.

4. Johnston, "Human Beings," 60.

5. E.g., Shoemaker, *Self-Knowledge and Self-Identity* and "Persons and their Pasts"; David Lewis, "Survival and Identity"; "Bodily Continuity"; Parfit, *Reasons and Persons*.

6. Jacqueline Trimier, "African Philosophy," in *From Africa to Zen*: ed. R. Solomon, K. Higgins *An Invitation to World Philosophy* (Lanham, MD: Rowman and Littlefield, 1993)

7. There is, however, a rich history of the self to be told in conjunction with (as well as in opposition to) the passions in Western philosophy. See Amélie Rorty, "The Coordination of the Self and the Passions," chap. 2 in this volume, 000–000.

8. Heine on Fichte, in *Reflections of Philosophy and Religion in Germany*.

9. For example, Voltaire defended Locke in his *English Letters* as the great defender of reason, apparently all but indifferent to the ferocious philosophical battles that were being carried on *within* the new Enlightenment tradition. He also rejected Cartesian metaphysics, which he had been force-fed as a student, but not Descartes's rational method.

10. See, e.g., P. F. Strawson's relatively conservative discussion of Kant and Hume on the "soul" in his *Bounds of Sense* (London: Methuen, 1966), 162–70.

11. I have tried to do so in my "Hegel's Spirit of Geist," *Review of Metaphysics* 23, No. 4 (1971) and in my book *In the Spirit of Hegel* (New York: Oxford University Press 1983). Those credentials stated, I hope I can avoid unnecessary obscurity without seeming the coward, but I will return to this difficult chapter in the history of philosophy, nonetheless.

12. E.g., H. A. Markus and S. Kitayama, "Culture and the Self: Implications for Cognition, Emotion, and Motivation," *Psychological Review* 98, no. 2 (1991): 224–53.

13. The hyperbole is not merely of the local speech-on-the-mall and comment-to-the-press variety. It is also promulgated by some very influential philosophers, many of them French, Michel Foucault and Jean-François Lyotard, e.g., or French wannabees. Much of the charm of Jacques Derrida and what—despite his frail protests—has come to be known as "deconstruction" is the fact that it calls the notion of selfhood into serious question and raises such "multicultural" questions. Of course, Derrida is as fond of mere puzzles as any post-Moorian analytic philosopher, many of them puzzling precisely because of their obscurity and self-undermining presentation. But there is no question in my mind which set of puzzles—A's brain in B's or the "logocentric" imperialism of the Western tradition—has had the greater influence and which now deserves our philosophical attention.

14. Philosophers who write about personal identity rarely seem to appreciate the effects on selfhood of even minor bodily changes. Physical incompetence, e.g., can devastate one's sense of self. (One remembers the difficulties of a six-week stint in a leg cast.)

15. One might well compare Kafka's story to other tales of transformation in which the subject knowingly *willed* or even just delighted in the change. All too often, problematic paradigms of personal identity are presented without any such specification of choice or agency. From the transcendental point of view, perhaps, it is supposed not to make a difference.

16. Jean-Paul Sartre, *Being and Nothingness*, trans. Hazel Barnes (New York: Philosophical Library, 1956).

17. G.W.F. Hegel, *The Phenomenology of Spirit*, trans, A. V. Miller (Oxford: Oxford University Press, 1977), pt. B. chap. 2. In the dialectic of the *Phenomenology*, the "master-slave" chapter follows the very short chapter on "self-certainty," which, along with much else, entertains and rejects as question-begging the Cartesian "certainty" of self. Hegel also considers, with equal brevity, the importance of the notion of "desire" in self-consciousness and, echoing Fichte, the ultimate awareness of oneself as "life." These more rudimentary forms of self-consciousness are then carried over (and *aufheben'd*) in the parable of "master and slave." (There is also a short discussion of the "I" as a matter of immediate acquaintance in the first chapter of the book, "Sense-certainty.")

18. P. F. Strawson, "Persons" and *Individuals: An Essay in Descriptive Metaphysics* (London: University Paperbacks, 1959). Johnston, "Human Beings."

19. These are the philosophies of Stoicism and Skepticism, respectively, but eventually the dialectic turns to an entirely different sense of personal identity that involves group identification (*Sittlichkeit*, "ethical substance") rather than the dubious independence of a competitive "state of nature." I have defended the idea that Hegel's discussion constitutes his contribution to the ongoing "state of nature" debate (and the nature of the so-called social contract that is formulated therein) in chapter seven of my book *In the Spirit of Hegel*.

20. Sartre's character Garcin in *Huis Clos* again provides us with an example. But his allegedly "out of character" behavior was a fatal blemish on his virtue. In the popular movie *Back to the Future*, a single spontaneous act, totally out of character, changes the future father of the hero into an entirely different person (though not in the extreme philosophical sense of this expression) and alters the future (in ways that are not, on reflection, altogether coherent).

21. Hegel, *Phenomenology*, pt C, 342ff.

22. For a particularly insightful and sensitive discussion of Augustine and Pascal in this regard, see Bas van Frassen, "The Peculiar Effects of Love and Desire," in *Perspectives on Self-Deception*, ed. Amélie Rorty and Brian B. McLaughlin (Berkeley and Los Angeles: University of California Press, 1988), 136f. What did perplex the Greeks, however, was the related problem of *akrasia* or incontinence. But *akrasia* presumes knowledge of what one should do even though one fails to do it, while self-deception involves a denial of what one should do. The latter, therefore, bears directly on the problem of personal identity in the way the former does not.

23. A protracted study of such a split, focusing on the difficulties of loyalty and integrity in corporate life, is Robert Jackall's *Moral Mazes* (Oxford University Press, 1988). See Nietzsche, *The Gay Science* trans. W. Kaufmann (New York: Random House, 1968).

24. This suggests the ongoing battle between Freud and Sartre and their followers, but it also emerges, with particular reference to the problem of self-deception, in Amélie Rorty's "Deception Liars, and Layers" in Rorty and McLaughlin, *Perspectives on Self-Deception*.

25. See, e.g., Thomas Nagel, *Mortal Questions* (Cambridge: Cambridge University Press, 1979).

26. Markus and Kitayama, "Culture and the Self," 224, notes.

27. Ibid.

28. In Kant's so-called Paralogisms of Rational Psychology. I have examined and defended this connection between Kant and Hegel in "Hegel's Concept of *Geist*," in *From Hegel to Existentialism* (New York: Oxford University Press, 1988).

29. M. Mauss, "A Category of the Human Mind: The Notion of Person, the Notion of Self," trans. W. D. Halls, in *The Category of the Person: Anthropology, Philosophy, History*, ed., M. Carrithers, S. Collins, and S. Lukes, (Cambridge: Cambridge University Press, 1985), 1–25.

30. E.g., A. Bloom, *The Linguisitic Shaping of Thought* (Hillsdale: Erlbaum, 1981), discussed in Markus and Kitayama, "Culture and the Self," 233–34. According to Bloom, 97 percent of Amerian subjects indicated that they saw no consequential difference in moral education between punishing a child for for "immoral" behavior and rewarding the child for "moral" behavior. Only 55 percent of Taiwanese and 65 percent of Hong Kong respondents agreed. Cf. Jerome Bruner, *Actual Minds, Possible Worlds* (New York: Plenum, 1986).

31. Johnston, "Human Beings," 60, italics and bracketed qualification added.

32. Donald Davidson, "On the Very Idea of Alternative Conceptual Schemes," in his *Actions and Events* (Oxford: Oxford University Press, 1980). Once again, the difference between a peculiarly philosophical problem, which can be readily reduced to paradox, and a parallel pedestrian problem—that is, one that nonphilosophers have to live with—comes into focus. There is nothing in the notion of "alternative conceptual schemes" that requires incommensurability. It is quite sufficient that there be systematic mutual misunderstanding. But if one "raises the ante" such that incommensurability becomes the criterion for alternative schemes, then, of course, the pressing problems of multiculturalism evaporate into philosophical confusion.

33. For an excellent account of the Maori-Pākehā disputes, see Andrew Sharp, *Justice and the Maori* (Auckland: Oxford University Press, 1990). The standard history of the preceding nineteenth-century "Maori Wars" is Keith Sinclair, *The Origins of the Maori Wars* (Auckland: Oxford University Press 1984). Several good philosophical accounts of the controversial Treaty of Waitangi of 1840 are in G. Oddie and R. Perrett, eds., *Justice, Ethics and New Zealand Society* (Auckland: Oxford University Press, 1992).

34. Sharp, *Justice and the Maori*, chap. 2.

35. See, e.g., articles by Moana Jackson and John Patterson in *Justice, Ethics and New Zealand Society*, and John Patterson, *Maori Values* (Palmerston North, NZ" Dunmore Press, 1992).

36. John Patterson, "A Maori Concept of Collective Responsibility," in *Justice, Ethics and New Zealand Society*, ed. G. Oddie and R. Perrett (Auck-

land: Oxford University Press, 1992), 11–26. While the term *corporate* suggests a perfectly plausible analog to the "loss of identity" (or, more positively, the acquisition of an identity) in adopting a role in the modern corporation, the term has a much wider meaning not (yet) wholly consumed in the embrace of entrepreneurial economics.

37. The problem of translating *utu* is itself symptomatic of the conceptual differences encountered at every stage of such cross-cultural comparisons. *Utu* is more than mere "getting even" and includes reparations and "setting matters right." While *utu* is a function of group pride or dignity (*mana*, another term that defies simple translation) vengeance is usually restricted to the individual offended. (One can avenge another, but one gets revenge for oneself.) And, of course, *utu* is considered not only legitimate but obligatory, while revenge is dismissed as mere irrationality by most Western theorists of retributive justice. E.g., Robert Gerstein writes: "Vengefulness is an emotional response to injuries done to us by others: we feel a desire to injure those who have injured us. Retributivism is not the idea that it is good to have and satisfy this emotion. It is rather the view that there are good arguments for including the kernel of rationality to be found in the passion for vengeance as a part of any just system of laws" ("Capital Punishment: A Retributivist Response," *Ethics*, 85 (1985): 75–79.

38. "Kairangatiura, when alone and surrounded by his enemies about to slay him, is reported to have said: 'you will kill me, my tribe will kill you and the country will be *mine*.' " Quoted by Roy Perrett, "Individualism, Justice and the Maori View of the Self," *Justice, Ethics and New Zealand Society*, ed. G. Oddie and R. Perrett (Auckland: Oxford University Press, 1992), 29.

39. Thus the awkwardness of the debates about whether or not the Treaty of Waitangi is a "social contract." The very idea of the social contract, at least in the Hobbesian version, that is the subject of much of the philosophical discussion relies on a strong notion of individual interests and group formation as a means to satisfy those interests. Or one can take as the "individuals" in question tribes or whole cultures rather than individual persons, but then it is not at all clear if the psychology—as opposed to the logic—of contract goes through. See Oddie and Perrett, *Justice, Ethics and New Zealand Society*, esp. articles by Stephen Davies, R. E. Ewin, Jindra Tichy, and Graham Oddie.

40. Andrew Sharp, "Being a Maori"; and Richard Mulgan, *Maori, Pākehā and Democracy*, quoted in Perrett, "Individualism, Justice, and the Maori View of Self," originally from Sharp, *Justice and the Maori* (Auckland: Oxford University Press, 1990), and Mulgan, *Maori, Pākehā, and Democracy* (Auckland: Oxford University Press, 1990).

41. Amélie Rorty, "The Historicity of Psychological Attitudes: Love is Not Love Which Alters When It Alteration Finds," in her *Mind in Action* (Boston: Beacon Press, 1988), 121.

42. Ibid., 122.

43. Ibid., 123.

44. Ibid.

45. Ibid.

46. I have pursued the kindred concept of what I call "shared identity" in love at greater length in two books, *Love: Emotion, Myth and Metaphor* (New York: Doubleday, 1981; New York: Prometheus Books, 1990) and *About Love* (New York: Simon & Schuster, 1988; Landam, MD: Rowman and Littlefield, 1993).

47. Such feeling theorists include, notably, William James, who in his essay "What is an Emotion?" defined an emotion as a set of sensations caused by a visceral disturbance caused in turn by an upsetting perception. This is by no means the whole of James's view (or views), but it is a view that has had enormous influence and also sums up a long-standing tradition of viewing the emotions in terms of bodily reactions and their phenomenal effects.

48. See Anthony Kenny, *Action, Emotion and Will* (Routledge and Kegan Paul, 1963).

49. Plato, *Symposium* trans. A. Nehamas and P. Woodruff (Indianapolis: Hackett, 1989).

50. See Rorty, "Coordination of the Self and the Passions," chap. 2 in this volume.

2

The Coordination of the Self and the Passions

Amélie Oksenberg Rorty

It is Descartes, of all people, who claims that "the good or harm of this life depends on the passions alone. . . . They dispose our soul to want those things which nature deems useful to us, and to persist in this volition" (PA. 212, 52). Like many of his predecessors, Descartes treated the passions as the body's emissaries to the mind, invasive and misleading at their worst, but at their best messengers bringing non-representational, highly fallible clues of the body's thriving or failing, set to begin the motions of its survival and flourishing.

In a speculative vein, Hume also links the passions—and in particular, the passion of pride—with the idea of the 'self'. There is a certain "peculiar impression or emotion, which we call pride: To this emotion. . . [nature] has assign'd a certain idea, *viz.* that of *self*, which it never fails to produce . . . Any thing, that gives a pleasant sensation, and is related to self, excites the. . . [agreeable]. . . passion of pride, which. . . has self for its object" (T. 287). But although any pleasurable property of the self excites joy, only those properties that are admired and prized by others generate the kind of pride that produces the idea of the self. The Look of the Other influences, though it does not wholly determine the construction of the idea of the self.

And in a continued inheritance from the Stoic tradition, Rousseau says, "Our passions are psychological instruments with which nature has armed our hearts for the defense of our persons and of all that is necessary for our wellbeing. [But] the more we need external things, the more we are vulnerable to obstacles that can overwhelm us; and the more numerous and complex our passions become. They are naturally proportionate to our needs" (Fragments for *Émile*).

35

Who is the self—the *we*—who is served or endangered by the passions? What are the self's real needs? How can the passions serve us, and how do they endanger us? What is the difference—if any— between the true self and the *idea* of the self that is "produced" by or constructed from a set of passions? Passions have been treated as the backdoor informants of the boundaries and the character of an individual's self-conception. Because passions were defined and identified as accidental guests or intruders on the mind's own essential activities, they serve as red-dye tracers of the line that differentiates what is essential and what is contingent to the self. They reveal the power politics of the faculties of the mind, the relative empowerment of reason, the imagination and fantasy to form action. The range of a person's passions indicates her conception of her boundaries and of what endangers or supports the maintenance of those boundaries. But laying down boundaries also reveals what is essential. It is not surprising that the passions serve as clues to the nature of the self: a person's passions are direct functions of what she is and of what she takes herself to be. To understand a person's passions, we must understand her history; and so too, to understand our conceptions of the passions and emotions, we must understand the history of the transformation of conceptions of the passions.

But it is, ironically enough, an accident of the metaphysical presuppositions of grammar—the assumptions imbeded in the contrast between the active and passive voice—that has fixed the correlation and coordination between the class of passions and an individual's self-conception. The origins of our intuitions concerning the passions lie in Aristotelian metaphysics, supported as it was by his grammatically based logical analysis of substantial predication. The term *passion* derives from Aristotle's general class of *pathē*, the passive reactions of a substantial individual as contrasted with the activities that originate directly from his essential nature, without needing a particular contingent event to set them in motion.[1] Aristotle's class of passions is clearly broader than our own: it includes wound scars, for instance, or startle reactions. Passions are changes, modifications, deviations in an individual's own essential activity; a condition is classified as a passion by reference to its etiology. But although certain sorts of conditions— like anger or fear—are typically passions, individual cases of anger or desire can arise directly from a person's own nature. For example, some cases of desire—those that are fortuitously occasioned—might be classified as *pathē*; but a particular desire can also be the expression of an endogenous activity. The natural desire for nourishment is, for example, not a passion but the expression of one of the species basic activities; but a well-nourished person's desire occasioned by a particularly tantalizing piece of pastry is a *pathos*.

Passions are not in themselves rational or irrational, harmful or beneficial, noble or ignoble, vicious or virtuous. And they are not necessarily felt or sensed. In their primitive forms, many but not all some *pathē* are protective though undiscriminating reactions of a biological organism. Nevertheless, since a *pathos* is often a deviation from the individual's essential self-fulfilling activity, it is more likely to indicate harm than benefit. For instance, fear is a reaction to what is perceived as dangerous, anger to what is believed to be an unjustified injury or insult. Still, because the reactions of human beings can also be cognitively or rationally mediated, it is possible to evaluate the rationality of a specific *pathos*—a specific instance of fear or anger— on a specific occasion. And while the passions do not in themselves have any specific moral status, a person's dispositions concerning the passions reveal not only her character but also the details of her virtues and vices. It is part of virtue to be disposed to be angry or fearful in the right way at the right time and at the right things. But knowing is *really* dangerous or insulting—what is really worth fearing or desiring—requires true self-knowledge, a true understanding of one's natures and ends.

Not surprisingly, the seventeenth- and eighteenth-century anatomists of the self and its passions absorbed and transformed their Aristotelian and Stoic heritage. The philosophical status of the passions— and the psychological roles accorded to them—changed dramatically in the period from Descartes to Rousseau. The class of passions acknowledged by Rousseau is a descendant—but a distant descendant—of those introduced by Aristotle: it excludes some Aristotelian passions (wound scars or startle reactions, for instance) and includes some conditions Aristotle would have considered virtues rather than passions, the sense of justice, for instance. During this period, Aristotelian *pathē* became *émotions*, that is, motives as the internal sources of motion and action. The class then expanded to include sentiments, modes of feeling and cognition that could serve as the sources of morality. Changes in the class of passions—the movement from passions to emotions and then to sentiments—mark shifts in conceptions of the self.

I want briefly to sketch some dramatic points in this transition: the point at which Descartes—not fully realizing the consequences of what he had done—unsuspectingly characterized the passions as motivating forces, directed to "those things which are useful to us"; and the point at which Hume acknowledged and traced the social contribution to the formation of pride and thus to the formation of a person's self-conception. With these dramatic but undramatized pivotal changes in mind, I want to turn to a more detailed examination of Rousseau's contribution to our story, the story of how a person's passions are coordinate with her conception of herself, how society coordinates the patterns of a person's agency with her conception of herself.

I

For all his struggles against scholasticism, Descartes could not entirely shake the Aristotelian inheritance that defined passions as externally caused contingent ideas, not essential to the mind as the true ego. By his lights, the mind is passive to the initial appearance of passions: they are nonrepresentational ideas attributed to the mind but caused by the body. Strictly speaking, they are not expressions of the mind's own essential intellectual activity. Since the mind *is* the ego, none of the passions, including perceptual images, are essential or necessary to the ego-mind as such. The mind does not have an essential interest in the welfare of the body, which is, after all, a distinct substance. Indeed the mind as such has no motives at all: its essence is fully expressed in thinking. Despite his Platonism, Descartes does not treat thinking as a reaching for or a moving toward. It is not a temporal process defined by its beginning, middle, or end, but a state that is well or ill formed. Nevertheless, we are not, at least in "this life," solely immortal mind-souls. We are also individual human beings, quasi-substantial unions of mind and a particular sort of body, a particular part of Extension. The passions serve the good and ill of *this* life, Descartes says; and by this he means the life of that curious hybrid substance, an individual person composed of the union of mind and body. The utility of the passions—particularly of the passion of desire—lies in their presenting motives to the mind, incentives to the will, to act on behalf of the compound union of mind and body. And here we have the unexpected, unsuspected point of change in the conceptions of the passions. To the extent that Descartes assigns the individual's self-preserving motivational structure to the passions, they have begun to move inward, to become an essential part the activity of an individual person. *Émotion* was originally a word that conveyed a condition of commotion and confusion; it began gradually to acquire a wholly different connotation, as conveying the sense of *that-from-which-one moves*. For Descartes, the passions-emotions are still, strictly speaking, conditions that the essential mind-self initially passively receives from the body. Left to themselves, the passions would act solely on behalf of the body's contribution to the hybrid individual. So it is the mind, rather than the body, that is authorized by the understanding and empowered by the will to determine the proper definition of what truly serves the compound mind-body. Like all neo-Stoics, Descartes accords the mind power over the passions. "There is no mind so weak," he says, "that it cannot, if well directed, acquire an absolute power over its passions" (PA. 50). Yet like all-Stoics, Descartes hedges his confidence: whether or not a mind is well directed is not always up to the mind's own powers. What Cartesian Stoicism guarantees is the mind's general essential *capacity*. It is not in the mind's own power to ensure the successful development and exercise of those capacities. That's up to the world.

Hobbes drew the consequences of Descartes's assigning motivational force to the passions. In denying Cartesian dualism, he operationalized the distinction between exogenous passions and endogenous desires as different stages in the human body's interaction with other bodies. A condition is classified as a passion when it is seen as a special kind of effect of the body's interaction with an external body; but when the same condition is regarded as a cause of a sequence that ends in motion and action, it can be classified as a desire. By a suitable intraorganic route, a condition that was originally an exogenous passion is among the causes of "external" action. With this analysis, Hobbes shifts the account of the motivational role of the passions: however, functional they might have been for preserving an organism, passion-reactions are strongly and directly linked with active desires. The way is prepared for relativizing the distinction between the inner and the external sources of motion and action. There is significant agreement between Hobbes and Spinoza on this issue. Each relativizes the distinction between passions and actions. Spinoza's vocabulary reveals this most clearly: rather than talking about passions and actions, he distinguishes passive and active affects, according to the degree of the adequacy of their ideas, that is, according to the extent to which the idea of the affect includes an account of the nexus of its causes.

Spinoza and Hobbes both express an uneasy irony about the ontological status of the individual. Spinoza's view of the conatus of an individual is exactly parallel to Hobbes attributing forces of self-preservation to individuals. But at a deeper reading, it turns out in both cases that the individual is analyzable as a product of all its causal interactions. For Spinoza, the individual mind is a section of Substance. The force and direction of an individual's conatus—its "essence"—is determined by its interactive relations to the totality of all other individuals.[2] For Hobbes, an individual body is a section of the system of the material world whose properties—its direction and force of motion—are determined by its interaction with the rest of the system of material objects. Ironically, the starting points that coordinate the (presumptive) boundaries of an individual with its range of passive passions are revealed to have no independent ontological status. For both Spinoza and Hobbes, the world is ultimately one complex system whose individual "parts" are not really independent ontological units: they operate—and can be understood—only through their interconnections. But despite the important similarities between Spinoza and Hobbes, there is an important difference. Spinoza remains within the Stoic tradition: knowledge—true self-knowledge—can liberate the individual from the bondage of the passive passions. An individual with a narrow and limited conception of his nature is passively subject to many affects; one whose idea of his own nature includes his patterns of interdependence on the system of causes no longer thinks of himself as passively affected: he recognizes his affects as the active expressions of his real nature. For all of that, Spinoza, like other Stoics, holds that it is the world as a total system—and not the individual himself—who determines whether he achieves self-knowledge.

Hume makes the next dramatic moves in our history. "We must distinguish," he says, "betwixt personal identity, as it regards our thought or imagination, and as it regards our passions or the concern we take in ourselves" (T. 253). The former idea—the self-as-observer—is composed of an associatively patterned series of impressions and ideas. The latter idea—the self-as-an-agent-with-a-specific-interest-in-his-future—is constructed from the patterns of a person's pride, whose causes are those pleasurable properties that he conceives as singularly *his* and that are particularly admired as "shining and visible" by his fellows. The socially formed passion of pride reveals what an individual considers most properly *his*, as central to his self-definition. Here again, we have the unexpected, unsuspected turning point in the coordination of the passions and the self. Hume introduced the social dimension in the construction of the fictional idea of the self: for the idea of the self that is "unfailingly produced" from the passion of pride is one that is marked by properties that are considered by others to be rare, "visible and shining, admired and prized" (T. 290–94). The pleasant properties associated with pride should be "very discernible and obvious, and that, not only to ourselves but to others also. . . . We fancy ourselves more happy, as well as more virtuous or beautiful, when we appear so to others" (T. 292).

The mechanism of sympathy enlarges our store of passion-emotions.[3] We are naturally prone, Hume thinks, to acquire the passions that we attribute to those whom we believe resemble us. There are two conditions for the operation of sympathetic resonance: for X to acquire the emotion or interest of Y, he must implicitly believe that

Y resembles him in some significant respect; and he must form an idea of Y's psychological state. The imagination so enlivens X's idea of Y's condition that the idea becomes a motivating passion in X's own psychology.

Without fully realizing the extent of his transformation, Hume adds yet another turn in our story. By now passions are no longer invasions: they are our very own motives, indeed they are all the motives we have. But the class of passions is further extended to include sentiments, motivating passions that have been formed by and from reflection, by "taking a general point of view." As he cryptically puts it: "Tis only when a character is considered in general, without reference to our particular interest, that it causes such a feeling or sentiment, as denominates it morally good or evil" (T. 472). And now—to what certainly would have been the astonishment and near incomprehension of Aristotle—the class of passions has been so extended as to become sources of our moral attitudes. The sense or sentiment of justice originally arises from the benign accidents of cooperative practices. These in turn provide the materials for the operation of the mechanism of sympathy. Sympathy enables us to acquire the passions and interests of those we believe to resemble ourselves, to take their welfare to heart as our own. Even though Hume does not think we have any natural altruistic motives, he thinks that we can, under the proper circumstances and with a well-trained imagination, take pleasure in the welfare of others as part of our own welfare. The way is set for making the educated sentiments motives that can in principle outweigh the narrow self-interest with which we begin. It seems that those passions that—like the sentiment of justice—have been sympathetically and imaginatively educated to take a general point of view can in principle enlarge the scope of a person's self-conception.

Corresponding to the expansion of the class of passions to emotions and then to sentiments are three-layered conceptions of the self. The "self as regards thought and the imagination" is passive to passions: they are simply impressions of reflection. But for the self "as regards . . . the concern we take in ourself"—the self as an agent—passions are emotions or motives. For the self that has been enlarged to include the welfare and interests of others, passions have become sentiments, modes of knowledge capable of moral evaluation. Hume's account of the origins of the idea of the self as an agent, his account of the origins of the idea of the self as a moral agent, gingerly avoids the problem of whether the constructed fictions of the self *are* the self or whether there is a truth of the matter, one that might provide a critique of a person's—or a society's—patterns of pride and sentiments of justice. His essay "On the Standard of Taste" gives criteria for evaluating fictions. We can, as Hume himself does not, extend those criteria to evaluating the fictions of the self. Learned historians and experienced critics will find themselves approving the attributes and properties that have provided a socially useful and pleasurable system of motivation. If historians and critics disagree . . . well, time and only time can tell.

II

But Rousseau thinks he can do better than time. We've been moving back and forth between metaphysics and poetry, between the self and the fictional construction of the idea of the self. Rousseau is obsessed with the question, What is the truth of the matter—what is the relation between an individual's true self and the self-conception that is coordinate with his passions? If the passions are affected by society, and if society is corrupt, the passions will be false and misleading indices of the true nature and boundaries of the self, of its real needs.

Rousseau attempts to provide a finely atuned account of the natural and the social contributions to the coordination between the self and the passions. There is, first, natural man as he might exist in a presocial world, the raw material, so to say, of the fully developed citizen that he can become.[4] As society develops, natural man becomes a socially formed self-conscious subject, one who is focused on issues of domination and subservience. By Rousseau's lights, society provides the necessary but disastrous stage or transition from natural man to his fulfillment as a rational, autonomous citizen, capable of generalized social sentiments. Each of these stages marks a distinctive coordination between the self and the passions. Nevertheless, although we are, so to speak, radically different persons with quite different psychologies as we find ourselves primarily defined by our social or political environments, our basic natural equipment and ends remain constant. They provide the grounds for evaluating social and political systems and for diagnosing their failures.

Natural Man: The Raw Materials of the Self

In *The Discourse on the Origins of the Sciences and the Arts* and in *The Discourse on the Origins and Foundation of Inequality*, Rousseau tells (his version of) the story of the origins and the corruptions of society. By providing a diagnosis of what he sees as the diseases of the self, that story is also meant to indicate the therapy of those diseases.

With an entirely different metaphysics and moral, Rousseau returns to Aristotle's primary contrast between activity and passivity. We are, he claims, constitutionally naturally active and independent sentient creatures, responding instinctively to what is present, without forethought, choice, or precautions for the future.[5] If—hypothetically—we could exist in a presocial state of nature, we would have an unselfconscious somatic *amour de nous-même*, a noncomparative sense of our own individual existence and well-being, a pleasurable sense of our own natural activity. *Amour de soi* is an unreflective "être bien dans sa peau." Natural life is difficult but healthy. The exercise of our constitutional activities—running, climbing trees, eating—carries unselfconscious delight. Natural life is difficult but healthy. It involves neither trusting sociability nor social distrust. Human encounters—including sexual encounters and partuition—are accidental and casual, without affective bonding. Infants are attended largely for the sake of the female's comfort, and children go their own way as soon as they become independently able to forage for their food. Alone, without the necessity—or the consequences—of bonding relations to others of his kind, presocial man does not develop language. His actions are unmediated impulsive responses to immediate needs: he does not yet have desires whose formation requires an active imagination for future contingencies or future possibilities. Since there is no thought for the future, there is no need for property, no need to regulate entitlement, no need for a formal political organization.

Besides the basic sentiment of his own existence, presocial natural man is endowed with *pitié*, a sympathetic responsive awareness of the suffering of other sentient creatures.[6] An unmediated precognitive reaction, not yet a motive for action, *pitié* nevertheless provides the raw materials for our eventual identification with our fellow citizens. Because men do not naturally define themselves by comparison, natural marginal physical inequalities do not generate the debilitating passions that accompany psychological and social inequality. Though presocial man is not malformed nor corrupt, he is also not yet genuinely himself, neither autonomously rational nor capable of genuinely moral sentiments. Bound to his impulses, he is only negatively free in not being subject to the will of another.

The Formation of the Social Subject

There is nothing in the state of nature, nothing within our own natures, that impells us to form societies. Because we are basically naturally self-sufficient, there is no press toward the division of labor that generates dependency. But "Man was born free yet everywhere we see him in chains." So why and how did free men enchain themselves, and what are the chains? Rousseau speculates that the events that brought men together in society were in a way accidental.[7] A series of geological accidents—an earthquake that enclosed a small valley, a flood or glacier that narrowed the scope of natural wandering—brought men into continued and close contact with one another in an environment that was sufficiently harsh to make survival an unending task and yet not so brutal as to set us desperately against one another. Rousseau envisages the accidental discovery of the preservation and utility of fire. The warmth and security it provides bring individuals closer together. They discover the benefits of cooperation: by combining their efforts, they can build better and more enduring shelters, secure their food and comfort more efficiently. The random mating that took place in nature is replaced by a more permanent bond between male and female in the care of their offspring. The relatively early separation between mother and child is replaced by a stronger and more protracted familial grouping. Sociability and language develop together, and the earliest form of the arts, arising from clustering around the hearth—storytelling, singing, and dancing—all appear together. But since there is minimal inequality of talents, men begin to compare and to rank one another's talents and skill. Instead of singing expressively, they begin to *perform* and to measure themselves by their success or failure in impressing or moving (what has become) an audience.

In becoming self-conscious, men become self-divided, objects of their own subjectivity. Gradually, *amour de soi* is replaced by *amour propre*, and men come to evaluate themselves by comparison to others and by reference to the esteem that others accord to them. They begin to construct themselves—to take on those skills and attributes—to conform to the patterns that they believe will gain them the esteem, and therefore the cooperation, of others. As their thriving comes to depend upon cooperation, their contributions become increasingly specialized. But the division of labor introduces a debilitating dependence. Physical and psychological passivity replaces animal activity. As men become observers and indeed self-observing spectators, the imagination is transformed. Always at the service of the satisfaction of needs and desires, the imagination had been a simple and short-term activity of direct imaging. In society, it becomes fantasy, still linked to the satisfaction of desire, but now constructing and exploring remote possibilities, whose conceptualization generates more desires, whose satisfaction creates even more refined possibilities. Men begin to live in a world of imagined fictions and hypothetical futures that radically transformed the self and its passions. A creature who had been content with a simple life, becomes feverish, perpetually dissatisfied, reactively busy without being genuinely—that is, independently—active. He is complicit in the process of his malformation.

And it is this—the dependency and passivity that develops from a reliance on the division of labor—that enchains us. The ills of social man are a function of the structures of dependency. The chains are those of the passivity and debility that dependence engenders. Dependency introduces relations of domination and subservience along with their numerous passions of defense and offense. Natural man has become a subject capable of taking himself as an object: in society, his sense of himself is now mediated through others.[8] Gradually the individual is transformed into the social subject, increasingly dependent on the perception, cooperation, and good will of others. Alternately servile and defiant, alternately grateful and resentful, proud and abject, social man is thoroughly ambivalent about those on whom his self-esteem depends. Ironically, the most social of men cannot have true, steadfast social sentiments.

Full of anxious forethought, beset by desires that he falsely believes represent his needs, the social subject is a creature of his fantasy-imagination. His language becomes increasingly fanciful and metaphorical. The arts—and particularly drama—command him. The theater inflames the imagination in such a way as to enlarge the possibilities of self-definition: it engenders a whole range of new passions. A calculating form of prudential rationality directed to satisfying desires develops in an uneasy oppositional balance to the fantasy-imagination—serving both to fulfill and to check it.

Together, imagination and prudence combine to invent the idea of property as a form of security. But it is quickly detached from its function of satisfying basic needs: it is absorbed into the materials for comparative *amour propre*. The marginal inequalities of nature are magnified by the institution of property, which in turn produces new forms of dependency and its consequences: envy, resentment, malice, jealousy, competition, servility. Whatever political institutions such a society might develop to protect their lives and their property reflect, reproduce, and augment the malformation and inequalities and inequities of social life. In such circumstances political institutions reproduce and solidify rather than correct social ills. Greed, competition, and envy become the dominant social passions. Men are no longer in any sense free: they are enchained to ever-multiplying passions that cannot be satisfied.

The Self as Autonomous Citizen: The Therapeutic Experiments

Having diagnosed the ills of our condition and traced their origins to dependency and to our plastic susceptibility to social formation, Rousseau conducts several thought experiments to investigate possible modes of therapy. There are basically three roads to the transformation of the debased social subject: the political solution is sketched in *The Social Contract*; the psychological and educative solution is sketched in *Émile* and the domestic/affectional solution is explored in *La Nouvelle Heloise*. All three therapeutic experiments have the same ends: reunite the subject and object in autonomous activity, promote equality, assure independence and block the formation of the structures of dependency; strengthen true universalizing rationality over the calculations of prudence; replace the tumultuous and fortuitous passions with stable, generalized sentiments. And all three have the same problems: they presuppose the conditions they are meant to achieve; they depend on the intervention of a benign, paternalistic, unflawed Legislator-Tutor; and they introduce elements that will undo the therapy.

In *The Social Contract*, Rousseau analyzes the principles and the institutions that would enable the social subject to become an autonomous citizen.[9] The principles of political life are directed to ensuring the equality of autonomous individuals. The institutions are to be designed in such a way as to enable man to regain a sense of his own activity, reuniting the self as subject and the self as object. The function of the state is to bring men to the fulfillment of their real natures. For this, it is necessary to reform both reason and the passions and to "force men to be free." By Rousseau's lights, this means that it is necessary to restrain the imagination, to censor the arts, to curb luxury. *The Social Contract* is an egalitarian transformation of Plato's *Republic*, one that substitutes the ideal of rational individual autonomy for the ideal of rational order.

Rousseau develops Hume's cryptic and tantalizing remarks about the role of "the general point of view" in developing the artificial virtues and the moral sentiments. The social subject's passions are to become the citizen's sentiments; the private subject comes to be moved by—and to identify himself with—the general will.[10] In any case, citizenship transforms rationality. The merely prudential thought that had been at the service of an individual's desires moves toward recognizing the necessities of universal laws. Nowhere is Rousseau's Stoic inheritance more forcibly stated: man fulfills his true nature by identifying himself with rational law, recognizing that his freedom can be achieved only by that identification. When man sees himself—

identifies himself—as a self-and-universally-legislating citizen, when his subjectivity and his objectivity are actively identical, his self-esteem is no longer slavishly dependent on particular social relations of domination and subservience. In principle, the sentiments that are coordinate with this transformation are equally generalized. The new man has also acquired generalized civic and religious sentiments, the sense of justice and of a civic religious piety. Those sentiments can be secured only by the structures of political equality in citizenship.

But the account of the just polity is riddled with manifest incoherence: it is a contractual account that depends on the initiative of a semi-divine external founder and legislator; it is a "social" contract that deliberately minimizes the social interaction of its citizens; its citizens suffer Janus-faced allegiances to the polity on the one hand and to their families on the other; it proclaims an egalitarian polity that excludes some of its members—the nurturing mothers—from the rights and obligations of citizenship; it is a thoroughly rationalized the secularized polity that nevertheless institutes the ritual observances and sentiments of civic-nature religion. In distinguishing agreement on the general principles of the polity—agreements that are to be accepted by universal consent—from the legislation of substantive decisions, it depends on a level of mutual trust. But how is this trust grounded and developed? Must the working assumption of the just polity be that distrust appears only in corrupt societies? The hidden implication of *The Social Contract* is that the best and most just political solution of social ills, the solution that restores (a rational and consensual version of) *amour de soi* is, at best, precarious. The formation of the social contract presupposes the very conditions it is meant to establish.

Rousseau presents his speculations about the educative-psychological therapy for the ills of the social self in *Émile*. He examines the sort of education that a truly well-formed human being might have, one who could become a free and rational citizen. In principle, no special social or historical conditions are required to carry on the experiment of Émile's education; in principle, the educative experiment should not presuppose the benign political conditions fixed by *The Social Contract*. Rousseau claims that his investigation will take men as they are to be found, anywhere and everywhere. In a sense this condition is met: Émile is a healthy but ordinary child; he is isolated in the countryside, but any countryside in a relatively temperate climate will do. And since he does not come into contact with political institutions, no particular political conditions are presupposed.

Émile is in many ways like natural man, and it is the Tutor's task to keep him that way as long as possible. He is independent and active; his sense of his existence is formed by a natural noncomparative sense of *amour de soi*. He has no passionate or idle curiosity, but inquires only when he has a particular practical need; and he is satisfied when that need is satisfied. Initially, he has no bent to generalize for its own sake. He is to learn from experience, by the consequences of his actions rather than from persons or books. If he were directly taught by the Tutor, the complex relations of power and dependence would be set in motion. He would become passive, anxious to please, secretly rebellious, biding his turn for tyranny. And if he were to learn from books, his "thought" would consist of ill-digested phrases that he would not understand. When he learns from his experience, he remains free and active. The development of the intellectual passions—the joys of playful comparison generalization and invention—are to be delayed as long as possible, until Émile is a genuinely self-reliant and self-sustaining person. The Tutor's maxims give the clearest account of Émile's psychology: Never tell Émile anything he doesn't ask about. Never tell him anything beyond his experience that he cannot actively use. Make things rather than persons his mode of education. Postpone his emotional development. Minimize self-consciousness. Maximize self-determination.

Like natural man, Émile has an instinctive sense of *pitié*. Unlike natural man, he also has a primitive sense of indignation, the key to a primitive and unarticulated sense of injustice. When his plants are uprooted, he senses himself wronged. By a series of lessons that connect his indignation with that of others, he devleops an understanding of the rights of others.

All goes well until adolescence and the wild host of passions that the appearance of sexuality brings. Émile encounters Sophie; he is of course enamored of her. The hope of his development as a free and independent citizen depends on his surviving this turmoil. It is at this point—and only at this point—that the Tutor presents himself as a commanding authority. He must call on Émile to leave Sophie for a time, to postpone their life together. He sends Émile off on his *wanderjahre* to explore the world. Sophie cannot, of course, accompany him. To begin with, if Émile is to come to a sound understanding of the world, he and Sophie must postpone their sexuality. Further, Émile must now develop a capacity to form his own judgment, to compare ways of life, to think in general terms. If the Tutor has done his job well, it is now safe even for Émile to go to the theater.

There is another crucial reason that Sophie cannot accompany Émile on the journeys that will prepare him for the last stage in his self-development. Sophie is not another Émile. She must be educated to tend to the welfare of others and to define her self through her capacity to nourish and to nurture. Far from a sense of active independence, Sophie is focused on her relation to Émile and to their children. Although hers is a life of sweet service, rather than one of rational autonomy, she nevertheless is accorded a certain sort of superiority. In time, Émile will not only depend on her sentiments but must, in certain instances, be guided by them.

Like *The Social Contract*, the educative therapeutic experiments presented in *Émile* presuppose conditions that—on Rousseau's theories—they are meant to produce. As the social contract presupposes a semi-divine legislator, so that Tutor appears to be new sort of autonomous divinity, simulateously devoted and detached. Without relations or affectional ties of his own, he has the education of Émile as his primary project. Yet he cannot become dependent on Émile or even on the hope that Émile's children will revere him. For all his devotion to his educative task, he cannot become dependent on his relation to Émile. And yet Émile is his primary and, it seems, his only "fruit."

Moreover, Émile must not compare himself with others, must not guess that he has been deceived or even manipulated. Yet since there are servants and peasant children, he would surely observe significant differences between them and himself. He must understand equality without having grown up among equals. Although Émile is clearly not given to psychological observation or speculation, and although everything is done to avoid his developing the habits—or even the ideas—of domination and subservience, he would surely become aware of the Tutor's orders to the servants and peasants. It is virtually impossble to imagine that Émile would remain wholly unaware of the theatricality of his condition.

But it is Sophie who presents the real problem for Rousseau's therapeutic experiments. Sophie is the new Eve in the Garden of Eden. She must be, and yet she cannot be, a citizen. The future mother of free men is nevertheless obedient or at any rate compliant, relatively ignorant of the world, educated for the particular nurturing sentiments of motherhood—and so unsuited to the disinterested universalizing rationality of citizenship. She is to have ribbons and she must learn to be coy. To maintain Émile's ardor for her, she must learn to refuse her favors. Vanity—innocent vanity, but vanity nevertheless—is introduced.

In any case, Émile's relation to Sophie introduces an internal division within himself, an obstacle for the unification of his subjectivity and his objectivity. His familial life—a life that is essential both to his welfare and that of his polity—leaves him with divided loyalties and a divided mind. As an adult citizen and *père de famille*, Émile must work through the contrast between the particularized interests of his devotion to Sophie and their children, on the one hand, and the generalized interests he develops as a citizen identified with the General Will, on the other. In principle, rationality should enable Émile to see the interconnection and perhaps the ultimate identity of these spheres. But he nevertheless initially experiences a distinction between his own inital responses and those that common life requires. Émile must express his private interest in order for the General Will to be formed: the particularity of his perspective are constitutively necessary for the formation of general policy. But to the extent that his sense of himself is particular and perspectival, it is not—at least initially—identical with the civic decisions to which he gives his rational consent. The contrast between the sentiments and generalized rational will remain, even though they are marked as contrasts between the psychology of Sophie and that of Émile.

Taken independently of one another, the therapeutic experiments—the political, the psychological-educative, the affectional-social—will be likely to fail. The psychological reforms of *Émile* need to be supported by those growing out of the political contract—but those in turn require the kinds of citizens formed by Émile's education. Each of the therapies appears to reintroduce the very diseases it was meant to avoid. The therapeutic projects cannot succeed in returning us to the unconflicted joys of our presocial condition. Nevertheless, although the therapeutic experiments sketched by Rousseau cannot assure the self's immunity against corruption, he believes that they will promote whatever little health our complex plasticity allows. While we can diminish our malaise, we can never be well. The self-awareness Rousseau has invoked to cure us reintroduces the very disharmony, the internal division it was meant to overcome. In any case, reforms are only as good as the reformers. But unlike the Tutor and the Legislator, we suffer malformed passions fed by imaginations excited by corrupt relations of dependency. Whether any aspects of the three therapeutic strands—the political, psychological, and social—can be appropriately combined will be a matter of historical accident. We are left in doubt and darkness, for it is not at all clear that the three domains can be combined. Superficially at any rate, there are barriers to the promised harmony of the inner and the outer man, of the familial and civic affections.

Rousseau's diagnosis of our ills and his therapeutic analyses express his divided mind and his struggles to unite it. He is metaphysically and morally committed to individual natural autonomy. Yet it is he who most stresses the social formation of an individual's conception of his freedom, his rationality, even his desires. He is a passionate egalitarian, and yet the social structure that he idealizes depends on women's political inequality. Sensitive to what he conceives to be the dangers of the power of language in forming the imagination, he nevertheless indulges in rhetorical outbursts, using the very methods he hopes to overcome, in the full realization that the processes of learning and transformation remain immanent in the outcome.

III

What is the pattern—if there is one—in this history that moves from Aristotle's *pathē* to Descartes's passions, to Hume's emotions and Rousseau's sentiments? The constant motif in the pattern is correlation between the self and the passions: a person's passions reveals her conception of her boundaries, of what she considers essential to her self. The shifts in the pattern are shifts in conceptions of the self.

Issues of strong individuation or subjectivity do not arise for Aristotle. *Pathē* are passive reactions contrasted with activities and actions that originate directly from an individual's essential nature without needing a particular contingent event to set them in motion. A person is primarily defined by the activities and potentialities that are essential to the species and by the ways in which his polity further specifies and actualizes those general potentialities. The fullest realization of an individual is his activity as a contemplator of what is eternal and unchanging; but an individual also fulfills his potentialities by developing and actively exercising his practical virtues, well-formed dispositions of action and passions. It is not passions as such but our dispositions concerning them that define our character.

Descartes introduces a complexly layered self: the essential ego is the mind, for whom passions are invasions. But "in this life"—the life of the hybrid individual composed of a mind and a body—the passions are self-preserving motives. Still for all of that, the passions are, in their first appearance, untutored effects of the body's action on the mind, they can therefore endanger as well as benefit us.

Hume adds a social dimension in the account of the formation of the concept of the self. The idea of the self is a fictional construct, a product of the passion of pride. But the "look of the other" is an essential antecedent of pride. Because he enlarges the range of the passions to include sentiments that have been formed by sympathy and by "a general perview," Hume enlarges the scope of the idea of the self to include the moral virtues, those sentiments that have gained general approbation. The self has centrally become a civil person, defined through his moral sentiments.

Rousseau speaks with many tongues. In a sense, he has returned us to our Stoic selves, fully ourselves only when we have achieved rational autonomy, identified our interests with those of the General Will, and transformed our passions into generalized and impartial civic sentiments. Rousseau answers the question that Hume leaves hanging: what is the connection between the self and any particular idea of the self? In a corrupt society, there is no relation; in a benign polity, they are identical. Nevertheless, Rousseau leaves us more conflicted, more divided than ever. Even setting aside the alleged miseries of the de-based social subject—miseries that might seem delightfully interesting to those not burdened by Rousseau's longing for unity and harmony— the autonomous citizen remains layered and conflicted. Descartes's dual self—the self as mind and the self as a hybrid of mind and body— has become a triadic self. There is the natural creature who somehow persists through his social and political formation/transformation. There is the private, familial man, and there is man as rational citizen. It would be a piece of false consciousness to deny any of these aspects; none can be transcended.

So much for the pattern. Is there room for asking, What is the truth of the matter? I believe that there is and that, despite the bizarre combination of a deplorable sentimentality and an equally deplorable Spartan regimen, Rousseau gives us the raw materials for answering the question. The truth of the matter is that we are multiple selves: we are wild animal creatures; we long for, and are committed to identifying ourselves with, a universalized rational autonomy. And even in the best of polities, we are also social subjects defined by the particular affectional relations that carry the dialectics of power relations in their wake. All these strata—and no doubt more—define our selves and our passions. There is no rest, no resolution, no pivotal point from which we can unify this many-headed beast. Each of the layers of our complex selves claims its own rights—and each claims the right to dominate the others. Each has its own definition of rationality; worse, each has its own definition of freedom and of thriving. At best—if we have the dubious good fortune of Émile's education and the genuine good fortune of living in a well-formed polity—we can learn to take joy in the complexity of our selves. But is the point of having a self to learn to rejoice in it?

BIBLIOGRAPHY

T. David Hume, *A Treatise of Human Nature* edited by L. A. Selby-Bigge (London: Oxford University Press, 1888 rep. 1989).

PA. Rene Descartes, *The Passions of the Soul: The Philosophical Writings of Descartes* vol. 1, edited by John Cottingham, Robert Stoothoff, and Dugald Murdoch (Cambridge: Cambridge University Press, 1984).

Jean-Jacques Rousseau, "Fragments for Émile" in *Oeuvres Completès* (Paris: Gallimard Editions Pléiade, 1969) vol. iv (my translation).

NOTES

1. Cf. Amélie O. Rorty "Aristotle on the Metaphysical Status of *Pathë*," *The Review of Metaphysics* 37, No. 3, March 1984. We do not, for instance, need external prompting to eat, to make friends, or to think; but something has to happen to us to make us sullen or nostalgic. Whether a certain sort of condition is a *pathos* or the realization of a species-defined trait—whether it is a passion or an activity—is a matter for scientific investigation. To determine whether a herd's imitative actions in following its leader's danger flight signals constitutes a specification of that species's natural, endogenous capacities and activities or whether those reactions are exogenous requires determining the essential characterization of a species. These are not merely academic questions. For instance, it is an important question for human beings to determine whether human reactions to charismatic figures are constitutional or contingently controllable responses.

2. Cf. Amélie O. Rorty, "The Two Faces of Spinoza," *Review of Metaphysics* 41, No. 2 1988.

3. T. 317ff. Hume's account of the operations of sympathy characteristically rests on two metaphors: a medical ("infection") and a musical metaphor ("consonance," "resonates"). The point of these metaphors is that the operations of sympathy do not require any intentional intervention. They operate whenever initiating conditions are met. See A. O. Rorty, "The Structure of Hume's *Treatise*," *History of Philosophy Quarterly* 10, No. 2 1993.

4. In discussing Rousseau's account of the relation between the self and its passions and sentiments, it is appropriate, indeed necessary, to use the masculine pronoun throughout. In *Émile*, it is clear that the ideal model of the fully developed human self is not a generalized, nongendered person. The model self is a man, who—to be sure—must have had a woman as his original nurturer and who will form a bond to a woman as his eventual partner. Though she is a moral teacher as well as a necessary complementary partner to her man, the model woman will never be fully autonomous or rational. Because her domain is that of particularized sentiments, she will not become a self-legislative citizen. Yet the fully developed citizen depends on her sentiments, her unmediated nurturance.

5. Rousseau derives the primary emphasis on activity from Aristotle. The constitution of the species carries a set of natural activities: no motives are required to develop or exercise these activities; the thriving of the species consists in their appropriate exercise. While Rousseau agrees with Aristotle about the centrality of practical reason and its connection with active citizenship, he strongly disagrees with Aristotle's elitist conception of practical rationality and with his strong separation between practical reason and the exercise of pure theoretical reason.

6. Because it connotes a sharp distinction between subject and object, because it presupposes a comparative judgment, "pity" is a poor translation of *pitié*.

7. Rousseau claims that Hobbes's description of men in the state of nature is in fact a description of man in prepolitical society. If Hobbes were right, he argues, the political contract could never have been formed. It is, of course, a long and complex issue whether Rousseau is entitled to make this criticism. To begin with, he is perfectly aware that Hobbes's account of the state of nature is as hypothetical and ahistorical as his own. And although Rousseau postulates an intermediate social stage between nature and political life, his criticism of Hobbes applies to his own account of the transition between social and political man. If the social subject is as deformed as Rousseau suggests, he would be incapable of the rational deliberation required to form the political contract.

8. In the *Confessions*, Rousseau deliberately reveals himself as a prime example of the effects of such malformation. Ironically, that corruption is often more clearly revealed in his unselfconsious accounts of his adventures than it is in his dramatic confessional proclamations. In the *Essay on the Origin of Languages* and in the *Lettre a D'Alembert*, he analyzes the complicity of the arts and letters in the processes of that corruption.

9. The title—*Le Contract Social*—is a misnomer. It is, after all, Rousseau who develops the contrast between society and the polity, between the informal psychological relations that grow without a person's explicit consent and the political relations founded on principles to which an individual has freely consented.

10. Despite his attempt to spell out the steps by which the general will is the rational expression of each individual's own interest, Rousseau's conception of the relation between the general will and civic sentiment remains obscure. That obscurity is marked by the fact that almost no two commentators agree about how best to interpret it.

11. Nevertheless Émile's education is placed in a specific and highly controlled social setting: he has no siblings; there are servants; there are peasants and gentry; there is property; the institution of promising is strongly in place. The peasants are manifestly not serfs but autonomous persons, and although the servants take their orders from the Tutor, they regulate the performance of

their tasks in much the same way that the Tutor himself does. Still so far as possible, the political basis for these conditions are not to affect Émile's development. Although Émile must acquire an understanding of promising and the proprieties dictated by property, no particular system of legislation or of inheritance is presupposed. But the Tutor nevertheless introduces a normative account of initial property entitlement: the control of property is explicitly linked to labor.

3

Rousseau, Hakuseki, and Hakuin: Paradigms of Self in Three Autobiographers

John C. Maraldo

In the course of reading it enthusiastically, I felt as if a self [*jibun*], something I had been unaware of until then, were being drawn out.

These remarkable words of Meiji novelist Shimazaki Tōson provide the starting point for my inquiry. Written in 1909 in an essay entitled "The Self That I Discovered in Rousseau's *Confessions*,"[1] Tōson's statement is all the more perceptive for being uttered, not by a philosopher seeking some articulated concept of the self, but by a man spontaneously expressing a new-found way to write in fiction of the truths of life and nature. Is it possible that Tōson had no model available to him, within Japanese culture, of what it is to be a self? And what is this "self" that Tōson discovers? In her work on the ideal of individuality in the Meiji novel, Janet Walker suggests that Tōson was "jolted into an awareness of his own self that existed, like Rousseau's, in the past and in the present, in the form of experiences, memories, and reflections." "The Japanese writers who created the first modern literature in the Meiji period," she claims, "discovered themselves as individuals through their reading of Western literature."[2]

In our present era of cultivated individualism, it is difficult to imagine that someone could be unaware of being a self-contained individual, existing "in the past and in the present, in the form of experiences, memories, and reflections." I want to show that this apparent lack of awareness is best interpreted as a confrontation with

57

certain Western paradigms of self which were undeveloped, or at least underdeveloped, in Japan. A survey of all possible models of self within Japanese and Western culture is far beyond the scope of this article; but a more modest sketch of self-identities in selected Buddhist, Confucian, and popular literature, juxtaposed against the heritage of Rousseau, will serve my present purpose. Following Thomas Kuhn's clue that a paradigm governs a group or practitioners who have certain training in common,[3] I will suggest that different methods of investigation were crucial to the formation of different paradigms of self. At the same time, my sketch will expose some of the difficulties of joining "paradigm" and "self" in one prepositional phrase, for a paradigm by definition functions to unify and identify a set of objects under investigation, but self-unity and self-identity are seen precisely as problems in modern Western thought, while much of Japanese thought sees the "self" as something that cannot be objectified.

Rousseau's Self-conscious Self

I have resolved on an enterprise which has no precedent . . . to display to my kind a portrait in every way true to nature, and the man I shall portray will be myself. Simply myself. [*Moi seul*].

These opening words to Rousseau's *Confessions*[4] declare his awareness of what we now call a "paradigm shift"—ostensibly, a shift only in literary genre, but at bottom a shift that established a newly emergent concept of self. In *The Modern Self in Rousseau's Confessions*, Ann Hartle argues that the solitary, self-centered individual actually depicted by Rousseau, more than the man he would portray true to nature, signals the modern understanding of human nature as mutable convention, rather than invariable essence.[5] Here I wish not to descend into and describe the inner sanctum of the self Rousseau exposes but only to point out the character and assumptions of the method he attempts.

At the beginning of the *Confessions*, Rousseau states his intent "to present myself before my Sovereign Judge, . . . [to bare] my secret soul as Thou Thyself hast seen it, Eternal Being." Rousseau's assumption that he commands an omniscient purview of himself was taken by Tōson as an admirable attitude of objectivity missing in Japanese literature, one that, Janet Walker surmises, was, associated with the introduction, around 1900, of Western scientific methods into Japan.[6] "I know my own heart," Rousseau writes, and he proposes to display himself as "vile and despicable, when my behavior was such, and good, generous and noble when I was so." The implication of self-omniscience is qualified only by some "defects of memory," but never by a lapse in sincerity or honesty: "I have never put down as true what I know to be false." At the end he proclaims, "I have told the truth. If anyone knows anything contrary to what I have here recorded, though he prove it a thousand times, his knowledge is a lie and an imposture."[7] Notwithstanding the self-righteous and rather defensive tone of this remark, it is hard not to hear it as a disclosure of belief in Cartesian incorrigibility: "I cannot go wrong about what I have felt, or about what my feelings have led me to do."[8]

It is important to realize that Rousseau's claim to be telling the truth about himself, however questionable it may be, is not identical with a claim to be representing facts or events as they are ascertained by others. Rousseau seems to believe that he can truthfully depict his inner or true self regardless of how factual or fictive his self portrait is. Although there is a fascinating controversy about the extent to which Rousseau understood his work to be fictional, his portrayed self to be his own creation,[9] we can separate this issue from that of the incorrigibility of self-knowledge. Rousseau's portrait can be an imaginative construct and still purport to present his true feelings and thoughts, all the more so when they include how he imagines himself to be. Rousseau's remarks show that he imagines a self that can know itself without error.

In similar remarks proclaiming his absolutely unique individuality, Rousseau belies a commitment to Cartesian privileged access: my inner self is invisible to others save by my voluntary confessions. "[My] readers . . . cannot have helped seeing, throughout the course of my life [that is, my *Confessions*], countless inner emotions of mine utterly unlike their own."[10] Yet Rousseau's method of disclosing the truth about himself is confirmation not of an inviolable Cartesian substance but of a Lockean self bounded by self-consciousness and memory. "I know nothing of my self till I was five or six," Rousseau confesses.[11] He reconstructs his life for us by remembering, recollecting, all the experiences he can (or will). "I trace my nature back in this way to its earliest manifestations."[12]

To be sure, his *Confessions* are not those of a mind simply spilling out its memories into a stream of consciousness by free association, but rather are self-consciously reflective and selective descriptions of himself and the others he encounters. Still, Rousseau's primary practice is remembrance; and in writing the *Confessions* it is a life *as remembered* that he presents for others to see as he confesses to see it. When Shimazaki Tōson writes his recollection, fifteen years afterwards, of his own experience of reading Rousseau and discovering his self, he is in fact already practicing writing according to the paradigm of a self constituted by its inner experiences, memories, and reflections. He is thus in a position to see Rousseau's life as the epitome of moral "self-discipline," as he calls it. For Tōson, Rousseau's self-scrutiny is totally modern and admirable.[13] Yet if there is something novel about Rousseau's willingness, and satisfaction, in exposing himself—vileness, virtue, and all—to the public eye,[14] still a scrutinized and recollected self is not without precedent.

The Heritage of Rousseau's Self: Locke

For it is by the consciousness it has of present thoughts and actions, that it is *self* to *itself* now, and so will be the same self, as far as the same consciousness can extend.

Locke, in his *Essay Concerning Human Understanding*, concludes that it is consciousness and memory, as opposed to spiritual or material substance, that constitutes the self. He is, of course, contradicting Descartes, but in the steps of his argument we find evident if unvoiced assumptions about the nature of self that both he and Descartes share. Locke argues that one could be the soul of Socrates, but unless one had Socrates' thoughts and memories, he would not be "the same person with Socrates."[16] To be a person here means to be unified by consciousness of a strictly personal, that is, individual sort. Reciprocally, consciousness signifies here a capacity to recollect a sameness throughout the various moments of its activity. For Locke, my identity is not jeopardized by interruptions of consciousness, lapses of memory, or absence of thought—these would only challenge a self made of thinking substance, although one wonders if psychological disorders such as multiple personality or ego-disintegration would not challenge Locke's thesis. (Though he might relieve those suffering from such disorders of personal moral responsibility, it is questionable that he would claim there is one person for each and every fractured personality, or, respectively, no person there at all.) But if Locke disputes substance as the identifying factor, just what notion does he share with Descartes?

"For as far as any intelligent being can repeat the idea of any past action with the same consciousness it had of it at first, and with the same consciousness it has of any present action; so far it is the same personal self."[17] Locke's rather awkward formulation here stipulates that identity is constituted by what is repeatable throughout my experiences; and what is repeatable is not, of course, an action as I once uniquely experienced it but rather the felt sense of its being, both originally and upon recollection, *my* action. The formulation is awkward, and suspiciously circular, only because Locke (unconsciously?) struggles to express a felt sense of something so seemingly self-evident that it nearly defies expression: there, behind every moment of consciousness, I am, always recallable by an act of reflection. Consciousness and, with it, self-identity are inherently egological. The problem Locke addresses is that of "personal identity"; but the "paradigm" he adopts is that of an "I" (eye) whose scope of vision defines the bounds of the self. That this "paradigm" is not universally self-evident is recognized easily enough in Tōson's remark at the beginning of this paper. And if it were universally self-evident, it would not be recognizable as a historically conditioned and perhaps culture-bound paradigm at all. (It is unlikely that Socrates, or any ancient Greek philosophers, lacking as they did a distinct notion of consciousness, would have understood Locke's views.) On the other hand, the fact that Locke took this recollective awareness of oneself for granted (it is just "plain experience" in his words), indicates the influence of a sweeping if unarticulated paradigm, whose cultural reign I cannot gauge here. What I do wish to point out, however, is the sort of method employed by Locke, the practice which is both governed by and creative of the paradigm.

"The understanding, like the eye, whilst it makes us see and perceive all other things, takes no notice of itself; and it requires art and pains to set it at a distance, and make it its own object," Locke says, in the opening passage of his *Essay*.[18] His statement reveals clearly enough his intent to distance himself from, to objectify, what is immeasurably near: "the understanding, that sets man above the rest of sensible beings" and, consequently, the self, which sets one man apart from all others. The "art and pains" Locke engages in are a prototype of what today is called "philosophical analysis": critical reflection at a distance from the immediate data of consciousness. To see remembered self-awareness as the identifying factor of the self, Locke cannot merely practice remembering his experiences, as Rousseau would do, much less present his awareness in a stream-of-consciousness mode. Although the paradigm of a self-conscious self made Rousseau's and Joyce's genres possible, neither of them could have articulated the paradigm, because neither puts sufficient distance between the writing and the writer. Locke isolates memory and awareness from their natural linkage to particular experiences and then reflects in detachment on the outcome. For this reason, Rousseau's work seems much more personal than Locke's; reading *The Confessions* makes us feel we know the heart of Rousseau, whereas the person John Locke, we feel, remains forever hidden behind his *Essay*. Locke is practicing a kind of reflection that may be said to be as creative of the paradigm of a self-conscious self as it is ruled by it. Once again, however, his detachment and isolation of this self are not without example and exaggeration. It was Descartes who meditated in his oven-room, who methodically detached himself from every worldly stimulus and discovered the thinking "I" (*ego cogitans*) at the root of a suspiciously solipsistic self that became the European paradigm, despite its controversial substantiality. That story, however, is beyond the confines of the present paper.

Arai Hakuseki and the Confucian Self

In the old days, when people had anything to say, they said it without unnecessary additions, expressing their meaning fully in as few words as possible. My parents were like that.

And so, too, is the author of these words, Arai Hakuseki, like that.[19] Great Confucian scholar and government reformer who advised the sixth and seventh Tokugawa shōguns, Hakuseki is more than reticent about the personal affairs he would consider unnecessary additions to the work that opens with the quoted passage. Composed in 1716, his *Oritaku shiba no ki* (*Told Round a Brushwood Fire*) is considered, for better or worse, the first proper Japanese autobiography and is often compared to Rousseau's *Confessions*.[20] The comparison would seem to be warranted. Both authors base their works on recollection, and both aspire to the honest truth. Both are driven by a felt need to justify their lives in the eyes of others. Rousseau writes to show himself as he actually was, and not as his enemies unjustly attempted to paint him. Hakuseki writes to "set down past events just as they occurred to me, with no thought-out plan. . . . I am the only man alive who knows the full story, so it would be inexcusable if, unworthy though I am, I did not set it down."[21] The full story Hakuseki will tell, however, is not a confession of his inner life but the story of the "details that concern His late Highness [Shōgun Ienobu]"[22] and that present Hakuseki as an exemplary public figure loyal to his lord and adept at right conduct. He writes so that his sons and grandsons "will not swerve from the path of loyalty and filial piety when they remember the laborious rise of their father and grandfather."[23] It is not surprising, then, that Hakuseki, a Confucian, begins his autobiography with a mention of his parents and a long account of his father and grandfather. When the author continues with a report of his own life, it is solely a life of external events, political consultations, and public administration that he presents. Though he hesitates not, he says, "to write . . . of delicate matters," the reader searches in vain for a glimpse of the secrets of the soul that Rousseau so readily reveals.

The few passages of unconscious revelation in Hakuseki's work are recognizable, for the translator at least, more by their tone than by their content.[24] Even if the "vehemence of Hakuseki's expression bears out the disturbed state of his feeling as he wrote," Hani Gorō's remark that his autobiography represents an awakening of individual awareness[25] seems a gross exaggeration when *Round the Brushwood Fire* is placed beside the *Confessions*. Hakuseki leaves but a trace of self-consciousness or awareness of himself, either as the author or as the subject matter of his "autobiography." "I shall now set down what I have seen myself since I reached years of discretion,"[26] he writes, and he proceeds to describe not himself but, once again, his father—"not a man who showed his feelings." Hakuseki is equally Confucian in betraying no hint of his own feeling toward his father's reticence. The few instances where he permits himself some introspection function as moral example, not as the confession of a hidden self:

> I was born quick-tempered, so my anger was harder to control than anything else. However, this also, as I have made my way through life's difficulties, is declining as my years increase, and now, perhaps, I am not as I used to be. I most earnestly desire that those who come after me should regard this [that it is necessary to learn to endure in everything, as my father taught] as an ancestral precept, and take it to heart above everything.[27]

Personal incidents where we today might expect an outpouring of elation or grief—or at least some expression of personal concern—deserve only a perfunctory, newscastlike report in Hakuseki's work. His marriage is not mentioned at all; and the first of three mentions of his wife occurs in a totally impersonal sentence: "Although I was attached to an unsatisfactory service and had barely enough to support a wife and family."[28] The death of his first child and illness of his son are recorded as interruptions in his plans to teach his lord the Confucian classics: "At that time [1694] my eldest daughter caught smallpox and died . . . Akinori also caught it. On account of these events, I did not begin lectures on the *Shih Ching* until the 8th of March."[29] The death of one child and birth of another, which occurred twice within a one-year period, go unmentioned.

When I focus on what Hakuseki does not write of, and contrast that silence with our modern sensibilities, I do not mean to imply that the Confucian author was cold-hearted or discompassionate. He is simply writing not in order to break the seal on the private confines of his heart but rather in order that "my posterity should understand the conditions of society."[30] And it is not that he chooses to conceal his inner self but that he does not recognize any such individual domain worthy of expression. As Joyce Ackroyd, the translator of Hakuseki's autobiography notes, traditions such as the Reformation that led to the exaltation of the individual's inner life [and] bore fruit in such writings as Rousseau's had no counterpart in Japan. "On the contrary, in that age in which the theoretic basis was Neo-Confucian ethics, the spiritual and material aspirations of the individual were schooled to subordination to social obligations." And even after Rousseau's type of self was discovered by people like Tōson in Meiji times, "the autobiographical genre attracted little attention. Unless self-revelation was transmuted into an experience of universal validity by art, the prejudice against enlarging on personal affairs was too strong."[31]

This assessment, however, makes an assumption that undermines the entire identification of the genre. For if the self-revelation proper to the autobiographical genre is essentially a revelation of personal affairs, then Hakuseki's work can hardly be called autobiography. If, on the other hand, the self that is disclosed (or hidden) in the Confucian work is not to be located essentially in personal and intimate matters, then it will be necessary to question accepted assumptions about what an autobiography, and the self it reveals, can be.

Hakuseki clearly did not live in a milieu where personal affairs could be experienced as the essence of self, but this does not mean that he lacked a notion of self. It suggests rather that a constant practice of alligiance to one's ancestors and principles, and service to one's lord and nation (identical when the lord was the shōgun), will create a different sense of self-identity and self-worth. The personal life that is recollected in this Confucian autobiography may not even look personal to someone nurtured on the model of a Rousseauean self. It may indeed appear to be a "selfless" life, an expression that certainly did not go unused in later Confucian literature. Within a century after Hakuseki's work, the old Buddhist ideal of "no-self" [*muga* 無我] was extolled in ethical *shingaku* manuals written for the populace. One such work, *Zoku Kyūō dōwa* (*Kyūō's Moral Discourses Continued*), written in 1835, asserts that

> if one had no selfish motives but only the supreme virtues, there would be no self. . . . If he serves selflessly, he does not know what service is [does not recognize it as service]. If he knows

what service is, he has a self. . . [to think] only of parents but not of yourself. . . is what I call no self.

This concept of "no-self" as Hiroshi Minami notes, "is identical with the spirit of service above self, where every spontaneous impulse is rejected as selfishness."[32] Even today, among the older, more traditional generation in Japan, the anthropologist Thomas Rohlen finds that "*ga* [我 ego-self]. . . is definitely related to *kokoro* [心] development. . . . In the training of children and adults, overcoming and controlling *ga* is an important goal. . . . Training ('to kill *ga*') and age. . . both serve to reduce the hold of *ga* on persons."[33]

Thirteen years after Hakuseki's work, the Confucian scholar Ishida Baigan founded the *shingaku* (mind-discipline) movement, later popularized by people like Kyūō. But Baigan's ideal of training did not stand unchallenged within Confucianism. Robert Bellah suggests that Baigan chose the expression *shingaku* in reaction to Ogyū Sorai, a contemporary of Hakuseki who had criticized such "mind discipline" as profoundly self-contradictory.[34] Sorai's criticism sounds suspiciously Zen Buddhist: "The Mind is without form. It cannot be controlled by itself. . . . To use one's own mind [*ga shin/waga kokoro*] to control one's own mind is like a lunatic controlling himself by means of his own lunacy." Sorai's aim, however, is not an enlightenment of no-mind or no-self but a way to ethical action. Slightly before Sorai and Hakuseki wrote, Kumazawa Banzan clearly pointed to the public sphere external to the self as the training ground for one who would investigate nature, regulate family and state, and live according to principle.[35] Such differences teach us that Hakuseki's *absence* of self-description is perhaps a clearer expression of the Confucian paradigm than is the phrase "no-self."

Equally controversial is the issue of consciousness of individuality in the Confucian paradigm I have delineated. Hakuseki's father and grandfather were *rōnin* (masterless samurai), and Hakuseki himself remained a samurai when he served his lord, not as a warrior, but as an educator. Various arguments have been advanced as to whether *bushidō*, the way of the warrior formed by the Confucian values of loyalty and submission to one's lord, actually killed a sense of individual self. The teachings of Yamamoto Tsunetomo, recorded the same year as Hakuseki's autobiography in the popular volumes known as *Hagakure* (*Hidden Leaves*), are often cited as evidence of an affirmative answer. Inatomi Eijiro recently blamed the lack of a clear sense of individual self among the Japanese on the long-reigning feudal system, quoting the *Hagakure* as expressive of the tradition: "Whenever one is taken into service to a lord, he should serve the lord without any consideration of his own self. Even if one . . . is ordered to commit harakiri, one should accept [it]."[36] (This quotation, as well as those above admonishing selfishness, imply of course that one naturally does have a sense of self—but only of an egoistic self [*ga* 我].) On the other hand, Uchimura Kanzō, a Meiji contemporary of novelist Tōson, a Christian and advocate of individualism, argued that the samurai obviously exhibited the kind of self-respect, self-assertion, and independence that formed the core of modern individualism[37] (and, I may add, still find expression in such sayings as *jibun ga aru* 自分がある).

Whether Hakuseki would have denied his self to the point of committing harakiri (which was by his time outlawed) or not, his self-protrayal fits both Inatomi's and Uchimura's descriptions. More than once Hakuseki demanded enormous sacrifices, in body and purse, of himself and his family by remaining for a time in the service of a dispossessed lord. Equally often he sought out opportunities to realize his own lofty ambitions.[38] Hakuseki, in other words, was not clearly committed to either selflessness or to self-assertion, nor are these necessarily opposed values.[39]

What seems to be decisive is that a widely shared paradigm of individual consciousness was not operative in Japanese Confucianism before Meiji times and so could not serve as a source of inspiriation for novelist Tōson.

Eighteen years before Tōson made his self-discovery, Fukuzawa Yukichi, the great educator and advocate of a new individuality, himself of samurai stock, had proclaimed that "Japanese warriors did not have any individuality."[40] Four years after Tōson read the *Confessions*, and probably uninfluenced by Rousseau, Fukuzawa published his own autobiography serially, which later was compared to the *Confessions* for its "freedom and directness."[41] It may seem curious, then, that Fukuzawa's autobiography did not also inspire Tōson to discover his personal self and write from its perspective. Fukuzawa freely reports of his virtues and vices; he writes that he is neither afraid of blame nor solicitous of praise, and is ashamed of his drinking habits, for example. Yet these occasional revelations are generalizations quite different in style from Rousseau's detailed self-exposé. Indeed Fukuzawa admits, as if telling the reader what to expect, that "my sociability did not go to the extent of opening myself completely to the confidences of others, or to share with them the inner thoughts of my heart."[42] If Fukuzawa's autobiography had nowhere near the impact of Rousseau's *Confessions* on Japanese writers like Tōson, it was perhaps because Rousseau had given them not merely a verdict about individuality but a whole new paradigm to emulate in their writing.[43]

Hakuin's No-self

Anyone who wants to attain the way of enlightenment must drive
forward the wheel of the four great vows.

The opening words to Zen master Hakuin's *Itsumadegusa* (*Wild Ivy*)[44]
announce the driving force of his own life as well as his intention in recounting it, but they hardly foretell the intensely personal nature of his
account. Hakuin's "spiritual autobiography," as translator Norman
Waddell calls it, is not entirely without precedent in Japanese Zen
literature; but compared to Dōgen's autobiographical remarks in the
Hōkyōki (1227) or (shortly before Hakuin) Bankei's memoranda, *Wild
Ivy* reaches a new height of style and self-revelation. Written in 1765,
Hakuin's work in seven-character Chinese verse was perhaps styled
after the "mad poetry" (*kyōshi*) popular in his day; but read according
to colloquial Japanese syntax, as it must be to make sense,[45] it does
not fail to engage the reader's constant attention.

Though his personal account is prefaced by a sermon on true versus false Zen, Hakuin quickly immerses the reader in what European
sentiment would call the "passions of the soul." He begins by vividly
describing his childhood fear of ending up in hell. Hearing a Nichiren
priest detail the torments of the eight Buddhist hells, his "whole body
shook with mortal terror. When I went to bed that night, even in the
security of my mother's bosom my mind was in a terrible turmoil. I lay
awake sobbing miserably all night, my eyes choked with tears."[46] He is
terrified at the sight of flames heating bathwater, overjoyed at his
mother's promise to resolve his anxiety and intensely preoccupied with
the problem of escaping the fires of hell.

The author's childhood obsession forms a textual occasion for revealing his innermost feelings as well as the actions that set him on his
spiritual path. The text is replete with psychological self-descriptions,
no matter what the event (though the recollection may be fanciful in
part). "I sweated and squirmed in distress," he writes of some childish
mischief.[47] "I can't possibly return to lay life. I'd be too ashamed. . . .
I am at the end of my rope. . . . Brooding, pondering my future over
and over, cudgeling my brain for an answer," he writes of his discovery
that becoming a monk did not exempt him from the fires of hell,[48] "I
was struck by an indescribable joy" at finding a stack of books that
might hold the answer.[49] Later, engaging in meditation practice "I
entered a cave of pitch darkness—when I walked, I didn't even know
that I was walking."[50] When *satori* first dawned, "my body and mind
dropped completely away. . . . Beside myself with joy, I cried out at the

top of my lungs. . . . Afterward, I was possessed by a feeling of enormous pride."[51] When rejected by Master Shōju, "I was totally disheartened and frustrated. I sat red-eyed and miserable. My cheeks burned from the constant tears."[52]

To such descriptions of extreme elation and depression we could add countless recorded memories of quiet sadness and burning desire, all of which form a pattern in Hakuin's account of his relentless search. The vehemence of his frequent condemnations of "silent illumination" (*mokushō*) Zen, a Zen of undriven quietude, equally reveals Hakuin's personality, as does the self-deprecation with which he ends the chapters of *Wild Ivy*: "I have constantly held up the ugliness of my house for others to see. . . . Call it filthy verbal refuse"[53] and "Any wise man who claps eyes on [my writings] will fling them to the ground in disgust, and spew them contemptuously with spit."[54]

Yet the "ugliness" held up for others to see and all the psychological self-descriptions serve quite different purposes than from Rousseau's, which were written just three years later but in an entirely different world. Hakuin is writing, not for personal display or self-justification, but to recollect a spiritual journey that might serve as an example to others. In this regard, his work parallels Augustine's *Confessions* and St. Teresa's *Life of Herself*, the two great Western spiritual autobiographies before Rousseau. Hakuin would demonstrate the necessity of an intense search, unrelenting struggle, and constant practice. He describes how he regretfully gave up his desire to live alone in the mountains and settled in his home temple, Shōinji, at the age of thirty-two. At the time of writing *Wild Ivy*, he has some three hundred monks practicing under his guidance, has written scores of letters, and made numerous trips to impart the Dharma. Other writings, in particular the *Orategama*, show us that his works were often directed to lay commoners and nobility, and they sometimes read like Confucian epistles, advocating "a humane government and the proper treatment of the farmers."[55] Even so, the intended audience of *Wild Ivy* is primarily other Zen monks, perhaps even limited to, the author admits, "a single superior seeker who has broken through the barrier. . . . I humbly and respectfully pass this work along to that patrician of the secret depths."[56]

Whatever the range of its audience, the intent of *Wild Ivy* and its presentation of self cannot be adequately discerned in a survey of psychological self-descriptions, explicit accounts of *satori* experience, or references to true practice. Despite its frequent interpolations of Zen stories and attacks on false teachings, Hakuin's work has a definite story line that advances the author from a fear-obsessed child to a fearless teacher, and this story line in general reveals the nature of his quest for something he never names and never finishes attaining. His years of wandering are stopped not by *satori* experiences but by circumstances compelling him to settle at Shōinji and, finally, by a resolve "to devote my energies to the countless suffering sentient beings of the world."[57] Clearly his task will never be finished, although the words that close *Wild Ivy*, depicting a visit one day by a monk, would aptly portray his life: "He pressed his hands together, bowed deeply, and then he was gone."[58]

What can be said of the self in Hakuin's work? The language of *Wild Ivy* is intensely personal and concrete, devoid of abstract or metaphysical terms like no-self, (except for the mention of "Dharma" and of the "Unborn," the false doctrine "that life ends with death"). But if the conceptual language itself is missing, the underlying theme of rebirth in *Wild Ivy* provides a clue to an inchoate concept, which becomes clearer when we look at his other works. Hakuin's childhood preoccupation with the thought of being reborn in hell is countered, at the age of fifteen, with a vow described in a supplement to the earlier *Orategama*: "Even if I should die, I will not cease my efforts to gain the power of one whom fire will not burn and water will not drown."[59] The same work recalls the first resolution of the problem, if not the final fulfillment of the vow, in details missing from the *Wild Ivy* account: "There is no cycle of birth and death through which one must pass."[60] Hakuin says he uttered these words upon his first *satori* experience, after grappling with the *Mu* koan[61] (*Wild Ivy* fails to mention the koan also). Later Hakuin presents his experience to Master Shōju, who asks, "What about the dog and the Buddha-nature." When Hakuin spontaneously replies, "There's no way at all for hand or foot to touch it," Shōju grabs his nose and twists it sharply. "How's that for a firm touch!" he declares. In *Wild Ivy*, Hakuin records his response as "I was incapable of moving forward. I couldn't retreat. I couldn't spit out a single syllable."[62]

Hakuin's reference to something untouchable and the master's attack on his body clearly indicate that the issue here is the self beyond birth and death. The koan that Shōju gives Hakuin after this rebuke is another case on rebirth: "What happened to Nansen after he passed away?" After a period of intense concentration, Hakuin resolves this koan, and others, upon being beaten senseless by a village woman. This time Hakuin gains the approval of master Shōju, who encourages him to engage in "after *satori* practice" and to strive "every minute . . . to revolve the great Dharma, pledging yourself to benefit and save all sentient beings, while having nothing—*nothing*—to do with fame or self-profit in any shape or form . . . then you will be a true and legitimate descendant of the Buddha-partriarchs . . . an even greater reward than being born as a man or a deva."[63]

Shōju's injunction expresses the ideal of self and the form of practice to which Hakuin was to devote his life. But again we must look to other works for a more conceptual description. *Orategama IV*, written fifteen years earlier, advocates the practice of concentrating on "one's True Self, which is No-Self, that Original Nature may come to Self-Awareness [*kenshō*]."[64] However, Hakuin writes,

> there are two kinds of "No-Self" [*muga*]. Thus one person, having always been weak of body, timid in spirit, and fearful of other persons, kills his feelings and yields to all external conditions. Even when abused he does not become angry, and does not become upset even though he is beaten. This habitual fool and dull-wit who [really] experiences nothing . . . believes. . . . As for me, I have fully attained this No-Self [but] if one wishes to achieve accord with the true and genuine No-Self in its purity, he must necessarily let go his hold on the steep precipice and then, after dying, come to life again. Only then will he directly experience the True and Real Self.[65]

The description of the first type of no-self may be heard in part as a criticism of the Confucian ideal popularized later. The typology itself, though it expresses a model of the true self, seems not as satisfying as the concrete story of *Wild Ivy*, precisely because of its more abstract and metaphorical terminology. "Letting go one's hold on the steep precipice" is further explained by way of analogy: finding oneself on "the steep face of a cliff, covered with slippery moss," where one "can neither advance nor go back." Because of its personal life context, however, I find the description in *Wild Ivy*, where Hakuin is incapable of moving forward, retreating, or spitting out a single syllable, more illustrative of the self-imposed barrier between one and one's "true self." At this precipice, *Orategama* continues, "only one thing remains: death. To break through the barrier of death of mind and will is the 'Way of Self-Awakening:'" "Brought to life again, suddenly one experiences a great joy like that of drinking water and knowing in his own self its coldness or its warmth. . . . We call [this] Original Nature come to Self-Awareness [*kenshō*]."[67]

Imagine, for a moment, novelist Tōson reading these words. Would they, or *Wild Ivy*, have struck him as forcefully as Rousseau's *Confessions*? I think his reaction, at least after reading Rousseau, would have been similar to Paul Tillich's in a conversation with Hisamatsu Shinichi in 1957:

> **Hisamatsu:** The Self is the true Formless Self only when it awakens to itself. . . it is always at once "one's own" and "not one's own"[68]. . . the Formless Self includes, in so far as it is Self, Self-awareness. But by this Formless Self (or Self-awareness) I mean the "Formless-Myself," which. . . expresses—or presents —Itself in its activities. . .[69] The True Awakening—or Formless Self—in Itself has neither a beginning an ending, a special place, nor a special time.
>
> **Tillich:** Then it cannot happen to a human being.
>
> **Hisamatsu:** . . . with this Self-awakening. . . one is no longer an "ordinary" human being. . . .[70]
>
> **Tillich** (later): Even so, you can't eliminate the "my". . . Is it that there is no centered self, no self-related self, which would be a hindrance?
>
> **DeMartino** (translator for Hisamatsu): The barrier is created by the reflectively self-conscious ego—or "I" which discriminates itself dualistically from "not itself"—or "not-I". *Muge* 'no hindrance' [is] the overcoming of this barrier. . . .
>
> **Tillich:** By the removal of individuality?
>
> **DeMartino:** No, by the fulfillment of individuality.
>
> **Tillich:** What is the difference. . . ?[71]

This conversation may be ironically called a "paradigm of the incommensurability of paradigms." Tillich's question is never answered to his satisfaction. At the end, Hisamatsu's translator intimates that the conversation reached an impasse because the theologian is pursuing an analytic approach, while the Zen teacher is attempting to express something ungraspable by this approach, but does not resort to methods appropriate to the expression of Formless Self. Tillich had admitted earlier in effect that even the kind of meditation he practiced was analytic: a reflection on problems, on the "contents of the universe." For Hisamatsu, on the other hand, "that which concentrates is that which is concentrated upon."[72] The two practices are quite distinct. The result is that Tillich is not only not "converted" to a different paradigm; he does not even understand it. How could such an unconditioned Formless Self be grasped as a historical paradigm at all?[73] One can trace the development of the notion and locate it in history, but its intention negates any specific location.

Tōson might surely have discovered something from Hakuin (or Hisamatsu), but it would not have been the individual "I" with an inner life (*naibu seimei*) of its own that was depicted in his novels. The awakening to true selfhood (*jiga e no mezame*) in his first novel *Hakai* (*Breaking the Commandment*) occurs when protagonist Ushimatsu reads the *Confessions* of a fellow *eta* (outcaste), Inoko Rentaro; acknowledges for the first time in his adult life who he is; and resolves to reveal his socially despised origins, which he has hitherto concealed and forgotten. "What Ushimatsu awakens to," Janet Walker writes, "is not the need for social freedom [the right to vote or to an education] but the need for a sense of self that he can be proud of and that he can show to others without fear."[74] Seeking this "spiritual freedom of the inner *kokoro* (heart),"[75] Ushimatsu's (and Tōson's) self would be like Hakuin's; in desiring moral justification it would be like Hakuseki's self; as a voice of conscience and critic of the abuses of society it would be Rousseau's self—and yet it withdraws from all three. The ambivalence of Ushimatsu toward himself is perhaps more characteristic of the author Tōson than the "selves" of any of our three autobiographers. The writing of Tōson provides a foil, not a realization, of Rousseau's vision. not to mention Hakuseki's or Hakuin's.

Conclusion

A paradigm is what the members of a . . . community share . . . A paradigm governs, in the first instance, not a subject matter but rather a group of practitioners.

Thomas Kuhn, *The Structure of Scientific Revolutions*

This sketch of three autobiographers has been a study in contrast. The autobiographies of Rousseau, Hakuseki, and Hakuin, and the writing of Tōson as a foil to all three, differ not only in emphasis, theme, and cultural assumptions. The methods of their writings as ways to narrate a self are different as well. Indeed their narrative practices seem sufficiently different to undermine universal notions both of self and of autobiography. What autobiography is becomes as questionable as what a self is. We noted that specialists have, for different reasons, disassociated Rousseau's *Confessions* and Hakuseki's *Told Round a Brushwood Fire* from the autobiographical genre, the first for being fiction rather than biography, the second for not being confessional.[76] And surely it would easy to locate Hakuin's *Wild Ivy* in another genre. Tōson's autobiographical novels, for their part, have been said to abandon both fiction and descriptive biography.[77] The lesson to be learned, however, is that autobiography no more constitutes a single literary genre than "self" names one kind of entity. I use the same name, *auto-biographia* (a writing of the life of oneself), for the three works simply because their authors purport to write of themselves; we might better say that each literally writes his self into life. The theme of investigation in each of these three autobiographies is not so much a unique self to be discovered as it is as a manner or method of writing, constructing from a singular perspective a model life for others.

These lifelike models necessarily vary, of course, with authorial innovation, cultural convention, and philosophical presupposition. Such conditions of life allow us certain generalizations: we read of a European intellectual, a Japanese Confucian reformer, a Japanese Zen monk. At the same time we might look for the unique person in each author: Rousseau, Hakuseki, Hakuin. But these are our identifications, not the perspectives of the authors, whether concealed or explicit. Each of them, however differently, constructs a model of how others beyond the bounds of such identifications might live their lives. These conditioned and self-constructing authors, seeking their own perspectives in writing, are each setting up a self that others could be. Their selves thus display the paradox of the paradigm, the model that is meant to describe something universal, but whose manner of describing is ineluctably particularized by conditions. Like a paradigm, moreover, the self emerges from social practices. The autobiographical self arises from narrative practices. The self that Tōson "discovers," for example, is not so much one already there as one he can now cultivate, or continue to cover up, through his writing.[78] A self abstracted from lived practices is no less questionable than the grammatical use of "self" as an independent substantive capable of being the subject of a verb.[79] Apart from such practices, "self" makes no sense at all.

NOTES

1. "Rusō no Zange chū ni miidashitaru jiko" in *Shimazaki Tōson Zenshū*. vol. 6 (Tokyo: Chikuma shobō, 1978), 10. See Janet Walker, *The Japanese Novel of the Meiji Period and the Ideal of Individualism* (Princeton: Princeton University Press, 1979), 145.

2. Walker, *Japanese Novel*, 144–45.

3. Thomas Kuhn, *The Structure of Scientific Revolutions*, 2 ed. (Chicago: University of Chicago Press, 1970), 176–80.

4. Rousseau, *The Confessions*, trans. J. M. Cohen (Harmondsworthy: Penguin Books, 1954), 17. All quotations of Rousseau are from this edition.

5. Ann Hartle, *The Modern Self in Rousseau's Confessions* (Notre Dame: Notre Dame University Press, 1983).

6. Walker, *Japanese Novel*, 96.

7. Rousseau, *The Confessions*, 605. For a deconstruction of Rousseau's disingenuous prose, see Paul de Man, "Excuses," in *Allegories of Reading* (New Haven: Yale Univeristy Press, 1979), 278–301.

8. Rousseau, *The Confessions*, 262.

9. Jean Starobinsky, in *Jean-Jacques Rousseau: Transparency and Obstruction* (Chicago: University of Chicago Press, 1988, 186ff) argues that Rousseau not only believes his account of himself is true because it comes from the inside, but also sets it up for others as a model of self knowledge. For Jean Guéhenno (*Jean-Jacques Rousseau*, London: Routledge and Kegan Paul, 1966, vol 2, 240), both Rousseau's attempt at self-knowledge, and the reading of his work in order to know the truth about him, are misguided. Ann Hartle, in *Modern Self*, presents the most nuanced account and tries to overcome the problem of Rousseau's self-knowledge by emphasizing the nature of the work rather than Rousseau's private person. She argues that Rousseau did not intend his work as factual biography and was aware of its fictional character; *The Confessions* bear witness to the nature of every man as private, inner self. Huck Gutman ("Rousseau's *Confessions*: A Technology of the Self" in *Technologies of the Self: A Seminar with Michel Foucault*, ed. Luther H. Martin, Huck Gutman, & Partick H. Hutton. Amherst: University of Massachusetts Press, 1988, 112) also points out Rousseau's references to the fictive quality of his work, but argues that he eventually undermines his strategy to individuate the self.

10. Rousseau, *The Confessions* 595.

11. Ibid., 19.

12. Ibid., 28.

13. Walker, *Japanese Novel*, 146.

14. The suggestion of exhibitionism is not accidental. Rousseau confesses that he was given to such behavior at the age of sixteen, and one wonders whether the whole of *The Confessions* is not a kind of vicarious outlet: "I haunted dark alleys and lonely spots where I could expose myself to women

from afar off. . . what they saw was nothing obscene. I was far from thinking of that; it was ridiculous" (Rousseau, *The Confessions*, 90).

15. John Locke, *An Essay Concerning Human Understanding*. ed. A. S. Pringle-Pattison (Oxford: Clarendon Press, 1924), 189.

16. Ibid., 192.

17. Ibid., 189.

18. Ibid., 9.

19. Joyce Ackroyd, trans., *Told Round A Brushwood Fire: The Auto-biography of Arai Hakuseki*. (Princeton: Princeton University Press, 1979), 35. The original text can be found in Odaka Toshio & Matsumura Akira, ed., *Taionki, Oritaku shiba no ki, Rantō kotohajime* (Nihon koten bungaku taikei 95) (Tokyo: Iwanami shoten, 1964), 149.

20. Ackroyd, *Told Round a Brushwood Fire*, 17. In a review of the Ackroyd translation (*Journal of Japanese Studies* 2, no. 1, Winter 1985, 170–77), H. D. Harootunian warns us of comparisons and translations that overlook the various ways narratives are constructed to support varying ideologies. He is critical of Ackroyd for virtually rewriting the *Oritaku*, a monologic narrative authorizing a single voice, as a confessional autobiography reporting the author's conversations and confrontations with others. Although I have relied almost solely on the translation, my analysis will suggest how far Hakuseki's work is from being confessional autobiography. On the other hand, even Rousseau's *Confessions* appear to some scholars, like Hartle above, to be other than autobiography. In my conclusion I suggest how the term must be used pluralistically. The preeminent scholar of Japanese autobiography, Saeki Shōichi, juxtaposes Rousseau and Hakuseki to place the writing of Futabatei Shimei, an older contemporary of Tōson, in Japanese literature; see the chapter "Rūsō to Hakuseki no aida" in his book *Kindai nihon no jiden* (Tokyo: Kodansha, 1981), 232–57.

21. Ackroyd, *Told Round a Brushwood Fire*, 35f.

22. Ibid., 36.

23. Ibid., 36.

24. Ackroyd notes that "so clearly does. . . his [irascible] personality emerge throughout his autobiography, that his style sometimes erupts into bitter invective and sometimes has an overtone of hysteria. Except at these points [which appear very seldom to this reader], it is dignified and grave as befitted a Confucian scholar. . ." (Ackroyd, *Told Round a Brushwood Fire*, 30).

25. Hani Gorō, *Arai Hakuseki & Fukuzawa Yukichi* (1936), cited in Ackroyd, *Told Round a Brushwood Fire*, 22.

26. Ackroyd, *Told Round a Brushwood Fire*, 46.

27. Ibid., 57.

28. Ibid., 70.

29. Ibid., 74. Contrast Hakuseki's reticence with Tōson's emotional depiction of the deaths of his daughters in his autobiographical novel *Ie*, written 1910–11. (See *The Family*, trans. Cecilia Segawa Seigle [Tokyo: Tokyo University Press, 1976].) This contrast in what is deemed fit for literary disclosure, however, should not mislead us to think that the family was of primary value for Tōson whereas for Hakuseki it was not. Seigle, p. xi, suggests that Tōson regarded the deaths of his daughters as sacrifices enabling him to work on his first novel. Tōson has a character in a later novel, *Spring*, rationalize leaving a job: "My family is of course important. But it is still more important that I find a way of life that is right for me. This is what all of us must do. What is the point of being a good son and brother when one does not even know the purpose of one's own existence." Quoted in Edwin McClellan, *Two Japanese Novelists: Sōseki and Tōson* (Tokyo: Charles E. Tuttle, 1971), 100. Tōson's works emerge out of a subtle revolt against family-centeredness; in that sense, his own newly found individualism is strongly related to the traditional value placed upon the extended family.

30. Ibid., 88.

31. Ibid., 19f.

32. Hiroshi Minami, *Psychology of the Japanese People*, trans. Albert R. Ikoma (Toronto: University of Toronto Press, 1971), 11.

33. Cited in Robert N. Bellah, "Baigan and Sorai: Continuities and Discontinuities in Eighteenth-Century Thought," in *Japanese Thought in the Tokugawa Period*, ed. Tetsuo Najita and Irwin Scheiner (Chicago: University of Chicago Press, 1978), 150. Recent nationwide surveys on the life philosophy of the Japanese people, however, suggest that the younger generation no longer holds such values, but rather is most interested in living "one's own life according to one's own tastes, without much regard for money or fame." (See Minami, *Psychology*, x.)

34. Bellah, "Baigan and Sorai," 145.

35. See Ian James McMullen, "Kumazawa Banzan and 'jitsugaku': Toward Pragmatic Action," in *Principle and Practicality: Essays in Neo-Confucianism and Practical Learning*, ed. Wm. Theordore de Bary and Irene Bloom (New York: Columbia University Press, 1979), 354f.

36. Cited in Furukawa Tesshi, "The Individual in Japanese Ethics," in *The Japanese Mind*, ed. Charles A. Moore (Honolulu: East-West Center Press, 1967), 236.

37. Furukawa, "Individual," 237.

38. Joyce Ackroyd, *Lessons From History: Arai Hakuseki's Tokushi Yoron* (St. Lucia, Queensland: Univeristy of Queensland Press, 1982), ix–xv.

39. Instead of selfless service versus self-assurance, the relevant issue in the controversy about the "individualism" of samurai may be the sense of individuality as separate self. George DeVos makes the apt generalization that the "Japanese sense of self is directed toward immediate social purposes, not toward a process of separating out and keeping the self somehow distinct, somehow truly individual, as remains the Western ideal." "Dimensions of Self in Japanese Culture," in *Culture and Self: Asian and Western Perspectives*, ed. Anthony J. Marsella, George De Vos, and Francis L. K. Hsu (New York: Tavistock Publications. 1985), 179.

40. Cited in Minami, *Psychology*, 17.

41. Shinzo Koizumi, "Introduction" to *The Autobiography of Fukuzawa Yukichi*, trans. Eiichi Kiyooka (Tokyo: Hokuseido Press, 1960), viii. Ishikawa Kammei's preface to the 1899 edition reports that the *Fukuō Jiden* was dictated at the request of a certain foreigner to share reminiscences of the period of the Meiji Restoration and was based on notes of memories recollected at random: "more an informal talk than an autobiography" (ibid., xiii).

42. *Autobiography of Fukuzawa*, 290, 327.

43. This does not mean that Rousseau's paradigm actually began to govern the methods of their writing, which some critics see as a continuation more than revolution of traditional Japanese literary forms. See Masao Miyoshi, *Accomplices of Silence* (Berkeley: University of California Press, 1974), 72; and Edward Fowler, *The Rhetoric of Confession: Shishōsetsu in Early Twentieth-Century Japanese Fiction* (Berkeley: University of California Press, 1988), 53. Janet Walker, who does see a strong connection between Rousseau and Tōson, Western naturalism and early Japanese "novels," suggests another reason that Fukuzawa did not inspire the new literary movement as did Rousseau and Zola at that time: Fukuzawa "considered the Western liberal ideal of individualism in a samurai context of ethical service to the state" (Walker, *Japanese Novel*, 62).

44. Norman Waddell, trans., "*Wild Ivy*: The Spiritual Autobiography of Hakuin Ekaku," *The Eastern Buddhist* 15, no. 2 (1982): 71–109; and 16, no. 1 (1983): 107–39. Unless otherwise noted, all quotations are from vol. 15 of *The Eastern Buddhist*. An edition of the original wood-block text can be found in *Hakuin oshō zenshū* (Tokyo: Ryuginsha, 1934), vol. 1.

45. Waddell, "*Wild Ivy*," 72.

46. Ibid., 81.

47. Ibid., 85.

48. Ibid., 87f.

49. Ibid., 89.

50. Ibid., 93.

51. Ibid., 95.

52. Ibid., 98.

53. Ibid., 109.

54. Ibid., 138 in vol. 16.

55. Philip B. Yampolsky, *The Zen Master Hakuin: Selected Writings* (New York: Columbia University Press, 1971), 17.

56. Waddell, "*Wild Ivy*," 109.

57. Ibid., 136 in vol. 16.

58. Ibid., 138 in vol. 16.

59. Yampolsky, *Zen Master Hakuin*, 116.

60. Ibid., 118. But in *Wild Ivy*, Hakuin reports that he cried out, "Old Gantō is alive and well!" (see Waddell, "*Wild Ivy*," 95).

61. The *Mu* koan, case 1 of the *Mumonkan* (Chin., *Wu-men-kan*) is in essence Jōshu's answer "*Mu!*" to the question, "Does a dog have Buddha nature or not?"

62. Waddell, "*Wild Ivy*," 98. Yampolsky's translation of the earlier account in the "Supplement to *Orategama* III," however, has Hakuin remaining "nonplussed" at Master Shōju's attack (see Yampolsky, *Zen Master Hakuin*, 118).

63. Waddell, "*Wild Ivy*," 101.

64. Winston King, Jocelyn King, and Tokiwa Gishin, trans., "The Fourth Letter from Hakuin's Orategama," *The Eastern Buddhist* 5, no. 1 (1972), 82.

65. Ibid,. 97.

66. Ibid., 98.

67. Ibid., 98.

68. "Dialogues East and West: Conversations between Paul Tillich and Hisamatsu Shin'ichi, Part One," *The Eastern Buddhist* 4, no. 2 (1971), 98, 101.

69. "Dialogues East and West: Conversations between Paul Tillich and Hisamatsu Shin'ichi, Part Two," *The Eastern Buddhist* 5, no. 2 (1972), 107.

70. Ibid., 124f.

71. "Dialogues East and West: Conversations between Paul Tillich and Hisamatsu Shin'ichi, Part Three," *The Eastern Buddhist* 6, no. 2 (1973), 94–97.

72. "Dialogues, Part One," 96.

73. Hisamatsu's words shortly before his death express the point poignantly: "I tell my family I do not die. I say that I am the formless Self. Therefore, I do not die. In fact, death never even crosses my mind. I have some work to do." (Quoted in Sally Merrill, "Remembering Hisamatsu Sensei," *The Eastern Buddhist* 14, no. 1 [1981], 129.)

74. Walker, *Japanese Novel*, 176. See Shimazaki Tōson, *The Broken Commandment*, trans. Kenneth Strong (Tokyo: University of Tokyo Press, 1974).

75. Ibid., 177.

76. See note 20 above.

77. Masao Miyoshi (*Accomplices of Silence*, 73) suggests that the writer of the so-called Japanese "I-novel" [*shishōsetsu*] set himself up not to invent, nor to report life, but to "live the very substance of his work." In a later essay, Miyoshi challenges the entire classification of *shōsetsu* as novels; as opposed to the art of the novel, the predominance of the first person in *shōsetsu* functions to conceal the narrator and to mark the continued suppression of the individual self. See "Against the Native Grain: The Japanese Novel and the 'Postmodern West," in Masao Miyoshi, *Off Center: Power and Culture Relations between Japan and the United States* (Cambridge: Harvard University Press, 1991), esp. 17–27. Edward Fowler's analysis of modern Japanese literature in *The Rhetoric of Confession* confirms the difference between the genres of novel and *shōsetsu*, and traces the development of *shishōsetsu* not from the Western "I-novel" but from Japanese genres.

78. Critical of Walker's *The Japanese Novel*, Fowler argues that early *shōsetsu* were anything but a celebration of individualism; Tōson's *Hakai* in particular is better seen as a "non-expression" of the so-called modern self [*kindai jiga*]. Fowler, *Rhetoric of Confession*, 75f.

79. On the grammatical "self" see Benard Mayo, *The Logic of Personality* (London: Jonathan Cape, 1952), 93–94; and Paul Ricoeur, *Oneself as Another* (Chicago: Univeristy of Chicago Press, 1992), 1–3.

PART TWO

Person in Japanese Theory and Practice

INTRODUCTION TO PART TWO

Thomas P. Kasulis

The three papers in this section of the book focus primarily on Japanese views of the self as person. Much of the ensuing discussion is necessarily comparative, however. Modern Japan is a particularly fruitful case for comparison, since it stands between the intellectual traditions of East and West. As an Eastern culture, Japan supplements its own indigenous ideas and values with Indian (especially Buddhist), Chinese, and Korean influences. On the other hand, as a twentieth-century culture profoundly affected by Western scientific and philosophical thinking, it draws mainly from the modern European continental tradition. A complex and fascinating issue, therefore, is how to sort out the diverse elements, examining whether they are integrated into a syncretic whole or coexist alongside each other without much direct interaction. This question has been important to both Japanese thinkers trying to understand their own culture and its origins as well as to scholars from the West trying to understand Japan as "other."

In the opening paper of this section, I sketch a general theory about how the self is formed and why the cultural study of self should be a collaboration between philosophers and anthropologists. I try to show that the anthropologist and the philosopher are acutely sensitive to different "strata" of the self as culturally formed. For the sake of convenience, we call these strata the "somatic" and the "intellectual." A comprehensive picture of the self within any culture would, I maintain, pay appropriate attention to both elements and their relationships. The paper briefly studies two traditional Japanese views of self, one drawn from the Heian Buddhism and one from a late eighteenth-century neo-Shintō movement. In both cases the distinction between somatic and intellectual seems to work well in explaining the dynamics within the model of self. The final section of the paper addresses how we might use the investigations of anthropologists and philosophers to analyze today's models of the self in Japan and perhaps even to predict the changes those models are currently undergoing.

The second paper in this section is by Takie Sugiyama Lebra, an anthropologist. Her paper analyzes the Japanese phenomenon of *migawari* (surrogation). Lebra shows how the surrogate is used in a variety of social contexts, ranging from religious healing practices, to interaction between overlapping social groups, to the management of aristocratic and imperial households. Although, as Lebra points out, the use of surrogates is a cross-cultural phenomenon, it may be especially prominent in Japan. In Japan, it seems, a way of being yourself is to let someone act in your place. Lebra speculates that the prominence of the *migawari* phenomenon in Japan derives from a nonintegral sense of self. The Japanese self is actually divisible into multiple selves that function differently according to context. As she puts it, the Japanese self may be said to be "dividual" rather than "individual." The rules of surrogation vary according to which part of the self is important in a specified social function. Hence, the Japanese self has a boundary more fluid and indeterminate than typically found in Western cultures. Lebra concludes her paper with specific information on how this fluidity is supported and utilized by the hierarchical structures of Japanese society.

Diane Obenchain, a historian of religion with both literary and anthropological interests, wrote the third paper in this section. She begins by developing a theory about a relationship between self and spiritual development. Her main thesis is that modes of the person include what she calls "expression out-in-the-world" and "nurturing-affirmation." Not only in our culture, but in other cultures as well, these modes are typically identified as being respectively masculine and feminine. According to Obenchain's theory, religious transformation can occur in the individual's movement from one of these modes to the other, without at the same time abandoning the former mode. She exemplifies her general theory with the autobiography of Ishimoto Shizue, a Japanese woman from earlier in this century who underwent such a religious transformation. Obenchain concludes with some general observations of her work with women in China and the United States, as well as Japan. In particular she observes that, compared with Japanese, contemporary Chinese males seem more adaptive in going beyond their traditionally "masculine" expressive mode to include "feminine" nurturing behavior. She surmises that such transformation in China may be easier because of the stronger emphasis placed there on the family as a primary unit in personal identity.

Although taking up a diversity of topics and disciplinary perspectives, this collection of three papers exemplifies some of the rewards accrued from the careful analysis of the meaning of the person in Japanese society. First, the Japanese case itself provokes many scholars to go beyond cultural description to theorize about the nature of self. The Japanese view is somehow both familiar and alien enough to provoke comparison. All the writers found in their research that the Japanese view of self is neither enigmatic nor irrational. Yet, to describe the Japanese perspective somehow takes one beyond the categories that have served so well to define the self in the modern West. Hence, the data from the particular cultural instance force a reevaluation of the universal claims so often made in the West.

A second theme emerging from papers is a rejection of any simple cultural relativism. The writers seem uneasy with any generalization that the Japanese view of the self works in Japan, and the Western (or North American) view functions well in our society. A subtle motif runs through many analyses suggesting that there is something "we" can learn from the Japanese. Sometimes the motif presents itself in an axiologically neutral way: comparing Western and Japanese views of the self gives us clues about the relationship between the universal and cultural aspects of constituting the person. At other times, however, there is less neutrality and more advocacy: the process of self-cultivation in Japanese society suggests aspects of humanity that might be better developed in our Western cultures. In other words, we might learn something about ourselves and our limitations by better understanding how the personal and cultural interrelate in Japan. Some of those most admired characteristics in the Japanese sense of personal identity include anti-egocentrism, loyalty for the sake of social harmony, taking responsibility for others, and an emphasis on intimacy. Yet, any scholar of Japan—even one who speculates on how modern Western culture might benefit from the cultivation of such virtues— must also recognize that those same Japanese virtues were manipulated by the totalitarian fascists in the 1930s and 1940s. Of course, we could also argue that American culture is particularly good at developing its own virtues, virtues that the Japanese might do well to cultivate more in their culture: a sense of individual rights and responsibilities, an emphasis on integrity as based in fundamental principles of law and morality, the encouragement of personal expression in a spirit of compromise. Yet, again, any cultural critic could trace how those very virtues can contribute to the anomie, loss of collective identity, and social dissolution so many observers find rampant in the United States today.

This presents us with one of the more sobering conclusions of intercultural comparison. It seems that many, perhaps all, societies or cultures can excel at developing a distinctive set of virtues that can be admired even by outsiders to that society. Yet that society will also, it seems, develop the political skills needed to twist or manipulate those same virtues into tools of oppression or dissolution. Perhaps this suggests the greatest benefit of intercultural, comparative studies. By studying the other, we find new options for *us*. In seeing those options, we free ourselves from being too strongly tied to only one tradition, a tradition—however noble in its origins—that can become fossilized or idolized into forms of oppression or dissolution. By studying the other, we defend ourselves from our greatest potential enemy—ourselves.

4

Researching the Strata of the Japanese Self

Thomas P. Kasulis

What is the nature of the Japanese perspective or perspectives on self? Before we begin to formulate our answers, we should first reflect on the question itself. We may find that we have different enough interpretations that our answers will be answers to different questions rather than different answers to the same question. For example, what should be our initial task in trying to respond to this issue? For some of us, mostly the more philosophical types, the question is to be answered by looking into books and seeing what the Japanese themselves have actually said about self. After all, if we want to know what the Japanese believe, it seems sensible to find out first what they themselves have said.

Others of us, those more social scientifically motivated, might chuckle at the naivete of such an approach. How many Japanese have written books about the meaning of self? Not many. And what sectors of the society did they represent? A small group of elitist, primarily male, literati. No, if we want to know what the real Japanese perspective on self might be, we should carefully observe what large samplings of Japanese tend to do, not what a few intellectuals happened to have said.

It is now the philosophers' turn to chortle. How can you possibly get from such observations of behavior to a theory of self? First, you will have to decide which data are even relevant to the question (which itself assumes you have at least a hypothetical answer already in mind), and then you will have to theorize on what the data mean. If there is theorizing to be done, let the philosophers of the target culture do it, not an outsider with no philosophical training.

The best way to resolve the conflict between these two approaches is to show how both are wrong. The text-oriented approach can reveal only the intellectual resources available to an individual in that culture who may want to articulate a theory of self. Whether anyone actually believes in that theory and acts accordingly will have to be empirically, not philosophically, established. Furthermore, the narrowly philosophical approach assumes that a cultural perspective on selfhood only occurs when a philosopher, head in hand, ruminates about the dark recesses of human being. But what about the perspective on self that emerges when an adult must decide how to weigh responsibilities to an aging parent against responsibilities to a developing child? Or when a person decides what criteria to look for in a spouse? Or when one has to decide on what values to consider in choosing a career or educating a child?

Such arguments suggest a culture's perspective on self may not have many direct connections to the philosophers' theories. Yet, it is just as wrong to assume those theories have no important connections at all. One does not need a Ford Foundation grant to discover that philosophical ideas live a life of their own outside the academy. When talking about his team's chances this year, the high school football coach—hardly a representative of either the intellectual or elite echelons of American society—will almost inevitably start talking about the players' collective and individual "potential." Without ever having read a word of Aristotle and perhaps without even knowing who Aristotle was, the football coach manages to use the Aristotelian concept of 'potentiality' to define his role as a coach, his relations with his players, and his plans for the future. We also can be fairly confident that in his interview with the news reporters the terms *dharma* and *jen* will not even come up. The coach is, in a profound sense, an *American* football coach, and he unconsciously draws on the ideas of philosophy available to him as a member of that society.

The purpose of this paper is to sketch an agenda for exploring the Japanese senses of self. The assumption is that both philosophers and social scientists have much to teach us in this enterprise, but they could teach us qualitatively much more if they would conceive their projects in a collaborative spirit, rather than as independent disciplines. The agenda assumes a dual-layered model for understanding the relation between self and culture, a model that can only be crudely presented here, but that will suffice to suggest how such collaboration can be beneficial. To illustrate how the model works, we will also analyze a few specific Japanese cases. These examples are not in themselves meant to be in any way definitive, but are developed just enough to show how the dual-layered model can shed light on our attempts to understand the Japanese senses of self, both in the past and the present. An adequate understanding of the self should include, to use a Zen Buddhist metaphor, "the skin, flesh, bones, marrow." Here we will have to settle for, at best, the bare bones.

In discussing a general theory for the relation between self and culture to apply to our Japanese case, we will call the two levels of self, the "intellectual" and the "somatic." On the intellectual level, we find reflective views of the self expressed through conceptual schemes: the self as understood through such culturally influenced resources as philosophy, religious doctrines, political ideals, theories of psychology, and expressed social values. We can use such conceptual schemes to think about, articulate, and relate to others both what we understand ourselves to be and the alternative paths to becoming what we would like to be.

If I am asked what is important to me as a person, for example, I will draw on ideas from within this culturally developed intellectual level of self-understanding. Similarly, if I want to criticize you for acting incorrectly and want to express reasons for my criticism, I may again utilize this level of meaning. In other words, the concepts on this intellectual level are the tokens for discourse among us as members of a particular culture. In one culture, a term like *satya* might be a token in that marketplace of ideas; in another, *chün tzu*; in another, *ego-integrity*. Although discourse on this level is public and shared, that discourse is not necessarily about my public self, however. Even in thinking about or discussing what is most personal, private, and intimate, I will do so in the conceptual vocabulary of my culture. In fact, even when reflecting silently on myself within conceptual frameworks, I utilize this dimension.

How do we learn this cultural form of discourse? We draw on a variety of sources: parents, teachers, religious leaders, books, folk narratives, political speeches, and so forth. Whenever we advocate, criticize, or explain a behavior, we operate on this culturally defined, intellectual level. Through such reflection we assimilate the conceptual and verbal vocabulary for formulating what is good or bad, valued or repudiated. We explain ourselves to ourselves on this intellectual level of selfhood.

Let us turn now to the so-called somatic level. Unlike the intellectual level, the somatic level is typically unconscious, although not unconscious in the usual psychoanalytic sense. As used here, "unconscious" refers to something neither individual (as in Freud's conception of the notion) nor universal (as in Jung's "collective unconscious"); it refers instead to the social forms acquired by the individual. Furthermore, we constitute this domain, unlike various psychoanalytic views of the unconscious, not through repression, but through habituation and conditioning, the process of behavioral acculturation. On this somatic level, our behavior, values, and ideas are so sedimented through our life in a particular culture that they are normally not the object of reflection at all. They seem to be more felt than thought.

To set the contrast, we can say that we evolve on the intellectual level through mimicking how others in our culture *speak* (or write) about their ideas, whereas we evolve on the somatic level by mimicking how others in our culture *act*. The intellectual lends us a lexicon of thought, but the somatic level develops a repertoire of behavior. To the extent I use certain words or concepts, I reveal the intellectual level on which I function; to the extent I display propensities to behave in certain ways, I reveal something of the somatic level on which I function.

This latter stratum of selfhood is somatic because it is sedimented or incarnated through repeated action: We habituate a mode of acting and interacting until it becomes, as we say, "second nature." This term is revealing insofar as what is second nature to us seems to be natural, and yet, upon reflection we know it was taught. As an adult male in a Western culture, for example, I find the handshake to be the most natural way of greeting another adult male. I hold out my hand spontaneously and without self-consciousness. If I do reflect, however, I know that I was not born a hand shaker. I remember being taught to act in that way by my father and I know I teach my sons in a similar way. I do not remember being given any *explanation* for the behavior except for something like "that is what we do" or "it is a way of being polite." I do remember, however, learning some rules about the behavior (do not shake hands with a lady unless she first offers her hand; look people in the eyes when you shake their hands; use a firm grip but don't clamp down too hard). Such instructions do not explain the handshake; they merely inform how to perform it. The purpose of the instruction is not to help us understand the behavior but indeed almost the opposite: We learn the instructions and habituate the behavior so that we will *not* have to think about doing it as we do it.

Another example of a simple, in this case less culturally influenced, somatic experience may make the relation between the intellectual and the somatic functions clearer. Suppose we ask a touch typist which finger strikes the *m* key on the typewriter. The typist can most readily answer this question not by picturing the keyboard and trying to remember where *m* is located, but rather by imagining oneself typing and feeling which finger moves as one goes to type the letter. Phenomenologically speaking, the right index finger is what seems to know the answer. As the touch typists do their work, they think about the words they want to type, not the keyboard. Their bodies (their fingers, in this case) "remember" where the keys are without recourse to reflection. The intellectual level is reserved for thinking about the words they wish to type, not the movement of the fingers on the keyboard.

Touch typing is certainly an individually, not culturally, learned activity, but the same mechanism applies to cultural forms such as speaking a native language. When I ordinarily speak in my native language, I think about what I want to say, not about the language itself. The experience can be described as my body knows how to speak English (my native "tongue"), but my mind has to think about what I want my body to say. Since this observation suggests something about how culture functions on the two levels of selfhood the intellectual and the somatic, let us look at it more carefully.

I am a native speaker of English. (Let us assume I know no other language.) English is second nature to me. It feels natural and comfortable to speak in English, and it seems as if I have always spoken it. I know, of course, that I was not born speaking English and that I had to learn it, but I have no memory of ever speaking anything else. My native tongue is English, and I do not have to think about English to think in English. This is all on my somatic level.

Let us now consider what I think about as I think or speak or write in English. I learned names and concepts along with the English words that express them. I think about concepts (that is, I manipulate and connect them in various ways) even as I express them in English. Although (except in extremely rare cases) my somatic level follows the standard patterns of English, my intellectual level is free to combine names and concepts into an infinite number of new expressions. I can say things in English—intelligible things—that none of the billions of English speakers through history have uttered before.

As free as this intellectual level of self-expression seems, however, it is restricted in two respects: the restrictions of the sedimented linguistic structures and the restrictions in my culturally inherited concepts with their accompanying vocabulary. For the sake of intelligibility there is a limit how far we may deviate from the grammar of our language, the semantic meaning of terms, and the generally accepted rhetorical forms of discourse. Similarly, we are limited in how far we can pursue thoughts that are inexpressible in the vocabulary of our language, however enriched it may be by foreign terminology. This is not to say we are *determined* by our language, only that we encounter limits within it. Reflection allows the current language to stretch beyond its present confines, but only to a certain extent. The evolution of any natural language proves we have the freedom to remake it to a certain extent to meet our needs; although restricted in how much we can stretch it, we are not determined by it.

Since we eventually want to discuss religious understandings of self in Japan, let us briefly examine a non-Japanese case first. It clearly exemplifies how a collective symbol system can successfully connect the intellectual and somatic dimensions, the theory and practice of a religious ideal.

Let us consider the meaning of Jesus' crucifixion for a tightly structured Roman Catholic community, one we might find in a Latin American village, for instance. On the intellectual level, we find a conceptualized doctrinal system that would include such formulations as "Jesus died for our sins." We should note immediately that a phrase such as "died for our sins" would have little, if any, intelligibility to a community untouched by Christianity. On the somatic level, on the other hand, we find a related communal behavior centering around such nonverbal symbols as the crucifix, for example.

How do the children in that society learn to understand themselves in terms of this matrix of doctrine and symbol? They learn about the doctrines in Sunday school, in sermons, in lessons at home, in reading the Bible. They learn to use the linguistic symbol system to express themselves and, in this case, to articulate their relation to God. The linguistic expression tells them, among other things, that they are sinners, that within them is a fundamental spiritual inadequacy that can be redeemed through self-examination, repentance, and faith. This obviously influences their self-understanding.

In contrast, those same children come to understand the nonlinguistic, symbolic meaning of the crucifix by participating in its communal use as an object of devotion to be kissed, as an image to instill the feeling of humility and repentance, as the icon that leads a procession through the village on a holy day. Here one comes to understand who one is by seeing oneself in communal action, by defining oneself through what one does.

What makes the crucifixion of Jesus work as a vehicle for self-definition is the way the two levels—the conscious, intellectual, conceptual level and the unconscious, practical, and somatic level—interact. The conceptualized need for repentance and redemption ("Jesus died for our sins") correlates with the tangible symbol (the crucifix) associated with the feeling of repentance and redemption.

The crucifixion example was picked precisely for its neatness and clarity, but of course, the range of religious phenomena in the world seldom has such a single correlation. In any culture, we do many things we cannot explain or justify, and we say many things we do not enact. Yet, the possibility for correlation, and the assumption that such correlations must exist even though we may have not worked them out fully, is important to our self-understanding. Without that possibility and assumption, we would find our entire view of ourselves—our thoughts, our feelings, and our way of life—to be groundless. When a situation occurs that sharply underscores a sharp separation between the intellectual and somatic, the members of the society become uncomfortable and wish to take some action, either personal or collective, to alleviate the bifurcation.

This seems to be what has recently happened in the United States in the controversy about burning the American flag as a sign of protest. The issue came to a head when the Supreme Court ruled that it is a constitutionally protected right for a dissident to burn an American flag publicly as a symbol of protest against government policy. The situation has created an odd tension for many Americans between our belief in the principle of freedom of expression (an idea operative on the intellectual level) and the feeling of patriotism attached to our communal actions toward the flag (behavior sedimented and affectively charged through the assimilation and habituation process). On the intellectual level, the ruling was understood to be consistent with our reflective rules of social interaction, including the rights set forth in the Constitution. Yet, many Americans—however much they may agree on this intellectual level—feel the ruling runs against our *practices* concerning the flag. As members of American society, we pledge allegiance to the flag, take our hats off as it passes by in a parade, present it to the family of a dead soldier, face it when we stand to sing the national anthem, even die on the battlefield in the attempt to keep it flying. This gives the flag meaning to us on a somatic as well as on an intellectual level. When the intellectual meaning of flag burning runs against its somatic meaning, we find ourselves in a quandary. Those who advocate a Constitutional amendment to prohibit the desecration of the flag hope to bring the reflective intellectual understanding and the unconsciously sedimented somatic feelings into accord. Those who support the Supreme Court's ruling hope to desacralize the use of the flag, making us conscious of the difference between patriotism and its symbols.

The flag-burning example in our society today displays well the dynamic to which I want to turn in analyzing the Japanese perspectives on self. When there is a dissonance between the intellectual and somatic level, or between the reflective understanding and practical enactment, or between the thought and the feeling, anxiety on both a communal and individual level is likely to arise. As human beings, we try to avoid anxiety. We try first to ignore the problem. When that fails (as when the Supreme Court deduces what follows from our intellectual level of understanding and we find it runs counter to how we act), a resolution is sought. We can change the intellectual system, alter our behavior, or both. Resolution of the incompatibility between the two levels brings stability and the lowering of the anxiety level.

Let us summarize the preceding points and see what they imply for our study of Japanese perspectives on the self. Such a study would seem to require the following. First, we need an articulation of the intellectual level of selfhood. What conceptual frameworks do the Japanese have as resources for reflection about who they are? Although the philosophers' full-fledged theories of selfhood may not permeate the society, many of the central philosophical ideas in the intellectual tradition become part of the parlance of everyday life. Second, and equally important, we must accumulate social scientific data about how the Japanese actually behave. What patterns of behavior do the Japanese culturally assimilate without resorting to reflective explanation? What symbolic forms and effects do those behavioral patterns display? Third, we must analyze the harmony and conflict between the two levels. What ideas reinforce which behaviors and vice versa? When conflicts have arisen, what strategies have been followed to bring the two levels into accord? In today's Japan, what conflicts between levels still remain such that the Japanese sense of self can be said to be still evolving in some direction?

To see how the dual-layered theory of selfhood can actually be used to analyze the case of Japan, let us briefly develop a few analyses. We will choose our cases to represent significantly different kinds of situations. Let us begin with a historical example.

Suppose our concern is to understand Kūkai's view of self, as he developed it in the early ninth century. Rather than simply trying to read his texts and derive from them the structure of such a theory, we will try to apply the dual-layered model.

On the intellectual level, what resources did Kūkai have available to him? First, there was a rather limited set of indigenous ideas on which he could draw: *kami* (sacred presences), *kotodama* (power of words), and various vague ideas about mystery, magic, and the forces of nature. From China, however, there was a vast store of philosophical terms and systems developed on the mainland over the previous millennium, especially the ideas of Confucianism and Buddhism. The former was by Kūkai's time already being used as a model for social and political relations. Confucianism had been brought into Japan as the literary tradition and the aristocrats learned their Chinese by studying the Confucian classics, histories, and poetry. Buddhism was originally the vehicle of artistic culture (painting, sculpture, architecture, music, dance) and thaumaturgy (rituals for health, prosperity, and control of the supernatural). During the eighth century, however, a network of Chinese Buddhist schools, each with its own epistemology and metaphysics blossomed in the major urban areas. In short, Kūkai had available to him a vast array of philosophical concepts from which to draw. The intellectual system was totally disorganized, however. There was no overarching philosophical system to clarify and evaluate the conflicting claims among the Confucianists and Buddhists or among the different Buddhist schools.

When dealing with a historical case from over a thousand years ago, it is somewhat more difficult to determine what resources on the somatic level of self would have been available. We are fortunate that we are not trying to make a general characterization of late Nara and early Heian Japan but, rather, are limiting ourselves to the biography of Kūkai. We know he grew up in Shikoku, even now a rural area of Japan. Undoubtedly, he participated in the local religious activities: festivals and prayers directed to the *kami*, the worship of natural awe-inspiring places having spiritual powers, and so forth. Linguistically, he would have learned Chinese as well as his native language, and we know that by the time of adulthood, his Chinese was excellent. We also know that as a person of aristocratic birth, Kūkai received an early training in the Chinese classics and enrolled in the *daigaku* at the capital at the age of nineteen to perfect his Confucianist training in preparation for a career as a bureaucrat. Within a couple of years, however, he dropped out of the college, giving up the possibility for a lucrative career, to go up into the mountains of Yoshino for ascetic practice. Although his writings show that he had a broad background in Buddhist doctrines (probably learned during his years studying in the capital), he would have encountered very little Buddhist practice in the city. In accord with ancient custom, spiritual disciplines were performed in the mountains. Yet, we also know that in Kūkai's time those spiritual disciplines were totally unsystematized, being collections of ascetic practices and thaumaturgic exercises originally derived from divergent sources: indigenous spirituality, Taoist alchemy, and a vast variety of Buddhist sources, both esoteric and exoteric. Kūkai spent at least a few years in the mountains practicing what scholars today call "*zomitsu*" ("miscellaneous" or "hodgepodge" esotericism).

We can see from all this that Japan was in period of great cultural transition. In coming to one's own perspective on self, an individual would find that the Japanese culture of the time had little to offer except the disjointed fragments broken off from a variety of traditions, both indigenous and imported. Kūkai would have to take those fragments and make a mosaic of his own, ultimately developing an image that would be a central paradigm for selfhood in Japan for centuries to follow. After a two-year trip to China where he studied under the

Chen-yen (Japanese: Shingon) master Hui-kuo, Kūkai returned to Japan and began to organize all the theoretical and somatic elements available in Japan at the time into a single, comprehensive system of theory and practice.

First, he structured the intellectual level of understanding by arranging all the known philosophical systems—secular, Taoist, Confucian, and Buddhist—into a single hierarchical system (the so-called ten mind-sets [*jūjūshin*]). This analysis put the available intellectual options into a spectrum, from profane hedonism at the bottom to his esoteric Shingon Buddhism at the top. Second, he manipulated the symbol system embedded in the somatic level so that, for example, Shintō *kami* were considered alternate forms of buddhas. Third, he articulated a comprehensive metaphysical system under the rubric of his Womb Mandala, the mandala of *ri*, "principle" (that is, the intellectual realm), and a system of practice under the rubric of the Diamond Mandala, the mandala of attaining *chi*, "wisdom," through somatic participation in the correct ritual forms, what he called "becoming a Buddha with and through this very body" (*sokushinjōbutsu*). Fourth, he developed a set of correlations that explained the superimposition of the two mandalas onto each other, the *ryobu* ("Dual") mandala. In short, he brought structure to both the intellectual and the somatic levels of the culture's resources and even developed a systematic correlation between the two levels.

Through the structure of this comprehensive world view, Kūkai's religious and philosophical system allowed a coherent sense of self. According to him, the self is inherently empty and achieves its meaning (indeed, its being) only as an expression of the cosmic buddha, Dainichi. All that exists is nothing but a symbolic expression (*monji*) of Dainichi's function (*yū*). That is, the universe is the activity of the enlightened cosmic buddha, but in our ordinary, self-delusory form of existence, we are unaware of this ontological, dynamic grounding in Dainichi's act (*gyō*). By performing the esoteric rituals of thought, word, and deed, we become intimate (*mitsu*) to Dainichi's function and experience ourselves as participants in Dainichi's own enlightenment. By participating in this enlightenment, we are attuned to the basic resonances (*kyō*) constituting the universe and find ourselves in harmony with all things.

Two historical points about this view of selfhood should be noted here. First, although Kūkai was the most comprehensive systematizer in his time, he was not the only one. Saichō of the Tendai school sent some of his disciples to study with Kūkai, and eventually there was a flow of ideas from Kūkai's Shingon esotericism (*tōmitsu*) into Tendai esotericism (*taimitsu*). In the long run it would be the Tendai tradition that would dominate the religious scene through most of the Heian period.

Second, the esoteric view of self was available only to the elite. Requiring the leisure time to practice complex rituals and to study arcane texts, the esoteric view of self lent itself readily to the Heian court, where the aesthetic way of life ruled. The denizens of this court celebrated the Buddhist view of transience (*mujō*) in their garden moon-viewing parties. Participating in the mystic resonances of the cosmos, their poetry addressed a secular *sangha* whose collective goal was to merge into the transience of things and to express that moment of mystic insight as *aware*, the "ah-ness" of things.

This aesthetic was not, I believe, what Kūkai originally had in mind as the final goal of esoteric Buddhism. At least, such effete elitism would not have been the focus of the compassionate Kūkai who established Japan's first public school open to all children regardless of class or gender (it closed a few years after his death) and who designed village irrigation reservoirs still used today. For the common people's spirituality, Kūkai's system also provided an intellectual defense. By interpreting Shintō through Buddhist concepts, the people could continue to practice their folk religion as always. Where the uneducated understood themselves to be worshiping *kami*, the intellectual saw in that same act the buddha. To show how Kūkai's ideas found their way into that elitist society would take us far afield of our purposes here. Our present purpose is to show how Kūkai forged one of the earliest coherent senses of self in Japanese culture and how his accomplishment can be understood in terms of the dual-layered model of self we have been developing.

The Kūkai example demonstrates how the theoretical layer was developed to give structure not only to itself but also to the diffused practices in the somatic layer of the society at the time. Sometimes, however, the somatic layer seems to give structure to the theoretical. Our case study in this regard will be Shintō. Shintō is a tradition that seems to defy philosophical analysis, at least initially. Consider the following bit of data from the modern culture:

Let's perch ourselves on a small hilltop in Ueno Park in Tokyo. We are no more than a couple of hundred meters from Ueno Train Station, a commuter center through which literally millions of Japanese pass every day on their way to work or way home. Below us is a small rectangular piece of land, perhaps seventy-five by twenty-five meters in size, covered with gravel. At one end is a small Shintō shrine, a simple hut of maybe four meters square, unpainted and containing no images or icons of any sort.

We watch from our observation perch the Japanese businessmen in gray suits hurrying to work. We focus on one running through the park. Reaching the shrine area, which stands between him and the station, he stops and then goes over to the spring-fed water trough to wash out his mouth and hands. Purified, he slowly walks up to the shrine, holds his hands together prayerfully, bows, claps, and pauses for perhaps ten seconds. He then claps again, turns solemnly from the shrine to the edge of the sacred area, and runs like the devil to the train station.

Here we find an enactment of self-definition that seems to operate almost entirely on the somatic, rather than intellectual, level. Shintō is something the Japanese do rather than think about. According to the 1986 statistics of the Japan Agency for Cultural Affairs, Japan has a population of 120 million people, of which 93 percent are Shintō and 74 percent Buddhist. Obviously, almost all Japanese see Shintō as part of their self-definition, yet at the same time, it seems to have little incompatibility with Buddhism and its sophisticated doctrinal systems.

Shintō grew out of the indigenous religion in Japan, the manaistic, animistic, magical religion that existed before the impact of Chinese high culture. We know of the prehistoric traditions through archaeological artifacts, ancient myths, and early poetic works. Shintō is an ethnic, rather than universal, religion that does not proselytize or seek converts. It is as tied to the Japanese sense of ethnicity as Judaism is to Jews and Hinduism to Indians. To be Shintō, many Japanese believe, is nothing more or less than being Japanese.

As a phenomenon of religious practice that can be observed sociologically or anthropologically, Shintō includes the following three aspects: (1) the primacy of feeling and intuition over logical explanation; (2) the inseparability of humanity from nature; and (3) ethnocentrism. Let us briefly consider each.

With certain minor qualifications, it is best to think of Shintō as having no creed or doctrinal system whatsoever. It is more a set of attitudes and customs. The primary religious focal point in Shintō is *kami*, often misconstrued in English as "gods." A *kami* may be a god—for example, the Sun Goddess Amaterasu is *kami*—but a *kami* can also be an extraordinary natural object, such as a special tree, rock, or Mount Fuji. A person, most often a great warrior or artistic master of some sort, may be *kami*, especially after death. Even a human-made article, a special sword, for example, may be *kami*. Thus, the word is perhaps best translated simply "sacred presence."

To a degree, Shintō does have an accepted set of myths, the stories of the gods in the *Kojiki* and *Nihonshoki* that justify the centrality of the imperial family, for example. Yet, Shintō generally functions as a folk religion: each locality has its special *kami*, distinctive festivals, and sacred objects. Shintō is more a set of somatically enacted feelings about purification, renewal, regionality, and communal spirit than it is any kind of philosophical or doctrinal system.

The second attitude mentioned was the Shintō emphasis on the closeness to nature. As we already pointed out, natural objects can be *kami*. It is important to bear in mind that the object itself is *kami*; the *kami* is not some spirit lurking invisibly in the tree or mountain. When the pilgrims reach the summit of Mount Fuji they will find the *torii* gate marking off the sacred presence. There is no shrine, no building, not even a sign. The pilgrim knows that the mountain itself is *kami*. Unlike the sacred places of Semitic religions (Mount Sinai, Mecca, Jerusalem), Mount Fuji is *kami* not for what historically happened but because it itself commands our respect and awe.

Finally, we turn to ethnocentrism of Shintō. Here is where our dual-layered analysis becomes most helpful. Perhaps the most striking way to pose the problem is in terms of the difference between the way Shintō is enacted on the everyday level and the way it is reflectively thought about. As a general rule, the Japanese have little ethnic exclusivity in their practices. *Gaijin* (foreigners, literally, "outsiders") are typically encouraged to participate in the local festivals. Women *gaijin* (usually Western anthropological researchers) have even been allowed to serve as assistants in Shintō shrines without any significant ethnic taboos. So, on the somatic level, although the practice of Shintō has a significant sense of bonding the Japanese people in some tribal fashion, there do not seem to be strong taboos against outsiders.

On the intellectual level, however, the ethnocentrism is much more marked. Shintō remains for many Japanese one of the distinctive aspects of their culture and ethnic identity. In the nationalistic years earlier in this century, Shintō served formally as a state religion. The question we must ask from our dual-layered theory of self is how this dissonance between the theoretical and the somatic emerged and what its significance has been.

There are two major stages in the development of Shintō on the theoretical level. In the Nara period, just before Kūkai's time, the state sponsored the recording of the ancient myths and histories as preserved in the oral tradition. This project resulted in the *Kojiki* (written in Japanese) and the *Nihonshoki* (written in Chinese). From our historical perspective we can see that one of the major reasons for recording these official texts was to establish historically/mythologically the centrality of the family line represented by the throne. The sun goddess of the imperial family, Amaterasu, became the central figure in the myth; the *ujigami*, and *kami* of the various major clans, were given subordinate but significant places in the pantheon. (Even the Tokugawa shōguns later used their supposed familial ties to one of these *kami* as a way of articulating their place in the Shintō pantheon.) This theoretical development probably had little effect on the ordinary people and their folk religious practices. The only significant difference would seem to be that they now knew of a theory that subordinated their local *kami* to the emperor's *kami* and symbolically connected all practice with reverence to the emperor. The emperor, like our crucifix example above, served as a symbol connecting the somatic and intellectual.

This is certainly a rather minimalist theoretical level of interpretation, and we might wonder how the somatic level could exist without a more reflective, intellectual underpinning. In particular, the introduction and emergence of Buddhism in Japan would seem likely to trigger some reflection on the essence of Shintō. Actually, we have suggested already how this intellectual problem was handled. As we noted in our discussion of Kūkai, the esoteric Buddhist traditions established metaphysical correlations between buddhas or bodhisattvas and the indigenous *kami*. If those correlations were accepted, as eventually was the case among classical thinkers both Buddhist and Shintō (who preferred to think of buddhas as *kami*, rather than vice versa), then the esoteric metaphysics of Buddhism could serve willy-nilly as an intellectual background for Shintō as well as Buddhism. Buddhism's intellectual embracing of Shintō relieved Shintō of having to develop a comprehensive philosophical understanding of itself.

This strange marriage continued until the Tokugawa period and the introduction of Neo-Confucianism, especially that of the Chu Hsi school (Japanese: *shushigaku*). Finding Neo-Confucianism amenable to its designs for restructuring and stabilizing the Japanese social order, the Tokugawa shogunate supported its development and promulgation. A side effect of introducing Neo-Confucianism in this way was that its writings, unlike those of the early Confucian tradition that had influenced Japan almost a millennium before, came prepackaged with critiques of Buddhism. (In China Neo-Confucianism arose in part as a response, both favorable and unfavorable, to Buddhism.)

The result was that for the first time since the early ninth century, the Buddhist worldview was called into question. Since it was that worldview that had also given intellectual respectability to Shintō practice, Shintō again found itself a somatically acculturated set of behaviors and attitudes without any clearly defined support on the intellectual level. In the late seventeenth century and throughout the eighteenth century, the intellectual debates within Japanese Confucianism and increasingly narrow sectarian scholarship within Buddhism drew the attention further away from Shintō. In reaction, an intellectual school of Shintō emerged: the so-called Native Studies movement (*kokugaku*). As the Confucianist school of "Ancient Texts Study" (*kogaku*) was trying to use philology to uncover the original meaning of the early Confucian classics in defiance of the later Neo-Confucianist interpolations, the Native Studies school developed its philology to study ancient Japanese texts such as the poetry of *Man'yōshū* and *Kokinshū*, novels like *Tale of Genji*, and the histories/myths of *Kojiki*. The last is our concern here, because of its connection with Shintō.

Kojiki is the oldest extant text written in the Japanese language, claiming to be the literary record of what had been the oral tradition in Japan up until the eighth century. It could first be recorded in the Nara period only because the Japanese had just begun to devise a way to write their own language with the use of Chinese characters. The philological problem was that the orthography used to transcribe the oral tradition dropped out of use within a few decades later in favor of a much more usable orthography (using *kana* to supplement the Chinese characters). The result was that within a century or two after the transcription of *Kojiki*, vast amounts of it had become undecipherable even to most intellectuals. This was the problem addressed in the latter part of the eighteenth century by the brilliant Native Studies philologist, Motoori Norinaga.

Motoori's biography shows that he was deeply influenced by popular Shintō piety. He attributed his own birth as the answer to his parents' prayers to a local *kami*. Throughout his life, Motoori prayed daily to that *kami* in gratitude. He considered his deciphering of the *Kojiki* to be a religious mission and spent more than thirty years on the project. What spurred him in his efforts was his fundamentalist belief that *Kojiki* contained the original *kami*-derived words about the creation itself. Picking up on the literary work done by his two immediate predecessors in the Native Studies movement, Motoori believed that the ancient poetic account of language was correct: In poetic expression the word and thing come into being together; they are word-things (*koto*). If that interpretation is correct, Motoori reasoned, to read *Kojiki* in its original sounds is to participate ritually in the act of creation itself. He came to see the original, pre-Sinified Japanese language (*Yamato no kotoba*) as the language of the gods, the source of all creativity, divine and human. He studied the spiritual power (*kotodama*) of the ancient language and saw it reverberating as a substrate in even his own latter-day Japanese language. He even argued that Japanese was superior to Chinese because its verbs inflect: Chinese is static, giving just the seed-meaning in the character; in Japanese that seed-meaning blossoms as the inflected suffixes locate the meaning-event in relation to time, activity-passivity, affect, and audience.

It is not difficult to understand Motoori's exuberance. He found himself thinking about the Japanese language even while he was writing in it. He was reflecting on the somaticity of linguistic expression. If we try to reflect on how we are capable of speaking our native language, it is indeed a wondrous event. The thing-word just "pops" into our mind in a form of spontaneity that gives every impression of being inspiration. How do we know when and how to use the pluperfect, passive, subjunctive of the verb *to do*? It just seems to conjugate itself miraculously, without the least effort on our part. This is not a unique experience. In Japan, Kūkai reflected on a similar experience of language a thousand years before; in the West, Heidegger did the same one-and-a-half centuries later. The difference, however, was that Kūkai and Heidegger thought they had understood something about language in general, whereas Motoori thought he had understood something about the ancient *Japanese* language in particular. Why? Because his experience of thinking about Japanese while writing in Japanese occurred as he was reading a text in Japanese that was purported to be the words of the gods. It was also the text that said the world was created with Japan as its origin and that the creator gods were directly related to only one group of human beings, the imperial family of Japan.

Motoori himself was not a simple nationalist or ethnocentrist. He did believe *Kojiki* correct in saying the creation site of the world was Japan and that the imperial family was related to the Sun Goddess. He was enthusiastically proud of his own culture. Yet, he was also careful to point out that all peoples in the world are brothers and sisters. Does the sun not shine equally everywhere? Why then was the true story of creation preserved only in Japan? Motoori argued that the story was known universally to all human beings but that only the Japanese were foolish enough to write it down in a script that they themselves would not be able to read. Meanwhile, everyone else in the world kept modifying the story every time it was rewritten, trying to make the miraculous sound more reasonable. It was a historical accident that Japan was the caretaker of a time capsule preserved from the moment of creation itself.

It did not take long for the next generation of the Native Studies school to work out the nationalistic syllogism, however. Hirata Atsu-tane, for example, argued that since the emperor is the tie to the gods, Japan must restore the control of power to the imperial family. This line of thinking contributed to the Meiji Restoration. Furthermore, since all the people in the world are one human family, the whole world would benefit from being under the rule of the link between the human and the divine, the emperor of Japan. How this originally philological movement led to Japanese fascism and imperialism is a fascinating story, but it takes us far afield of our present concerns. So, let us return to how Motoori's case illumines the dual strata of Japanese selfhood.

In Kūkai's case we saw how the intellectual was hierarchically structured into a system that reinterpreted and integrated the somatic layer of self. The intellectual and somatic were integrated via the intellectual. In Motoori's case, however, the impetus was in the opposite direction. The somatic aspects of speaking a native language, of affectivity, of ethnic and cultural identity were pushed into the theoretical level of self. For Motoori the self lives in community and is capable of speaking the creative language of the gods, a language preserved (albeit only partially) in the cultural tradition of Japan. This is a language not of theoretical grammatical structures but the spontaneous, affectively charged, expression of the genuine heart (*magokoro*). In our aesthetically formed community (the Heian court culture was Motoori's ideal), the poetic, creative, god like aspect of the human self comes to the fore. Our intention-mind-heart (*kokoro*) resonates with the intention-mind-heart of things and events (*mono no kokoro* and *koto no kokoro*) in the spontaneous recognition (*aware*) of the wondrous quality of each creative moment. Freed of the restrictions imposed by the "masculine" (*masuraoburi*) influence of society and its rationalistic tendencies (*kara no kokoro*—the "Chinese mind-heart"), all of us can manifest our genuinely "feminine" (*taoyame buri*) nature in the spontaneous expression of creativity and feeling. The significance of this view is that it articulates the somatic level as intellectual and, in so doing, creates an emotivist anti-intellectualism.

Where does this leave the Japanese perspective on self today? Although this cannot be answered without further research, let us apply the dual-strata model to see at least how that research in both philosophy and the social sciences might be structured. Before we even do that, however, we should mention one lesson from the examples we have discussed. There is no single Japanese perspective on self. Not only is no culture monolithic in its view of self, but any such views are temporary and volatile. A theory satisfying to the intellectual stratum may run directly counter to the behavior in the somatic stratum or vice versa. Furthermore, change in the view of selfhood does not only occur at time of cultural crisis. To return to the example from the first part of this paper, if the flag-burning case had gone to the Supreme Court during the era of the Vietnam War protests, it would have triggered a heated and divisive reaction. Instead, it arose in a period of relative calm, and Americans will have the leisure of considering more coolly the relations between the principle of freedom in self-expression and patriotic feeling as enacted in our social behavior.

One purpose of cultural criticism—whether it takes place in the philosophers' forum or in the streets, whether in the students' complaints about school or in a person's complaints about one's in-laws or boss—is to bring the inconsistencies to light. These inconsistencies may be within the intellectual stratum alone, the somatic stratum alone, or in their interface. In any case, the words we use to talk about it will be somewhere expressible in intellectual stratum. In Motoori's case, for example, he had to dig deeply to find them, but he did find them; in the vocabulary of his culture he could not have found the ideas necessary to developing a Western-style sense of psychoanalysis or a Marxist sense of class consciousness, however.

At the same time, the feelings we have about our inconsistencies will be somewhere expressed in our somatic behavior. Whereas the philosopher can help us see the range of possibility for reflection within the culture, the social scientists can specify the conditions under which the behavior can take form. In the case of Japan, for example, one may theorize a democratic view of self (the ideas for it are there in Buddhism as well as ideas borrowed from the modern West). But how can such a view be enacted if the somatics of Japanese language are such that (1) I can eavesdrop on a conversation on the subway between two workers in the same corporation and by their language alone know which has seniority, if even by only a year or two and (2) the language spoken to me by a woman, regardless of age, resembles the language I as a man use only when showing deference to my senior? The theoretical level of selfhood may allow democratization and the elimination of gender distinction, but at present the somatic level of Japanese selfhood does not. I hasten to add again, however, that the perspective on selfhood, even in the somatic level, is in flux. There is an increasing usage of *boku* by younger women, for example, a first-person pronoun that has been used until recently only by men. Are we seeing a shift in the somatic level of selfhood expressed in the gender-specific terms of the ordinary language? Only the data from social linguistics can answer that.

In terms of a project for understanding the Japanese perspectives on self, the self not as something defined and fixed by tradition but as something evolving before our very eyes, we need to do at least the following. For the intellectual stratum, we need a comprehensive philosophical cataloging of key ideas available for the Japanese definition of selfhood. The range is truly staggering. At one time or another, the Japanese have developed philosophically for their own purposes the theories of Buddhism, Confucianism, Western philosophy (especially the modern continental European and American traditions), and their own Native Studies tradition. Aspects of all these systems have worked their way into the parlance of the everyday. Simultaneously, the social scientists need to gather more information about how the somatic level of selfhood is being enacted. What changes seem to be occurring? Third, and this is in many ways the most important part of the enterprise and the part least developed so far, the behavioral trends on the somatic level must be compared to the discourse on the theoretical level in academic forums, the intellectual journals, newspaper editorials, and so on.

To take one example from current phenomena in Japan, the "theories of Japaneseness" (*Nihonjinron*) seem to be developing at an extraordinary rate. Two decades ago, this was a topic seldom discussed. Now the large bookstores have whole sections devoted to the "field." What is the meaning of this phenomenon in terms of the evolving sense of self in Japan? The majority of the literature seems clearly right wing, an attempt to return to the ethnocentrism of the Native Studies movement in some of its more diabolical forms. But is that all it is? If we look at the theoretical level alone, we can see the inevitability of the return to this topic. One of the lasting effects of the Native Studies movement is that it made ethnicity and culture into an ontological category. Virtually no major Japanese philosophy in the twentieth century has been able to avoid incorporating some theory of culture into its system. If philosophy is to have a theory of reality, the modern Japanese philosopher assumes, the reality of culture must be included. Not all modern philosophies took up the problem of Japaneseness; some tried to define culture broadly enough to be universally applicable. If we define culture in terms of Japaneseness, we have ethnocentrism; but if we define Japaneseness as one instance of culture, we can have a broad philosophical theory more in line with Wilhelm Dilthey or Max Weber than the fascist thinking of wartime Japan.

How do we know in which direction the *Nihonjinron* phenomenon will go? Although the philosophers may like to speculate strictly in terms of logic and intellectual history, the data about trends in the somatic stratum of self enactment are crucial. As the Japanese travel more in the world and have more contact with the outside, do they feel more a part of it or more apart from it? What does the behavioral phenomena tell us about the unconscious and affective tendencies in the Japanese context? Finally, we must ask each other in a collaborative sense about the interactions between the two levels.

Are the right-wing intellectuals undermining or underpinning the behavioral trends? How do Western-borrowed terms (*gairaigo*) about self operate on the level of popular discourse? Does the language use show a move toward individual expression or cultural identity?

Only as we start asking these questions and start working in a truly interdisciplinary and cross-disciplinary manner will we even begin to have some clear idea about the Japanese perspectives on self, the *changing* and *evolving* perspectives on self.

5

Migawari: *The Cultural Idiom of Self-Other Exchange in Japan*

Takie Sugiyama Lebra

Self-Perception as Socially Contextualized

Many observers of Japanese, while they differ in specific emphases, concur that the Japanese self (or personhood) is *socially* defined, contextualized, or embedded. To the extent that the social construction of the self is a universal fact, it may be restated that the Japanese person not only acts in response to but also *perceives* his/herself as contingent upon a given social nexus. The result is the consciously socialized self. If viewed through the Western lens for perceiving the self as non-contingent, autonomous, or intrinsic, the Japanese self indeed appears situationally circumscribed or *on/giri*-bound (Benedict 1946); dependency prone (Doi 1971), rank conscious, and group-oriented (Nakane 1967); empathetic (Aida 1970), differentiated into *uchi* and *soto* or *omote* and *ura* as pointed out by Doi (1985) and many other authors, mindful of *sekentei* (Inoue 1977); indeterminate (Smith 1983); relativistic (Lebra 1976a); hanging "between" persons (Kimura 1972; Hamaguchi 1977); uncertain, multiple, moving, or shifting (Minami 1983; Rosenberger 1989; Kondo 1990; Bachnik 1992). All these characterizations correspond to the linguistic absence of the fixed "I" (or "you") as well as the lexical variety of "I" substitutes.

Given the current ethos of Western intellectuals against their own (or, more accurately, their colleagues') ethnocentrism, including self-critique among reflexive anthropologists, it is unnecessary to remind ourselves that the socially contingent self as described above should not be equated with emotional or cognitive immaturity just because

107

such is typical of non-Western, particularly preliterate, tribes. Citing one recent work may suffice. On the basis of free-response test results on self-perception, Cousins (1989) refutes the notion that the socially situational self is incapable of thinking in abstract terms. Compared with American responses, Japanese self-perceptions, which were indeed found to be more sociocentric, surpass American counterparts in both concreteness and abstractness. This finding suggests that the boundaries of "social contexts" are quite variable, contracting and expanding, immediate and remote, interpersonal and global, which in turn confirms the "indeterminacy" of self.

The foregoing picture of the socially compact self has been repudiated by some authors as a "stereotype" or "group model" (Befu 1980). It is true that social contextuality, while characterizing the Japanese self as measured by the Western yardstick, does not exhaust it. In a paper (Lebra 1992a), I identified three levels of self as follows: the social or "interactional" self is at the basic level, where Japanese find themselves most of the time; above this level is the "inner" or reflexive self, which centers around the *kokoro* (heart/mind) and engages in monologue, with a leave of absence from dialogic involvement; at the highest level, there is the "boundless" or chaotic self, where the boundary disappears between subject and object, self and other, or the inner and outer self, so that both the social and inner self are upgraded into an empty self. The point, however, is that the three levels are far from undercutting one another. The higher levels of self sustain the basic, social self not only by compensating, remedying, or counterbalancing the excess of the social self but reenergizing it when it is deemed deficient. Thus the Japanese emphasis upon *seishin* (spirit), singled out by Befu (1980) as a proof of Japanese individualism, is in fact mobilized in group training, as witnessed by Rohlen (1973). While critical of the group-model and in partial agreement with Befu, Moeran (1984) nevertheless concedes that the Japanese "individuality" is immune to "individualism" and instead can be allied with groupism via *seishin* and *kokoro*.

This paper pursues the socially contextualized, indeterminate, multiple self even further by focusing on identity exchange between self and other, where self assumes another person's identity or vice versa. The exchangeable or substitutable self is in striking contrast to the Western idiom of self as consistent, continuous, unique, intrinsic, or clearly bounded (see Shweder and Levine 1984; Marsella, DeVos, and Hsu 1985). By the Western standard, this extensibility of self to other might appear as a delusion. Needless to say, it has nothing to do with mental disorders, since it is only temporary, conscious, and even obligatory. I choose this topic because in my view it throws the social contextuality of the Japanese self into relief.

The Idiom of Identity Substitution

I became keenly aware of this kind of identity exchange while doing fieldwork in the early 1970s on the cult called "Gedatsu." This particular cult has spirit possession as a main ritual, and it is not surprising that identity exchange between self and a supernatural entity takes place during possession. What aroused my curiosity was that members of the cult explained many instances of their behavior or experience outside possession as manifestations of identity substitution.

As I have reported elsewhere (1976a, 237–40; 1976b; 1986), my Gedatsu informants would visit shrines to apologize for sins committed not by themselves but by ancestors or other supernatural agents. Apologies were offered, in other words, by "vicarious" sinners who were most likely to be victims of vicarious retribution such as illness. Identity exchange was articulated in the written and recited formula of apology: I am here, turned into so-and-so (*nari-kawatte*), to apologize for his (her) sin from the bottom of (my) heart. For X to "become" Y in surrogacy (*kawaru, naru, narikawaru*) was a common idiom. Such identity exchange involved the human self and a variety of others, supernatural and human, dead and alive, known and unknown: My wife's illness is mine; I am just borrowing her body. You really can't tell whose illness it is. Surrogacy thus amounts to the mirror reflection, mutual replication, or fusion between self and other: My ancestors, I, and my descendants—we are one and the same; "Ancestor worship means self-worship" (Lebra 1986, 362).

This extent of surrogacy is quite bizarre, even by Japanese standards. Nevertheless, through exposure to the cult's idiom of identity exchange in this extreme form, I became aware of how often ordinary, "normal" Japanese speak in a similar language without raising anybody's eyebrows. Anecdotes are legion. When I paid air fare to a travel agent who took the trouble to come to my residence, he gave me a receipt, but not the ticket itself, assuring, "Don't worry. I will become you, my honorable customer [*okyaku-sama ni nari kawatte*], to get your boarding card ready at the airport." Indeed, he was there as promised.

In interviewing a woman in her sixties, I found her firmly dedicated to a Shintō sect without being a member of it. It turned out that her action had nothing to do with her own faith but was a surrogate devotion for the sake of her deceased mother, who had been a devout member. She missed her mother deeply and became a religious successor to her without, however, losing her own nonreligious identity. The latter example, as well as the Gedatsu example, shows that identity exchange can occur not only to serve expedience as in business transaction (e.g., the travel agent) but also to express a person's inner subjectivity, like faith or sincerity.

To add another anecdote: in a popular weekly television program, in 1989, I happened to see a famous twenty-two-year-old boxer who, after retiring from the ring because of injury, was training and coaching his followers. He said, "When my trainee is in the ring, I am the one who is fighting the game. I become the boxer." (By the way, the same athlete said, in answer to the question what had been sustaining him throughout, "I thought of those people who have helped me, my parents, my mentors, and countless others. This is a very important point in winning the game. Those who don't think this way, those who think they have made it by themselves are sure to lose." The socially loaded self thus emerged out of a boxer whom we would ordinarily expect to be dependent on nothing but his own body, skill, and will.)

Identity substitution may take a more subtle, less detectable form. One day when I was looking for a computerized library service in Japan, I asked for help from Professor A at X University, whom I happened to know. Professor A in turn asked his colleague, Professor B, about my request, whereupon Professor B designated Professor C at Y University as the most appropriate person to ask, because Y University was equipped with such computer services. B assured A that all I should do would be to tell C that B was the introducer. Understanding my apprehensiveness, Professor A wrote a letter of introduction addressed to C, mentioning B as the introducer. In order to get an appointment I called C, telling about this chain of introductions. C was too busy to help me in person, but introduced his colleague D. When I went to meet Professor D, he received me warmly, and bothered to guide me over to the library and introduce me to E, the computer specialist, and bowed to him with the request to help me. Mr. E was very kind and helpful. This was an unexpected and moving experience. I knew Professor A only, but each person at a chain link acted as if he knew A personally, or as if he were A himself and my friend because of the previous introducer. Sensitized to the prevalence of identity exchange at that time, I was tempted to see a series of that practice in this chain from A to E. A's kindness did not cool off in the course of serial substitutions but was rekindled and warm.

It may be that this sort of behavior, as an objective phenomenon, occurs in the West as well, but the subjective reasoning channeled by the culturally available idiom is likely to be quite different, different enough to suggest something noteworthy about the Japanese sense of self and other. I have been in a quandary over how to translate the Japanese expressions of identity exchange or surrogacy. Words like *delegate, proxy, representative, deputy*, or even *surrogate*—none of them convey the meaning of the Japanese *kawari* or *migawari* (the person, the act or state of substitution) to my satisfaction. The verb forms such as *naru, kawaru, narikawaru, mi ni naru*, which appear more frequently in conversation and were translated above as "become" short of a more fitting alternative, seem even less translatable. This linguistic problem alone hints that a clue to the Japanese self underlies the idiom of *migawari*. As Doi (1985) says about *amae*, whether this term or its equivalent is available in a culture makes difference in the way the universal emotions of dependency are released. Similarly I argue that the availability of the idiom of identity exchange for common usage does make a difference in the perception of self.

To continue on the linguistic discrepancy relevant to our discussion, another term should be mentioned as lacking an English equivalent, namely, *honnin*. There are many English terms for the person taking the surrogate role such as *substitute, deputy, delegate*, and other words listed above, but there is no English word for the person who is substituted for, delegated, and so on, that is, for the "true" self-person. The Japanese *honnin* stands for such a nonsubstitutive, authentic self, used in implicit or explicit distinction from the surrogate (*kawari* or *dainin*). Let me illustrate this by another experience of mine. About to begin fieldwork in Tokyo, I called a ward office to ask what I should bring over for alien registration. The office clerk, after answering my question, reminded me, obviously as a matter of routine, that the *honnin* should show up. In this situation, he meant "you yourself," saying implicitly that a surrogate would not do." *Honnin* is thus well marked in Japanese, more so than *dainin*, the latter usually being implied as a reference for *honnin*. This linguistic practice substantiates rather than weakens the above argument that *migawari* is quite common among Japanese, so common that the *honnin* marking is necessary.[1]

It may be further noted that, in the absence of the constant "I," the speaker may call him/herself, particularly in addressing a child, by the term likely to be used by the listener. Thus a schoolteacher calls himself "*sensei*" in speaking to his pupils, a father "father" in speaking to his child, an adult man "uncle" in speaking to an unfamiliar child, and so on (see Suzuki 1976 on terms for self and other). For a psycholinguistic moment the speaker may be said to "become" the listener. The self-other reflexivity in this sense is doubled in honorific terms like *gozen*, *kakka*, and *heika*. These are for addressing or referring to someone much higher in status than the speaker and may be translated as "my lord" or "your (his) highness" or "your (his) majesty" (*heika*). Literally, these terms indicate the speaker's humble self present "in front of" or "down below" the venerable personage seated high above. Psycholinguistically, the speaker A addresses B by looking down upon himself from the height of B.

Substitution may be more institutionalized as in the practice of adoption. Japanese are known for their readiness to adopt a child or even an adult, as a child substitute, particularly when an heir is needed.

As my latest research on the aristocracy got under way, the *migawari* came into even sharper focus, since this class had been practicing it more frequently and in a more theatrical manner. It is as if it were symbolic of status. Below, I attempt to highlight a few salient features of *migawari*, drawing upon a variety of sources of information, including aristocratic informants.[2] The emperor as a key self or a key mirror of the Japanese self will also appear as a major actor on the *migawari*-stage in the following analysis. Three features of *migawari* are singled out as salient: protection, authentication, and implementation.

Protection

First, the *migawari* is necessary when the *honnin* is physically or mentally disabled, sick, or too old, or young, helpless, or immobile to perform his/her role. There is nothing particularly Japanese about this. Substitution of the *honnin* in litigations by abundantly available lawyers is among the most common aspects of American life. The difference lies in the modes of such substitution. For Japanese, the *migawari* is supported by the culturally sanctioned dependency, the expected availability of nurturant substitutes, the representational capacity of fellow members of a group like a household, and the general acceptability of substitution as legitimate. This aspect of *migawari* involves protective nurturance.

Consider person A who wants or feels obligated to attend the funeral service for his friend B or B's kin, C. If A is too old, sick, or out of town, expectations are that substitutive attendance be made by A's wife, son, or other available kin, even though B is a stranger to the substitutive attendant. A hospitalized patient becomes a passive care receiver supported by a *migawari* taking an active role in communicating "on the *honnin*'s behalf" with the doctor, nurse, and other hospital staff or in hosting well-wishing visitors. It is against this backdrop that the true diagnosis, if devastating like cancer, can be kept secret to the patient as *honnin* while disclosed to his caretaker as *dainin*. When I was hospitalized in this country, I became painfully aware of the difference: it was entirely *my* responsibility to let the hospital staff know how I was doing, to ring a bell if I needed emergency help, to ask for pain killer when I was in pain. It was a chilling revelation that the American health-care system assumes the patient as a nonsubstitutable *honnin*. When a Japanese child is studying day and night for entrance examinations, it may be his mother who commutes to a shrine every morning to offer a surrogate prayer for his success. It is as if Japanese gods are responsive to such surrogate worshipers.

In the imperial institution, a sick emperor like Taishō (1912–26) was substituted for by the Crown Prince (Hirohito, Taishō's son) as *sesshō* (regent). Historically, the *sesshō* office was politically abused by the Fujiwara clan from the ninth through the eleventh centuries. But such abuse was inevitable in view of the status of the *sesshō* as nothing less than "the substitute for the emperor," which amounted to the emperor-*sesshō* equation: "the *sesshō* is the emperor himself" (Ishii 1982, 148–49).

Authentication

When a "true" inner state or feeling of the self is to be convincingly demonstrated, the *honnin*'s action alone may not be taken as sufficient. At issue here is "sincerity," held by Japanese as a key moral value. The receiver of a favor expresses gratitude, but his sincerity is to be authenticated by words of thanks from his family or fellow members of his group. The same holds true when a request is made, in that the requester's mentor or anybody that counts more than the requestor *honnin* is expected to authenticate his sincerity by requesting the same on his behalf.

The function of the *migawari* for authentication is particularly important when a person commits a serious offense. He owes an apology to the victim, for whatever pain he has caused him, or to the public, for disrupting society (*seken o sawagasete*). Particularly if the offender is regarded as too young or low in his status to have his word taken seriously, the Japanese public expects the *honnin*'s apology to be backed up by a *migawari* apology from someone who is senior or superior to the offender, such as his father, mentor, or boss. A recent incident will illustrate the *migawari* for authentication.

The Self-Defense Forces submarine *Nadashio* collided with a sport-fishing boat in August 1988, resulting in the death of most of the boat's passengers. While the cause was under investigation and guilt was yet to be determined, the *Nadashio* captain called rounds of the victims' families to apologize in tears. And something inevitable soon took place: the director of the Self-Defense Agency, Kawara, resigned. This incident was picked up in the popular "Sunday Morning" show, where a social critic expressed his approval of the director's resignation as reactivating the *bushidō* (samurai chivalry) tradition of harakiri as well as the Japanese esthetics of *isagiyoshi* (gallantry). It looked for the time being (before the case was brought to the court) as if Kawara's resignation concluded the whole issue involved. An American participant in the show, however, said that Americans would not understand why Kawara had to resign, because he had no responsibility for the disaster. Only the person(s) in direct charge of the submarine operation, he argued, should be punished. For the Japanese, that was not enough. What mattered most, at least in the initial reactions of the Japanese public, was not the technical error but the alleviation of the stress through social management. The situation required that the sincerity of apology by those directly involved be authenticated by the self-punishment of an official whose status was high enough.

Another, more recent incident may be cited. In April 1989, a photographer of *Asahi Shinbun*, a major national newspaper, while taking pictures under water near Okinawa, inscribed two initials on the coral reef, apparently to leave this aquatic adventure recorded for good. This was exposed and severely criticized as a grave destruction of the marine environment; it led to the company's dismissal of the photographer and punitive action against a fellow-diver and several others deemed as responsible for this "vandalism." To conclude this incident, the president of *Asahi* resigned (*Japan Times* May 27, 1989).

It is in view of this overload of vicarious responsibility "traditionally" assumed by superiors as a price of high status that the Recruit Scandal, exposed in 1988, appeared so offensive and, indeed, scandalous. Politicians, faction leaders in particular, alienated the Japanese public not so much because of their corrupt financial deals as because they blamed the corruption on their subordinates, such as managerial secretaries; their behavior was diametrically opposed to the rule of *migawari* for authentication.

There are cases where the *honnin* has no regrets about his conduct, as would be the case with radical students in the 1960s and 1970s. Many fathers came out to present themselves as *migawari* offenders, apologized, and resigned from their jobs, and some committed suicide. A typical statement made by a parent was "*Musuko ni kawatte owabi shimasu"* (I apologize as a substitute for my son). In this situation, the *migawari* apology is not for authentication but for a total replacement of the *honnin*'s identity.

Implementation

Status is an important determinant of who is to substitute for whom. In authentication, it is the superior who steps into a *migawari* role on behalf of the *honnin* holding a lower status, authenticity stemming from the substitute's status. But the correlations of high status to surrogate role, and low status to *honnin* role, do not always hold; they can be reversed when substitution serves other purposes. Note, too, that the status for authentication does not go upward indefinitely: it was the Defense-Force Agency director, not the prime minister, who resigned.

According to Linton (1936), status is coupled with role. Status as a cluster of rights or privileges to be claimed subsumes role as a cluster of duties or responsibilities to be performed, the two constituting the passive and active side of the same coin. In actuality, however, they are often mismatched. It is possible that a given status is either too low or too high for its holder to perform a certain role incumbent on the status. A third feature of the *migawari* is for implementation to fill in the status-role gap when the status is too high or when it carries too much symbolically loaded weight, as happens to an eminent public figure.

Relevant here is what a sample of aristocratic informants had to say. The hereditary aristocracy has been out of existence since 1947, but since 1976 I have been in occasional contact with more than one hundred survivors or their descendants. In interviews, they were asked to recall their prewar life-style (see Lebra 1993 for comprehensive research results). The single most striking feature of their recalled life-styles was the omnipresence of servants to discharge almost all the responsibilities that the ordinary househead and housewife would have done by themselves. Domestic chores and child rearing in the residential section of the "interior" were performed primarily by maid servants, while the male staff of the "exterior" managed the household in relation to the outside or "public." Even poor members of the nobility, which numbered not a few, had several servants to buttress their aristocratic status. For the children, the personal maid servants were constantly available as surrogates for their mothers, which often, if not always, resulted in a closer bond with the former than the latter. While they spoke to the children with honorifics, they also "became" disciplinarian parents or even *kyoiku-mama* (Lebra 1990). Fathers and husbands were often blind to the matter of the household treasury, which was under the jurisdiction of their surrogates. This accounted for the masters falling prey in the early postwar period to the former servants who took advantage of their masters' naivete. These stories demonstrate that the mundane household responsibilities, both internal and external, were beneath the status of the nobility and left to those of inferior status.

The main role in the household left to the aristocratic head and wife was ceremonial. Here, particularly among large, wealthy households of *daimyō* origin, some rituals were conducted by top servants. The managerial male servants were central actors in the ceremonial theater of marriage engagement, conducting the exchange of gifts for a son or daughter of the house. The wedding announcement was made in the name of the head manager. Periodical visits to temples, shrines, and mausolea to pay respect to the master's ancestors as well as to their caretakers (priests) were mentioned as the most important job of the head maid. This ritual action was called *godaihai* or *godaisan*, meaning "surrogate worship."

Even the sacred tradition of a household, which would appear embodied by the househead, was carried on by his surrogate. In some court-noble houses (*kuge*), styles of arts were transmitted, such as poetry, calligraphy, flower arrangement, incense art, court dressing, court music, and so on. Supposedly inherited from father to heir in secrecy, the art was not necessarily learned or practiced by the head of the house. Due to economic necessity combined with cultural revivalism, various house arts have been recently recaptured by the *kuge* descendants who now personally practice and teach them. "In the seven-hundred-year history of this house," said one of these descendants, "I, the twenty-eight-generation head master, am the first to make a living out of this art through teaching it." His predecessor, interested in perpetuating the art, nonetheless remained aloof from it, relegating the role of preserving and teaching it to a house retainer and commoner followers.

Interestingly, among the jobs taken up by the aristocrats were surrogate ones for the imperial house, including the role of surrogate parenthood for royal children. If the aristocratic househead recruited surrogate role-takers from among commoners to implement his status, so did the emperor from among aristocrats. Ritual roles were specially important. Imperial messengers called *chokushi* were, and still are, sent to various places, such as imperially sponsored shrines, as *migawari* for the emperor, that is, as the emperor himself, and they are to be treated as such. Except for major rites requiring the emperor's personal presence, chamberlains take turns every morning substituting for the emperor as the presiding priest for Shintō ceremony at the palace shrine. The chamberlain on duty purifies himself (*kessai*) by bathing, appears in full court-priest garment, and receives all the courtesy due to the emperor. "He becomes the emperor." It is in this sense that, according to a palace worker, the emperor goes to the palace shrine every day to pray and "keeps all day long wishing peace for the whole nation."

The imperial rituals conducted since Emperor Shōwa's death on January 7, 1989, gives further insight to this institutionalized surrogacy or the imperial self in connection with death pollution. I must digress a little to offer some detail on the background of imperial rituals. Upon Emperor Shōwa's death, the initial simple ceremony of imperial succession (*shokei*) was conducted for Crown Prince Akihito as the new emperor. Thereafter, all members of the royalty, including the new emperor, went into mourning, which would last for a year. Only after the passage of the mourning period, which coincided with the deceased emperor's maturity into the "pure" status of a god and his spiritual relocation to the *koreiden* (one of the three palace subshrines that houses all the imperial ancestors), could the truly grand ceremony of enthronement (*sokui*) be held. The ceremony was scheduled in the fall, subsequent to the completion of the mourning cycle. This coordinated with the harvest of new rice, so the enthronement ceremony was combined with the *niinamesai* (the annual imperial rite for tasting new rice), which was thus specially designated *daijosai* (grand tasting rite). The reason for this double ceremony as well as the interval between the two rituals was because the mourning emperor was disqualified from presenting himself in the palace shrine, particularly the most sacred subshrine, called *kensho* (or *kashikodokoro*), which enshrines the Sun-Goddess, the primordial imperial ancestress. This is where the *daijosai* ceremony was held.

Is it because the new emperor was polluted? A Shintō scholar, hesitating to say yes, explained to me that the emperor in grief "refrains" from attending the shrine, and he added that Shintō rites are *matsuri* (festivities), all for celebrations (*hare*), not for grief: Shintō gods welcome only those worshipers who are in a joyous mood. However explained, it is certain that the idea of pollution is essential to the shrine taboo, since shrine attendance requires body purification (*kessai*), abstinence from "four-legged" animal meat, as well as being out of the menstrual period, in the case of a woman.

The death-polluted emperor was thus supposed to stay away from the "pure" palace shrine as well as from the Shrine of Ise, where the "original" symbol of the Sun-Goddess, *the* mirror, is enshrined. This means that he could not even send his close *migawari*, like a chamberlain, to the shrine as he usually would. And yet, the shrine could not be left unattended even one day.

The dilemma was resolved by the presence of another category of imperial attendants, ones not affected by death pollution. There are a number of palace-shrine priests called *shoten*, who assist the emperor (or his surrogates) and other members of the imperial family with conducting shrine rituals. It was the *shoten*, specifically the head *shoten* (*shoten-cho*), who stepped into the role of the "pure" emperor while the imperial *honnin* was impure, and this began at the very moment of the previous emperor's death, immediately followed by the simple succession ritual.

Succession involves the transmission of three regalia: the jewel, sword, and the mirror. While the first two items (*kenji*) were handed over to the new emperor directly, the mirror, the symbol of the Sun-Goddess enshrined at *kensho*, was not. It was the head *shoten* who, substituting for the emperor (*tenno ni kawatte*), took over the *kensho* ritual of succession and read the *otsugebumi* (an oath to the imperial ancestress to be read by the emperor himself).

From this beginning until the expiration of the mourning period, the imperial postmortem rituals were bifurcated between the impure (in connection with the late emperor) and the pure (in association with the Sun Goddess and other Shintō deities). The latter domain was inhabited exclusively by the *shoten* priests taking over the "pure" self of the emperor. It was the *shoten* who visited the Ise Shrine or conducted daily rituals at the palace shrine. In an informant's words, a *shoten* "becomes the emperor." The new emperor had not lost his pure self but while impure, he could not act out the pure phase of himself, relying instead upon the pure priests to assume his identity.

Beyond the Self-Other Opposition

The above discussion on the imperial self in rituals leads to our conclusion. Three points have emerged. First, the self-other exchangeability presupposes the double, multiple, or split self. I referred to the double self of the emperor, pure and impure. Complementarily, those retainers, secular and religious, who substitute for the emperor, also assume double selves—substitutive and nonsubstitutive (*honnin*). In this sense, the Japanese self may be said to be "dividual," instead of "individual."

First, since Japanese say that the *kami* (deity, supernatural entity, spirit) resides within the *kokoro* of each and every person, it may be conjectured that the dividuality of the human self relates to the dividuality of the supernatural. The Sun-Goddess, the sacred mirror, is housed at the Shrine of Ise, but we also have seen the *kensho*, which is the most sacred section of the palace shrine, enshrining her. The Sun-Goddess at the palace is said to be a *bunshin* (split deity) of the Sun-Goddess at Ise. After the imperial funeral, the center of the mourning ritual moved to the burial site, the mausoleum under construction, in rural, western Tokyo, where daily services were held by a group of lay ritualists (*saikan*) recruited for this purpose. But there was another center constructed within the palace, called "*gonden*," the temporary shrine for the deceased emperor. The *saikan* thus took turns alternating between the two sites. The *gonden*, according to one of the *saikan*, enshrined a *wake-mitama* (split spirit) of the buried emperor. *Wake-mitama*, *bunshin*, and *bunrei* all refer to a split portion of the stem spirit or deity. Most local shrines all over Japan house *bunrei* invited over from major national shrines. Is it that the human self imitates the supernatural self in such divisibility without losing its identity, or vice versa?

Second, the *migawari* phenomenon has much to do with status hierarchy in ranks and age. As we have seen, substitution can occur upwardly and downwardly. In authentication, it is a higher-status holder who is expected to substitute, while implementation involves a lower-status holder as a substitute. In protection, the hierarchy can run in either direction. It is often the case, however, that protective substitution overlaps implementation. When a chamberlain, for example, substitutes for the emperor, we are not quite sure whether he is protecting the emperor or implementing his responsibility. Probably both. The same may be said to hold for the wife substituting for the husband. In a previous work (Lebra 1984) on women residents of a Japanese town, it was often found that the wife, as *the* home manager, substituted for her husband, the househead, in representing the house. She performed, for example, the role of officer for a neighborhood association in the name of the househead and formal officer. She seemed at once to be implementing his status and protecting him from the mundane chores of the neighborhood. It is interesting to note in this connection that Japanese gods are not only revered and worshiped but "protected."

The superior, including the emperor, who is substituted for by the inferior in implementation and protection, can be thus kept out of touch, "elevated" (or shelved) to a pure symbol, or have his authority usurped. This situation can give rise to the vagueness of the locus of responsibility for action. While excessive responsibility of a superior is noted in authentication, the opposite (insufficiency in his sense of responsibility) can occur as a result of protective implementation. The latter situation seems to underlie the refusal by the faction leaders implicated in the Recruit Scandal to admit their own guilt. This leads to the next point.

Third, that the nonsubstitutive self is well marked and recognized in the Japanese idiom as *honnin* implies its marginality in relation to the *dainin* that prevails in actual social life. In both protection and implementation, the higher person has a better chance to be a *honnin*, but is he really himself? Idiomatically he may be one: nobody talks about the emperor being a substitute for someone else except probably for high deities like the Sun Goddess. But psychologically he is far from being a *honnin* himself. To be remembered is the symbolic load of status: the higher the status, the more heavily guarded with symbolic meaning. In this sense the emperor may be said to be a pure symbol dissociated from his natural body.[3] As a symbolic being, his existence may allow no room to express his own self. Those of my aristocratic informants who were close to Emperor Showa in person pointed out that they had met nobody as "pure" and "selfless" as the emperor. To a lesser degree, aristocrats played a symbolically heavy role accompanied by the inhibited or nonself self. In other words, the elite, too, play(ed) a substitutive role on behalf of those below, inasmuch as a symbol stands for something else. It may be said that the *migawari* is a widespread cultural style adopted across classes.

I mentioned substitution of the *honnin* by lawyers as a common feature of American society. The lawyer, offering professional service in exchange for monetary fees, relates to the *honnin*, his/her client, by a voluntary, interest-motivated contract. Difference in self-perception between Japanese and Americans may have to do with the difference between the obligatory, diffuse type of identity exchange that involves status asymmetry, and the contractual, right-defensive exchange as exemplified by the lawyer and client.

In an additional note, it is tempting to say that attention to the Japanese idiom of self-other exchangeability may lead one beyond the structuralist horizon of the self-other opposition, where self claims primacy over other. I could claim to be a deconstructionist in this sense if I were receptive to fashionable poststructuralism. I am resistant to this brand of Western intellectual fashion, probably because I am like other Japanese who, too sensitized to the situational, multiple contingency of perception and action to be fully converted into structuralism, have been practicing poststructuralism prestructurally and therefore have nothing to deconstruct.

NOTES

Research for this paper was undertaken while I was a recipient of grants from the Social Science Research Council, University of Hawaii (Fujio Matsuda Scholar), and Wenner-Gren Foundation. The support is gratefully acknowledged.

1. In connection with *honnin*, I should mention another interesting case of marking. In kinship terms, the Japanese speaker often qualifies the identity of his/her kin with "real" (*jitsu*), such as *jippu* (real father), *jikkei* (real brother), *jisshi* (real child), in distinction from adoptive father or father-in-law. The kin category like "father" includes both the natural and simulated type, or both *honnin* and *dainin*, and because of the high frequency of the latter type, the former is marked as real. See note 2.

2. Here it may be pointed out that I found a greater frequency of son-adoption among aristocratic than commoner families, sometimes over three or more generations in a row, for the obvious reason that the hereditary aristocracy was more compelled to perpetuate the patriline (see Lebra 1989 for aristocratic adoption). Here a man, an incumbent househead adopted another man (who could be an adult or a daughter's husband) and "became" his father and predecessor, while the adopted man "became" a son and heir to his adoptive father. The ease with which such adoption was practiced is another indication, I believe, of readiness for identity exchange.

3. In discussing the British monarch, Hayden (1987) recognizes two bodies of the king or queen: "body natural" and "body politic," one to be hidden within the private realm, the other to be on public display. This seems to suggest a feature shared by the two monarchies. But in the eyes of the Japanese public, the Japanese emperor, as exemplified by Emperor Shōwa, seemed much more hidden and inaccessible than his British counterpart. At the same time, the Japanese emperor seemed more constrained in being his natural self (Lebra 1992b).

BIBLIOGRAPHY

Aida Yuji. 1970. *Nihonjin no ishiki kozo*. Tokyo: Kodansha.
Bachnik, Jane. 1992. "The Two 'Faces' of Self and Society in Japan." *Ethos* 20:3–32.
Befu, Harumi. 1980. *The Group Model of Japanese Society and an Alternate Model*. Rice University Studies Series 66. Houston.
Benedict, Ruth. 1946. *The Chrysanthemum and the Sword: Patterns of Japanese Culture*. Boston: Houghton Mifflin.
Cousins, Steven D. 1989. "Culture and Self-Perception in Japan and

the United States." *Journal of Personality and Social Psychology* 56:124–31.

Doi Takeo. 1971. *Amae no kozo*. Tokyo: Kobundo.

———. 1985. *Omote to ura*. Tokyo: Kobundo.

Hamaguchi Eshun. 1977. *Nihon rashisa no saihakken*. Tokyo: Nihon Keizai Shinbunsha.

Hayden, Ilse. 1987. *Symbol and Privilege: The Ritual Context of British Royalty*. Tuscon: University of Arizona Press.

Inoue, Tadashi. 1977. *Sekentei no kozo*. NHK Books. Tokyo: Nippon Hoso Shuppankai.

Ishii, Ryosuke. 1982. *Tenno: Tenno no seisei oyobi fushinsei no dento*. Tokyo: Yamakawa Shuppansha.

Kimura Bin. 1972. *Hito to hito to no aida*. Tokyo: Kobundo.

Kondo, Dorinne. 1990. *Crafting Selves: Work, Identity and the Politics in a Japanese Factory*. Chicago: University of Chicago Press.

Lebra, Takie Sugiyama. 1976a. *Japanese Patterns of Behavior*. Honolulu: University of Hawaii Press.

———. 1976b. "Ancestral Influence on the Suffering of Descendants in a Japanese Cult." In W. H. Newell, ed., *Ancestors*. The Hague: Mouton Publishers.

———. 1984. *Japanese Women: Constraint and Fulfillment*. Honolulu: University of Hawaii Press.

———. 1986. "Self-reconstruction in Japanese Religious Psychotherapy." In *Japanese Culture and Behavior: Selected Readings*, ed. T. S. Lebra and William P. Lebra. Rev. ed. Honolulu: University of Hawaii Press.

———. 1989. "Adoption among the Hereditary Elite of Japan: Status Preservation through Mobility." *Ethnology* 28:185–218.

———. 1990. "Socialization of Aristocratic Children by Commoners: Recalled Experiences of the Hereditary Elite in Modern Japan." *Cultural Anthropology* 5:78–100.

———. 1992a. Self in Japanese Culture. In *Japanese Sense of Self*, ed. N. Rosenberger. Cambridge: Cambridge University Press.

———. 1992b. "The Spatial Layout of Hierarchy: Residential Style of the Modern Japanese Nobility." In *Japanese Social Organization*, ed. T. S. Lebra. Honolulu: University of Hawaii Press.

———. 1993. *Above the Clouds: Status Culture of the Modern Japanese Nobility*. Berkeley and Los Angeles: University of California Press.

Linton, Ralph. 1936. *The Study of Man: An Introduction*. New York: Appleton-Century.

Marsella, Anthony J., George DeVos, and Francis L. K. Hsu, eds.

1985. *Culture and Self: Asian and Western Perspectives*. New York: Tavistock Publications.

Moeran, Brian. 1984. Individual, Group, and *Seishin*: Japan's Internal Cultural Debate. *Man* 19:252–66. Reprinted in *Japanese Culture and Behavior: Selected Readinas*, ed. T. S. Lebra and W. P. Lebra. Rev. ed. Honolulu: University of Hawaii Press, 1986.

Minami Hiroshi. 1983. *Nihon teki jiga*. Tokyo: Iwanami Shoten.

Nakane Chie. 1967. *Tate shakai no ningen kankei*. Tokyo: Kodansha.

Rohlen, Thomas. 1973. "'Spiritual Education' in a Japanese Bank." *American Anthropologist* 75:1542–62. Reprinted in *Japanese Culture and Behavior: Selected Readinas*, ed. T. S. Lebra and W. P. Lebra. Rev. ed. Honolulu: University of Hawaii Press, 1986.

Rosenberger, Nanct R. 1989. "Dialectic Balance in the Polar Model of Self: The Japan Case." *Ethos* 17:88–113.

Shweder, Richard A., and Robert A. LeVine, eds. 1984. *Culture Theory: Essays on Mind, Self, and Emotion*. Cambridge: Cambridge University Press.

Smith, Robert J. 1983. *Japanese Society: Tradition, Self, and the Social Order*. Cambridge: Cambridge University Press.

Suzuki Takao. 1976. Language and Behavior in Japan: The Conceptualization of Personal Relations. *Japan Quarterly* 23:255–66. Reprinted in *Japanese Culture and Behavior: Selected Readings*, ed. T. S. Lebra and W. P. Lebra. Rev. ed. Honolulu: University of Hawaii Press, 1986.

6

Spiritual Quests of Twentieth-Century Women: A Theory of Self-Discovery and a Japanese Case Study

Diane B. Obenchain

Introduction

This paper essays to articulate some discoveries as regards "self," which surfaced for women who participated in a seminar I conducted over the past five years in the United States, Japan, and China entitled "Spiritual Quests of Twentieth-Century Women: A Comparative Literary Study." The paper has five parts. The first four parts develop sequentially a theory concerning the process of becoming increasingly "self"-aware. Part one offers an integrated way of conceiving what is "sacred" and what is "self." Part two explores the essential human process of storytelling as a vehicle by which one becomes consciously aware of one's presence in the world, of who one is, of self. Storytelling involves two persons or presences, the teller and the listener. Part three traces how these two roles or patterns of activity, to which we give the names "expression out-in-the-world" and "nurturing-affirmation," most often in history have been taken up by men and women respectively, regardless of culture. Part four concerns the religious or spiritual transformation that takes place when those learned in one of these roles or patterns "cross over" to cultivate the part of the other. The final section of the paper focuses on Japanese women as they move into "expressive out-in-the-world" patterns of behavior *without abandoning* skills of nurturing-affirmation that they have learned first as their primary role in society. Shizue Ishimoto's autobiography, *Facing Two Ways*, will serve as a case study and illustrative example of the theory developed in the four preceding sections.

Our exposition will also include some remarks concerning

Chinese women, who differ somewhat from Japanese women in that the affirmative-nurturing role for women in China has not been as highly valued or articulated to the same degree as in Japanese society. Nonetheless, both groups of Asian women appear in sharp contrast with increasing numbers of Western women who, due to a Western cultural emphasis on "expression out-in-the-world," have felt more socially valued the more they abandon the affirming-nurturing role.

We are somewhat critical of attempts to define 'self' solely in terms of expressive out-in-the-world patterns of behavior, which are associated quite often with dominant Western males and seem everywhere in the world to be "in fashion" these days. Our own view is that men and women discover more of who they are, of self, by opening out, by learning the part of the other, while at the same time holding onto a good part of their first acquired role behaviors. Over a lifetime, men and women realize more of who they are by finding a balance of both modes of living within each person. Whether expanding into expressive out-in-the-world patterns of behavior or expanding into nurturing-affirming patterns of behavior, *both involve religious transformation*. Some have argued that symbols of major religious traditions are most helpful for cultivating nurturing patterns of behavior to round out expressive patterns, but *not* necessarily the other way around. We shall challenge this claim.

We are not attempting here to present in all variety the literature written by women since the turn of the century in the three cultural areas in which we have worked. In this short paper, we endeavor only to present *one* thread connecting the writing of some leading women, a thread that not only has held the material together meaningfully for us but also continues to offer new insights, new congruities, as we live our lives. We are at the beginning. The discovery in the course of human history of who we are as human beings, female or male, is, in the vastness of our universe, just underway and may, if we are wise enough in practicing the best of what we have learned, have a long way to go. The process will continue to involve, as it does today, opening out, through our cumulative traditions, to more.

Self As Presence of What Is Sacred in the World:
Some Conceptual Correlations

Work in the field of comparative history of religion suggests that perhaps there are as many conceptions of 'self' as there are conceptions of what is 'sacred'.[1] Both notions are considerably shaped by specific language and cultural systems, geographic locations, and historical events. Coming up with any one definition of self is as difficult as coming up with one definition of what is sacred: one's concept of self or sacred either is universalized to the point of losing existential meaning or is so specific as to invite rejection on the basis of cultural, social, political, or gender bias. This correspondence in range between understandings of self and of what is sacred is perhaps not coincidental.

When we look at the variety of shape and form that human reverence of something "more," something sacred, has taken in our relatively short term on this earth, one conviction in all this variety stands out to which the eminent scholar of religion Wilfred Cantwell Smith cogently calls our attention: "There is more in human life than meets the eye."[2] Following this line of thinking, religion might be defined generally as giving care to, paying heed to, paying attention to, more *in* human life than meets the eye.[3] What is more in human life is already within us and around us in the world; we are already, in some sense, participating in it. Hence, transcendence (more) is also immanence.[4] When we pay attention to or give care to what is more, which is already within and around us in the world, *we give it priority in our lives*, we are in *awe* of it: it is sacred to us. Insofar as we give priority to more in human life than meets the eye, we desire to live and move *with* it, not against it.[5] We are willing to let it take the lead.

The history of religion is the history of human efforts to symbolize, in sometimes more and sometimes less humanlike terms, what is more in human life than meets the eye. In whatever way we conceive of more, included in this conception or symbol is a way for us to participate in it, to bring more of it out in our lives. We sense, know, intuit that it is in living and moving *with*, rather than against, what is more in which we already participate, that we enliven more wisdom, more harmony with others, and more personal joy in the world. In other words, we embody the best of what we can humanly be. In this sense, then, *humanism*, as a focus on what we humans can do and be, and *religious living*, as giving priority to more in human life than meets the eye, living and moving with it so as to give expression to more wisdom, compassion, joy in all that we do, go very well together indeed.[6]

Let us use the term *self* to refer to one's notion of who one is in answering the question, who are you?. As one increasingly opens out to more in human life than meets the eye and gives it priority in one's life, one's understanding of who one is, one's notion of self, one's response to the question, who are you? deepens or changes. This may be revealingly stated from the other direction as well: one's awareness of self, of who one is, is the process by which more in human life comes into great conscious realization here-in-the-world. *How* one conceives of more in human life to which one yields and gives priority, is conceptually correlated with *how* one conceives of "who one is," one's "self." Additionally, *how* one actively expresses in the world, through intentions, thoughts, words, conduct, more in human life than meets the eye is also conceptually correlated with one's conception of "more." All three conceptions—of more, of self, of living and moving in a sacred manner—move together.

For example, if one conceives of more in human life as *dao* (a Chinese conception of more as the spontaneous way of the ten thousand things), then, one's conception of who one is parallel: a vessel through which *dao* expresses itself spontaneously in-the-world. Who one is, one's awareness of self, is one relatively momentary shape or form of constantly changing *dao*. Moreover, one's conception of living and moving in a sacred manner will be parallel as well: one is to live and move naturally and spontaneously, without reflection or intentional effort (*wu-wei*) to force actions to conform to prescribed standards.[7] If we take up the Judeo-Christian concept of more in human life than meets the eye to which one gives priority, then one's entire conceptual understanding of participating in more, of who one is as presence of what is sacred in the world, shifts. Following one Judeo-Christian conception of more, God is "Creator," "Master," "Lord." Humans, given dominion over the created domain, are "servants" of the master who are instructed to follow the master's commands. Living and moving in a sacred manner, then, requires considerable reflection and intentional effort to submit to the lord and to know and follow the commands of the master.

Other examples could be given for each human conception of what is sacred. Viewed in this way, the terms *sacred* (or what is more in human life than meets the eye and to which one gives priority) and self have no specific conceptual content that is always the same. The specific meaning and use of these terms will vary from culture to culture, person to person, time to time, even within one person's lifetime. Our purpose here is simply to take note of the persistent correlation among (1) conceptions of what is sacred, (2) conceptions of who one is, one's "self" as participating in what is sacred, and (3) conceptions of how we live and move in a sacred manner to realize *more* here and now: intellectually, emotionally, practically, psychically, physically.

Here we would offer a word of caution. Many today do *not* use the term *self* in the *humanistic* and *religious* sense, which we have just set forth. Instead, one's understanding of who one is, one's awareness of self, often gets carried along in the secularizing flood of "modernity." Caught up in this flood, ironically, one knows one's self *less* for one's participation in "more," which interconnects all, and *more* for one's being cut off, separate, utterly unique, "less," as it were. This recent attention to self as individual uniqueness is in great part a response to increasing invasion of our lives by mass media and authority in every possible form. But dividing off, limiting, drawing boundaries—these methods of the secular world for taking control are subtle. While on the surface appearing to give an individual power over his or her life, the secularizing stream actually moves in the opposite direction, as we find ourselves too isolated and alone in our understanding of who we are to mount a challenge to those forces that sap our life. In our view, life and strength are in interconnecting, exchanging, sharing. This is the core of our entire argument.

Because the term *self* may be used with both secular and sacred orientations, we need to make clear our use of the term. In this paper we shall be concerned with self as one opens out to more in human life than meets the eye, that is, with self as presence of what is sacred in the world. In this regard, then, we are more concerned with what we share and the very process of sharing itself than with what makes us unique and the process of isolating uniqueness.[8]

To Be Present Here in the World Is to Be Known

Most of us know that we are, that we are in-the-world, that we are present here. This sense of presence is important, although we are not often aware *of* it, that is to say, it does not frequently become an object upon which we reflect conceptually. Some of us have discovered that our sense of presence can increase as others give witness to us, that we feel more present in the world the more we are known and affirmed by others. In turn, we are more able to be present to yet others, affirming or increasing their awareness of their presence in the world.

The startling fact about presence is that one knows one's self as present in-the-world because *someone else* does. In addition, *what* one knows about one's self is what at least one other knows. Thus, one's conscious realization of who one is, is shared. If conscious realization of who one is, is always a shared realization, then to be aware of self is to be engaged to some degree in intimacy. To know who one is, to know one's self, is impossible without the loving gift of affirmation from another. Presence, as we know it, is copresence.

Conversely, to withhold affirmation of another is to keep what he or she has said or done out-of-the-world. If carried out to an extreme, withholding affirmation is tantamount to denying him or her presence in-the-world, to denying life. It is the opposite of being loving and generous. Consistent withholding affirmation of another may retard the other's conscious realization of who he or she is, his or her sense of self. Moreover, as we have set forth in the previous section, if knowing one's self is the conscious realization, to some degree, of who one is, as one opens out and gives heed to more in human life than meets the eye, then to discourage, through withholding affirmation, another's discovery of who he or she is puts limits on another's conscious realization of what is sacred, which is, in effect, to put limits on the presence of the sacred in the world.

On these several points, the well-known anthropologist Barbara Myerhoff, in her prizewinning studies of elderly Jews in Venice, California, and of Huichol Indians in New Mexico, among others,[9] offers extensive evidence as she argues throughout that telling one's story is the vehicle through which one becomes known and affirmed in the world. In her lectures at Kenyon College five years ago, Myerhoff asked us to consider what the shortest story might be. As we wondered to ourselves, she offered an example: "Kilroy was here." Similarly, Ursula LeGuin locates the minimum story in notch-cutting:

> She tells about the cathedral in northern England in which a stone was found in the transept a few feet up from the floor. There, carved laboriously in the stone, were some marks which, translated, read, "Tolfin carved these runes in this stone." Tolfin, she said, bears witness to the existence of Tolfin. He was a human being unwilling to dissolve into his surroundings.[10]

The shortest story is simply a testament of being. Its purpose is to draw witness (the Latin word *testimonium* means "witness") to one's existence so that one is known by another. A witness, upon hearing the story serves as a mirror, reflecting back the story to the teller and in so doing affirms: Yes, I hear you; yes, I know you; yes, you exist; yes, you are in-the-world. Myerhoff states: "I am keenly interested in how one is 'made' as a person and how one 'makes a world' by the acts of preservation and witnessing. Finally there is the issue of 'bearing witness,' of surviving, of becoming visible and thereby achieving existence in the eyes of others; that is, coming to be."[11] Myerhoff's *Homo narrans*, humanity as storyteller—"relentless, intractable storyteller"—is a subtle observation with profound implications.

Most of us know the experience of having something incredible happen to us and then rushing to find someone to tell about it. If the person to whom we tell our story does not believe it, it is as though, for a time, he or she has denied our being in-the-world. Our very best friend is the person who really does listen, who really does understand, who really does say yes to us. When we are with this friend, we feel truly here in-the-world, relaxed. One who is not our friend is one who does not listen to and affirm what we say or, worse, insists on *changing* what we say so that it is no longer our story. Often for such a person, we exist only when we fulfill what he or she thinks *ought* to be our story or wants to be our story, for only then do we receive his or her recognition. In its extreme form, this is subjugation.[12]

Telling one's story, expressing who one is, can be narrated with movements of the body as one gestures and acts out who one is for another to see and reflect back. Or, one might formulate a concept of who one is and argue it philosophically. Or, one might paint a picture, mold a sculpture, write a symphony. In whatever form, one is giving "voice" or "image" to who one is in order to draw witness and affirmation back. That witness may well be oneself. Over a lifetime, one's awareness of who one is, of self, changes, expands, deepens—sometimes gradually, sometimes suddenly. So, also, one's story changes.

Throughout the process of discovering who one is, the affirming presence of another is essential. When we are young, affirmation comes from parents or "significant others" who generously affirm us and, in so doing, bring us increasingly into the world. Much of what they affirm in us draws out the behavior patterns, the values, the thinking processes that will enable us to fit into a cultural, social order. Myerhoff explains:

> Cultures include in their work self-presentations to their members. On certain collective occasions, cultures offer interpretations. They tell stories, comment, portray, and mirror. Like all mirrors, cultures are not acccurate reflectors; they are distortions, contradictions, reversals, exaggerations, even lies. Nevertheless, the result—for both the individual and the collectivity—is self-knowledge.
>
> The self-portraits of these people range from delicate and oblique allusions to fully staged dramatic productions in the course of which members embody their place in the scheme of things, their locations in the social structure, their purposes and natures, taking up the questions of who we are and why we are here, all things that, as a species, we cannot do without.
>
> Such performances are opportunities for appearing—an indispensable ingredient of being itself—for unless we exist in the eyes of others, we may come to doubt even our own existence. Being is a social and psychological construct; it is something that is made, not given. Thus, it is erroneous to think of performances

as optional, arbitrary, or merely decorative embellishments as we in Western societies are inclined to do. In this sense, arenas for appearing are essential, and culture serves as both stage and mirror, providing opportunities for self and collective proclamations of being.[13]

In discovering who we are, our first understanding of self comes from the playing out of rituals, roles, behavior patterns that have been told to us. We become who we are expected to be by our families, by our social groups, by our culture. We exist in the world in so far as we enact this rituals, roles, behaviors, for when we do so, we are affirmed, "stroked," given being in the world. Who others understand us to be becomes our understanding of self.

However, who we are and our conscious realization of who we are, that is, of self, may be more than what others tell us initially. It may happen that as we open out to more in human life than meets the eye, as we give it priority in our lives, we discover more of who we are than social roles, rituals, and language have revealed to us. For this more to be present in the world, telling one's story and being heard and affirmed by another is again essential. This exchange may take any variety of form.

One of the more intriguing examples of telling one's story and being heard and affirmed by another is the course of instruction between a Chan (Japanese *zen*) master and a disciple. The master's one intention is to affirm the Buddha-nature as it unfolds in a person. His skill-in-means as a teacher is his choice of words to affirm and not distort:

> One made of clay and decorated with gold.
> Even the finest artist cannot paint him.
> The one enshrined in the Buddha Hall.
> He is not Buddha.
> Your name is Yecho.
> The dirt-scraper all dried up.
> See the eastern mountains moving over the waves.
> No nonsense here.
> Surrounded by the mountains are we here.
> The bamboo grove at the foot of Chang-lin hill.
> Three pounds of flax.
> Lo, the waves are rolling over the plateau.
> See the three-legged donkey go trotting along.
> A reed has grown piercing through the leg.
> Here goes a man with the chest exposed and the legs all naked.[14]

D. T. Suzuki explains: "we live in affirmation and not in negation, for life is affirmation itself; and this affirmation must not be the one accompanied or conditioned by a negation; such an affirmation is relative and not at all absolute . . . Absolute affirmation is the Buddha; but somehow you do not recognize it until you, like Gutei's little boy, lose a finger."[15] Life never repeats itself exactly, so the master's task is to affirm it, the Buddha-nature, exactly as it expresses itself at any given moment.[16] The master's affirmation sparks "self"-knowledge as the master mirrors back the Buddha-nature as it comes into expression within one. One's expanded awareness of self, who one is, is now *present* in the world.

Perhaps the oldest recorded story of discovering more of who one is, more of self, beyond role, ritual, and linguistic predeterminations is the *Epic of Gilgamesh*. In one version of this story, Gilgamesh, having conquered all within his realm, becomes destructive of that social order as he attempts to live within it, for there is more to him than that social order can tolerate and still remain intact. So the celestial powers send down the almost-equal Enkidu, whom, in hand to hand combat (another way of telling one's story), Gilgamesh conquers, but not easily. At last he has discovered someone who "knows" him. They become fast friends and set off away from the social order and its prescribed roles, the known world, to face the unknown. What happens to them is somewhat paradigmatic for all those who set off to discover more: the encounter with evil, the confrontation with mortality, the rejection of solitude, and then the final leaving behind of one's story, in Gilgamesh's case, the engraving in stone of what happened: "Gilgamesh was here" (with a few particulars). And so his presence, narrated and alive in each of us as we listen to and empathize with his story, continues in us. Presence is copresence.

A very recent story of discovering more of who one is is Alice Walker's *The Color Purple*. We shall discuss this story in some detail here, as it illustrates much of what we shall be considering in the next two sections.

As Shug befriends Celie, she listens to all that has happened so tragically to her: she has been beaten, raped, and robbed of all dignity. Prey to her family and to her husband, she and others knew her "self" only for her manual labor, her female body, her stupidity, her ugliness. However, in contrast to what others have affirmed, Shug starts to take joy in Celie's sense of humor, her gentleness, her intelligence, her loving nature. Slowly, Celie comes to realize more of who she is, more of her "self." One can almost feel Shug's love pulling Celie into-the-world.

Significantly, as Celie discovers more of who she is, more of her "self," her image of God shifts, as does the way in which she relates to God. She used to write to God, whom she imaged as "an old white man." Despite how negatively she conceived of him, still he was the one "person" to whom she could talk (presence is copresence), and in this manner she was able to hold onto life, being here in the world, however tenuous that sense of presence may have been. Then, as she starts to receive Shug's love and affirmation, she takes in from Shug more about God:

> God is inside you and inside everybody else. You come into the world with God. But only them that search for it inside find it . . . God ain't a he or a she, but a It . . . God is everything . . . Everything that is or ever was or ever will be. And when you can feel that, and be happy to feel that, you've found It . . . God love everything you love—and a mess of stuff you don't. But more than anything else, God love admiration . . . Not vain, just wanting to share a good thing. I think it pisses God off if you walk by the color purple in a field somewhere and don't notice it . . . People think pleasing God is all God care about. But any fool living in the world can see it always trying to please us back . . . It always making little surprises and springing them on us when us least expect . . . Everything [even God] want to be loved. Us sing and dance, make faces and give flower bouquets, trying to be loved. You ever notice that trees do everything to git attention we do, except walk?[17]

As Celie is increasingly loved, affirmed, brought into the world, she starts to relate to God differently. She ceases to write to him, but rather begins to affirm "It" in the delights of life that she comes to experience for the first time. She no longer feels she is at "his" mercy. She has a friend; she is loved; she is in-the-world. Having awakened into more, she starts to speak out who she is, something she has never done, and in so doing, curses her husband to his face. He laughs: "Who you think you is? he say. You can't curse nobody. Look at you. You black, you pore, you ugly, you a woman. Goddam, he say, you nothing at all . . . I probably didn't whup your ass enough . . . I should have lock you up. Just let you out to work."[18] A rush of dust stops the fight. Shug shakes Celie and she comes to her "self"—consciously, verbally, out loud for all to hear—for the first time: "'I'm pore, I'm black, I may be ugly and can't cook,' a voice say to everything listening. 'But I'm here.'"[19] Shortly thereafter she signs her name for the first time in a letter to her sister Nettie.

Her next letter to Nettie starts out: "I am so happy. I got love, I got work, I got money, friends and time. And you alive and be home soon. With our children."[20] Let us note well that what brings Celie into fuller awareness of who she is in-the-world is not just affirmative love, although love is by far the most essential. Work, money, time, in addition to loving, affirming friends and her sister, became part of her story. It is greater opportunities for self-discovery through work, money, and time that the present, far more than the past, is offering to many more women and members of minority groups. We cannot overlook or underestimate the role of these factors, alongside loving affirmation, which must come first, in making possible greater realization of who one is, of self. We shall return to this issue in more detail in the next section.

Nurturing and Expressing: Gender-free, Learned Patterns of Behavior

Affirming and validating actions, gestures, expressions of others is what we, in our research, haved called "nurturing" behavior. In nurturing another, one witnesses, authenticates, receives who another is. Often one nurtures selectively in that one sees or hears some things, which one views as true and good according to accepted values of one's family, social group, and culture, but not others. Affirmed for some activities, we learn certain prescribed roles or patterns of action. However, as we turn in the direction of more, which is both within and beyond us, to learn more of who we are beyond these roles, then, perhaps, our best nurturer, our best friend, is one who is not as selective, but, rather, lets us try out alternatives. In a word, nurturing says (perhaps without saying) simply, yes. And the profound effect of this yes is that, when heard, we are in-the-world.[21]

Nurturing behavior is loving behavior. It encourages and supports life in all ways: physical, mental, emotional, spiritual. In addition, it would seem that the deeper the level on which one is able to lovingly support the expression of another, that is, the being in-the-world of another, the deeper is one's love for him or her. Nurturing comes naturally, although it is quite possible, by choice or lack of attention, to let this natural inclination run slack. The spontaneous inclination to nurturingly affirm another is like one corner of the real leaping up in joyous recognition of another; it is the tendency of what is true to seek, to know, more of itself. One could almost say that, in this sense, what is true is naturally "social."

Asserting, telling, narrating, demonstrating, expositing—these are all examples of what we, in our research, have called "expressive" behavior. Expressive behavior projects who one is out-into-the-world to be witnessed, validated, and received by others as true, valuable. It draws energy and attention to one with words, gestures, movements that say, "See me, feel me, touch me, hear me."[22] Expression out-in-the-world requires risk, will, courage, determination, for one can be rejected, not witnessed, not received. It also involves making choices as regards the way in which one might express who one is and being responsible for these choices. For one's being received in-the-world, one's being present in-the-world, one's being consciously aware of "self" in-the-world, is dependent upon such choices.

Both nurturing and expressive patterns of behavior are essential to the process of bringing more in human life than meets the eye out into conscious realization. Expression without affirmation cannot know its self, who it is. On the other hand, nurturing-affirming love without another's expression has nothing to witness, enjoy, love; it wants to say yes but there is nothing or no one to say yes to. Being in-the-world requires the coming together of expression and affirmation. Meaning in life also involves both and is deepened as expression and affirmation become more profound.

To this point in time, in virtually all known cultures, the nurturing pattern of behavior has been most often linked with women, women as mothers in-the-home. The expressive pattern of behavior has been linked primarily with men and their moving about out-in-the-world outside the home. There is good evidence that these roles are to some extent biologically set.

Young human beings need a tremendous amount of encouragement, support, nurturing, on all levels—physical, mental, emotional, spiritual—to draw them increasingly into the world and to help them discover more of who they are here in-the-world. As has been the case for most of human history, the mother (or surrogate), who has physically given birth to a child, has been the first primary caretaker of a child, providing physical support, mental stimulation, loving affirmation; she offers what she has and the youngster takes all up into his or her growing, deepening, being in-the-world.

Valerie Saiving, in a most illuminating article written in 1960, draws upon the research of Margaret Mead. Saiving notes that in every culture young girls, in discovering who they are, imitate their mothers, knowing that eventually, being of the same sex, they will grow up to take their place. Young boys, however, in discovering who they are, quickly recognize that they are sexually different from their mothers. They cannot physically give birth as she does. And taking, we think mistakenly, nurturing to be primarily or altogether a physical activity, the young boy turns away from mother and her nurturing-affirming way of being to discover who he is as distinctly different from her. This discovery requires trying out different possibilities through expression, performance, and achievement out-in-the-world. In the process, he learns to undertake risk, challenge, choice, and uncertainty.[23] We shall return to more of Saiving's argument in a moment.

While, no doubt, women and men are, to some extent, biologically pushed in the direction of nurturing and expressive patterns of behavior, we would like to suggest that there is more to being human than our physical bodies.[24] Discovering more of who we are in addition to our biological gender might well take us into learning patterns of behavior that the other gender already knows quite well. In so doing, each discovers more of what it is to be human. Perhaps there is yet more beyond these two patterns of behavior, nurturing and expressing, for us to discover; but let us start with what is close at hand.

Going beyond a set of learned behaviors does not necessarily require abandoning these behaviors. Taking them with one, one cultivates, *in addition*, new patterns of behavior that bring out even more of who one is, thereby broadening, deepening, integrating one's "self" knowledge.

Virginia Woolf's writing, both in prose and fiction, during the first half of the twentieth century, addresses precisely this emergence out of first-learned roles, nurturing for women and expressing for men, into something more as one also learns the part of the other. Woolf argues that to become expressive out-in-the-world, women require the same sorts of preconditions that men have had—time away from family, money, and "a room of one's own." In a complementary way, to cultivate affirming, loving, and validating others, men require preconditions that women have had—time with family members, an environment encouraging sharing on all levels, freedom from the hustle and bustle of the world.

With great wit in *A Room of One's Own*,[25] Woolf argues the case that quite often a man's expressive ego, his confidence to express who he is, draws its sustenance, its life, from a woman. However, her energies may be so depleted in nurturing and affirming him, as she does her children, that there is no energy, time, money left with which she can express who *she* is. In this manner, one side of humanity has sacrificed its own expressiveness to enable the expressiveness of the other.

In her novel *To the Lighthouse*, Woolf wonders whether it might be possible for both sides, male and female, to take up both tasks, nurturing and expressing, within one and the same person.[26] At length Woolf portrays the marriage of Mr. and Mrs. Ramsey and their three children. He is a distinguished university professor, somewhat overly dependent upon her affirmation for his confident ability to write, to express himself. She is the perfect mother, offering all she has, physically and emotionally, to her husband and children, so that each might draw from her energy, time, and love the resources each needs to be more fully present in-the-world.

Mrs. Ramsey dies. Ten years pass. Mr. Ramsey then marries Lily, a personal friend of the family and an aspiring artist who never seems able to finish a painting, to find its center. As the pace of the story begins to move away from what has felt like a still life and races towards a bursting finish, Lily attempts on the beach to finish her painting of a lighthouse in the distance. Mr. Ramsey hovers over her begging for affirmation, attention. She holds back, keeping her energies focused on her painting.

Just as she is sure that all of Hell will rain down on her for her denial of comfort, time, and attention to Mr. Ramsey, for her holding onto some of her energies to express her vision, she looks down at his boots and notices they are untied. Unlike Mrs. Ramsey who always felt herself unworthy even to tie his shoes, Lily encouragingly compliments Mr. Ramsey on his choice of boots and never gives even a thought to tying them. As small as this point is, it gives rise to an earthshaking discovery on the part of Mr. Ramsey: that he is quite capable not only of making his own choices but also of validating himself for his choices, as he had done on his own with his boots. He is terribly pleased and proud of himself, somewhat like a child who has discovered that he can tie his own shoes. And with this discovery of his own power of self-affirmation, the next moment he is off to offer loving affirmation to his children, something he has rarely, if ever, done before.

From here the novel opens out in a rush as Mr. Ramsey and his children head off in a boat to the great lighthouse at sea, a point that has always been in front of them but to which a journey was never successfully made when Mrs. Ramsey was alive. Along the way he compliments his son for his courage and skill. "Well done!" he says for the first time. Just as they reach the lighthouse, Lily standing on the far shore finds the center of her painting: the lighthouse. Her *vision and its expression* are complete.

Woolf's point is that women will not be able to envision for themselves the meaning in life, nor will they be able to give full expression to their visions, until men cease to take so much time and energy from them. This will require that men discover that having been affirmed by others, they, in turn, can be their own source of energy and affirmation for themselves as well as for others. As Woolf portrays it, there is required a simultaneous moment of shift on the part of both men and women. When Lily took the courage to hold onto some of her own resources for her own expressive work, just then Mr. Ramsey discovered his own inner resources for self-affirmation and nurturing others.[27] For both the moment of shift or crossing over required great courage to face the unknown upon which followed a powerful, new orientation to the world, what we would call a "religious" or "spiritual" transformation.

Crossing over: Passing through the Same Door Heading in Opposite Directions and Ending up in the Same Place

Valerie Saiving has argued that our inherited religious teachings, by and large, have been directed toward those whose expression out-in-the-world has gone to some excess: pride, will to power, exploitation, aggression, self-centeredness, psychological dependence.[28] If we were to give example to Saiving's point, Judeo-Christian symbols address these excesses by encouraging sacrificial love. Buddhist symbols likewise encourage compassion and the letting go of grasping desire. So also Confucian cultivation of benevolence (*ren* 仁) seeks to curb drawing too many resources, too much power, time, and attention, to any one person or family and encourages, instead, extending familial, nurturing care and concern out-of-the-home into the market place and government leadership.

What, then, will these symbolic resources offer the woman who already is perhaps overly skilled in sharing, sacrificing, giving her life to others? One-sided nurturing has its own excesses: diffusion of physical, emotional, and mental energies, refusing others privacy, and indiscriminate, nonreflective acceptance or tolerance of whatever is offered by a loved-one.[29] There are many awe-inspiring symbols of more in human life that image nurturing, compassion, and loving devotion as feminine: Mother Mary, Kuan Yin, and Radha, to name three who are known to many; and there are countless other highly personal but less well known symbols of the source of life as feminine in fields, valleys, and sacred alcoves in homes of every region. While these symbols inform us, male and female alike, of the transcending dimension of giving love, care, and nurturing to others, because these images are feminine, they have tended to suggest to women that nurturing is *all* of who they are. Rarely, in the major religious traditions of the world, do we find symbols of awe-inspiring, rational, responsible, risk-taking, expression out-in-the-world imaged as female. Quite the contrary! Saiving states:

> theology, to the extent that it has defined the human condition on the basis of masculine experience, continues to speak of such de-

> sires [to devote time, energy, and focus to expressing more fully
> who one is out-in-the-world] as sin or temptation to sin. If . . . a
> woman believes the theologians, she will try to strangle those im-
> pulses in herself . . . [thinking] she has no right to ask anything
> for herself but must submit without qualification to the strictly
> feminine role."[30]

The "feminine role" to which Saiving refers here is the role into which
females have been traditionally and culturally instructed. However, we
would argue that there is nothing necessarily "female" to the nurturing
and loving role as witnessed by the fact that many religious teachings
are precisely for the very purpose of cultivating these qualities *in
males*!

To move beyond excesses of either expressive or nurturing behavior, men and women both need symbols of more in human life than
meets the eye, symbols that encourage them to move beyond what
they already do well, to be spiritually transformed into deeper and
broader realizations of all that we humanly are. Significantly, movement beyond known roles into new ways of being in-the-world is equally uncertain, equally terrifying for both men and women. To cross over
safely in a manner *integrated* with what has come before, questers in
either direction require true, reliable, religious—spiritual—guidance
and instruction.

The last several decades have been marked by increasing numbers of women going beyond the walls of the home and its home "in-
dustries" to work out-in-the-world.[31] For some, this going beyond the
walls has been desired; for others, it has been required, given economic or political demands. In either case, passage beyond the walls has
meant, more or less through trial and error in different forms of expression out-in-the-world, discovery of more of who one is.[32] This discovering of more of who one is necessarily involves (although one may
not always be aware of it) reconsideration of what traditional religious
symbols reveal to us. For some women, such reconsideration has resulted in outright iconoclasm. For others, efforts have been undertaken
to invent, almost from whole cloth, new religious traditions.[33] Still
others have let their spiritual quests slide into neglect in the face of too
many unanswered questions and no clear path that rings true. In our
seminar, we endeavored to let what we *in fact are doing*, rather than
theoretical thinking, lead the way to a possibly tru*er* fathoming of our
passage into more.

The history of religion is the course of our human attempts to
grasp through symbol *more* within and beyond us in order that we
might bring *more* out in our lives.[34] These attempts have been con-

siderably influenced by factors from our space-time dimension—social, economic, political, and environmental. This is true not only in our choice of symbols but also in what we choose to find *in* a symbol, that is, how we interpret a symbol and render it meaningful in our lives. In every generation, every person reinterprets, reunderstands, inherited symbols in search of more truth to inform one's life. So it is quite natural that many women stepping out into *more in* their everyday lives have sought *more in* the religious symbols which have already meaningfully shaped their lives. (Recall Celie's new discovery of God.)

Symbols that have been handed down by the generations are not only shaped by exigencies of space-time, they also convey truth—not all of truth, which is not possible—but surely some enduring facet of it. Some symbols do this better than others.[35] If a symbol has withstood the test of time, say a millennium or two, and still reveals to many, more about what is true, more about how the sacred lives and moves in-the-world, it must be of great flexibility in speaking what is true to many generations of tens of thousands of persons. This being the case, we wonder if there is not yet more to be discovered *in* these symbols handed down by the generations—undiscovered corners, unnoticed facets, unattended dimensions—that might, when explored more closely, illumine and inspire *more* than was at first thought. We wonder if this might be especially so for women crossing over into what has been to them largely unknown, new terrain: expression out-in-the-world.

To take one example, God, a symbol of what is within and beyond us from the Judeo-Christian tradition, is described in the Bible not only as love but also extraordinary power for creative expression. He created the world. He is not only forgiving but also disciplining and commanding. He is not only patient but also capable of righteous anger and sudden bursts of willful, awesome power. Jesus, believed by his followers to be God's son, is portrayed in the New Testament as embodying the latter of each of these pairs of attributes as much as the former. Then why is the focus for those desiring to be like God's son, to be in Christ, centered almost entirely on cultivating the former qualities and rarely the latter? Could not those who are already skilled in nurturing and affirming gain spiritual direction not only from Jesus' nurturing, healing love but also from his rationally discriminating, assertive, commanding, courageous, expressive out-in-the-world activity as well? Often these are just the qualities women need to offer their best at work out-in-the-world, but rarely have symbols of more in human life than meets the eye been interpreted to give encouragement and instruction to women to cultivate precisely these qualities. Once again, we are *not* suggesting the substitution of these qualities for their

already well-cultivated nurturing qualities, but, rather, we are searching for ways to integrate more into women's understanding of who
they are as they increasingly *must* go out of the home and into the
larger world of work in which *more* is asked of them.

Another example might be found in the Chinese *yin-yang* 陰陽
symbol.[36] In its earliest usage, *yang* referred to the side of the river in
the sun; *yin* the side of the river in the shade. By extension, *yang* is the
source of more in life emerging from light; *yin* is the source of more in
life emerging from darkness. Again, *yang* has the qualities of warmth,
dryness, movement, while *yin* has the qualities of cold, moisture,
quiet.[37] The *yin-yang* symbol came into greater range of meaning during the Han period (206 B.C.–A.D. 220), when its cosmological explanations were mixed in with those of the *Yi Jing* (*Book of Change*).[38]
The oldest parts of *Yi Jing* present a primal complementarity of yielding, indicated by a discontinuous line (– –), and firmness, indicated by
a continuous line (—). In full hexagramic form, *yang* is represented in
six continuous lines (☰), known as the hexagram *qian* and having
the qualities of "continuous actualization and differentiation of form."
Yin in hexagramic presentation is six discontinuous lines (☷☷),
known as *kun* and having the qualities of gentle, accommodating re-
ceptivity that nourishes the unfolding of *qian*'s ten thousand forms.[39]

We find here a very close affinity between *yang* and *yin* modes of
action and the two modes of action, creative expression and nurturing
affirmation, which emerged out of the Western sources we have portrayed above. *Yang* activity, like creative expression out-in-the-world
in general, has been ascribed most often in human history to the male
gender, and *yin* activity has been ascribed most often historically to the
female gender. However, we would argue here against any *necessary*
association of certain qualities or modes of action with either the male
or female gender. Certainly sets of qualities and activities are to some
extent biologically and culturally encouraged, as we have already
affirmed, but these sets of qualities are by no means *essentially* or *ultimately* of one gender or the other. *Yin* and *yang* are qualities of being
and are not necessarily linked with either physical gender. Similarly,
expression and nurturing are qualities of being, which males and
females both can cultivate and put into practice. While role differentiation associated closely with physical gender has played a clear and
well-defined role in our traditional and cultural stories, which tell us
who we are, our human story (which is more than meets the eye) continues to unfold.[40] In this regard the symbol of mutually interpenetrating *yang* and *yin* is highly instructive to us: each mode of action has the
presence of the other *moving within* it. Life is a changing, balanced
harmony of *yang* and *yin* modes of being, not as separate halves, but

as interpenetrating modes of activity, which through learning and cultivation may become present in all persons who so desire.

As in other civilizations, China's major religious traditions speak far more to males crossing over to cultivate the *yin* dimension of life in the midst of *yang* activity than to females crossing over to cultivate the *yang* dimension of life in the midst of *yin* activity. Both the Confucian tradition and the Daoist tradition encourage cultivation of the nurturing, affirming, receiving, caring, empathetic side of life.[41] The Daoist tradition does this far more thoroughly than the Confucian tradition, but the intention to round out excessive expressions or projections of individual self-interest, will to power, arrogance, greed, and pride through cultivation of nurturing affirmation of others is made quite explicit in both traditions.[42] Nurturing affirmation (*yin*) moving within creative expression out-in-the-world (*yang*) has been socially encouraged on the part of Chinese men for thousands of years. While we commend the cultivating of *yin* to harmonize with *yang* on the part of Chinese males, we feel there has not been as much encouragement given to Chinese women to cultivate *yang* (creative expression out-in-the-world) in integration with their already abundant *yin* (nurturing affirmation).

To cultivate *yang* expressive out-in-the-world qualities (rational discrimination, making independent choices, taking risks, taking the lead) women will need symbols of more in human life than meets the eye which tell them that they as female human persons are *yang* as well as *yin* (the latter fact they already know quite well). More symbols of women as *yin* alone (the Dao on the unseen level, the Great Mother, the fertility goddess) cannot possibly encourage in women the cultivation as *integral* to who they *truly* are, to self, of these expressive out-in-the-world ways of being necessary to their work outside of the home. Quite the contrary, limiting the feminine gender to only the *yin* side of life, no matter how ultimate or primary one might consider it to be, will stymie her spiritual growth, not open it out to more.[43] For political reasons, Chinese women since 1949 have just recently begun to express out loud and in writing their individual spiritual quests to discover, express, affirm, validate more of who they are as human persons, both nurturing at home and expressive out-in-the-world. It will be sometime yet before they will be fully free to write of the spiritual transformation involved in their quests to realize more of who they are as *yang* as well as *yin*. Yet already we see such themes emerging.[44]

To this point in human time our combined social, economic, and cultural contexts are just beginning to yield the kinds of conditions that would allow more persons to open out to more beyond activities or roles into which women or men have been initially patterned. All this makes for interesting variations on our spiritual quests to embody an integrated unity of nurturing and expressing. *How* we get to this unity, *which* facet of more in human life than meets the eye receives our focus as we seek to augment or broaden our realization of who we are, may vary from gender to gender, person to person, culture to culture. In our view, it matters not whether religious symbols of more in human life than meets the eye are masculine or feminine in gender. That is *not the issue.*[45] What is far more important than the gender of a symbol is whether a man or a woman finds in a symbol a door *into more* in one's life, more revelation of all that one can humanly be such that one is moved to *be more*, to *realize more* of who one is, more of self here-in-the-world.

For the moment, focusing on different or complementary dimensions of more in human life than meets the eye, it may seem that men and women are ships passing in the night heading in opposite directions. But this is to look only at the surface of what each is working on *now*. Into religious or spiritual transformation of any kind, into discovering more of who one is, one does not go empty-handed. One takes with one who one already is. In the end, we may end up in much the same place, with much the same sense of self-harmonizing both expressive and nurturing modes behavior. The *China Daily* recently printed the following article about female managers, whom it called "heroes" at work:

> This is one of the secrets of the success of the women. They see the workers as brothers and sisters and gather opinions and suggestions from them. Emotional involvement by these women is especially common. Some psychologists think that this is the natural expression in enterprise management of female care and tenderness. These women care about everything concerning their worker's life and work, from protection policies for female workers to caring for the sick and the injured; from the establishment of kindergartens to vocation and tour programmes.[46]

This is one of the best modern articulations of Confucius's instruction in *ren*, that is, family-modeled benevolence toward and empathy with others, together with assertive, creative leadership and management of others out-in-the-world, that this writer has read![47]

Thus, we would caution any final definition of self in terms of what men or women in a culture *are seeking now*. One's conscious realization of self is the whole of who one is discovered over a lifetime, as Shizue Ishimoto's story below will confirm. Likewise our understanding of what it is to be human comes from the whole of our cumulative, worldwide, human experience, not just from one culture. Unfortunately, we have not found this cumulative approach to self or self-understanding prevalent among prominent Western theories of "self-discovery," which tend to limit the definition of self to expressive/ assertive patterns of behavior of dominant males in Western society.

"You are the Buddha!" Shizue Ishimoto Faces Two Ways

The fascinating autobiography of Shizue Ishimoto, *Facing Two Ways*, gives illustrative example to the theory of self-discovery that we have been developing. As she turned from the past to face women of her day and Japan's future, what qualities did she seek to bring out in her "self" as she struggled on behalf of others here in-the-world? What images of more in human life than meets the eye inspired her to realize these qualities? Why was religious transformation essential to her "self"-discovery? To answer these questions, we shall consider Japan's central religious symbol, which has the feminine gender, and social in-the-world roles of Japanese women who are to embody this sacred power depicted as feminine. In the conclusion of this paper, we shall suggest some similarities and differences between Shizue's story taken together with the recent unfolding story of Chinese women and the story of many outspoken Western women today.

Hiratsuka Raicho (1886–1971) in the first issue of her magazine, *Seito (Bluestocking)*, published in 1911, offers the following lament: "In the beginning, women in truth were the sun. We were authentic human beings. Today, women are the moon. We live dependent and simply reflect the light that emanates from another source. Our faces are pale blue, like the moon, like the sick."[48] In Hiratsuka's view, the status of women has changed over time. Some archaeological and historiographical evidence does suggest that women in Japanese society may well have enjoyed a social status in the past quite different from their social status since the founding of the Meiji era.[49] Early mythological stories and the highly regarded cumulative tradition of literature written by Japanese women convey a subtly powerful feminine presence in-the-world, which is distinctive of Japanese women.[50]

We know very little about the origin of the *kami* (upper) Amaterasu, Japan's central image of more in human life than meets the eye, which has the female gender. Nor do we know a great deal about Japan as a matriarchal society before the advent of written language, which came to Japan from China along with Confucian, Daoist, and Buddhist thought in the sixth and seventh centuries.[51] Nonetheless, it is clear from the *Kojiki* and *Nihonshoki*,[52] as well as from

Shintō rites involving female virgins at holy shrines, that the gender of the source of life, water, and the sun rising from it, the symbol of Japan, is female.[53] Moreover, so is fire: "Izanami gives birth to fire and dies as a result."[54] The eminent psychologist Kawai Hayao argues that this sacrifice of Izanami in giving birth to fire indicates "how old the Japanese cult of the sacrificing mother must be."[55]

Japanese imaging of the source of life—water, sun, fire—as feminine is mirrored in the role of woman in Japanese society as first and always mother: the central source of bodily comfort and nurturing, affectionate affirmation.[56] George DeVos, in his well-known studies of Japanese psychology, has similarly discerned that "the Japanese woman tends to be resigned to a more non-reciprocal nurturant relationship with a dependent husband . . . with a dependent child."[57] Dependency on mother, which is encouraged in children and continues to be encouraged for males over their entire lives, becomes the model for social behavior that lacks much of what has been called in the West "individual independence."[58] Takeo Doi, a well-known Japanese psychiatrist, has argued that childlike dependence on the mother "writ large," so to speak, is the key to understanding the Japanese personality.[59] Similarly DeVos asserts that the nurturant-dependency relationship between mother and child, with its potential for guilt, is at the root of the Japanese sense of self as belonging to a group.[60]

We might describe this nurturing dependency in yet another way as the "glue" that holds together the imported Confucian teachings concerning family, which came from China to Japan in the seventh century and received particular attention in the Tokugawa period (1600–1868).[61] What resulted when these Chinese teachings on patriarchal family order were assimilated into Japanese culture was a kind of wrapping of patriarchical order around the outside with maternal nurturing-dependent bonding on the inside.[62]

Some, working from a Western perspective, have labeled the Japanese woman as "weak," "confined," "submissive."[63] However, if we look again, it is easy to see how the nurturing role of mother can take too much control of a child, such that the source of life that is imaged as sacrificing itself for the other becomes a voracious demon.[64] Buruma's work *Beyond the Mask* traces in film and fiction the entire range of images of woman or mother who has become too powerful—and, therefore, too threatening—and must be brought into some kind of submission whence come all types of sadistic sexual activities on the part of the male.[65] Perhaps one could say that whereas in the West we may be witnessing these days a one-sidedness of expressive-independent behavior, in Japan there has been a one-sidedness of nurturant-dependence.[66] In this peculiarly Japanese pattern, the female is restricted to the nurturing role, although she holds *great power* in that role. The male, while yet bounded in all relationships by nurturing-dependency, which keeps him from exhibiting expressive individuality, attempts to balance feminine motherly power with his position of superior in the male/female hierarchical order set by the Confucian tradition, but he is not always successful.[67]

From the beginning of the Meiji era, the nurturing skills of Japanese women were to be put to new use in rendering Japan a rising star in the world economic order. As Sharon Nolte's work on "The 'New Japanese Woman'" informs us: "the home ministry, especially in its organ magazine *Shimin*, prescribed [for women] hard work, self-restraint, savings, public contributions and the socialization of children in those traits essential to the discipline of the industrial workplace."[68] Japanese women were to play a key role in Japan's surge toward productivity by staying at home and performing functions essential to Japan's economic expansion, such as overseeing household spending and saving as well as education.[69] Yet, in contrast to the leading role she was to play at home (and the house truly is the woman's domain in Japan), the Japanese woman, after the Meiji Restoration, found herself more systematically barred from all political activity. The same leaders, having opened Japan to Western ideas and promulgated the Meiji Constitution of 1890, barred all women, regardless of class, from attending political meetings. The message was loud and clear: "Save the family and enrich the nation."[70] In other words, stay at home, nothing has changed for you.

However, there has been some exploration by Japanese women themselves as to how things might change for them as they venture into regions beyond their socially prescribed role of mothering, no matter how essential that role may be to modern Japanese economic success. There is tremendous variety in these explorations to which we cannot possibly give justice here. Instead, we shall focus on one autobiographical story of Baroness Shizue Ishimoto, *Facing Two Ways*,[71] as an illustrative example of one kind of choice Japanese women are making as they open out to what is beyond the role of nurturing mother *without necessarily leaving this role behind*.

The recognition that one has a choice marks the beginning of the discovery of more of who one is. Of her education, of her instruction in proper feminine conduct, Shizue writes, "We were taught what we ought to do and to be, but never did we discuss questions of personal freedom and independent thinking or the right to be guided by one's own conscience."[72] Her mother lectured her too on *kafu ni somaru*, "to be dyed in the family ways," of one's husband, "to crush her desires and ambitions" and "submerge her individuality in her husband's personality and his family's united temper."[73] A noblewoman by birth, Shizue's recognition of alternatives came with exposure, through her husband's work, to the conditions of men, women, and children laboring in coal mines of western Japan (1915) and through her taking some coursework, at her husband's insistence at first, when they both were in the United States, to become more self-sufficient (1919). After graduating from the Business Training School of New York, she viewed her "self" anew: "To me, the winning of this certificate seemed like gaining an invaluable treasure. I had struggled through the long winter battling with loneliness. An inner voice whispered triumphantly: "Now you can be a self-supporting woman, whenever your wish to."[74]

Over a period of time, however, she found that this education could not simply be used to make her a more alive, liberal and understanding companion to her husband. She felt that she was called to more. After meeting Margaret Sanger in New York, one of the early advocates of birth control in America, she decided to take the program of birth control to Japan.[75]

Managing a small knitting business to raise funds to support a leper hospital at Gotemba, Shizue found requests for her to talk on the birth-control principle every place she visited. But her activity was felt by others to contrast sharply with the role women ought to take:

> It was taken as the fancy of a romantic person or of one not quite sound in her head. They called me "Madame Control" and drew caricatures of me in papers and magazines. It was not seldom that people hissed, pulled one another's sleeves secretly or smiled ironically at me when they met me on the street or at any other place. Some reactionary countrymen considered me a hateful woman who brought shame on her ancestral house. Instead of urging my sex to bear as many soldiers—noble patriots—as they possibly could, I was even belittling the military glory of the nation, so they said.[76]

The prewar years brought more ostracism, privation, jail, and finally divorce from her husband, who backed down from his earlier socialist ideals and could not cope with a wife who expressed her self out-in-the-world.

Following the war, she married Kato Kanju, a socialist, and both became advisors to the occupation government. As the top vote-getter in the country, she was elected to the Japanese house of representatives in 1946 and served in the Japanese Diet until her retirement in 1974. Since then, she has served as president of the Japan Family Planning Federation and, as of 1984, was still active at the age of eighty-seven, lecturing around the country.

Throughout these expressive and noble efforts of Shizue out-in-the-world beyond the family walls, Shizue was also questing inwardly to be known, affirmed, nurtured on a level perhaps deeper than any human being could go: "I longed for unbetraying truth and spiritual contentment. If Buddha would but open his benign arms, I felt that I could throw myself upon his infinitely wide and deep bosom and find peace. My heart was being starved by lack of nourishment. In the hope that it might develop harmoniously with my reason, giving new strength for life, I drew nearer to Buddhism."[77] However, the ritualistic and dogmatic faith of Amida Buddhists, to whom she first turned, did not give witness to her expanding rational capabilities. Turning, then, to Zen she confronted the sutra: "You are Buddha." "I am Buddha?" "Yes, you yourself are Buddha!"[78] Zen practices for the purpose of realizing "self" as the creative strength of the universe (conceived of as Buddha) brought inward fortification and discipline to her, but because practitioners of Zen with whom she became familiar seemed too ready to deny the reality of the world she knew all too well as real, in the end she turned to Nichiren Buddhism, where she found a way of "social righteousness requiring action under persecution and every difficulty."[79]

Specifically, it was in Nichiren the person, both historically existent and, in some manner, transcendently present still, that Shizue found the spiritual companionship, the knowing and being known, for which she had searched. Nichiren embodied the strength and courage, which never failed him even when he faced the threat of death,[80] that she so desperately longed to realize in her self. If he could do it, she could:

> since I was deeply inspired by the spiritual power of Nichiren, who feared neither hunger nor death, who never worried about shelter or clothing, I reached a wonderful calmness of mind, never to be disturbed again by uncertainty, grief, anger or momentary pleasure.
>
> The calmness of my mind is, I should say, an attainment not be explained to others by words, . . . This satori, may be defined as an intuitive looking into the nature of things, in contradistinction to the intellectual and logical understanding of life . . . Or we may say that with satori our entire surroundings are viewed from quite an unexpected angle of perception. In the midst of financial problems, I could now take a deep breath as if under the shining spring sun.
>
> . . . Satori is a revolution—a revaluation of the spiritual aspect of one's existence. This change of mind came to me, not through my hard practice of za-zen meditation, but as the balance

sheet or gross sum of my years' hard thinking and labor, and the various experiences of my early life.[81]

Through years of turning inwardly toward more in human life than meets the eye and of expressing her energies outwardly in-the-world to better the living conditions of others, Shizue increasingly came to know more of who she was, an ever-expanding "self" becoming ever more consciously aware. With this inward illumination opening out, Shizue resolved to take her message, her story, ever further out-into-the-world even if the road be filled with thorns.[82]

If we take a closer look at Shizue's spiritual quest, we discover that it is woven together by much the same thread that we have traced in the first four sections of this paper. Having been born in an upper-class family and sent to upper-class schools for women that cultivate the fine art of nurturing and affirmative behavior (and one might add here that Japanese women are a most exquisite expression of nurturing behavior taken into the dimension of aesthetics), Shizue first knew her "self" firmly embedded in the nurturing role, a role of great power, deeply appreciated and subtly articulated throughout Japanese culture. Prerequisites—such as "a room of one's own," time, money to study, write, go to school in order that she might become capable of self-support (which prerequisites the modern era is slowly but surely opening out to more women in a manner unlike any other time in human history)—enabling Shizue to expand beyond her nurturing role into something more, were, as with Virgina Woolf as well, not a problem.

The more Shizue became practiced in the skills of expression out-in-the-world, that is, rational judgment, independent and responsible choice, risk taking and determination, the more she *harmonized* these skills with her first learned role behavior to nurture and affirm others. That is, she did not abandon the nurturing role but incorporated the expressive role into it.

As she took up expressive out-in-the-world activity, women such as Margaret Sanger and the historian Mary Beard were significant inspirational friends. Unfortunately, her first husband was not interested in hearing her expanded story, and so also was the case with many other upper-class men and women in prewar Japan. So she remained, in a sense, "outside the accepted story." Put another way, Japan's collective story was not yet ready to include hers. Those she worked with were her "affirmers" as she promoted the birth-control project as well as other projects to assist the disadvantaged. Later, her second husband became her main "nurturer" as she pressed on with her expressive work on behalf of others out-in-the-world. But these human sources of nurturing affirmation, although absolutely essential to her survival in a world who "knew her not," did not serve as models for the kind of creative-expressive rational judgment, independent responsible choice, and risk-taking determination she needed to continue her out-in-the-world struggle for the dignity and care of others, particularly disadvantaged women.

For this inspiration and affirmation of more of who she was, she turned to more in human life than meets the eye, to a presence she felt deeply within that knew her in all her depth, far beyond whatever cognitive realization she might have of her "self." Her quest involved a series of "trials" as she searched for a symbol of more, a religious symbol, and for instruction that could bring out more of the personal courage, wisdom, and care for others she so desired to realize, to express in her "self." Finally, she turned to Nichiren and found there the door into more in human life than meets the eye for which she had been looking. Emulating Nichiren, she crossed a threshold into greater realization of "self." Crossing into more, an ongoing religious or spiritual transformation, she struggled for better social conditions for women, a struggle that increasingly asked more of her "self." Emulating Nichiren as she read and reread his words, she found the wisdom, strength of independent choice, and courage of her convictions she required to keep going in the midst of tremendous pressure against her.

For Shizue, imaging more in human life than meets the eye as the source of life and nurturing within the home—this image *alone*—would not have inspired a greater discovery and realization of more of who she was as she worked on behalf of others out-in-the-world. To realize more in her self as well as in others, she needed a symbol of her self as more than nurturing fertility goddess. This was especially so given her birth-control program, which said to women, you are the source of life *and more*.

Let us remember that for the first half of her life, Shizue had already cultivated and practiced well the nurturing role. As she moved out-into-the-world, Shizue's story was not one of abandoning this role for another but, *more positively*, one of taking nurturing behavior out-into-the-world and *adding* to it creative, expressive patterns of behavior necessary to living and moving beyond the physical domain of the home. Thus, the step out-into-the-world was a step into a *cumulative more* of who she was, more of her self, an integration of past and present, rather than an abandonmnet of what had come before for something else. To take this step into more, she required knowledge of more of who she could be: greater range of rational agility, greater independence for responsible choice, greater courage to take risks. The greater person she could be was conveyed to her in the divine-human person of Nichiren, symbolizing more in human life than meets the eye, in which she understood herself as participant as she cultivated his example of living and moving in-the-world.

Quite powerfully Shizue's spiritual quest illustrates Valerie Saiving's profound suggestion that women who are moving into *greater* discovery of who they are need symbols of more in human life than meets the eye that *do not bring out more sacrificing, nurturing behavior* on the part of women (with which most women are by childhood instruction quite familiar) but, rather, bring out greater expressive rationally discriminating, risk-taking, decision-making, assertive behavior *to balance nurturing* skills as one offers the best of one's inborn talents and acquired knowledge out-in-the-world. Notice that we are saying emphatically *not* that these expressive qualities are *all* that define "self." Rather we are saying that these are the qualities of self that many women, like Shizue, have not at first been encouraged to bring out in their "selves" but later desire to cultivate to augment whatever "self"-realization has taken shape in character and conduct already.

Conclusion

Our studies of spiritual quests of twentieth-century women have offered us several insights. First, as human beings we continue to become more consciously aware of who we are. Our image of self, our knowledge of self, continues to change, deepen, expand. This is especially true when we open out beyond acquired roles and patterns of behavior that cultures, and to some extent biology, have set for us. Expressive-assertive patterns of behavior and nurturing-affirmative patterns of behavior have often been called "masculine" and "feminine" respectively. Our own view is that linking these patterns of behavior with one gender or the other so as in some way to define that gender is misleading and limiting. Initial learning of who one is gives men and women each a place to start, but their full sense of who they are, their greater realization of "self," comes when each crosses over, transcends, opens out to more in human life than meets the eye.

We have noted how men in going beyond expressive behavior have relied on traditional religious symbols of more in human life that encourage nurturing, care and concern for others. Many contemporary women in going beyond nurturing role patterns have argued that they are not as easily helped by such traditional symbols. We have contended here, however, that insight into more of the expressive out-in-the-world qualities of life that women seek to embody in themselves may yet be found in inherited or traditional religious symbols such as Shizue Ishimoto found in Nichiren. Moreover, in *Facing Two Ways*, Shizue did not leave behind the old but added to it the new: she combined her newly cultivated creative and expressive work out-in-the-world with already well-cultivated skills of nurturing and affirming others.

In closing, we would like to take note of a major trend in the West: that, for a complex variety of reasons, there is a culture-wide lessening of attention to nurturing and affirming others. Family is receiving less emphasis than it once did, and this is having an effect on our children in terms of their own interest in and ability to nurture others. Modern, secular emphasis on expression out-in-the-world has resulted in extreme stress on uniqueness and newness, on each person having his or her statement to make in fashion, work, attitude, relating to others. Every sort of public media—magazines, advertisements, television, radio, film—encourages this. In the wake of this trend, for the last several decades increasing numbers of Western women have begun to leave behind the nurturing role to join men in public marketplace competition to "out express" each other in all sorts of achievement.[83] The result has been "self" defined one-sidedly as "expressive, discriminating, choosing, risk taking, assertive, unique" without any nurturing balance. Such a self is often lacking in care for and empathy with others and slips easily into "selfish."

It is not that creative out-in-the-world expression is not positive. Indeed, we have argued throughout that such expression is one of two strands that interweave to give us meaningful presence in-the-world. Moreover, it is within this expressive dimension of life that many women, already well versed in the nurturing side, are endeavoring now to discover more of who they are, and we applaud this.[84] Yet we are concerned that these efforts on the part of women to realize more of who they are expressively out-in-the-world are adding (unintentionally perhaps) to the modern, secular, unidimensional emphasis on the expressive out-in-the-world, unique side of life and self, which is so prevalent in Western culture today, with the result that neither women nor men in Western society are taking seriously enough the nurturing-affirming side of life and self, which is so necessary for the whole to survive.

What to do? Here we want to be most careful. Our concern is *not* to send women back inside the walls to be the sole dispenser of nurturing care and concern for others. Nor do we want to see nurturing abandoned altogether.

In our studies of recent stories of Japanese and Chinese women, we have found some encouraging leads to another alternative. Family remains extremely important throughout Asia, and as Asian women move beyond home's gate to expression out-in-the-world, they tend to take their nurturing care and concern for others with them. Shizue Ishimoto's story is an outstanding example, as are the Chinese female factory workers and managers referred to at the end of section four. Interestingly, as increasing numbers of Chinese urban women *must* go out of the home to work, rather than sacrifice the family, which has often happened in similar circumstances in the West, we find Chinese men beginning to pick up more of the nurturing tasks at home. While one sees this crossover on the part of some (mostly younger) males in the West, it is still quite rare in Japan. Why does it seem to come more easily for Chinese men?

We would suggest the main reason is that in China, family truly is the central symbol of more in human life than meets the eye. As a member of a family, stretching from the finite here and now into infinity backward and forward in time, a Chinese person is always aware that who he or she is, is family. Knowledge of self is knowledge of family. Cultivation of self is cultivation of family. Nurturing of family is nurturing of self. It is this nurturing of family that is at the core of Chinese cultural learning, past and present, and is the reason why when a mother cannot make it home to feed a child, a father will. And society, his neighbors, his workplace, will commend him for it.[85]

What fascinates us about these Japanese and Chinese examples that we have been considering is their suggestion that cultural emphasis on nurturing may in the end lead to *more* discovery of who we are—as *both* men and women in our contemporary world are increasingly called to integrate *both* expressive and nurturing roles within one and the same person—than does the modern, secular, one-sided emphasis on the expressive individual that is so prevalent in the West today.

As we stated at the start, *both* creative expression and nurturing affirmation are essential to discovering who we are, fathoming our presence in the world, knowing our "selves." The more we express who we are and affirm each other, the more what is sacred, what is more in human life than meets the eye, comes up to conscious realization in-the-world. The more we discover who we are as we share our stories, the more we discover self not as a singular presence in the world but as a copresence, or "shared-in-common presence," living and moving in a sacred manner both here and beyond. It is this conscious realization of participating *together* in something *more*, in something sacred, that is what true self-realization is all about.

NOTES

1. During a seminar at Harvard University which commenced my doctoral work there in 1974, Wilfred Cantwell Smith surprised me by saying that

there are as many conceptions of God as there are Christians. Smith's position is that symbols or words do not have absolute meanings. Whatever meaning a symbol or word has comes from those who give meaning to it. The history of religion is the history of what symbols of more in human life than meets the eye have meant to different persons and how these symbols, thereby, have served differently to transform people's lives.

2. This is the first line of W. C. Smith's "Religion as Symbolism" in *Encyclopeadia Britannica*, 15th ed, *Micropaedia* (Chicago: Encyclopaedia Britannica, 1985), 498–500. During the fall of 1989, while teaching in Mandarin an introduction to comparative history of religion at Beijing University, I found it more fitting with the Chinese language and worldview to change the preposition *to* in this aphorism to *in*, which Smith, also in Beijing during May 1989, received positively.

3. In the notes to chap. 2 of his *Meaning and End of Religion*, W. C. Smith explores two possible roots of the Latin term *religio* from which the English term religion is derived. First, there is the Latin root *ligāre*, meaning "to bind." It is this verb that many scholars use to define religion as a "binding of humans to that which transcends" them. Smith also explores another possible understanding of *religio* derived from the Latin root *lig*, meaning "to pay attention, to give care." Putting together this notion of religion as "to pay attention or to give heed to" with the aphorism "there is more in human life than meets the eye," what results is the definition of religion presented here (which is quite coherently communicated in Chinese).

4. To image this for my Chinese students I used to create a circle with my arms and place human beings as a dot within this circle. Facing inward and focusing on what we already know and increasing our mastery over what we know is the secular orientation. Facing outwards toward the ever-expanding circumference of the circle, giving priority to more beyond what we know and consciously realize, is the religious or sacred orientation. Opening out (in Chinese *kai fang* 開放) or yielding or giving heed to (*rang* 讓) what is more in human life than meets the eye does not necessarily require an understanding of more, of transcendence, as altogether "other than" human.

5. The best statement I know of this idea of living and moving with more in human life than meets the eye comes from Black Elk, the Oglala Sioux medicine man: "This was the ceremony, and as I said before, the power of it was in the understanding of its meaning; for nothing can live well except in a manner suited to the way the Power of the World lives and moves to do its work." This comment was transcribed by John G. Neihardt in the 1930s in *Black Elk Speaks* (Lincoln: University of Nebraska Press, 1978), 180. My students in China were entranced with this work and a few set about translating it into Chinese. Black Elk's vision lives on.

6. The focus of the modern era on human mastery of the material or physical world or others has been interpreted in two ways as regards religion. Some assess such human mastery as "humanistic," in contrast with "religious,"

which they might describe as "reverencing and depending on powers which transcend the human." Accordingly, in the modern age in which we seem to be able to master matters of the world on our own, some no longer have any use for religion defined in this way. Others use the term *"humanistic"* to refer to efforts to master human nature rather than to master the environment or others. This latter understanding of humanism is not necessarily in contrast with religion, especially if religion is defined in a manner similar to that which we have offered above.

7. To get a feel for *Daoist* embodiment of spontaneous, effortless, natural *wu-wei*, one might image a Chinese landscape painting with a range of mountains disappearing in the misty distance. Usually the mist, clouds, and water combine into some weaving continuity that represents *dao* on an unseen level. The trees, rocks, mountains, and perhaps one or two small figures climbing a long, narrow, and winding path to a monastic retreat on an oddly shaped, lofty peak are momentary expressions of *dao* on the seen level.

8. Of course, there are and always will be differences among us, and we delight in this. Our point here is that in seeking to understand who we are, these differences are *not sought out in themselves* primarily but, rather, *are the effect* of our turning primarily toward a shared brilliance, to choose a metaphor, which is filtered differently by each of us into many shades and shapes. The whole array of color and form is the very nature of our collective existence in space and time and is beautiful. If, however, in attempting to discover who we are, we turn our focus away from our common source of light (and life) and focus, instead, on our differences, work to accentuate these differences, or take one difference and make it the fundamental standard for the rest, we find that, quite ironically, everything starts to become dull and lifeless.

9. Barbara Myerhoff, *Number Our Days* (New York: Simon & Schuster, 1980).

10. Barbara Myerhoff, "Telling One's Story," *The Center Magazine*, March 1980, 29.

11. Ibid., 27.

12. Myerhoff offered another illuminating example. At the University of Southern California, she requested her students to find a person in their lives who, in a sense, "did not exist." Each student was to listen to the story of this other person by writing it down. She told of a male student who went home to interview the family maid, someone he knew by last name only. Over a period of several weeks, she recounted everything that had ever happened to her. In the process, he came to know her by her first name. He looked forward to greeting her at the end of a day. The more he heard her story, the more she became increasingly present to him in the world. Finally, he asked how she could remember so vividly all that had happened to her. She replied that every night she had gone over and over the details of the day, memorizing them and

repeating them, just in case some day some one might ask. Such is our hope for life. Presence in the world is copresence, shared knowing, intimacy, communion.

13. Ibid., 24.

14. D. T. Suzuki, *An Introduction to Zen Buddhism*, (New York: Grove Press, 1964), 77.

15. D. T. Suzuki recounts the story: "Gutei's favourite response to any question put to him was to lift one of his fingers. His little boy attendant imitated him, and whenever the boy was asked by strangers as to the teaching of the master he would lift his finger. Learning of this, the master one day called the boy in and cut off his finger. The boy in fright and pain tried to run away, but was called back, when the master held up his finger. The boy tried to imitate the master, as was his wont, but the finger was no more there, and then suddenly the significance of it all dawned upon him. Copying is slavery. The letter must never by followed, only the spirit is to be grasped" (Ibid., 72).

16. Ibid., 54.

17. Ibid., Alice Walker, *The Color Purple* (Great Britain: Women's Press, 1983), 166–68.

18. Ibid., 176.

19. Ibid.

20. Ibid., 182–83.

21. Nurturing-affirmation in this sense "gives birth," but lest "birth" be given too physical a connotation, we choose to limit our use of this term.

22. An adaptation of a line from the song "Tommy" by The Who, a British rock group popular over the last two decades.

23. Valerie Saiving, "The Human Situation: The Feminine View" in *Womanspirit Rising*, ed. Carol P. Christ and Judith Plaskow (San Francisco: Harper Row, Publishers, 1979), 25–42.

24. Anyone watching contemporary Western television or film these days might find this hard to believe.

25. Virginia Woolf, *A Room of One's Own* (New York: Harcourt Brace Jovanovich, 1929).

26. Virginia Woolf, *To the Lighthouse* (Great Britain: Hogarth Press 1927; London: Grafton Books, 1977).

27. Anecdotal evidence confirms Woolf's point here: when I asked Japanese women and Chinese women in considerable numbers over the last

two years what is the hardest thing for them to do, invariably the reply was "take time and energy away from the family and give it to work (whether desired or not) out-in-the-world."

28. Saiving, "Human Situation," 35.

29. Ibid., 37–39.

30. Ibid., 39.

31. We might note here that the traditional term for wife in Chinese and Japanese is "person inside-the-house" (*neiren* 內人 and *kanai* 家內, respectively).

32. We might add here that as women go outside of the home to discover more of who they are and to share their discoveries, their stories are coming together as bits and pieces are being taken up into the "public" out-in-the-world story, which is certain to have an impact on the overall socioeconomic-political shape of culture but will take considerable time to discern. The same is true for any minority moving beyond previous social roles, expressing more of who they are out-in-the-world, and narrating this passage into more in stories, written and oral. Women inside the walls have always expressed who they are, told their stories to each other. Women are wonderful storytellers as every child inside-the-walls knows. Japanese female writers, in particular, have a rich tradition of writing about intimate matters, inside-the-walls. In fact, Japanese women writing about "interiors" have been said to have given earliest form to the novel as a genre of writing that narrates interior "psychological" space as well as exterior surfaces of a story.

33. For succinct examples of these sorts of efforts on the part of women during the past two decades, see Carol P. Christ and Judith Plaskow, eds., *Womanspirit Rising* (New York: Harper Row, 1979); see especially section 4, "Creating New Traditions," with essays describing several directions in which women are putting their attention. Mary Daly has been one of the most vocal of those in the "us versus them" (female versus male) mode of feminist theology. Her three most famous books are *The Church and the Second Sex, Beyond God the Father*, and *Gyn/Ecology*. Recently there have been many more specific attempts to generate religious traditions around Great Mother as symbol of more in human life. See in particular the following: Rosemary Radford Ruether, *Womanguides: Readings toward a Feminist Theology* (Boston: Beacon Press, 1985); Clarissa W. Atkinson, Constance H. Buchanan, and Margaret Miles, eds., *Immaculate and Powerful: The Female in Sacred Image and Social Reality* (Boston: Beacon Press, 1985); Susan Cady, Marian Ronan, and Hal Taussig, eds., *Sophia: The Future of Feminist Spirituality* (San Francisco: Harper & Row, 1986); Barbara G. Walker, *The I Ching of the Goddess* (San Francisco: Harper & Row, 1986).

34. Wilfred Cantwell Smith, more than any other scholar I know, has argued this view of religious symbols. This perspective finds illustration in

every piece of his writing. See, e.g. his Ingersoll Lecture, delivered March 10, 1988, at the Harvard Divinity School, entitled "Transcendence." In his opening remarks, he states: "My thesis is that there have been throughout history and across the world a general human awareness of transcendence; and a general human propensity to perceive it, and to express and to nurture the awareness of it, in and through specific forms" (printed in *Harvard Divinity Bulletin*, Fall 1988).

35. See again W. C. Smith's careful articulation of this point in "Religion as Symbolism" in *Encyclopaedia Britannica*, 15th ed., *Micropaedia* (Chicago: Encyclopaedia Britannica, 1985), 498–500.

36. While the precise origins of this symbols remain obscure, traces of a *yin-yang* school of thought are found in the *Lu-shi Chun-qiu* and the *Dao De Jing*, both compilations of the Warring States period (403–221 B.C.). See Fung Yu-lan, *A History of Chinese Philosophy*, vol. 1, trans. Derk Bodde (Princeton: Princeton University Press, 1952), 159–69, 382–87.

37. Ibid., 159.

38. The latter work traces its origin to the dawn of the third millennium and the legendary emperor Fu Xi.

39. See Sukie Colegraves for an interpretive discussion of *yang* and *yin* and their expression in two forms of human consciousness in her *Spirit of the Valley* (London: Virago, 1979), particularly chap. 3.

40. Many who have listened well to our cumulative inherited human story and learned much from it desire to continue writing that story, as previous generations always have.

41. On this point, let us consider first the Confucian tradition that teaches that the family hierarchical system is structured throughout by one main principle, which has two intimately connected faces: that elders are superior to and therefore *responsible for* all those who are younger; that those who are younger and receive the care and protection of elders should respond with *respect, reverence, and loyalty* toward their elders. In this pattern, the relationship of males to females is generally that of elder to younger, except when two different generations are involved. The principle that joins these two faces is *xiao* 孝 (usually translated in English as "filial piety"). On the one hand, *xiao* is a reflective hierarchical principle and, on the other, it is an emotion, an affection, a shared feeling of tenderness, love, and mutual concern expressed in specific degrees, depending on hierarchical relationship. One could say that it is this affectionate bond of *xiao* that holds together the entire Chinese world. Behaviors that express hierarchical family order are codified into prescriptive modes of conduct known generally as "ritual" or "custom" and are found in distinctively different variations throughout Asia.

In principle, this system of family behavior was very much supported by Confucius but certainly not invented by him. Confucius's contribution to this early tradition was not this family system per se but rather (1) a method of cultivating, deepening, extending *xiao* within and beyond the family to give an inner spiritual dimension of *ren* 仁 to outward ritual forms of family behavior, which often were performed perfunctorily and empty of heart, and (2) a source of encouragement to "family ordering," in principle and in affection, of the world shared in common beyond the walls of the (biological) family compound.

Inner depth of feeling rooted in *xiao* and heightened through cultivation into a reflective-felt care and concern for others at the core of all activity was what Confucius called "*ren*" (benevolence toward others). At the core of *ren* is a nurturing and empathizing with others out-in-the-world as one serves in a position of expressive leadership. We view this Confucian cultivation of *ren* as an effort to bring out more of the nurturing-affirming side of life to balance and round out assertive, self-interested expressive behavior both within and beyond family walls.

42. See Roger T. Ames's carefully argued presentation of Daoist teachings (in the *Lao Tzu* and the *Chuang Tzu*) as advocating *not* the primacy of the "feminine" but rather a balance of "masculine" and "feminine" gender traits in those of political leadership position. Roger T. Ames, "Taoism and the Androgynous Ideal," in *Women in China*, ed. Richard W. Guisso and Stanley Johannesen, (Lewiston, Edwin Mellen Press, 1981), 21–45. I think Ames is positively correct that these teachings are meant to compensate for an imbalance of "masculine" (assertive, authoritarian, rigid, and violent) traits on the part of the king and to encourage the "preserving" or cultivating of "feminine" character traits such as softness, weakness, noncontentiousness, flexibility, genuineness on the part of the ruler who is to balance both in order to rule effectively.

While I agree with Ames in his conclusion that the Chinese "organismic definition of person" lacks the connotations of "separate individuality of person" often found in the West, I differ somewhat from the conclusion he draws from this that any one "individual" need not develop "the full complement of masculine and feminine gender traits within the parameters of one person." I think the teachings of the *Lao Tzu* and *Chuang Tzu* are very definitely arguing that any one individual person in position of ruling or in his or her own life generally needs to cultivate both within one and the same person. Each person can embody a balance of *yin* and *yang*, as does the entire cosmos. Such a balance of *yin* and *yang* may not involve what Ames calls "the full complement" of each gender trait, but a considerable integration or harmony of both is required if any one is to be an "analogue" to the natural cosmic harmony of Dao.

It is for this reason that I tend *not* to label the creative-expression role as "masculine" or the nurturing-affirming role as "feminine." I think these are culturally and historically learned associations, which are not necessarily biologically determined (although perhaps, as I have suggested above, they are somewhat biologically encouraged). By not linking these two roles with gender, it becomes much easier to suggest that a man become nurturing and affirming, than to suggest that a man become "feminine." Similarly, it is much easier to suggest that a woman become creatively expressive out-in-the-world than to suggest that she become "masculine." Our concern is to broaden out and to integrate these two modes of behavior as we *each* discover more of who we are as persons, but this is *not* to say we are "androgynous." If modes of behavior are *not*, in any ultimately determining way, biologically gender linked, the issue of androgyny (that is, being of both biological genders) no longer pertains.

43. In our view, "feminist" efforts to argue for the *primacy* of Dao and of the feminine side of life are ironically in keeping with the historical tendency to offer valuable instruction in *yin* to males expanding beyond their already quite cultivated *yang*, while offering *little or no instruction to females*, already quite cultivated in *yin* qualities, as to how to expand into a balanced harmony by cultivating *yang*. The *Lao Tzu* and the *Chuang Tzu* texts are excellent examples of how major religious traditions have spoken, to males, encouraging them to cultivate nurturing-affirming qualities to balance excessive expressive-assertive traits. Such texts more often than not, keep women embedded in nurturing behavior or *yin* qualities and do not encourage their balancing of these traits with attempts to cultivate *yang* or expressive-assertive qualities. Spiritual instruction for women crossing over to achieve a balance of *yin* and *yang* is often quite difficult to find.

Parallel to Dao or *yin* symbols of amorphous, nondiscriminative, Great Mother—quite literally more in human life than meets the eye—is the traditional role for women in China: mother amorphously, nondiscriminatingly nurturing within the walls of home, not seen or visible to the outside world. Symbols of woman as "invisible," nurturing mother abound, but what about ones for the visible, out-in-the-world side she is called to display in today's China?

When asked, many young Chinese urban women today will respond that what is most important to them is that they will eventually marry and have families. However, since all women in socialist China are encouraged—politically, socially, economically—to work, putting time and energy into work as well as family has caused hardship. Recently Chinese girls lament that, although called out into the world to work, they have few inspiring images, models, symbols of who they are out-in-the-world: rational, discriminating, determined, assertive, risk taking. In cultures where family and nurturing still receive great emphasis and encouragement, women do not want to have to choose between nurturing and expressive activity. They want to and *must* do both.

In this apparent vacuum of images of women as expressive out-in-the-world, many Chinese young women have sought to copy the expressive career-ism of Western women, but lacking any conceptual scheme for assimilating this to the Chinese emphasis on family and nurturing, they have become quite confused. I have been told by these urban women, young and old, from all over China, to whom I lectured last year in China, that the model we have been developing in this paper of women holding onto their nurturing skills while *adding and integrating* more creative-expressive out-in-the-world skills as they work in the world beyond the home is most helpful. "Like solving a puzzle!" they say.

44. Again in my teaching and lecturing in Beijing last year, students and colleagues brought forth many examples in writing by women in several genres of their search to be strong, assertive, and expressive in the workplace, as men have been encouraged to be, and their efforts combine these behaviors with socially desired nurturing family activity. One poem by a student spoke poignantly of having become strong as a great oak tree yet inwardly longing to be accepted as a soft red flower, which she felt her "self" to be as well. There were other similar struggles expressed by loving mothers who have found great usefulness and success out-in-the-working-world. One of the best examples of combining the *yin* and *yang* roles, nurturing and expressive, within the Chinese tradition is found in the semi-autobiographical story of Maxine Hong Kingston, an American Chinese, in her *Woman Warrior* (New York: Knopf, 1976).

45. All symbols of what is sacred are to some degree anthropomorphic. It seems to us off the point to insist that as women we necessarily must be inspired by "feminine" symbols of more, however this "more" might be conceived. If symbols of feminine gender that truthfully inspire greater creative expression out-in-the-world already exist, all the better for women and men, but we see no use in requiring or creating them specifically *for* women. For reasons that are not our purpose here to explore, this manner of approaching spiritual quests of women may not find outspoken acceptance among "feminist" women in the West. Arguments and debates on this issue are multiple and varied. Perhaps the most well-known collection of these arguments can be found in Christ and Plaskow, *Womanspirit Rising*.

46. *China Daily*, November 1988 (date not recorded).

47. See note 41 above for a discussion of Confucius's *ren*.

48. Hiratsuka Raicho, *Hiratsuka Raicho Jiden* (Hiratsuka Raicho's Autobiography), vol. 1, ed. Kobayashi Tomie (Tokyo: Daigetsu Shoten, 1971), 328; quoted in Mikiso Hane, *Reflections on the Way to the Gallows* (Berkeley and Los Angeles University of California Press, 1988), 1. Mikiso Hane movingly recounts several of the true stories of Japanese women who, in early twentieth-century Japan, fought to improve the position of women in that society.

49. Sharon Nolte, "The 'New Japanese Woman': The Home Ministry's Re-definition of Public and Private, 1890–1910" (Paper presented at the conference "Japanese Women" Kenyon College, April 1987). Sharon, a professor at DePaul University, was just coming into the strength of her work when she died suddenly during the summer of 1987. We all miss her. She had much to tell us about Japanese women. See also Mikiso Hane's discussion of the evidence of a shift from matriarchy to patriarchy in his *Reflections on the Way to the Gallows*, 4–7.

50. G. B. Sansom, *Japan, A Short Cultural History* (Stanford: Stanford University Press, 1931), 22–36. Edwin O. Reischauer, *The Japanese* (Tokyo and Rutland, Vt.: Charles E. Tuttle Company, 1977), 205, 209.

51. Eiichiro Ishida, *Japanese Culture A Study of Origins and Characteristics* (Tokyo: University of Tokyo Press, 1974), 29, 39.

52. The standard translations of the *Kojiki and Nihonshoki* are Donald L. Philippi, *Kojiki* (Tokyo: University of Tokyo Press, 1968), and W. G. Aston, *Nihongi* (Reprint, London: George Allen & Unwin, 1956).

53. Sansom, *Japan*, 45–62.

54. Ian Buruma, *Behind the Mask* (New York: Pantheon Books, 1984), 4, 226.

55. Cited in Buruma, *Behind the Mask*.

56. See Takie Sugiyama Lebra, *Japanese Women* (Honolulu: University of Hawaii Press, 1984), chapter entitled "Mothering," 158–216, for the most informative study on this subject that this writer has found.

57. Anthony J. Marsella, George DeVos, and Francis L. K. Hsu, eds., *Culture and Self: Asian and Western Perspectives* (New York: Tavistock Publications, 1985), 156–57.

58. George DeVos states: "Mothers tend to 'suffer' their children rather than to forbid or inhibit their behavior by using verbal chastisement or even physical punishment. The child, while this form of discipline is going on, learns gradually the vulnerability of the loved one and that control of an offender is exercised not by doing anything to the offender but by self-control . . . In a positive sense, the mother expresses the capacity for self-exhaustion on behalf of her child but in so doing creates an awesome sense in the child that aggressive behavior is destructive. As a child is learning the awesomeness of his own capacity to destroy by deviant behavior, he is also learning that he can make others feel bad by dedicating himself to an inordinate degree. If one expresses suffering, another will react with guilt" (ibid., 155).

59. Doi Takeo, *The Anatomy of Dependence* (Tokyo, 1971); cited in Buruma, *Behind the Mask*, 21, 228 and Marsella, DeVos, and Hsu, *Culture and Self*, 142.

60. Marcella, DeVos, and Hsu, *Culture and Self* 143, 152, 162. See also Takie Suiyama Lebra's discussion of "belonging" in *Japanese Patterns of Behavior* (Honolulu: University of Hawaii Press, 1976), 22–37. Buruma also illustrates this: "It goes on in adult life too; juniors do it to seniors in companies, or any other group, women do it to men, men do it to their mothers, and sometimes wives, the Japanese government does it to stronger powers, such as the United States" (Buruma, *Behind the Mask*, 21).

61. For a description of the Confucian patriarchal, hierarchical pattern of family, see note 41 above.

62. See my discussion of differences between Chinese and Japanese sense of family in "The Moon and the Sun: Explorations into Some Cultural Differences behind the Code of Confucian Filial Piety (paper presented at Association for Asian Studies Annual Meeting, Chicago April 5–7, 1990). Briefly here, the Chinese familial patriarchy is entirely male. *Tian* 天 (usually translated in English as "Heaven"), the central symbol of more in human life than meets the eye in the Chinese tradition, is male: the great, "ancestral" father of all, the epitomy of knowledge, moral rectitude, leadership, and proper affection who mandates and sets example for all under Heaven. Moreover, *xiao* 孝 (family-clan affection, often referred to in English as "filial piety"), the glue that holds the family (and all its extensions) together, is a form of affection derived not so much from mother/son relating (as in Japan) as from father/son relating. In China, the father, by virtue of his position, is to be a paragon of knowledge and moral leadership, whether as the head of a family or of a state, and he is to serve as a didactic example to all, whether his sons or his people. The son is to follow and yield to the father in listening/learning obedience and awe-filled reverence. The affection of a father is instructive as it supports and affirms worthy behavior. Different from the father's, a mother's affection in China is viewed as noninstructive, for it lacks discrimination. *The Book of Rites* sets forth these differing descriptions of affection in father and mother: "Here now is the affection of a father for his sons—he loves the worthy among them, and places on a lower level those who do not show ability; but that of a mother for them is such, that while she loves the worthy, she pities those who do not show ability—the mother deals with them, on the ground of affection and not of showing them honour; the father, on the ground of showing them honour and not of affection (*Rites 33/11 in Harvard-Yenching Institute Sinological Index Series*, trans. James Legge, in *Li Ki, Book of Rites*, vol. 2, 341; quoted in Allison Black, "Gender and Cosmology in Chinese Correlative Thinking," in Caroline Walker Bynum, Steven Harrell, and Paula Richman, eds., *Gender and Religion: On the Complexity of Symbols* (Boston: Beacon Press, 1986), 171.

63. Indeed, there is a great deal of vocabulary within the Japanese language that corroborates this point. A new and immensely helpful book on what Japanese words say about women is *Womansword* (notice the pun), by Kittredge Cherry (New York: Kodansha, 1987). Anyone learning the Japanese language, customs, and society and/or interested in Japanese women should consider this "must" reading.

64. See Buruma, *Behind the Mask*, chap. 4, "Demon Woman."

65. See Buruma, *Behind the Mask*, 47, who discusses these rebellions against mother that can be epitomized in the aggressive exhortation "please die, mother," a line of a play by poet-playwright Terayama Shuji. In fact,

Buruma's entire book is a spectral presentation of deviant behavior of all types that occur in efforts to break out of these nurturing maternal bonds.

The term *kyoiku mama* (educational mama) is now in common parlance; it refers to the constant nurturing a mother gives to a child throughout his (sometimes also her) education. The purpose is to have the child achieve high placement at Japan's top universities. Thereby, the family's social position and status are confirmed. But sometimes pressure from mother can be too great, as witnessed in the increasingly more frequent cases of children, usually young boys, killing their mothers or parents due to too much educational and social pressure coming from them.

Politically radical groups might also be looked at in this light of breaking out of the confines of the nurturing mother/son relationship that allows for little growth and change.

66. This one-sidedness of "expressive independent" behavior in the United States and of "nurturing dependent" behavior in Japan may help to explain why current economic talks between the two countries are often difficult. Whereas once Japan was in a dependent position upon the United States, the situation is now reversed somewhat, with the United States economically dependent upon Japan. The problem in this context is that the United States does not recognize Japan's "superiority" and so does not assume the part of a dependent. Instead, the United States continues to insist "expressively" on its independence, while the Japanese keep nurturingly patient as they wait for the United States to see it more accurately, like a mother waiting patiently for a child to conform to accepted dependent behavior patterns.

One in a dependent position does have power to get want one wants in the following manner. The parent (mother/father), by virtue of her/his position, is expected to nurture, take care of, the child-dependent. Those younger/subordinate, whose duty it is to remain entirely loyal to and dependent upon those older/superior, lack any "rights" in the Western sense and must find other means to move their elders or superiors. This is often done by finding a way to publicly shame the superior by indicating that she/he has not shown enough care and concern for a younger/subordinate as a parent should. Such a suggestion, with evidence to prove it, carries with it the inference that the superior is *no superior at all* and very quickly brings the desired kindness and benevolence on the "parent's" part to put off any challenge to her/his superior position. See George DeVos's discussion of the power of one in the dependent role in *Culture and Self* (159–60).

67. One other aspect of Japanese culture, the way of the warrior (*samurai*) has received very little mention in recent studies of the Japanese sense of self (DeVos and Lebra barely touch on it), but anyone living in Japan for any length of time cannot help but constantly hear the word *gambate* (compete with all your strength) on every street corner. Ritualized shouts repeated over and over again, resound like ancient chants of samurai drilling their combative skills and can be heard in every *kyudo* (archery) range, *aikido* (a form of spiritual boxing), and *karate* hall, as well as on every baseball field and ten-

nis court. Japan as a whole is extraordinarily competitive, whence comes their current global economic victory. Some might contend that this is a form of Japanese "expressive independent" behavior. We would suggest that, in fact, it is a form of "rebellion" against their constant sense of dependency on others. While on the surface, rebellion appears "expressive" or "assertive," it remains rooted in dependence as its "inversion" and so is *more of the same* dependency, rather than a separate and distinct pattern of behavior, like creative-expressive activity, which complements or balances nurturing behavior, as we detailed in section four.

68. Nolte, "New Japanese Woman."

69. Ibid. The more frugal Japanese women are, the more money goes into savings. As family savings are added to other family savings, large sums for research and development are accumulated for family companies and for the nation. Women's frugality at home, therefore, is a linchpin in Japan's economic success. Most Japanese men are quite aware of this, although they do not admit it openly.

Additionally, women put primary attention to children's education and become what is called "*kyoiku* mamas" or "educational mothers" as they go to school with and even study for their children, principally their sons. The purpose of all this is to enable the son to test into the best university, after which his and the family's future success in socially high status and work is guaranteed. Finally, Japanese women at home inculcate the values that fuel the expanding workplace that now consumes most of a Japanese men's waking hours.

70. Ibid.

71. Ishimoto Shizue, *Facing Two Ways* (Stanford: Stanford University Press, 1965 reprint).

72. Ibid., 56.

73. Ibid., 78.

74. Ibid., 185.

75. Her concern for working women and their conditions, which started in the mines, later developed into her program for birth control: "While I was at the Miike mines, wives and daughters of miners went down in a half-naked condition, mingling with the naked men laborers. They followed the men and carried out the coal as the men loosened it with their picks. It was ridiculous to expect morality in such circumstances. Women who worked in the darkness had a pale complexion like the skin of a silkworm; they spoke and acted shamelessly, the last sign of feminine dignity sloughing off. Often pregnant women, working until the last moment, gave birth to children in the dark pit" (ibid., 160).

Later Shizue turned to the institution of geisha, the causes of its existence, and how to bring about an end to this form of subjugation of women:

"Only where security is assured to those who work can love and marriage properly exist. Conversely, only where love and marriage are both enlightened and possible to all can prostitution disappear. The welfare of the state is intimately bound up with this issue" (ibid., 296).

76. Ibid., 232.

77. Ibid., 323. One is reminded here of Confucius's "Only Heaven knows me!" (*Analects*, trans. Arthur Waley [New York: Random House, 1938), 127] and Jesus being known fully only by God (see Gospel of John in particular). What Shizue was experiencing may be true for all of us, in that on our spiritual quests to discover more of who we are, it is necessary to be known validated, affirmed, although this nurturing may not, on the deepest level, come from a human hand.

78. Shizue, *Facing Two Ways*, 333–34.

79. Ibid., 341. Moreover, Nichiren Buddhism took action against social injustice and was, according to Shizue, the only sect of Japanese Buddhism at that time that did not rank women below men.

80. Ibid., 342–44.

81. Ibid., 345–46.

82. Ibid., 346. We should emphasize that Shizue's story is somewhat unusual in Japanese society. The *Japan Times* frequently offers articles on the difficulties of working women in Japan. Japanese men and perhaps women, too, for the most part still see a necessary separation between those who are mothers in-the-home and those women who work out-in-the-world. Shizue's bringing together in one person both the nurturing and expressive roles is rare on the part of women in Japan. Working women who are also mothers receive little public support and are discouraged by management in companies that, more often than not, promote only women who do not care about their families and work harder than men.

83. The modern, secular trend to focus *one-sidedly* on expression out-in-the-world has led increasingly to greater forgetfulness or loss of the nurturing side of life. This has shown up not only in the loss of concern for family but also in a loss of concern for tradition, those tried and true cumulative heritages that "nurture," "affirm," and instruct each succeeding generation into what it is to be human.
The modern, secular trend, while given perhaps greatest emphasis in the West, is spreading everywhere in the world with the same symptoms: letting go of family, letting go of tradition, letting go of the nurturing side of life.

84. According to our theory, developed in sections one through four of this paper, self-discovery as religious or spiritual quest involves crossing over into more. Put much too simply, for we all are more complex than this: women versed in nurturing skills cross over into more as they work on the expressive

side of life and men versed in expressive skills cross over into more as they work on the nurturing side of life.

85. Time and again I have watched one Chinese male colleague after another suddenly disappear from a meeting and head home early to prepare lunch or dinner for a child. Even more moving perhaps are the Chinese papas "riding" their children to school on the crossbars of their bikes, singing songs along the way. Many might object to the lack of safety features involved in this form of travel or that fathers really cannot take time from work for this kind of nurturing. But which is open to greater risk: a child embraced in his father's nurturing arms with his melodious hum gently accompanying the way to the neighborhood school or nanny or a child braced and strapped into a child's seat in the back of a car as mother up front, trying to do all nurturing tasks and late for work, speeds sixty miles an hour down the freeway, with the radio blaring, to a city day-care center?

PART THREE
Person in Chinese Theory and Practice

INTRODUCTION TO PART THREE

Roger T. Ames

The five articles that constitute the Chinese contribution to reflections on self for this volume begin from Tu Wei-ming's "Embodying the Universe: A Note on Confucian Self-realization." Tu's first sentence announces a theme that is a point of departure for all of the articles in this section: "Personality, in the Confucian perception, is an achieved state of moral excellence rather than a given human condition." This theme of creative self-transformation, further echoed and elaborated in the philosophical papers of Ames and Hall, is a cultural warrant for a rather regimented conception of contemporary Chinese preschool education as it is described by David Wu, and it is an object of concern for Margery Wolf, an anthropologist, who sees in this definition of person a basis for exclusively male gender construction in traditional Chinese society that has consistently ignored the Chinese woman.

Tu Wei-ming begins from the physical site of human development. Human flourishing begins from the cultivation of one's physical nature as integral to the religious and aesthetic expression of one's self. The body, far from being an impediment to self-realization that must be overcome through the rigors of asceticism and self-denial, is in fact the locus of self-transformation. This observation returns us to elaborate discussions in the first volume in this series on self: *Self as Body in Asian Theory and Practice* (1993). Self-transformation proceeds through the conscious "ritualization" of self, physical and psychical, in which the seemingly linguistic and cultural impositions of the Confucian tradition are activated as instruments of both personal and communal realization. Holistic ritual practices involving one's entire person function like a social grammar to shape interpersonal relationships, to extend and deepen them, and to make them meaningful and important. It is feeling expressed as intimacy and sensitivity, rather than as rationality, volition, or intelligence, that defines the ultimate quality of the human being. Body and world, through one's cultivation of the dis-

171

tinctively human heart-and-mind, assume profound spiritual significance. It is this capacity of the human being to contribute spirituality
to the world that makes the Confucian vision "anthropocosmic," where
"humanity in its all-embracing fullness forms one body with Heaven,
Earth, and the myriad things."

Roger T. Ames in the second article attempts to articulate a classical Confucian model of self that will at once distinguish it from dominant Western notions of self and, at the same time, accommodate the
terms of Confucian realization laid out in Tu Wei-ming's article. To do
this, he first surveys four current explanations of the Confucian self to
identify their contributions and their inadequacies.

Ames argues that the "hollow men" model of self, which takes
"selflessness" as a fundamental Confucian value, perpetuates the
stereotype of absolute obedience to some external central authority
promoted by Hegel in his description of the "*geist-less*" Chinese. The
overcoming of "selfishness," clearly a desiridatum in the Confucian
project of self-realization, cannot be equated with "selflessness." The
goal of classical Confucianism is a ritually construed community that,
by the very nature of ritual itself, demands personal participation and
investment rather than self-abnegation.

The second model that Ames sets aside is the "autonomous individual," suggesting in its place a notion of "unique individual." There
is an equivocation with the term *individual* between one member of a
class of like entities, and something which is entirely unique in itself.
Autonomy, a necessary condition for the freedom and self-expression
of the liberal democratic self, is anathema to the irreducibly social
Confucian model of person. Ames argues that in spite of the relational
nature of the classical Chinese conception of person, it is still very
much an individualism in subscribing to the second sense of individual
as an unsubstitutable participant in a network of unique roles and relationships.

Although an "organic" conception of self has explanatory force in
delineating Confucian presuppositions, there are also limitations to this
metaphor, which, according to Ames, derive mainly from Aristotelian
associations, such as the actuality/potentiality distinction, teleology,
the hierarchy and immutability of species, and so on.

The final depiction of self critiqued by Ames is the mereological
part/whole system proffered in recent discussions of Confucianism
because of its assumptions about "wholeness" and the integrity of its
"parts."

Borrowing the "field" vocabulary central to the natural sciences
during the first half of this century and more recently appropriated by
the human sciences, Ames attempts to construct a "focus-field" model

of self. He begins from the assumption that human beings exist as constitutive elements in a natural and social field. The field concept, always reflexive, eschews the assumption of some exterior, objective vantage point from which to make observations or some internal, essential agency, and as such it precludes the possibility of foundations and the totalizing theories they support. Dualisms such as agent and act, self and other, mind and body, are not relevant. Instead, persons are seen as integral to a communal field, constituted through the very interactions and life forms they seek to define. These interactions are authored through a pattern of roles that shape and are shaped by the various strata of discourse constituting community: language, rites and ritual practices, embodiment, social institutions, and so on. This ongoing process of shaping or "focusing" a self precludes familiar notions of a superordinate, unitary self, and instead defines self as an inventory of events, desires, and beliefs transacted through an ever shifting construal of relationships, at some times tightly focused, while at others, more loosely construed.

David L. Hall's contribution, "To Be or Not to Be: The Postmodern Self and the *Wu*-forms of Taoism," shifts the emphasis within the Chinese tradition from Confucianism to Taoist philosophy. "Self" as a concept, reports Hall, is painfully recondite, having a cluster of often contrasting and conflicting associations. Similar in spirit to Amélie Rorty's celebration of Rousseau's "failure," Hall's essay too embraces this ambiguity of meaning, claiming that far from subverting our exploration, it is the promise of it. Our hope for a truly robust conception of "self" lies in aesthetic complexity and underdeterminacy rather than logical consistency.

Hall sees self as coming into being *pari passu* with culture-bound ways of thinking and living. His survey of the historical origins of the Western concept of self begins from the analogical relationships among *pysche*, *polis*, and *kosmos* in the articulation of aesthetic, ethical, political, and metaphysical explanations. Our mature Greek conception of self emerges out of a chaotic and unintegrated welter of unstable vital functions to find order in the tripartite structure of self in Plato and Aristotle. This now increasingly unitary self is further fortified with Augustine's contribution of autonomous will, preparing a foundational structure of reason (knowing, science), passion (feeling, art), and will (acting, morality) for the eventual transition to the various permutations of a modern self and its distinctive "self-consciousness" and "self-understanding."

Maturation of this modern self, shaped and enriched by the each of the early modern philosophers in turn, culminated in Hegel's grand claims for arriving at an integrated cultural self-understanding. It was the attack on Hegel mounted by philosophers such as Kierkegaard, Marx, and the existentialists that led to the diremption of the value spheres which Hegel had tried so keenly to keep intact, and to the fragmentation of the superordinate self.

As Hall points out, it is the valuation of this "fragmented" and "decentered" self that demarcates the late moderns from the new spokespersons of postmodernism: for the late moderns the incompleteness and incoherence of self issues forth in negativity and alienation; for the postmoderns this same condition entails the possibility for complex aesthetic satisfactions and the appreciation of difference. With apologies to Parmenides, there is no Being (presence); only beings are (difference).

Hall then turns to philosophical Taoism as a resource for ruminating on the philosophy of difference. For classical Taoism, in the absence of any foundational ontological claims, there are only "this's" and "that's." Hence, "knowing" (*chih*), "feeling" (*yü*), and "acting" (*wei*) as a vocabulary of self have no reference to "presence"—to underlying "Being"—but only to the difference of "this's" and "that's" as particular perspectives on the totality. Applied to the notion of self, Taoism gives us the insistent particularity of a pluralistic and aesthetic self-consciousness (a "we" instead of an "I") without the dialectical tension that attends the postmodernist's break with modernism.

The next essay, David Y. H. Wu's "Self and Collectivity: Socialization in Chinese Preschools," provides us the opportunity to explore the characterizations of self described in the preceding articles in the concrete world of the Chinese preschool. What recommends the preschool experience as a locus of investigation is that it is a profoundly formative period in the life of any culture. It is at this stage in the career of a person that the cultural construction of the self is perhaps most evident and the profile of the person-to-be is most clearly articulated.

Of particular notice in David Wu's study is that the distinctive features of the socialization process that occurs in the Chinese preschool emerges from comparisons and contrasts among three cultures, China, Japan, and America, and from comparisons and contrasts between more traditional models of Chinese family and the present single-child policy. As Wu observes, "our research allows the understanding of the three cultures' preschools but also of the three cultures as seen through their preschools."

The traditional goal of Chinese education in constructing a socially viable person is captured in the slogan, "to sacrifice smaller self to accomplish greater self" (*xisheng xiaowo wan cheng dawo*). With the present-day single-child policy, there has been particular concern that the stereotypical selfishness and self-centeredness of the only child would undermine the originally Confucian values of social responsibility in a fiduciary community. The seemingly restrictive and regimented attitudes popular in Chinese preschools need to be understood in a wider context, including the child's home life, in which doting parents and grandparents provide too little control to foster socially responsible citizens. Life at the preschool—preferably a boarding school—is seen as a sustained societal corrective that, through praise for model behavior in a collective environment, works to dissolve the "smaller self" and establish a foundation for the "greater" social self. The teachers assume important moral responsibilities for the socialization of children who belong not only to the family but also to the community at large: "The promotion of selflessness and collectivism lies at the core of the Chinese preschool's mission." Under present conditions, there seems to be some consensus among both parents and teachers that "auntie" teachers in the "big family" preschool can be more effective "mothers" to the children than the mothers at home.

The final article in this section, "Beyond the Patrilineal Self: Constructing Gender in China," is contributed by Margery Wolf, an anthropologist, who is critical of a traditional Confucian model of self as an "openly gendered perspective" that has failed to give even minimum notice to women's voices. Wolf's critique on the Confucian tradition is informed by recent feminist scholarship in which the historical "invisibility" of women has become a major cross-cultural concern.

Margery Wolf's analysis of the Confucian model of self begins from a fundamental question: of what real relevance is the Confucian self, an intellectual ideal of the Grand Tradition, for the semiliterate rural woman who has, both then and now, been largely excluded from this cultural legacy? Gender becomes deeply implicated in the comparison between the male child, who is socialized as a son, a father, a grandfather, and then an ancestor in the continuing lineage of a resolutely patriarchal family, and the female child, whose sense of self is problematized by her only temporary residence in the home, the relationships into which she is born, and her anticipation of an almost wholesale transfer of identity on marriage. The Confucian world of familial roles and relationships, which guarantees not only material well-being and spirituality but also personal identity itself, has meaning and security for the man child alone. It is only when a woman gives birth to a son and establishes a uterine family of her own that she can exercise some personal control over her own identity and status.

To demonstrate the fragility of the woman's sense of self, Wolf is able to use suicide patterns to show a woman is most vulnerable on the occasion of her own marriage and of the marriage of her son(s), occasions on which her sense of self is most threatened with disintegration. Because the construction of those human relationships that ground the complex Chinese social order is a thoroughly gendered process, Wolf asserts persuasively that gender difference is the most critical variable in understanding Chinese behavior. Traditional models of Confucian self-realization have ignored this variable and have promoted a wholly masculine set of importances as defining of Chinese society broadly. Given the inescapable constraints imposed upon the Chinese woman by her gender, there is a real question as to whether she would respond to a notion like "self-realization" with anything short of a weary cynicism, for her best interests lie elsewhere in the success and happiness of her progeny.

Each of these five articles on the Chinese conception of person bring additional illumination to a tradition that has been historically distant from European civilization, a distance that has made it both curious and exotic for Western observers. Perhaps the greatest benefit we can derive from this investigation lies with the rich contrast we find between the diverse Chinese and the European models of self, for it is in this contrast, whether we are Chinese or European or something in-between, that we can develop a keener understanding of our own particular senses of self and of the alternative possibilities. And, as Robert Solomon underscores in his opening essay in this volume, self is not primarily or most importantly a philosophical "puzzle" but an issue that has relevance to and implications for every moment of our ordinary life experiences.

7

Embodying the Universe:
A Note on Confucian Self-Realization

Tu Wei-ming

Personality, in the Confucian perception, is an achieved state of moral excellence rather than a given human condition. An implied distinction is made between what a person is by temperament and what a person has become by self-conscious effort. A person's natural disposition—whether introverted or extroverted, passive or aggressive, cold or warm, contemplative or active, shy or assertive—is what the Confucians refer to as that aspect of human nature which is composed of *ch'i-chih* (vital energy and raw stuff). For the sake of convenience, we may characterize the human nature of vital energy and raw stuff as our psychophysiological nature, our physical nature, or simply the body.[1]

The Confucian tradition—in fact, the Chinese cultural heritage as a whole—takes our physical nature absolutely seriously. Self-cultivation, as a form of mental and physical rejuvenation involving such exercises as rhythmic bodily movements and breathing techniques, is an ancient Chinese art. The classical Chinese conception of medicine is healing in the sense not only of curing disease or preventing sickness but also of restoring the vital energy essential for the wholeness of the body. Since the level of vital energy required for health varies according to sex, age, weight, height, occupation, time, and circumstance, the wholeness of the body is situationally defined as a dynamic process rather than a static structure. The maintenance of health, accordingly, is a fine art encompassing a wide range of environmental, dietary, physiological, and psychological factors. The delicate balance attained and sustained is the result of communal as well as personal effort. To become well and sound is therefore an achievement.

However, the centrality of the physical nature (the body) in the

177

Confucian conception of the person is predicated not only on the irreducibility of the vital energy and raw stuff for personal growth but also on the potentiality of the body to become an aesthetic expression of the self. The wholeness of the body, often understood as allowing the vital energy to flow smoothly, is not only a measuring standard but also a unique accomplishment. Indeed, the idea is laden with ethico-religious as well as psychophysiological implications.[2] When Mencius defines the sage (who has attained the highest moral excellence in the human community) as the person who has brought the bodily form to fruition,[3] he assumes that the body is where the deepest human spirituality dwells. Yet, it is important to note that the Mencian conception of sagehood involves much more than our physical nature.

It seems that the conscious refusal to accept, rather than the lack of conceptual apparatus to perceive, the exclusive dichotomy between body and mind prompts the Confucians to endow rich resources to the idea of the body as the proper home for human flourishing. The ascetic rigor deemed necessary for reaching a higher spiritual state in virtually all major religions is practiced in the Confucian tradition, but the attention is not focused on self-denial, let alone immolation of the body. The Confucians do not take the body as, by nature, an impediment to full self-realization. To them, the body provides the context and the resources for ultimate self-transformation.

Understandably, Confucian education takes the "ritualization of the body" as the point of departure in the development of the person.[4] Lest the purpose be misconstrued as the imposition of well-established societal norms of behavior upon the innocent youth, "ritualization" as a dynamic process of interpersonal encounter and personal growth is not passive socialization but active participation in recognizing, experiencing, interpreting, and representing the communicative rationality that defines society as a meaningful community. In other words, through ritualization we learn not only the form of the accepted behavior but the grammar of action underlying the form as well. Surely, on the surface at least, it seems that we are socialized unsuspectingly, if not totally against our will, to become members of a linguistic and cultural community. We really do not have much choice in adopting the linguistic specificities of our mother tongue and the cultural particularities of our fatherland. Nevertheless, the Confucians believe that if we make a conscientious effort to actively incorporate the societal norms and values in our own conduct, we will be able to transcend the linguistic and cultural constraints of our society by transforming them into instruments of self-realization. Like poets who have mastered the subtleties of the language, articulating their innermost thoughts through them, Confucians who have become thoroughly proficient in the nuances of the ritual are said to be able to establish and enlarge others as well as themselves by bringing this personal knowledge to bear on daily practical living. The seeming naivete of the Confucians in accepting their own linguistic and cultural universe as intrinsically meaningful and valuable is based on the collective judgment that the survival and continuation of their civilization is not a given reality but a communal attainment. This judgment is itself premised on a fundamental faith in the transformability and perfectibility of the human condition through communal self-effort.

Actually, for the Confucians, the intellectual recognition and experiential acceptance of the body as the point of departure for personal growth are the result of a strong commitment to a holistic view of self-realization. The body, as our physical nature, must be transformed and perfected so that it can serve as a vehicle for realizing that aspect of our nature known as the nature of *i-li* (rightness and principle), the moral nature, or simply the heart-mind (*hsin*).[5] Even though the body is a constitutive part of our nature, it is the heart-mind that is truly human.

A person's temperament may significantly determine his natural disposition in a social environment. Whether he is introverted, passive, cold, contemplative, and shy, or extroverted, aggressive, warm, active, and assertive may very well be a reflection of his native endowments. Quite a few Chinese thinkers, for pragmatic and bureaucratic considerations as well as for social and aesthetic ones, have been fascinated by the classification and evaluation of distinctive character traits. A third-century treatise on the categorization of human beings according to talent and disposition remains to this day a comprehensive treatment and sophisticated analysis of personality types.[6] However, despite the importance and irreducibility of the vital energy and raw stuff (the physical nature or the body) that we are endowed with, the main concern of Confucian education is the process through which we realize ourselves by transforming and perfecting what we are born with.

The Heart-Mind and Human Sensitivity

As Mencius notes, in regard to physical nature, the difference between humans and animals (birds or beasts) is quite small. What truly distinguishes human beings from animals is not the body but the heart-mind. Since the body is the proper home in which the heart-mind dwells, it is perhaps more appropriate to say that the heart-mind (in addition to the body or the body fully informed by the heart-mind) specifically defines the uniqueness of being human. Learning to be human means that the self-consciousness of the heart-mind initiates a process by which the body is transformed and perfected. The ritualization of the body can thus be understood as the active participation of the heart-mind to help the body to become a fitting expression of the self in a social context. To be sure, an act of the will or an existential decision is required when the heart-mind becomes fully aware of its role and function in bringing this process to fruition. For Confucius, the critical juncture occurred when he "set his heart upon learning" at fifteen.[7] However, even the very young, when involved in simple rituals such as sprinkling water for the adults to sweep the floor or giving answers of yes or no to easy questions, exercise their hearts and minds in ritualizing their bodies. It is precisely because the heart-mind is housed in the body (although in practice it can be absent from it) that the human body takes on the profound spiritual significance that distinguishes it from the physical nature of birds and beasts. As a corollary, the body devoid of the heart-mind, is, strictly speaking, no longer human and can easily degenerate into a state of unreflexivity indistinguishable from the physical nature of birds and beasts.

The most prominent feature of the heart-mind is sympathy, the ability to share the suffering of others. This is why the Chinese character *hsin*—like the French word *conscience*, which involves both cognitive and affective dimensions of consciousness—must be rendered as "heart-mind": For *hsin* signifies both intellectual awareness and moral awakening. By privileging sympathy as the defining characteristic of true humanity, Confucians underscore feeling as the basis for knowing, willing, and judging. Human beings are therefore defined primarily by their sensitivity and only secondarily by their rationality, volition, or intelligence.

Expanding Sensitivity: The Perfection of the Self

Learning to be human, in this sense, is to learn to be sensitive to an ever-expanding network of relationships. It may appear to be a consciousness-raising proposition, but it entails the dynamic process of transforming the body as a private ego to the body as an all-encompassing self. To use the Confucian terminology of Master Ch'eng Hao (1032–85), the whole enterprise involves the realization of the authentic possibility of "forming one body with Heaven, Earth, and the myriad things."[8] Concretely, for Confucians, in learning to be human beings by cultivating the capacity to empathize with the negative feelings of one's closest kin—namely, by directly referring to our own hearts and minds—we should understand the reasonableness of the following dictum: "Do not do unto others what I would not want others to do unto me!"[9]

The ability to feel the suffering of others or the inability to endure their suffering empowers us to establish an experiential connection with another human being. This provides a great resource for realizing our moral nature (the nature of rightness and principle). The Confucians believe that our sympathetic bonding to our parents is not only biologically natural but morally imperative, for it is the first step in learning to appreciate ourselves not in isolation but in communication. Indeed, since the Confucians perceive the self as a center of relationships rather than as an isolable individuality, the ability to show intimacy to those who are intimate is vitally important for allowing the closed private ego to acquire a taste for the open communicating self so that the transformation of the body can start on a concrete experiential basis.

But if we extend sympathy only to our parents, we take no more than the initial step toward self-realization. By embodying our closest kin in our sensitivity, we may have gone beyond egoism, but without the learned ability to enter into fruitful communication outside the immediate family, we are still confined to nepotism. Like egoism, nepotism fails to extend our sensitivity to embody a larger network of human relationships and thus limits our capacity for self-realization. Similarly, parochialism, ethnocentrism, and chauvinistic nationalism are all varying degrees of human insensitivity. In the dynamic process of self-realization, they are inertia or limitation. In either case, they are detrimental to the human capacity for establishing a community encompassing humanity as a whole.

Confucian communitarianism, far from being a romantic utopian assertion about equality, unity, and universality, takes as its theoretical and practical basis the natural order of things in human society: the family, neighborhood, kinship, clan, state, and world (figure 7.1). In fact, it recognizes the necessity and legitimacy of these structures, both as historically evolved institutions and socially differentiated organizations. They are natural to the human community not only because they enable us to define ourselves in terms of the breadth and depth of human relatedness but also because they provide both material and spiritual resources for us to realize ourselves. The Confucians do not accept the status quo as necessarily rational. Actually their main mission is to improve on the current situation by bridging the gap between what the status quo is and what it can and ought to be. Confucians are in the world but not of the world. They take an active role in changing the world by managing it from within; instead of adjusting themselves to the status quo, they try to transform it according to their moral idealism.

A salient feature of Confucians' moral idealism is their commit-

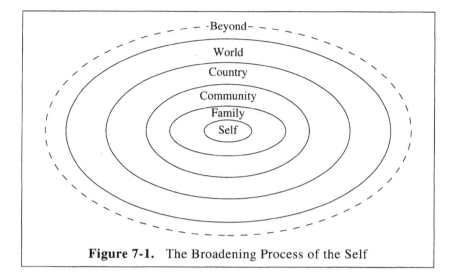

Figure 7-1. The Broadening Process of the Self

ment to the efficacy of education as character building. The Confucian faith in the transformability and perfectibility of the human condition through communal self-effort implies that personal growth has not only ethical value but political significance. The ritualization of the body is relevant to political leadership as well as to social harmony in the family, neighborhood, and clan. Since Confucians believe that exemplary teaching is an integral part of political leadership, the personal morality of those involved is a precondition for good politics. Politics and morality are inseparable. What political leaders do at home is closely linked not only to their styles of leadership but also to the very nature of their politics. Self-realization, in this sense, is not a lonely quest for one's inner spirituality but a communicative act empowering one to become a responsible householder, an effective community worker, and a conscientious public servant. Confucians may not be successful in their political careers or may choose not to seek office, but they can never abandon their vocation as concerned intellectuals.

A concerned intellectual, the modern counterpart of the Confucian *chün-tzu* (nobleman or profound person), does not seek a spiritual sanctuary outside the world. He is engaged in this world, for total withdrawal from society and politics is not an option. Yet, although to be part of the "secular" world is the Confucian vocation, the Confucian calling is not to serve the status quo but to transform the "secular" world of wealth and power into a "sacred" community in which, despite egoistic drives, the quest for human flourishing in moral, scientific, and aesthetic excellence continuously nourishes our bodies and uplifts our hearts and minds.

The Ceaseless Process of Human Flourishing

Understandably, to become a mature person (an adult), in the Confucian sense, is not to attain a limited professional or personal goal but to open oneself up to the ceaseless process of human flourishing. The becoming process, rather than an attained state of being, defines the Confucian personality. One's critical self-awareness in the later stages of one's maturation (e.g., at the age of fifty, when Confucius confessed to have known the Mandate of Heaven)[10] ought to be directed to the authentic possibilities of further growth in moral development. Unlike scientific and aesthetic talents, sensitivity in ethics never declines and, properly cultivated, it becomes more subtle and refined.

Nevertheless, a person becomes a personality not by conscientiously obeying conventional rules of conduct but by exemplifying a form of life worth living; indeed by establishing a standard of self-transformation as a source of inspiration for the human community as a whole. The interchange between an exemplary teacher and the students aspiring to become householders, community workers, or public servants is never one-way. As fellow travelers on the Way, they form a community of the like-minded so that the project of human flourishing becomes a joint venture, mutually admonishing and mutually encouraging. The exemplary teacher as an achieved personality in the eyes of the students must continue to cultivate his inner resources for self-transformation. Confucians do not believe in fixed personalities. While they regard personalities as accomplishments, they insist that the strength of one's personality lies not in its past glories but in its future promises. Real personalities are always evolving. This is why fundamental improvement in the quality of existence is possible for even a human being a breath way from death: "Thou shall not judge the person conclusively before the coffin is sealed!"[11]

This faith in and commitment to the transformability and perfectibility of the human condition through communal self-effort enables Confucians to perceive each person as a center of relationships who is in the process of *ultimate* transformation as a communal act. The "ultimacy" in this seemingly humanistic enterprise is premised on the ability of the human heart-mind, without departing from its proper home (the body), to have the sensitivity to establish an internal resonance with Heaven by fully comprehending its Mandate. Sensitivity so conceived is a "silent illumination." It is neither a gift from an external source nor a knowledge acquired through empirical learning. Rather, it is an inner quality of the heart-mind, the shining wisdom that a ritualized body emits for its own aesthetic expression. Such an expression is neither private nor individualistic, but communal.

As mentioned, for the Confucian to bring self-transformation to fruition (to its ultimacy), he must transcend not merely egoism but nepotism, parochialism, ethnocentrism, and chauvinistic nationalism. These undesirable habits of thought, perceived as varying degrees of human insensitivity, limit the full potential of the silent illumination of the human heart-mind to manifest itself. The Confucian insistence that we must work through our families, communities, and nations to realize ourselves is not at all incompatible with the Confucian injunction that we must go beyond nepotism, parochialism, and chauvinistic nationalism to fully embody our humanity. Actually, the seemingly contradictory assertions signify a dynamic process that defines the richness of the Confucian way of learning to be human.

On the one hand, Confucians, in contrast to individuals, take the communal path by insisting that, as a center of relationships, a personality comes into being by fruitfully interacting with its natural human environment—the family, kin, community, and the state. This process of continuously communicating with an ever-expanding network of human relationships enables the self to embody an increasingly widening circle of inclusiveness in its own sensitivity. On the other hand, Confucians, as opposed to collectivists, firmly establish the "subjectivity" of the person as *sui generis*. No social program, no matter how lofty, can undermine the centrality of selfhood in Confucian learning. After all, Confucians see learning for the sake of the self as the authentic purpose of education. To be sure, the self as an open and communicating center of relationships is intimately connected with other selves; far from being egoistic, it is communal. However, by stressing the centrality of the self in learning to be human, the Confucians advocate ultimate self-transformation, not only as social ethics but also as the flourishing of human nature with profound religious significance.

Forming One Body with Earth and the Myriad Things

For Confucians to fully realize themselves, it is not enough to become a responsible householder, effective social worker, or conscientious political servant. No matter how successful one is in the sociopolitical arena, the full measure of one's humanity cannot be accommodated without a reference to Heaven. The highest Confucian ideal is the "unity of Man and Heaven," which defines humanity not only in anthropo-

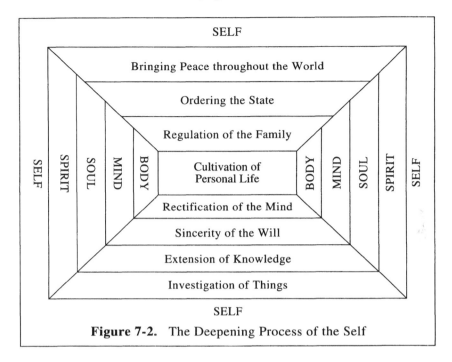

Figure 7-2. The Deepening Process of the Self

logical terms but also in cosmological terms. In the *Doctrine of the Mean* (*Chung-yung*), the most authentic manifestation of humanity is characterized as "forming a trinity with Heaven and Earth."[12]

Yet, since Heaven does not speak and the Way in itself cannot make human beings great—which suggests that although Heaven is omnipresent and may be omniscient, it is certainly not omnipotent—our understanding of the Mandate of Heaven requires that we fully appreciate the rightness and principle inherent in our heart-minds. Our ability to transcend egoism, nepotism, parochialism, ethnocentrism, and chauvinistic nationalism must be extended to anthropocentrism as well. To make ourselves deserving partners of Heaven, we must be constantly in touch with that silent illumination that makes the rightness and principle in our heart-minds shine forth brilliantly. If we cannot go beyond the constraints of our own species, the most we can hope for is an exclusive, secular humanism advocating man as the measure of all things, By contrast Confucian humanism is inclusive; it is predicated on an "anthropocosmic" vision. Humanity in its all-embracing fullness "forms one body with Heaven, Earth, and the myriad things." Self-realization, in the last analysis, is ultimate transformation, that process which enables us to embody the family, community, nation, world, and cosmos in our sensitivity (figure 7–2).

NOTES

1. According to Chu Hsi (1130–1200), the idea of "physical nature" originated with Chang Tsai (1020–1077). For a general discussion on this, see Wing-tsit Chan, "The Neo-Confucian Solution to the Problem of Evil," *Bulletin of the Institute of History and Philology* 28 (1957): 780–83.

2. For a thought-provoking attempt to formulate an Eastern mind-body theory, see Yuasa Yasuo, *The Body*, ed. T. P. Kasulis (Albany: State University of New York Press, 1987). It should be noted that Professor Yuasa's attempt is based on his understanding of Japanese Buddhism in general and the thoughts of Dōgen and Kūkai in particular.

3. *Mencius*, 7A:38.

4. For a general discussion on ritualization as humanization, see Tu Wei-ming, "Li as Process of Humanization," *Philosophy East and West*, 22 no. 2 (April 1972): 187–201.

5. *Mencius*, 6A:7.

6. Unfortunately, Liu Shao's *Treatise on Personalities* (*Jen-wu chih*) is still not yet available in English translation.

7. *Analects*, 2.4.

8. See his essay on "Understanding the Nature of *Jen* (Humanity)," in *A Source Book in Chinese Philosophy*, trans. and comp. Wing-tsit Chan (Princeton: Princetion University Press, 1963), 523.

9. *Analects*, 15.23.

10. *Analects*, 2.4.

11. This common expression is still widely used in China. Although it is a popular idiom rather than an assertion in the Confucian classics, it vividly captures the Confucian spirit that self-realization is never completed and that, as long as a person lives, he is still redeemable.

12. *Chung-yung* (*Doctrine of the Mean*), 22. For a discussion of this idea in the perspective of Confucian "moral metaphysics," see Tu Wei-ming. *Centrality and Commonality: An Essay on Chung-yung* (Honolulu: The University Press of Hawaii, 1976), 100–41.

8

The Focus-Field Self in Classical Confucianism

Roger T. Ames

Arthur Danto, a distinguished philosopher (and friend), in the context of discussing the difficulty in interpreting a philosophical text, remarks:

> one of my favorite passages in the *Analects* is where Confucius says that if he gives someone *three* corners who cannot find the *fourth* corner for himself, he cannot teach that person.[1] (Emphasis mine)

Of course, the passage that Danto is referring to in fact reads:

> If I have shown someone *one* corner of a square and he is not able to infer from it the other *three*, I will not show him a second time.[2] (Emphasis mine)

Apart from the rather obvious and amusing irony of getting the passage wrong when you are trying to tell people how to read a text, Danto is certainly understating the effort required to put the square together.

In this essay, I want to begin by looking critically at several interpretations of the Confucian conception of self, claiming that none of them is successful in giving Confucius his square. I then want to develop my own model of the Confucian self, and to argue that, in fact, what Confucius was really looking for was a circle, anyway.

Model 1: The Hollow Men

In the early nineteenth century, Hegel, witnessing the European assault on a seemingly passive China, read the situation from a distance. I cite him at some length here because, although the tenor of his commentary might be blunt and offensive, in substance, it resonates rather closely with much of what is being said today. Describing the traditional Chinese conception of self, Hegel reports:

> moral distinctions and requirements are expressed as Laws, but so that the subjective will is governed by these Laws as by an external force. Nothing subjective in the shape of disposition, Conscience, formal Freedom, is recognized. Justice is administered only on the basis of external morality, and Government exists only as the prerogative of compulsion. . . . Morality is in the East likewise a subject of positive legislation, and although moral prescriptions (the *substance* of their Ethics) may be perfect, what should be internal subjective sentiment is made a matter of external arrangement. . . . While *we* obey, because what we are required to do is confirmed by an *internal* sanction, there the Law is regarded as inherently and absolutely valid without a sense of the want of this subjective confirmation.[3]

Hegel's perception of the Chinese as animated by a top-down "totalitarianism" and hence as being shaped and justified entirely from without, is hardly obsolete. In fact, its most recent application is in the contemporary discussions on the Chinese response to human-rights talk.

Much if not most of the contemporary commentary available on Chinese attitudes toward human rights has interpreted the fundamental presupposition that the Chinese "self" is qualified by a kind of self-abnegation or "selflessness" in a manner that, in a more modern and subtle way, echoes the Hegelian "hollow men" characterization of the Chinese person cited above. Donald J. Munro, for example, argues that

> selflessness . . . is one of the oldest values in China, present in various forms in Taoism and Buddhism, but especially in Confucianism. The selfless person is always willing to subordinate his own interests, or that of some small group (like a village) to which he belongs, to the interest of a larger social group.[4]

R. Randle Edwards combines the presumption of a Chinese homogeneity with his observation of preestablished social pattern to reinforce Munro's interpretation of the Chinese ideal:

> most Chinese view society as an organic whole or seamless web. Strands in a web must all be of a certain length, diameter, and consistency, and must all be fitted together in accordance with a preordained pattern. . . . The hope is that each individual will function as properly as a cog in an ever more efficient social machine.[5]

Both Munro and Edwards construe the Confucian model as a collectivism in which individual interests are insignificant, except when they are of service to those of the group.

Mark Elvin brings a similar model into his interpretation of specifically a contemporary Marxist-Maoist conception of self. In describing the revolutionary self of modern literature, Elvin delineates what seems revolutionary but what he sees as having characteristics that bear comparison with the tradition:

> Independence of thought or perception is an illusion. Thought has a class character. . . . Only the minds of those who have a working-class standpoint can reflect reality unimpaired by selfishness. (Compare the Neo-Confucian idea that selfishness could block the individual mind with contact with the universal mind.)[6]

Elvin derives this interpretation from a variety of sources, including the contemporary idéologue, Ai Ssu-ch'i (1910–1966):

> If you are able to be like this, without the slightest individual selfishness, and in no degree affected by the influence on thought of the selfishness and vileness of the large landlord or large bourgeois classes, then, when you examine a question, you will have no prejudices, no anxieties, to impede your understanding the true nature of the question to the bottom, and you can obtain a correct knowledge of everything.

Thus, Elvin, by making the working-class mentality "other" and equating *the eradication of selfishness*, with *selflessness* arrives at the same conclusion as Munro: "The individual remains of significance only as the locus of an ever-renewed moral struggle whose aim is the extinction of individuality."

C. K. Yang represents this model from a sociological perspective:

the Western concept of individualism . . . runs directly counter to the spirit of the traditional Chinese family and is incompatible with the traditional loyalty to it. Self-cultivation, the basic theme of Confucian ethics traditionally inculcated in the child's mind from an early age, did not seek a solution to social conflict in defining, limiting, and guaranteeing the rights and interests of the individual or in the balance of power and interests between individuals. It sought the solution from the self-sacrifice of the individual for the preservation of the group.[7]

Munro, Edwards, Elvin, Yang, and the legion of scholars who seem to share this interpretation are certainly right in assuming that the Chinese tradition has been largely persuaded by a Confucian-based relational—and hence social—definition of person, rather than by any notion of discrete individuality. And they are again unassailable in their assumption that this fact has profound implications for the way in which China has responded to any doctrine of human rights. But where we must take issue is with the assumption that, in the Chinese context, community interest and self-interest are mutually exclusive.

We can allow that there does not seem to be an adequate philosophical basis to justify self as a locus of interests independent of and prior to society. Under the sway of this relational understanding of human being, the mutuality and interdependence of personal, societal, and political realization in the classical Chinese model can and has been generally conceded.[8] But it certainly does not follow that the consequence of this interdependence is selflessness. Under scrutiny, the consequence of attributing "selflessness" as an ideal to the Chinese tradition is to sneak in both the public/private and the individual/ society distinctions by the back door. To be "selfless" in the sense presupposed by these commentators requires that an individual self first exist and then, as C. K. Yang states explicitly, that it be sacrificed for some higher public interest. And the suggestion that there are "higher interests" on the part of either person or society covertly establishes a boundary between them that justifies an adversarial relationship. The "selfless" interpretation of these commentators does not support the claim that "person" in the Chinese tradition is irreducibly social; ironically, it vitiates it.

These several commentators, in imposing a "selfless" ideal on the Chinese tradition, are appealing to a contest between state and individual—the struggle between advocates of group interests over the priority of individual interests—that has in large measure separated collectivist thinkers from the liberal democratic in the Western experience, but has perhaps only limited applicability to the Chinese model.

While it is true that for the traditional Chinese model, self-realization does not require a high degree of individual autonomy, it does not follow that the alternative to autonomy is capitulation to the general will. Rather, Confucian "personalism," to use William Theodore de Bary's felicitous term,[9] involves benefiting and being benefited by membership in a world of reciprocal loyalties and obligations that surround and stimulate a person and define a person's own worth.

This attribution of "selflessness" to the Chinese tradition, both ancient and modern, seems to arise out of an unfortunate equivocation between "selfish" and "selfless." To eschew selfish concerns does not necessarily lead to self-abnegation. The classical Confucian position, as I understand it, contends that, because self-realization is fundamentally a social undertaking, "selfish" concerns are to be rejected as an impediment to one's own growth and self-realization.[10]

In Chinese philosophy, a perennial issue that has spanned the centuries has been the likelihood of conflict between the pursuit of selfish advantage (*li* 利) and negotiation of that which is appropriate and meaningful to all concerned (*yi* 義), including oneself. Concern for selfish personal advantage is associated with retarded personal development (*hsiao jen* 小人) while the pursuit of what is broadly "appropriate"—including, of course, one's own interests—is the mainstay of the self-realized and exemplary person (*chün tzu* 君子).

This question as to whether "selflessness" has been and still is a Chinese ideal hinges in important measure on the corollary assertion that the project of self-realization is in fact to be pursued through "obedience . . . to the chief relevant authority," where each higher level of authority takes precedence over the one below it, until one reaches the emperor in imperial China and the party leadership in that country today.[11] Such a combination of "selflessness" and externally imposed order, if true, would bring this model perilously close to Hegel's characterization of a Chinese totalitarianism and its "hollow men."

This top-down interpretation represented by Hegel and others is encouraged by the relative absence of the adversarial tensions that arise in the separation of private and public interests, yet is belied by the basic trust that colors the relationship between person and state in what Tu Wei-ming describes as the "fiduciary community."[12] The coterminous relationship between strong person and strong state presumed in the Chinese model contrasts with the liberal Western concern to limit state powers as a precondition for individual autonomy.

In China, the traditional assumption has been that personal order and the order of society and the state entail each other, with the broader configuration always emerging out of the more immediate and concrete.[13] When the country succumbs to disorder, the exemplary person returns to the more immediate and substantive precincts of home and community to begin again to shape an appropriate order.[14]

On being asked by a rather unsympathetic second party why he did not have a formal position in government, Confucius replied that the achievement of order in the home is itself the basis on which any broader attainment of order depends.[15] The central doctrine of graduated love and ritually ordered community in which family plays such a vital role—in fact, where all roles are reduced to the familial[16]—is predicated on the priority of participation in the immediate and concrete over determination by more general principles and ideals. Even when a higher order of social or political organization is deferred to, it is given definition and represented in the concrete embodiment of a particular person—a specific ruler or leader with whom one can assume a personal relationship.

This traditional Chinese prejudice for the immediate and concrete tends to preclude the acknowledgment of any concept of universal human rights. Witness the fact that the Chinese have had at least a dozen draft constitutions in this century, and there seems to be no end in sight. At the same time, the assumption of the "rite" of immediate and substantive participation does not permit the sanctioning of absolute state power. In the classical political rhetoric, a symbiosis between government and people is presumed in which the people have been construed as the more primary value: "the people as root" (*min pen* 民本) or "the people as mainstay" (*min chu* 民主), an attitude that is still very much present in the way in which "democracy" as a concept is understood in the contemporary Chinese world. The participation and tolerance characteristic of a bottom-up emergent order provides, at least ideally, an internal check on totalitarianism.[17]

It is commonly noticed that in China, from ancient times to the present, conflicts have been generally dealt with through informal mechanisms for mediation and conciliation that are as close to the dispute as possible.[18] Society has been regulated largely through ritually defined relationships, and thus it has required relatively minimal government. It is this same communal harmony that defines and dispenses order at the most immediate level that is also relied upon to define and express authoritative consensus without more obvious formal provisions for effecting popular sovereignty. Clearly, to the extent that the Confucian model is a project of cultivation directed at self-realization, the social and political order is derived from the participants themselves, who cannot be fairly construed as self-abnegating.

Having set aside the Hegelian stereotype that the Chinese are selfless "hollow men" manipulated externally from above, we shall turn to a model that purports to be a variation on this same theme but in fact anticipates a more fundamental issue: how different is the Chinese conception of self from those models dominant within the Western tradition?

Model 2: Autonomous Individuality

Underlying the preceding interpretations are the assumptions that the Chinese conception of self necessarily entails "individuality" and that if the Chinese have ever chosen to acknowledge this fact, they have also chosen to reject it. Frequently, the assumptions are couched in a language that privileges the aims of "modernity." Donald Munro, for example, argues that differences identified between the West and the Chinese are largely a function of inadvertently comparing a modern Western concept with a traditional Chinese counterpart:

> there is also the danger that he will assume that Chinese and Europeans have always had radically different world views and values associated with them and, consequently, that they are likely to in the future. In contrast, mindful that our individualistic values are relatively modern, the reader may then find himself free to ask the question: If we compare Europeans before the Enlightenment with premodern Chinese, will we find that their world views were also similar in important ways? I believe that the answer will be that they were.[19]

For Munro, the Chinese conception of self is transitional and premodern, and, allowing that we were once burdened with something similar, we now have a concept that is both modern and enlightened.

Marcel Mauss, a sociologist who has surveyed the development of the concept of self across a wide range of cultures and epochs, provides a more self-conscious statement of Munro's position. He maintains that the Western consciousness of the autonomous and sacred individual emerges out of archaic notions, such as those owned by the American Indian and the Chinese, as the fragile product of high science and culture:

> It remained to make of this rational, individual substance what it is today, a consciousness and a category. . . . Who knows even whether this "category," which all of us here believe to be well founded, will always be recognised as such? It is formulated only for us, by us. Even its moral strength—the sacred character

of the human "person" (*personne*)—is questioned, not only throughout the Orient, which has not yet attained the level of our sciences, but even in the countries where this principle was discovered. We have great possessions to defend. With us the idea could disappear.[20]

It can be argued that "self" does necessarily entail a notion of individuality. But, exposed in the differences we have discovered between being "nonselfish" and being "selfless," there is an unnoticed conceptual equivocation on the term *individual* that plagues this whole discussion. "Individual" can mean either one of a *kind*, like one human being as a member of a class of human beings, or *one* of a kind, like Turner's unique *Seastorm*. That is, "individual" can refer to a single, separate and indivisible thing that, by virtue of some essential property or properties, qualifies as a member of a class. By virtue of its membership in a "kind," it is substitutable—"equal before the law," "entitled to equal opportunity," "a locus of unalienable rights," "one of God's children," and so on. It is this definition of individual that generates notions like autonomy, equality, liberty, freedom, and individuated will. By virtue of both its separability and its indivisibility, it relates to its world only extrinsically and hence, where animate, has dominion over its own interiority.

Individual can alternatively also mean uniqueness: the character of a single and unsubstitutable particular, such as a work of art, where it might be quantitatively comparable to other particulars but where it has literally nothing qualitatively in common with them. Under this definition of individual, equality can only mean parity—a comparable excellence.

In the model of the unique individual, determinacy, far from being individuation, lies in the achieved quality of a person's relationships. A person becomes "recognized," "distinguished" or "renowned" by virtue of one's relations and their quality. Much of the effort in coming to an understanding of the traditional Confucian conception of self has to do with clarifying this distinction and reinstating the unique individual in the Confucian picture. While the definition of self as "irreducibly social" certainly precludes autonomous individuality, it does not rule out the second, less familiar notion of unique individuality.

Mark Elvin, in pursuing an understanding of the Chinese conception of self, is sensitive to the importance that unique place has in the traditional Chinese world: "The Chinese believed, by and large, in a unique personal existence, no doubt fortified by the concept of a structure of kinship ascendants and descendants, stretching indefinitely forward into the future, in which the individual occupied his unique place."[21] This Chinese conception of unique individuality stands in contrast to that of the autonomous individuality, which attends "the isolation of the European soul" from other souls and, ontologically, from the illusory world of sensual perception. The uniqueness of the person is embedded in a ceaseless process of natural, social, and cultural change.

Herbert Fingarette, in his research and published work on Confucius, has done more to stimulate discussion on Confucian philosophy among philosophers than any other contemporary Western scholar. The surge in philosophical studies on Confucius since the appearance of Fingarette's small book *Confucius: The Secular as Sacred* reflects the extent to which Fingarette, in lending the authority of his name and reputation, has helped to make Confucius a respectable area of philosophical inquiry.

Fingarette's appreciation of Confucius is nuanced and complex, and in exchanges with him both personally and in print, I have usually come away persuaded either that we are substantially in agreement, on which occasions I have been much encouraged to have the corroboration of someone so deeply respected, or alternatively, that Fingarette has been able to take the interpretation one step further. This is certainly the case in our previously published exchange on the Confucian notion of self that I want to recount briefly here and then continue.[22]

I suggested that in Fingarette's attempt to define the Confucian conception of self, he falls prey to this equivocation between autonomous individual and unique individual. First, he seems to me to beg the question of his analysis by assuming that if Confucius has a notion of self that is importantly different from Western constructions of self, it is to be found by isolating and exploring precisely that cluster of concepts that are generally relevant in translating *Western* conceptions of self: "I will lay the foundation for my own theses by examining in some detail four terms that are used with frequency in the *Analects* that seem explicitly to refer to self and to willing: *chi* 己, *shen* 身, *yü* 欲, and *chih* 志."[23] In appealing to this particular glossary of terms for self, I think Fingarette underestimates the magnitude of the problem in the translation of Chinese culture into the Western tradition. Because Confucius did not use these specific terms as the basis for a doctrine of self-cultivation, Fingarette concludes that he did not regard self-cultivation as a central concern:

> It is the *commentator*, rather than Confucius, who is tempted to generalize these teachings by focusing on the "self" as an overarching or basic rubric, and summing it all up in terms of

"self-cultivation." . . . Would Confucius himself have generalized on his own teachings, or summarized them, by taking the consummately cultivated self as his focal concept? The fact is, of course, that he did not. Why not? . . . My answer is that he did not say it because he did not mean it.[24]

Although one can give good reasons for taking exception to Fingarette's analysis, it is worth reviewing carefully, because there are several insights of this always sensitive scholar that can be disengaged from his conclusions and have importance for our discussion.

First, Fingarette comments on the absence of an "inner psychic life" in the Confucian model of self:

Confucius' usage reveals no explicit doctrines of a metaphysical or psychological kind about the details of structure of will, or the processes internal to the individuals' control of the will. There is, for example, no reification of a Faculty of Will, . . . no theatre in which an inner drama takes place, no inner community with ruler and ruled. This absence of an elaborated doctrine of an "inner psychic life" is consistent with theses that I have argued elsewhere.[25]

Fingarette's explanation is that it is because the exemplary person (*chün tzu* 君子) in Confucius does not express his own egoistic will, but wills the noncontingent, nonpersonal *tao*. In Fingarette's own words:

If one seeks to understand deeply the content of an egoistic will, one must necessarily understand that particular person, the motives, anxieties, hopes, and other personal data that go to make intelligible the conduct of that person. But the more deeply one explores the *chün tzu*'s will, the more the personal dimensions are revealed as purely formal—the individual is the unique space-time bodily locus of that will; it is *that which* controls, but it is nonsignificant regarding why, specifically, or in what specific direction, the control shall be exercised. To understand the content of the *chün tzu*'s will is to understand the *tao*, not the *chün tzu* as a particular person. The ego is present in the egoist's will. The *tao* is present in the *chün tzu*'s will.[26]

Fingarette's conclusion, then, is that the self of the exemplary person, insofar as we may call it a "self," is an empty room, a transparent medium through which the *tao* is expressed: "Not my will, but Thine be done."[27] In these terms and in this sense, argues Fingarette, Confucianism is consistent with the pan-Asian ideal of selflessness.[28] To me, we seem to come back full circle to Hegel where *tao* replaces despot in explaining the absence of the Chinese "self."

In Fingarette's response to the reservations summarized here, he makes the following points.[29] We are disagreeing not in substance, only in terminology. We both agree that the uncultivated person is ego bound, and thus, individuated. And we both agree that the cultivated person represents a set of concerns that go beyond any sense of private self. The distance between us lies in Fingarette's use of the word *self* with its normal English meaning as the private egoistic self, the individual ego. It is in reference to this sense of self that Confucius advocates cultivating a notion of person who is "selfless," namely, one who has transcended egoistic motivations. Such being the case, the absence of selfishness is, in fact, the absence of self. I, on the other hand, use the term "authoritative person" (*jen*) to express this same consummately human ideal, which I take to be an unselfish "authoritative self" rather than an ego self. My motivation in doing so, and in suggesting that Confucius has a notion of unique individuality rather than autonomous individuality, is to save the particular. Let me explain.

My primary reservation concerning Fingarette's interpretation of Confucius' cultivated person has had to do with what I have taken to be his depersonalization of *tao* and his suggestion that the cultivated person is transparent, where *tao*, devoid of any personal content, uses this cultivated and thus "empty" person as a medium through which to shine. I read this as a familiar Brahmanistic or even Platonic collapse of the many into the One, the particular into the universal, with, of course, a bit of a Confucian spin. For me, Fingarette was introducing a notion of single-ordered world into Confucianism where it doesn't belong, "metaphysicalizing" classical Confucianism by separating *tao* from the world and making it into some unifying principle that, while independent of particular persons, disciplines their world.

I take *tao* to be *always* "personal" in the sense of being emergent as the pattern or "way" in which specific historically and culturally bound people contextualize themselves in the dynamics of community living, and I take it as *always* being viewed from one unique perspective or another through *this* complex of roles or *that* matrix of relationships. Thus I took Fingarette to be understating the important place that the unique and site-specific person has in expressing *tao*.

It is the further development in Fingarette's position that has returned me to his other writings to rethink my reading of his original position and, I think, get clearer on what he has tried to say. In any event, the language that he uses to describe the "selfless" Confucian is worth repeating; I agree with it entirely.

> The point is: Why should we reify "self" by giving it the independent noun form in English, and thus impute to Confucius the notion of some inner entity, some core of one's being—whether egoistic or ideal? If Ames and I are right in our basic view of Confucius' ideas in this area, we ought to make it a point to avoid speaking of "the self" in Confucius. We ought to speak of a person as acting, but not suggesting by "person" this notion of an Actor who somehow embraces inwardly a moral or psychic core which is then expressed in action. On the contrary, the fundamental moral-human reality is (as Ames and I agree) the social nexus, and person along with many other things receive their specific, humanly relevant nature, as well as their humanly relevant location, by reference to and as a result of the communal life-forms. "Person" is an abstraction, a set of complex attributes conceptually abstracted from the social reality; social reality on the other hand is not an abstraction but is the concrete reality.[30]

In understanding the Confucian person in this way, we resist the familiar move to separate *that which orders* (the self, rationality, volition) from *that which is ordered* (specific thoughts, desires, experiences). We abandon notions of a unitary self, which makes our many experiences one, in favor of a more underdetermined range and locus of experiences expressed through specific roles and relationships. We will return to this in the focus-field conception of self outlined below.

Model 3: The Organic Self

Another model frequently posited in explanation of the Confucian conception of self is that involving the metaphor of "organism." This position has become increasingly influential because of Joseph Needham's application of it.[31] In this view, the nature of the self is construed as a whole with parts that functionally interrelate to achieve a purpose or aim. The Aristotelian language of "potentiality" and "actuality" is frequently appropriated to articulate this notion. The acorn is *potentially*, and may *actually* become, an oak tree. Although there is much in the organic metaphor that one may associate with the Confucian model of self, there are several reasons why, despite its surface attractiveness, this model might be problematic.

First, organism entails a sense of wholeness. In the classical Western tradition, this wholeness is modeled along cosmogonic lines. The world is an organic whole, a *kosmos*. In the absence of cosmogonic beginning in the Confucian tradition, the power of creativity and the responsibility for creative product resides more broadly in the phenomena themselves in their ongoing interactive processes of becoming. Phenomena are not marshalled (*kosmeo*) into a unified whole (*kosmos*), like Homeric leaders marshalling their troops for battle, but exist as interdependent yet self-disciplining *kosmoi*.[32]

Where a phenomenon—in this case, the self—is initiated by and dependent upon some externally derived or "given" creative principle for the "nature" of its existence, and, said another way, where it is other than self-generative (*tzu-jan* 自然), the creative contribution of that phenomenon itself tends to be diminished. The existence of some antecedent and preassigned creative principle—be it Plato's abstract *eidos*, the Judeo-Christian deity, *phusis*, or the like—does in fact serve to account for natural and moral order. At the same time, such an explanation tends in some degree to delimit the dynamic possibilities of phenomena themselves in the natural world.

The difference between the "nature" of self in a cosmogonic tradition and in a noncosmogonic cosmology is suggested by the kinds of questions that the philosophers in these contrasting cultures are inclined to ask. Cosmogonic concern generates metaphysical questions, a search for essential principles: How did the cosmos begin? What are its first principles? What is the origin of the existence and growth of natural phenomena? What are their essential defining principles, and how are they actualized?

Noncosmogonic cosmology, on the other hand, will generate primarily historical and rhetorical questions: Who and what are our historical antecedents that have given us our present definition? What are their achievements that we can appropriate to enculturate ourselves? How can we further cultivate ourselves so as to contribute to the appropriated tradition as it is embodied in our contemporary exemplars? How can we turn this historical and cultural interdependence to maximum benefit? The thinker's role in the noncosmogonic tradition, then, will not be as much to discover and define self as to create a model of self that is persuasive and evokes emulation.

A related implication of this distinction between a cosmogonic and noncosmogonic worldview is that in the absence of some overarching *archē* (beginning) as an explanation of the creative process, and under conditions that are thus "anarchic" in the philosophic sense of this term, although "nature" might indeed refer to "kinds," genus and species as categories would be dependent upon generalizations made by analogy among *sui generis* phenomena. Difference is prior to identified similarities. For example, as Mencius states explicitly, what distinguishes a person from a human beast is not some inviolate natural endowment but a tentative and always particular cultural refinement.[33] Even for Confucius, who insists that he cannot gather with the birds and beasts because he is, after all, a human being, he still makes it abundantly clear that he will associate with only *some* human beings—only those who are refined and cultured.[34]

For A. C. Graham, the dynamic force of "human nature" (*jen hsing* 人性) is evident in the metaphors Mencius employs to characterize the concept: growing trees and animals, ripening grain, flowing water.[35] In extending the dynamic implications of nature to the human being, Graham is keen to correct his earlier understanding of human nature as "that which one starts with," revising it instead to cover the entire career of a person's existence. In the human context, then, the nature of the self denotes the entire process of being a particular person. Strictly speaking, a person is not a sort of *being*, but first and foremost a *doing* or *making* and only derivatively and retrospectively something done. For this reason, at least in reference to the human being, I would question the wisdom of translating *hsing* as "nature," not only because it invokes unwanted associations that more properly belong to a cosmogonic tradition and invites us willy-nilly to impose the presuppositions of alien models on the Chinese self but also because this translation fails to capture the sense that self is an ongoing poietic process. For the human being at least, the *hsing* of self seems to come closer to "character" "personality," or "constitution" than what we generally understand by "nature."

A second caution that we need observe arises from the frequent use of "cultivation"—a term that also suggests the organic metaphor. "Cultivation" usually translates the character *hsiu*, as in "cultivating oneself" (*hsiu chi* 修己)[36] or "cultivating one's person" (*hsiu shen* 修身).[37] The character *hsiu*, translated "cultivate," is most commonly glossed as "effecting proper order" (*chih* 治) in a sociopolitical rather than in an organic sense. The point that I want to make is that the cultivation of self as a cultural product allows for a greater degree of creativity than a more restricted horticultural or husbanding metaphor might suggest.

Further, Aristotelian associations with this "cultivation" metaphor conjure forth a potentiality/actuality distinction that is not appropriate. Such a distinction is fundamentally progressive, entailing as it does an efficient, a formal, and a final cause. By contrast, there is a real question as to whether the classical Chinese notion of self can be most clearly understood by appeal to systemic teleological models. In the classical Chinese world, it is entirely reasonable to conclude that most acorns become squirrels. The reason that teleology does not fit the Confucian model is that it introduces a goal that "instrumentalizes" the process. Progressionist theories suggest a steady advance toward a predetermined perfection. It is the degree to which this Confucian model of self is aesthetic, free of any definite and specified goals, that gives it its flexibility and creative range. In describing the emergent order that is self, one must distinguish between *a posteriori* generalizations and goal direction. The physiological functions of the person can, perhaps, be discussed in terms of some teleonomic behavior-regulating "program" that controls a process and leads it toward a given end. This would appear to be goal directed and hence teleological. But it is precisely the contrast between such programmed behavior and the creativity of the human being that the early Confucians appeal to as being distinctively human. A self does not qualify as a self on the basis of its natural functions.

A common biological heritage has, by defining the human life in terms of a familiar set of problems, set constraints on the degree of difference evidenced by cultures and the semiotics that articulate them. But even at the biological level, there is good reason to proceed with caution when assuming the existence of some universal and unchanging predicament. As Steven Collins observes:[38]

> technological changes in biochemistry—notably in test tubes— might introduce novelty even here. Similarly, the use of speech for human communication, mutual identification and cooperation could perhaps also be construed as a basic predicament. But again, technological changes—in the past the transition from oral to written culture, in the future possible transformations of informal technology—might cause "categorial changes" in language-using human organisms. . . . [We] should beware the too-easy identification of bio-social universals.

Model 4: Part of the Whole as Self

The fourth model constructed to explain the Confucian self that I want to critique originates itself as a challenge to the kinds of explanations we have encountered above, especially what I have called the "autonomous individual." Chad Hansen claims that philosophical Chinese has a part-whole structure rather than a one-many structure. Allowing Hansen to speak for himself:

The difference is that in one-many structures, the units are treated as interchangeable, fixed in "size," and only externally related. Thus, with individuals comes the notion of a fixed unit—the atom, the quark, the person, the U.N. member, and so forth. To increase the scope of reference we increase the number of units or individuals. . . . The contrast between Western languages and Chinese can be explained by focusing on how individuation is related to the notion of thing-kind. Built into English count nouns is a single principle of individuation. We treat that kind of thing as having natural, fixed, and functionally similar individuals.[39]

Hansen sets up a contrast here between our one-of-a-*kind* individual—the autonomous individuality described above—and our unique *one-of-a-kind* individual. What we have called "unique individuality" he describes in the following terms:

Parts, by contrast, are of variable size. Some parts may be parts of parts. One can refer to more and less inclusive parts of the same whole. A finger is part of a person. So is a hand, an arm, a trunk. Mereological sets—sets which consist of, rather than contain, their members—are part-whole systems. . . . In the Chinese case, both the parts and the wholes are concrete—the general is also the concrete. In speaking, we tend to assimilate "concrete" and "particular" as well as "abstract" and "universal." . . . The Chinese part-whole contrast is, on the other hand, on just one level (by hypothesis, nonabstract). . . . For the Chinese writer, then, the world need not be presented as sets of interchangeable objects (substance or particulars) which instantiate properties. It can be structured on part-whole distinctions which are variable. Parts have no given "basic" configuration—no single, inherent principle of individuation. What counts as a part in a part-whole explanation is relative to the context.[40]

I cite Hansen at length here because a critique of his position will help identify elements in the construction of my own model.

One ironical aside here is that if we want to identify uniqueness as *the* defining characteristic of "individuality," it can be argued that the Chinese come out far more individualistic than the Western one-many model. In the part-whole model, all parts are concrete and *one* of a kind; in the one-many model they are each categorially kinds of things—human beings with defining essences—and on that basis, are interchangeable. In the Chinese case, however, the fundamental "uniqueness" of each person is tempered by the degree to which the weight of a shared cultural tradition is, through patterns of deference, constitutive of each member of the community.

In evaluating the adequacy of Hansen's part-whole model, the first criticism would be that this assumes the existence of a "whole" that makes the "part" in some sense instrumental or subordinate in its relationship to the meaning of the whole. Along the lines of an Augustinian "aesthetic argument," the constitutive piece in the jigsaw puzzle achieves its meaning from the meaning of the whole. The whole is greater than its parts. The alternative, then, is "just parts"—each of them a perspective on the amorphous field of parts to which they belong, where each part is also its whole. In this reading, you have as many wholes as parts, but no single whole.

Second, the part-whole model gives an integrity to the part that is perhaps misleading. "Partness" can alternatively be focal and elastic—merely one specific and contingent interpretation among many possibilities. Given that each part also has its whole, the wholes are also specific and contingent.

Third, the part-whole model does not do justice to the intrinsic relatedness of the particulars—the sense that in each particular "focuses" all particulars, that each particular requires every other for its explanation and sustenance.

Fourth, the part-whole model, by suggesting that the whole is bounded and complete, establishes a nonpart perspective from which the parts can be entertained. Even where the parts are contingent, the single whole is itself necessary. It thus limits creativity in a way that is inconsistent with the notion of autogeneration (*tzu-jan* 自然). Neither synchronic nor diachronic "wholeness" is consistent with a tradition in which the cosmogonic is inoperative.

Fifth, Hansen misses the equivocation in the way in which "abstract" applies to his own model. The familiar formal abstraction is the abstraction of certain univocal qualities from two or more particulars that qualify them as members of a set. It is the expression of the quality in the absence of any particular object. The less obvious sense of abstraction involves isolating one part from the whole to which it belongs. Hansen's "finger, hand, arm, trunk" are selective abstractions from a concrete body. Formal abstraction involves abstraction from actuality; selective abstraction involves abstraction from possibility. Neither formal nor selective abstraction yields a complete meaning.

Finally, in calling this a "part-whole *system*" (emphasis mine), Hansen assumes an underlying and ordering principle that precludes in the same degree intrinsic relatedness. "System," at least in common parlance, presupposes unity and, hence, univocality. A system is a universe. Of course, the absence of system in this sense does not preclude a particular coherence and regularity, as it is construed from the perspective of each part.

Model 5: Self as Focus and Field in a Focus-field Model

As I have noted above, the Chinese assumption is that personal, societal, and political order are coterminous and mutually entailing. One method of outlining the focus-field model of self, then, is to follow Plato in using the analogy of political order to describe the articulation of the particular person.

The first volume of the *Cambridge History of China* describes the career of the Han empire from its emergence under Liu Pang to its gradual disintegration three and a half centuries later.[41] In this volume, Yü Ying-shih uses the "five zones" (*wu-fu* 五服) of submission as a device for describing the dynamics of the Han world order:

> According to this theory, China since the Hsia dynasty had been divided into five concentric and hierarchical zones or areas. The central zone (*tien-fu* 甸服) was the royal domain, under the direct rule of the king. The royal domain was immediately surrounded by the Chinese states established by the king, known collectively as the lords' zone (*hou-fu* 侯服). Beyond the *hou-fu* were Chinese states conquered by the reigning dynasty, which constituted the so-called pacified zone (*sui-fu* 綏服 or *pin-fu* 賓服, guest zone). The last two zones were reserved for the barbarians. The Man and I barbarians lived outside the *sui-fu* or *pin-fu* in the controlled zone (*yao-fu* 要服), which was so called because the Man and I were supposedly subject to Chinese control, albeit of a rather loose kind. Finally, beyond the controlled zone lay the Jung and Ti barbarians, who were basically their own masters in the wild zone (*huang-fu* 荒服) where the sinocentric world order reached its natural end.[42]

This hierarchical scheme also describes the descending degree of tribute—local products and services—provided to the court at the center. Although this five zone theory seems more complex, it is really a distinction that defines the relative focus of an "inner-outer (*nei-wai* 內外)" circle:

> China was the inner region relative to the outer region of the barbarians, just as the royal domain was, relative to the outer

lords' zone, an inner zone, and the controlled zone became the inner area relative to the wild zone on the periphery of Chinese civilization.[43]

This solar system of a centripetal harmony with patterns of deference articulating a central focus seems pervasive in Chinese society. These concrete, functioning patterns of deference "contribute" in varying degrees and are constitutive of the authority at the center, shaping and bringing into focus the character of the social and political entity—its standards and values. This determinate, detailed, "center-seeking" focus fades off into an increasingly indeterminate and untextured field. The attraction of the center is such that, with varying degrees of success, it draws into its field and suspends the disparate and diverse centers that constitute its world. The dynamic tension that obtains among these various centers articulates and inscribes the Han character. Importantly, the quality of these suspended centers are constitutive of the harmony of the field.

This sense of order in which all of the diversity and difference characteristic of the multiple, competing centers of the Warring States period are lifted into the harmony of the Han dynasty translates readily into intellectual world. The intellectual geography of the Hundred Schools in the pre-Ch'in period gives way to a syncretic Confucianism-centered doctrine that absorbs into itself and to some degree conceals the richness of what were competing elements to articulate the philosophical character of the period. This shift is better expressed in the language of incorporation and accommodation than of suppression.

As the centripetal center weakens in the second century A.D. and as the political order gradually dissolves into a period of disunity, the disparate centers precipitate out of the harmony to reassert themselves, and what was their contribution to the now-weakened center becomes the energy of contest. What was a tightening spire in the early Han becomes a gyre, disgorging itself of its disassociated contents. In the same period, there is a resurgence and interplay of competing philosophical schools and religious movements that reflect a disintegration of the centrally driven intellectual harmony.

Reflection, I believe, would persuade us that this focus-field notion of order is precisely that captured in the fundamental Confucian concept of ritually ordered community, where ritual (*li* 禮), defined at the center by the authority of the tradition, not only demands personalization and participation but, further, is always reflective of the quality of its participants. Similarly, the extent to which a "zone" is active or passive with respect to configuring order is a function of its own distinctive achievement and the quality of its contribution. In fact, in the language of this tradition, the meaning of ritually ordered community itself is made literal from the image of *she-hui* 社會 : "a deferential assembly gathering around the sacred pole erected in the center of the community." Nishijima Sadao tells us:

> Such community life, based on the hamlet, had its religious center in the altar (*she* 社) where the local deity was enshrined. In the same way there was an altar for the state community (*kuo-she* 國社), and each county and district also had its own altar. The religious festivals which took place at the hamlet altar (*li-she* 里社), at which meat was distributed to the participants, helped to strengthen the community spirit.[44]

Above we have employed the Han court analogy as a means of articulating the Confucian self as a "field of selves," but then the court analogy is itself derived from the all-pervasive family model. The "family" as the Chinese model of order is a variation on this notion of a graduated, centripetal harmony. Ambrose King argues persuasively that in the Chinese world, all relationships are familial:

> Among the five cardinal relations, three belong to the kinship realm. The remaining two, though not family relationships, are conceived in terms of the family. The relationship between the ruler and the ruled is conceived of in terms of father (*chün-fu* 君父) and son (*tzu-min* 子民), and the relationship between friend and friend is stated in terms of elder brother (*wu-hsiung* 吾兄) and younger brother (*wu-ti* 吾弟).[45]

The family as the "in-group," is determinate and focused at the center, but becomes increasingly vague as it stretches out both diachronically in the direction of one's lineage and synchronically as a society full of "uncles" and "aunties." It is articulated in terms of *lun* 倫, a ritual "wheel" (*lun* 輪) of social relations that "ripple out" (*lun* 淪) in a field of discourse (*lun* 論) to define the person as a network of roles. King's critique on this model is insightful:

> What must be emphasized here is that while Confucian ethics teach how the individual should be related to other particular roles through the proper *lun*, the issue of how the individual should be related to the "group" is not closely examined. In other words, the individual's behavior is supposed to be *lun*-oriented; the *lun*-oriented role relations, however, are seen as personal, concrete, and particularistic in nature.[46]

While King's insistence that the Confucian model of self is constructed in concrete, particular, and differentiated relationships between self and "other" is certainly on the mark, this allowedly parochial self is not entirely devoid of a sense of group. We must give King the observation that the concreteness and immediacy of one's own definition is, like graduated love, necessitated by the unwillingness in this tradition to disengage the theoretical from experience. A role is not something you "are" but something you "do." But King goes too far in suggesting that the self's sense of group is so vague as to preclude the possibility of a broader civil ethic. He states:

> It seems to me that Confucian social ethics has failed to provide a "viable linkage" between the individual and *ch'ün* 群 , the non-familistic group. The root of the Confucian *Problematik* lies in the fact that the boundary between the self and the group has not been conceptually articulated.[47]

King, in missing the link, echoes Bertrand Russell's reservations about the weight given to family relations in the Chinese world:

> Filial piety, and the strength of the family generally, are perhaps the weakest point in Confucian ethics, the only point where the system departs seriously from common sense. Family feeling has militated against public spirit, and the authority of the old has increased the tyranny of ancient custom. . . . In this respect, as in certain others, what is peculiar to China is the preservation of the old custom after a very high level of civilization had been attained.[48]

The link that both King and Russell overlook here is that although the family, the society, the state, and even the tradition itself, as the extended "group" or "field," is indeed ambiguous *as a group or field*, the vagueness of the abstract nexus is focused and made immediate in the embodiment of the group or field by the particular father, the social exemplar, the ruler, and the historical model. The meaning of the group is made present in my father, my teacher, Mao Tse-tung, and Confucius. Each *lun* as the focus and articulation of a particular field of roles is holographic in that it construes its own field. Although the concreteness and immediacy of the centripetal center precludes any but the vaguest and indeterminate definitions of "Chineseness," this notion comes alive *to me* in the image of a Tseng Kuo-fan or a Yang Yu-wei.[49] The totality is nothing more than the full range of particular foci, each focus defining itself and its own particular field.[50]

A final foray. And here I return to the Fingarette engagement earlier in this discussion. We really must question the appropriateness of using "concept" language to discuss the Confucian self. Concept belongs to the one-many model, where "self" can be understood as having some univocal and hence formal definition—it reifies or entifies self as an ego or an ideal. Concept is dependent upon formal abstraction. Given the dependency of the Confucian model on the particular image, then, we might have to allow that the Confucian self is precisely that particular and detailed portrait of Confucius found in the middle books of the *Analects*, where each passage is a remembered detail contributed by one of the disciples who belonged to the conversation. And this portrait, as it attracts more disciples and plays a role in shaping unique self-images in the tradition, does the work of concept.

In our *Thinking Through Confucius*, David L. Hall and I argue for the dominance of what we call an "aesthetic" order as the signature of the Confucian sensibility. It is this aesthetic sensibility that demands the particular detail and precludes the definition of self in abstract terms. It is not unexpected, then, that Rudolf Arnheim, in his reflections on the visual arts, provides us with a useful vocabulary for exploring the Confucian model of order. Arnheim is persuaded that the nature of composition in the visual arts reflects an underlying cosmological tendency: "Cosmically, we find that matter organizes around centers, which are often marked by a dominant mass. Such systems come about whenever their neighbors allow them sufficient freedom."[51] This phenomenon, observes Arnheim, is true of both the vast astronomical space and the microscopic realm. The center that is so constituted is "the center of a field of forces, a focus from which forces issue and towards which forces converge."[52] These centers, then, relate to each other as a calculus of centers, which, from their interplay, produce a balancing centripetal center, which tends to distribute the forces of its field symmetrically around its own center:

> Overcoming the egocentric view amounts to realizing that a center is not always in the middle. . . . More often, the environment is dominated by other centers, which force the self into a subordinate position. . . . Speaking generally, one can assert that every visual field comprises a number of centers, each of which attempts to draw the others into subservience. The self as viewer is just one of these centers. . . . The overall balance of all these competing aspirations determines the structure of the whole, and that total structure is organized around what I will call the balancing center.

The notion of composition that Arnheim is elaborating here describes abstractly the composition of the Confucian self and the various foci that define that world. But the clearest expression of this Confucian self is not abstract or theoretical. It is available only at the interface between the inspirational biographies and models that define a particular cultural tradition and the unique individuals that populate any particular historical moment.

NOTES

1. See Arthur Danto, "Postscript: Philosophical Individualism in Chinese and Western Though," in *Individualism and Holism: Studies in Confucian and Taoist Values*, ed. Donald Munro (Ann Arbor: University of Michigan Press, 1985), 385.

2. *Analects*, 7.8.

3. F. Hegel, *Philosophy of History*, trans. J. Sibree (Reprint, New York: Dover, 1956), 111–12.

4. Donald J. Munro, "The Shape of Chinese Values in the Eye of an American Philosopher," in *The China Difference*, ed. Ross Terrill (New York: Harper & Row, 1979), 40.

5. See R. Randle Edwards, "Civil and Social Rights: Theory and Practice in Chinese Law Today," in *Human Rights in Contemporary China*, ed. R. Randle Edwards, Louis Henkin, and Andrew J. Nathan (New York: Columbia University Press, 1986), 44. This position is widely held. Cf. Louis Henkin, "The Human Rights Idea in Contemporary China: A Comparative Perspective" in ibid., 39 and Andrew J. Nathan, "Sources of Chinese Rights Thinking," in ibid., 141–47.

6. See Mark Elvin's article, "Between the Earth and Heaven: Conceptions of the Self in China," in *The Category of the Person: Anthropology, Philosophy, History,* ed. Michael Carrithers, Steven Collins, and Steven Lukes (Cambridge: Cambridge University Press, 1985), 185.

7. C. K. Yang, *Chinese Communist Society: The Family and the Village* (Cambridge: MIT Press, 1959), 172.

8. See *Analects*, 6.30, and the *Ta-hsüeh* as the classic statement for this coextensive relationship.

9. See William Theodore de Bary, "Neo-Confucian Individualism and Holism," in *Individualism and Holism*, ed. Donald J. Munro (Ann Arbor: University of Michigan Press, 1985), 332.

10. See *Analects*, 12.1: "Authoritative humanity proceeds from oneself —how could it come from others."

11. Munro, "Shape," 41.

12. Tu Wei-ming, "Confucianism: Symbol and Substance in Recent Times" in *Value Change in Chinese Society*, ed. R. W. Wilson, A. A. Wilson, and S. L. Greenblatt (New York: Praeger, 1979), 46.

13. See *Analects*, 12.17. See also 13.6, 13.13.

14. Ibid., 8.13, 15.17.

15. Ibid., 1.2, 2.21.

16. Ambrose Y. C. King, a sociologist, makes this point in his paper "The Individual and Group in Confucianism: A Relational Perspective," in *Individualism and Holism: Studies in Confucian and Taoist Values*, ed. Donald Munro (Ann Arbor: University of Michigan Press, 1985), 58.

17. In describing this "people-as-root" rhetoric, Nathan discounts any association between it and the sovereignty of the people, regarding it rather as a passive people being served by benign rulers. See Nathan, "Sources of Chinese Rights Thinking," 150–51. Traditionally, however, there was a great emphasis placed on the education of the rulers and officialdom to insure that those in positions of authority were enculturated in the norms of conduct and values derived broadly from the popular experience.

18. See Victor H. Li, *Law Without Lawyers* (Boulder: Westview Press, 1978), esp. chap. 4.

19. Munro, Introduction to *Individualism and Holism*, 2.

20. Marcel Mauss, "A Category of the Human Mind: The Notion of Person, the Notion of Self," trans. W. D. Halls, in *The Category of the Person: Anthropology, Philosophy, History,* ed. Michael Carrithers, Steven Collins, and Steven Lukes (Cambridge: Cambridge University Press), 20–22.

21. Elvin, "Between the Earth and Heaven," 170.

22. See Roger T. Ames "Reflections on the Confucian Self: A Response to Fingarette," in *Rules, Rituals, and Responsibility: Essays Dedicated to Herbert Fingarette,* ed. Mary I. Bockover (La Salle, Ill.: Open Court, 1991).

23. Herbert Fingarette, "The Problem of the Self in the *Analects*" *Philosophy East and West* 29, no. 2 (April 1979), 131.

24. Ibid., 130.

25. Ibid., 133.

26. Ibid., 135.

27. Ibid., 136.

28. In fairness to Fingarette, one should note that he does qualify this position, using the distance between a musical score and a personal performance of it as an analogy for the distance between the *tao* concept and the particular manifestation of it. See ibid., 137.

29. See Herbert Fingarette's response in *Rules, Rituals, and Responsibility: Essays Dedicated to Herbert Fingarette*, ed. Mary I. Bockover (La Salle, Ill.: Open Court, 1991), 194–200.

30. Ibid., 198–99.

31. Joseph Needham, *Science and Civilisation in China*, vol. 2 (Cambridge: Cambridge University Press, 1954–), 18–26.

32. See Jonathan Barnes, *Early Greek Philosophy* (London: Penguin, 1987), for a discussion of the cosmological vocabulary of the classical Greeks.

33. See *Mencius*, 4B.19.

34. See *Analects*, 18.6, which needs to be qualified with 5.10, 4.25, 4.3, and so on.

35. Angus Graham, "The Background of the Mencian Theory of Human Nature," in *Studies in Chinese Philosophy and Philosophical Literature* (Albany: State University of New York Press, 1990), 43.

36. *Analects*, 14.42.

37. *Mencius*, 7A.1, 7B.32.

38. See Steven Collins in "Categories, Concepts or Predicaments? Remarks on Mauss's Use of Philosophical Terminology" in *The Category of the Person: Anthropology, Philosophy, History,* ed. Michael Carrithers, Steven Collins, and Steven Lukes (Cambridge: Cambridge University Press, 1985), 73.

39. Chad Hansen, "Individualism in Chinese Thought," in Munro, *Individualism and Holism*, 36, 41.

40. Ibid., 36–37, 41–42.

41. Denis Twitchett and Michael Loewe, eds. *The Cambridge History of China,* (Cambridge: Cambridge University Press, 1986), vol. 1, *The Ch'in and Han Empires 221 b.c.–a.d. 220.*

42. Yü Ying-shih, "Han foreign relation," in ibid, 379–80.

43. Ibid., 382.

44. Nishijima Sadao, "The Economic and Social History of Former Han," in ibid, 522.

45. King, "Individual and Group," 58.

46. Ibid., 62.

47. Ibid., 62.

48. Bertrand Russell, *The Problem of China* (London: George Allen & Unwin, 1922), 40.

49. Yang Yu-wei is my teacher and has taught my best students from his grotto in Taipei.

50. This model of centripetal harmony is pervasive in the defining literature of the Chinese tradition. It explains Mencius's point in claiming that "all of the myriad things are complete here in me" and "one who applies exhaustively his heart-and-mind realizes his character, and in thus realizing his character, he realizes his field [*t'ien* 天]." *Mencius*, 7A.4, 7A.1. Again, it describes the relationship between the fields (*tao* 道) and foci (*te* 德) that we are familiar with from the Taoist cosmology. It is also the vision of the Hua-yen notion of *shih-shih wu ai* 事事無礙—a field of interpenetrating particulars in which each construes its own field.

51. Rudolf Arnheim, *The Power of the Center: A Study in the Visual Arts* (Berkeley and Los Angeles: University of California Press, 1982), vii.

52. Ibid., 2.

53. Ibid., 5.

9

To Be or Not to Be: The Postmodern Self and the Wu-*Forms of Taoism*

David L. Hall

Our Interlexical Age

A sensible approach for anyone who seeks the precise meaning of a controversial term is to begin with the dictionary. Sometimes, of course, this exercise may be futile, owing to the presence in one's lexicon of such an array of meanings as to confound rather than clarify. One of the notorious terms whose principal meanings hide in the interstices of its myriad senses is the word *culture*.

One despairs in the face of the complexity presented by even a modestly comprehensive dictionary entry for *culture*. After all, a dictionary has value only to the extent that the denotative sense is not swallowed up by disparate connotations. One may discover no appropriate dictionary sense of a word such as *culture* if the important meanings increasingly depend upon specific contexts of application as yet unregistered by the dictionary. In such a case, novel connotations threaten to outrun the denotative significance which grounds the dictionary sense.

Another troublesome word, as a recent excursion through the relevant citations of the *Oxford English Dictionary* has shown me, is *self*. A perusal of its laundry list of meanings demonstrates that the *self* entry (if one includes the various reflex terms—*self-love, self-abnegation, self-interest, self-denial, self-affirmation,* and so forth) is among the more diversified and incoherent of *OED* entries.

We gain nothing by searching out the origins of the term, for, as we are darkly told at the beginning of the entry, the etymology of *self* is "obscure." Of course, it is unlikely that the obscure origin of *self* is

213

responsible for its dictionary entry reading like Borges' version of the Chinese encyclopedia entry for "animal". The reasons are far more likely associated with the history of the concept and its referents, whose philosophical transmutations over time are in part due to the transmogrifications of the notions of 'soul', 'person', 'individual', 'human being', 'citizen', and allied terms.

As a philosopher of culture called to reflect upon the meaning of self, it does appear, therefore, that I am twice damned by the limitations of the dictionary. If we survey the fate of the notion of the self within the context named by the term *culture*, we soon recognize that because the sense of culture is as problematic as that of self, we cannot easily construe the meaning of the latter in terms of the former. Since, however, any coherent concept of self presupposes some coherent sense of culture, it would appear that we certainly should proceed to characterize the one in terms of the other. The process, however, leads us to many equally viable senses of self that entail the existence of incoherent notions of cultural context.

We must, then, accede to the fact that any resort to dictionaries to uncover the meaning of the self and its culture will offer us but little comfort. Fortunately, however, we are not limited to the use of a dictionary by reference to its internal entries. Therefore, I shall urge that, instead of using a dictionary to search for the meaning of our problematic term, we should first ask after *the meaning of the dictionary itself*. This question certainly cannot be answered in any trustworthy manner by recourse to a dictionary. We must ask for the metalexical meaning of "dictionary." And this is a question for the philosopher of culture.

My claim is that a more relevant employment of the dictionary with respect to the topic I am seeking to unravel is as a *metaphorical* rather than as a *literal* standard. I would contend that, in our contemporary situation, the dictionary as metaphor provides the appropriate standard for the interpretation of both self and culture and of the relations of the two.

Historical ages, or cultural epochs—indeed, culture itself—may be defined by attitudes toward the dictionary. There are periods characterized by the *creation* of dictionaries and those content with the consultation and emendation of them. At the beginning of the Enlightenment, for example, *philosophes* were intent upon the gathering and appropriate classification of the new knowledge; subsequently, over a much longer stretch of time, modern cultural activity has largely depended upon the consultation and emendation of those dictionaries. The latter phases of modernity are outworkings of the recorded insights of its beginnings.

Transitional periods in a culture are signaled by the collapse of dictionaries. The dictionary crumbles at both ends. On the one hand, words begin to dissolve into their etymologies; on the other, they are ramified by their myriad textual associations. The pretextual and intertextual loci of the meanings of important terms renders the dictionary a problematic resource. Things fall apart.

Where are we, where does our present age stand with respect to the "dictionary question"? I would argue that we are neither creators nor emenders of dictionaries. Indeed, as "postmoderns" we conceive ourselves to be "postlexical" or "interlexical." We are beyond the comforts of the dictionary. To think of ours as an interlexical age is to grasp the sense in which meaning lies both outside or beyond any dictionary or, to say much the same thing, in the interstices among the meanings listed seriatim in a dictionary. Whether we are but temporarily without the standard of the dictionary or shall ultimately find a place that permits us to survive without that resource is currently a question of some rather agitated debate.

We who live in an interlexical age no longer define ourselves by recourse to the dictionary as meaning resource. We no longer feel ourselves enjoined to arrive a univocal definition of the principal notions we employ in achieving cultural self-consciousness. We are equally prevented, however, from taking the easy way out by celebrating the complex relativities of meaning associated with these notions. The chief aim of the dictionary—that of including alternative meanings in order to permit the selection of the best definition relative to context—has been subverted in favor of the recognition that all of our interpretative categories are, in fact, "cluster concepts." By the term "cluster concept" I mean to indicate a complex of associations that can neither be reduced to a coherent or internally consistent meaning nor seen individually in their respective context-relative meanings. A cluster concept is a permanently ambiguous notion.

As an example of such a concept, consider the word *freedom*. What does that notion *mean*? This question is hardly a dispassionate, detached query since, in the United States of America, we hold "freedom" to be a precious possession, whose benefits are essential to our condition as citizens. Yet we seem to mean a great deal more by the term than we can in fact *logically* mean.

Freedom certainly means, to those of us who share the liberal democratic heritage, "free choice amidst limiting circumstances." But, in addition—and *at the same time*—it means a host of other things: the knowledge that breaks the bonds of ignorance ("You shall know the truth, and the truth will set you free"), the power to effect one's will, to guide or alter events by rational (read *rhetorical*) suasion. Finally, for our purposes (though the list is certainly much longer), freedom carries the paradoxical meaning, "freedom from responsibility," in the sense that one may feel determined by circumstances and thus free from accountability.

One is tempted to say, Well, freedom can't mean all these things. Which is the *correct* view? Not only is there no consensus as to the correct view, most of us are quite content to hold these divergent notions together in a single, gloriously inconsistent notion. With every use of the term *freedom*, we are as likely as not to express the entire cluster of associations, unaware of the logical tensions among the variant meanings. Freedom is a cluster concept.

I will argue that self is a cluster concept, as well. In our interlexical age, searching out the sense of self, therefore, means escaping the boundaries of the dictionary and moving among the uncollected, initially uncoordinated sense of things. We can evoke a viable sense of self only by calling together the relevant connotations that own their meanings by virtue of a complex of associations that, as a cluster, may very well lack any logical or semantic coherence.

What *meaning* can a cluster have if the semantic elements are mutually inconsistent and yet in some complicated manner may be shown to possess their meaning by virtue of the clustering process? We can answer this question only by "redefining" the meaning of "connotative sense." For even terms characterized by recourse to a cluster indifferent to the question of logical coordination are, nonetheless, contextually defined.

Such "definitions" must result from aesthetic juxtapositions that highlight the tensions of contrasting and conflicting referential associations against the background of an aesthetically complex, if logically inconsistent, context. Our understanding of such terms would have to be closer to the experience of "enjoyment" and "appreciation" than to that of an act of grasping cognizable import.

Language betrays one attempting to speak in this fashion. I certainly do not wish to imply that the understanding or appreciation of the meaning of cluster concepts entails the existence of a coherent agent of appreciation or understanding. Indeed, the basic impulse of my argument leads to the conclusion that self, above all, is a cluster concept. The only hope of accommodating the incoherence, incongruence, and inconsistencies embedded in cluster concepts is that the self appropriating these notions must be of the same flexible form as the notions themselves. Aristotle's doctrine remains intact: There is a real sense in which we become that which we know.

I have not spent these pages speculating upon the fate of the dictionary merely as a means of easing my audience into an arcane subject. On the contrary, I hope to show that much can be learned about the self and its present circumstances by understanding the status of the dictionary. This status is in fact a symptom of the fate of the notion of self in our late modern culture. I shall demonstrate this claim straightaway by looking now at the extremely problematic history of that notion.

Self, Culture, and History

If we are to avoid serious anachronism in the discussions of the subject of the self we must acknowledge that self, in the most meaningful sense, already involves consciousness. Without articulate self-consciousness, there is no self. In the strictest sense of self—namely, as self-conscious—self is a modern invention, since modernity is the place of the discovery of subjective consciousness.

Of course, the less stringent sense of self, as "agent" or "knower" who acts or understands in the outer world of things and events, has a much older origin. It would appear that one may with plausibility trace the *historical* origins of the concept of the self within Anglo-European culture. The historical contingency of self provides some evidence for the culture-bound character of the concept. The self is accidental, in the sense that it is not a necessary product of the chronological development of any particular cultural milieu. This claim is underwritten by the fact that the articulated notion of self, in anything like our contemporary senses of the term, is demonstrably absent from some cultural milieus.

I have argued in other contexts that our cultural self-understanding depends upon the recognition that ours is a tradition based upon the cosmogonic motivation of construing order from out of chaos.[1] One best tells the story of our cultural development by indicating the specific manner in which our cosmogonic tradition articulated the cultural significances we have drawn upon to establish the meanings not only of self but also of the notions of God, Nature, Power, Law, and so forth.

With respect to the sense of self, one finds a fairly coherent notion beginning with the philosophic syntheses of late Greek antiquity. Plato's recognition of the analogical relationship between *psyche* and *polis* was based upon a long history of the articulation of the relationships between the person and context that establishes a pattern of historical permutations of the understanding of the self. The self came into being *pari passu* with social and cultural organization.

It is a truism of the interpretation of ancient Greek culture that the analogy established between *kosmos* and *polis* had its origins in the sense of *kosmos* as referenced to social and political structures. The verb *kosmeo* (to set in order) was used in a number of quite ordinary contexts from household to military before it came, as a noun, to be used by Pythagoras as a characterization of the natural world. *Kosmos*—"World"—came into being modeled, as it were, upon social organization. The cosmos is the *polis* writ large, just as the *polis* is the soul writ large.

The analogical relationships among *psyche*, *polis*, and *kosmos* are exploited in the mature phases of Greek philosophy to develop the general structures of aesthetic, political, ethical, and metaphysical understandings. The same process is more obvious, of course, with respect to the cosmological employment of the concept of *dike*, "justice," which was a term of art in the courts before Anaximander applied the notion to the interaction of opposites within the Boundless (*to apeiron*).

In the discussion of putatively "naturalistic" concepts, therefore, one does well to seek a social and cultural ground for the tools permitting their articulation. This principle certainly must be applied to any consideration of the meaning of self within the Western tradition. *Psyche* developed in Plato as a tripartite structure owning the functions of spirit (*thymos*), appetite (*epithymia*), and reason (*nous*). These notions were manifest in conventional contexts associated with disparate and uncoordinated human activities and expressions and only later came to have what was held to be an essentialistic reference to psychic structure. Aristotle used these same notions in his organization of the disciplines: theoretical (*theoria*), practical (*praxis*), productive (*techne*).

This structure is adumbrated already in the senses of person or individual suggested by the Homeric texts. The terms Homer used to refer to the essential, living aspect of the individual human being were variously *psyche*, *noos*, and *thymos*. Construed as functions, these elements express the characteristics of "life, perception and (e)motion."[2] There is in the beginning no reason to posit a self-conscious being aware of its various functionally specialized potentialities.

One of the most telling developments in the creation of a coherent conception of self comes about with the transition from the Greek to the Judeo-Christian cultural context. It is arguably the case that until Augustine's ruminations upon the soul's relationship to God, the notion of will (*voluntas*) was not a part of the conception of the personality.[3] The notion of "will," after all, requires a sense of "over againstness," which derives from a central power—God or Divine Caesar—who embodies or instantiates absolute authority. Another way of saying this is that to own *intention* one must be *in tension* in a significant manner.

I have said enough, I believe, to demonstrate the plausibility of the thesis that, from the sense of a chaotic matrix of shifting uncoordinated and unintegrated vital functions to the expression of the tripartite structure in Plato and Aristotle to the final articulations of the three modes of functioning as reason, passion, and will, there was an obvious and traceable historical transition in which the circumstances of the Greek, Roman, and Judaic elements of Anglo-European cultural traditions contributed the contingent factors that eventuated in the modern conception of the self.

This brief rehearsal of the notion of *psyche* from the ancient Greeks to the present suggests that the modern conception of the self is dependent upon the modalities of knowing, acting, and feeling associated with the development of human personality in the Anglo-European culture. We find more than echoes of this psychic structure in Kant's critiques of the value spheres of the aesthetic, moral, and rational and in Hegel's dialectical analysis of consciousness, as well as in Freud's psychoanalytic categories of ego, superego, id.

Whatever permutations of the self one might wish to highlight, the three general notions expressed by terms such as *knowing*, *acting*, and *feeling* will be involved at some level. No coherent or adequate analysis of these terms is possible, of course, for the reason alluded to at the beginning of this essay. There have been too many theoretical proposals made with respect to these modalities of psychic activity to make any analysis either possible or desirable. Nonetheless, a general analysis will serve to provide a background against which we might more fruitfully discuss the fragmentation of the modern self and the postmodern celebration of that fragmentation.

Knowledge has resort to concepts or principles involving class concepts that cannot but deny the idiosyncratic character of particulars. Whether knowing is said to precede or to be consequent upon praxis, it has, nonetheless, a shaping character, since the practical forms of construing the world are but reflections of the theoretical forms of shaping antecedent chaos in terms of the structures of mythopoetically described cosmos. The first philosophic question—the question to which *physis* (Latin, *natura*) was the answer is, What kinds of things are there? Understanding the world in terms of a *kind* or *kinds* of things is the paradigmatic expression of knowledge in our tradition.

"Action" has its origins in the heroic model of the *agon* (contest), which involves the assertion of an agent of such quality or magnitude as to certify either the agent's superior strength or courage in the face of the strength of an other. This model derives from the Homeric tradition and continues to serve as one of the crucial interpretations of action in our tradition. An alternative, paradigmatically expressed by

St. Augustine in the fifth century of the common era, involves obedience to the all-powerful will of God. The elements of *greatness* and *humility*, or excellence and deference, define the modalities of human action. In either case there is the notion of assertion, be it that of the hero or the divine agent.

The Greek concept of *agon*, which defined the context for the heroic notion of the individual, did not provide a stable, continuous focus of authority in tension with which the notion of will could be established. That notion, as I noted above, did not originate in our tradition until action was interpreted in relation to an authoritative divine will. Modernity, then, charts the detachment of that notion from its theological context and the association of action with the volition of autonomous human beings.

The element of "feeling" is more diffuse in its signification than the other two modes of psychic expression. Perhaps it is best focused by the notion of "desire." The difficulty in understanding the mode of desiring lies in a failure to grasp the psychological underpinnings of the mode. Desiring is a wanting and, as the ambiguous word "want" suggests, it is predicated upon a lack. When Plato defined desire (*eros*) as the "stepchild of abundance and need," he captured the essentials of passion. Absence of the desired object leads to desire; its presence or possession—ostensibly the goal of desiring—mitigates or cancels the desire. We want what we do not, perhaps *cannot*, have.

One of the serious problems associated with the element of desiring concerns the contradiction between the need to possess a desired object and the even more primordial need to create an *object* out of that which is desired. The poignancy of desire is that in objectifying the goal of our desiring we cancel the desire. This self-contradictory character of desiring is, of course, a major theme in most Buddhist and some Western psychologies.

This broad survey of the contextualization of the self from out of the classical cultural resources highlights the elements which the Age of Enlightenment will take up in its effort to build the subjective autonomy and rational self-consciousness of the modern self. For we do not have a real concept of the self until we arrive at subjective, self-conscious experience as the principal mode of self-interpretation. This is, as I have said, a peculiarly modern occurrence.

The Modern Self

The easiest way to tell the story of the strictly modern self is by rehearsing the reading Hegel provided of Immanuel Kant's philosophic program.[4] According to Hegel, Kant's three critiques were in fact conscious attempts to ground the autonomy of the value spheres of art, science, and morality. Taking the analogy from Plato, Kant recognized that reason, passion, and (in the post-Augustinian age) will as modalities of human experience were focused by the cultural interests of science, art, and morality. The three critiques provided an account of the nature and limits of rational inquiry vis-à-vis the investigation of intellectual and practical culture.

Hegel claimed, however, that Kant was not sufficiently aware of the threat to the cultural autonomy of the value spheres and it was his—Hegel's—mission to provide a philosophic rationale for the protection of these individual and cultural interests. Hegel's speculative system rehearsed in the most complete form the means of coming to cultural self-consciousness. With the advent of this exercise in cultural self-articulation—that is, the mediation through cultural forms of the various modalities of self expression—the modern self, at least in principle, realized its apotheosis.

It was certainly the case that the modern world had already manifested other agents of self-interpretation. Descartes is often singled out as the first truly *modern* philosopher, by virtue of his discovery of rational subjectivity; Francis Bacon may be said to provide a supplement to Descartes's project through the invention of the self as assertive agent, as a shepherd of technological progress. David Hume found in the passions of pride and envy, love and hate, the source of self-awareness and the meaning of individuality. Baudelaire, ringing the aesthetic variation of Hume's economic interpretation stressed the creative, novelty-seeking artist as the paradigm of selfhood. And so forth.

These thinkers could easily be understood as having stressed in their theories the importance to self-understanding of the elements of reason, volition, and passion respectively. But there is a sense in which, the obvious limitations of Hegelian philosophy to the contrary notwithstanding, the full conscious recognition of the complexity of the self is a post-Hegelian phenomenon that depends in some skewed manner upon the grandiosity of the Hegelian project.

The Fragmentation of the Modern Self

I have been presupposing throughout this essay that one may be a self in some inchoate sense without *having* a self. Being a self, in the sense that one is a thinking, acting, and feeling creature, is possible without full self-consciousness. It is self-consciousness, however, that permits one not only to *be* but to *have* a self.

If it is true, however, that one has a self only if one is self-

conscious—that, in other words, consciousness is the manner of holding onto, of owning, a self—it is also true that the dissolution of the integrated self presupposes a kind of consciousness—namely, that sort of
consciousness which advertises the internal diremption of the elements
of the self.

The assault upon the Hegelian project came from numerous
quarters, of course, but none was so devastating in its consequences as
the critique offered by Søren Kierkegaard. It is one thing, said
Kierkegaard, to realize in some abstract and speculative manner a
vision of the harmony of the value spheres and of the modalities
of self-expression that resonate with them, and quite another thing to
come to grips with the concreteness of temporal experience.

At the level of lived experience, there seems no way to discover a
means of overcoming the concrete conflicts among the knowledge-
bearing institutions, the propertied interests, and those technological
activities that order the instrumentalities of society. Life is one thing,
philosophy another.

Hegel's resolution of the diremption of the value spheres is a resolution in theory. It is comprehensive in itself, but remains essentially
unrealized in the sphere of praxis. Other proposed resolutions, such as
those offered by the Marxists or existentialists, constitute, insofar
as they are realized, resolutions in practice. But these practical
approaches are both reductive and partial. That is, they require that
concrete personal and institutional choices be made that exclude real
alternatives without providing an adequate rationale for this exclusion.

For example, though Marx's indignation at the alienated condition of the newly emergent proletariat is a justifiable decrying of the
reduction of the self to the interests of property acquisition and ownership, the Marxian alternative errs in the opposite direction by col-
lapsing the distinction between the theoretical and practical spheres in
a manner that effectively cancels the life of disinterested intellectual
activity. Relevance is gained at the cost of comprehensiveness.

According to the relativist, there appears to be no means of
establishing a preference of one view over another. Unfortunately, for
the modernist, however, we cannot simply be content with settling
upon whichever theory or mode of praxis best suits us. The dominant
views of the self, derived from the specialized, reductive construals of
selfhood in accordance with the rational, volitional, and affective paradigms are not merely mutually incompatible, they are incompatible
components in effective tension within each self-conscious self.

Faced with the alternatives of either narrowness or incoherence,
the only "rational" choice seems to be that of attempting to avoid
inconsistencies by accepting one of the various modalities of self-

expression as the focus of one's sense of self. Even if this were possible, it would only result in externalizing the otherwise internal conflicts that come from attempting to modulate the tripartite self. Institutions and movements within a society will be in conflict the more individuals refuse to recognize the need to supplement within themselves the full range of the modalities of self-expression.

In late modern culture, to be a self is to be incoherent or narrow; moreover, to *have* a self in these times is to recognize our incompleteness or our incoherent forms of self-articulation and expression—that is, to experience fragmentation, manyness, internal contradictions, a variety of centers, a plurality of foci. Whether this condition is experienced as *alienation* and *anomie* or as a complex aesthetic satisfaction is the question that divides the late moderns from the advocates of postmodernism.

The Postmodern Celebration of the Decentered Self

Postmodernism offers an alternative to both narrowness or the negative construal of incoherence through a transfer of the criteria of relatedness away from the logical or rational to the aesthetic. On these terms, what was once unacceptable because expressive of divisiveness, inconsistency, and incoherence is desirable because of its expression of aesthetic contrast and intensity.

Also, the paradigm of self-understanding has shifted in postmodernism from the ego-based, substance view to that of the self as process. And the processive understanding of the self permits the serial realization of conflicting modalities of self-expression. The self as process is concerned with its "career" rather than its self-identity at a moment. This career is one in which various dimensions of expression are possible.

The denial of authorial presence, the absence of the omniscient narrator, and the general suppression of linear narrativity in fiction, along with the celebration of multiple personality constructs, the announcement of the "death of man" in the human and social sciences—all challenge the modern concept of the self as free, subjective, autonomous consciousness.

Each of these phenomena is an expression of the general disillusionment with the so-called philosophy of presence, which, according to Heidegger, Derrida, and the poststructuralists, has dominated philosophic discourse from the beginnings of Greek philosophy. The desire to make Being present through the beings of the world, to advertise the logos or structure of that which is conceptually entertained has created a profound bias toward the recognition of the sameness of the otherwise different, the pattern in the flux of passing circumstance. In the idiom of the philosophy of presence, self is that logos which makes present the putative being of consciousness.

With the failure of the philosophy of presence, however, comes the new project of thinking based upon the claims of difference. To think difference is to think in postmodern terms. With respect to the self, one thinks difference by attempting what Kierkegaard said could not be done—namely, to think the becoming of the self. One attempts to think process, to think temporality.

By attempting to think self-difference rather than self-sameness, one denies the need for a logos, pattern, or structure that makes the self present to itself. In place of such a logos one celebrates the ever-not-quite, the always-only-passing character of experience.

Though the project of thinking change is not more easily realizable today than when Parmenides and Zeno advertised its rational impossibility, something has been gained by virtue of the critiques of Kierkegaard and others. At least this much has changed: Whereas after the Parmenidean gambit, the principals of our cultural articulation chose reason and logos over the intuition of process and becoming, contemporaries faced with that same choice are apt more readily to forego reason if it precludes access to the temporal, processive character of concrete experience.

Being, Nonbeing and the Senses of Self

One of the most fruitful themes characterizing postmodern philosophy is that of "ontological difference." Martin Heidegger and Jacques Derrida and many other of the French poststructuralists have discussed this issue with a great deal of subtlety. One cannot exhaust the relevant implications of this term, however, without moving beyond the immediate interests of Heidegger and his epigoni.

The question of difference ought not be limited to that of the difference(s) between Being and beings. It is feasible on a completely cosmological reading of the way of things to ask after the differences among beings without admitting the possibility of any ontological contrast. On such a reading there is no ontological ground. There is no *Being*—only beings. This form of radical cosmology is, with appropriate terminological changes, exemplified by philosophical Taoism.

Likewise, a completely *ontological* view may be found in Parmenides. "Only Being is. . ." On this view the question of difference resolves itself into a difference between Appearance and Reality, between the Way of Truth and The Way of Opinion. In the Realm of Being no differences obtain.

Between this radical cosmology and radical ontology there lies the position that has dominated Western philosophy—one that eschews (or attempts to) the single-sidedness of either radical solution. Being is privileged over both beings and nonbeing. God as being may serve as creator; from the emptiness of nonbeing come the beings of the World. In religious mysticism there may seem to be an approximation to Parmenidean mysticism, but the sense of the important contrast between beings and Being is not lost even here.

A fourth possibility lies in that metaphysical nihilism which claims that Nonbeing is the ultimate. Beings are illusory as is, *a fortiori*, Being-Itself. On this view nothing exists. There can be no true difference(s)—only Indifference. The question of difference arises with respect to the contrast between the merely apparent beings of the world and the Nihil that guarantees their illusory status. This is the reverse of the Parmenidean vision, which leads to an equally radical question—this time a *dis*ontological one: Why is there Nothingness—the Nihil—rather than Being or beings?

These four possible manners of construing the question of difference vis-à-vis the question of Being, beings, and nonbeing provide a resource both for the interpretation of cross-cultural phenomena and for the assessment of the relevance of those phenomena for issues within the Anglo-European context. We shall attempt to exploit this typology with respect to the issue of "selfhood."

In the first place, movements away from "logocentric" interpretations of the self associated with postmodernism may be interpreted by recourse to the alternative senses of difference presupposed by the break with the philosophy of presence. If the philosophical program based upon difference suffers the same fate as that of the philosophy of presence, either the mysticism of the Parmenidean vision or metaphysical nihilism will be found applicable. At present, in anticipation of the success of a philosophy of otherness and difference, the experimentation lies with the form of radical cosmology associated with the denial of ontological grounding and with the implicit claim, "Only beings are."

The Resort to Alternative Cultures

Comparative philosophy has, as one of its primary functions, the provision of novel resources for speculation. Visions, theories, or models developed and articulated over several centuries may be employed in order to test the implications and applications of an untried insight. The obvious value of such comparative work is the ability to see the outworkings of a nascent theory or value orientation within an alternative culture as a means of sorting out the possible consequences within one's own milieu.

And quite apart from the question of the relevance and viability of an insight or vision newly aborning in one's own cultural context, there is the question of the inertia of the past and the manner in which it might prevent the internal development of that idea in anything like a pure form. Thus, one might well have a truly original and creative idea that is strangled, stunted, or buried by language and methods wholly inappropriate to its expression and application.

Given the state of ruminations upon the self in the postmodern West, it is clear that the insight relative to the sense of "difference" is receiving only partially apt expression and articulation in the language and methods employed by the postmodernist thinkers. Comparative philosophy, therefore, ought lead one to the search beyond one's cultural resources for contexts in which such ramifications are evident.

Where might one look for such resources with respect to the notion of the self? The Buddhist no-self doctrines presuppose a concept of emptiness in which the ontological character of things is either dissolved or held to be ultimate. *Śūnyatā* has been given the questionable interpretation of "mystical eternalism"—a variety of the Parmenidean vision. Cosmological entities are empty with respect to the ontological ground. Alternatively, a form of metaphysical nihilism may be expressed by the *śūnyatā* doctrine.

Neither of these interpretations allows for an exploitation of the question of difference in any meaningful way. In the latter alternative, the sense of indifference may be said to rule absolutely. Nothing finally exists (has "own-being"), so indifference is all. In the former alternative, indifference is still the ultimate consequence: Cosmological characters are ultimately unreal and all differences dissolve in the singularity of nirvana.

The best resource, I would claim, for the postmodern seeking cultural supplementation is to be found in the vision of the philosophical Taoist. Taoism is an articulated and ramified philosophy of difference rooted in a radical cosmology.

Self, No-Self and the *Wu*-Forms of Taoism

The most provocative characterization of *tao* 道 in the *Tao Te Ching* is as both "nameless" and "nameable." If *tao* per se is the Way of things, construed as all of the processes of becoming,[5] then nameless and nameable *tao* characterize the functions of "Nonbeing" and "being" respectively, as abstracted from the process of Becoming-Itself. *Tao* is the *That Which*. That which *is* and that which *is not* are the polar elements of Becoming-Itself.

It would be easy to misunderstand this interpretation as claiming a far greater coherence for the Taoist vision than is likely. One must look carefully at the meaning of *wu* 無 in this context. As Angus Graham has argued, the "being" and "nonbeing" have strikingly different associations than do the notions of (*yu* 有) and *wu*.[6] For example, *wu* means "have not" "there is not," which readily contrasts with the sense of nonbeing as "nothing" or "no entity." The sense of *wu* is of the absence of concrete things. The correlative sense of *yu* in this context is the presence of these same concrete things.

For the beginning student of Chinese language and culture, one of the very real mysteries is the fact that the same verb can mean both "to have" and "to be." The recognition of the concrete references of both *yu* and *wu*, however, accounts very well for this fact. For the classical Chinese, *yu* indicates that "something is present." "To be" is "to be around." Likewise, "not be" means "not to be around."

With reference to the subject of self, the distinction between being a self and having a self, which was made earlier, would not be a legitimate one for the Chinese to make, since "to be" and "to have" are one and the same thing. In fact, having is the more helpful sense here since it more definitely indicates some concrete thing that is present to be "had."

If one looks at Taoism with the appropriately adjusted sense of being and nonbeing, the notion of *tao* as the That Which loses its ontological tone. There is only "this" and "that." To translate this idea as "Only being*s* are" is quite appropriate, provided one not look for any Being standing behind or beneath or beyond these beings. Beings are "thises" and "thats." *Tao*, construed as That Which Is and That Which Is Not—Nameable and Nameless *tao*—characterizes the process of existence and experience as Becoming-Itself. This reflexive notion, however, does not name an "Itself" that becomes; rather, the locution "Becoming-Itself" refers to the processes of becoming per se. It is these processes that constitute *tao*.

Each particular element in the totality has its own *te* 德. *Te* is best understood as a particular focus—that which orients an item in a field of significances such that it achieves its own intrinsic excellence. The *te* of an element provides the perspective from which it construes all other items in its environs. In this manner each item, with respect to its *te*, "names" and creates a world.

Tao and *te* are related as field and focus, respectively. The relations of *tao* and *te* are "holographic"—that is, each element in the totality of things contains the totality in an adumbrated form. The particular focus of an item establishes its world, its environment; the totality as sum of all possible orders is adumbrated by each item.

Wu-chih 無知, as "no-knowledge," means the absence of a certain kind of knowledge—specifically the sort dependent upon ontological presence. Knowledge grounded in a radical cosmology must be "unprincipled knowing," the sort of knowing that does not appeal to principles as the logos determining the meaning of an item. *Wu-chih* provides one with a sense of the *te* of a thing—its particular focus—rather than yielding some understanding of that thing in relation to some concept or universal. Ultimately *wu-chih* is expressed as a grasp of the *tao-te* relationship of each encountered item that permits an understanding of the totality construed from the particular focus (*te*) of that item.

Wu-chih, "knowing without principles," is tacit and, though inexpressible in literal terms, may be communicated though parabolic and imagistic language. A Confucian critic challenged the Taoist claim that begins the *Tao Te Ching*—"The Way that can be spoken of is not the constant way"—by asking: "If the Way cannot be spoken of, how is it that the *Lao-tzu* used several thousand characters in speaking of the Way?" The Taoist replied: "I make for you a beautiful embroidery of drakes and pass it along to you for your admiration. I cannot, however, show you the golden needle by which it was made." Such parabolic language is distinctive in a radically cosmological context, since metaphor and imagery cannot presuppose a literal ground. Parabolic language, therefore, is constitutive of discourse itself. Language is, from the beginning, a language of difference and particularity.

Wu-wei 無為, often translated as "no action," involves the absence of a specific sort of action—namely *principled* action. If one acts in an "unprincipled" manner, one must take up the perspective of that in accordance with which or in relation to which one is acting. These actions are *tzu-jan* (自然) "spontaneous," "so-of-themselves." As such, they are unmediated by rules or principles. Thus, the relations of *wu-chih* and *wu-wei* ring interesting changes on the relations of knowledge and action in most Western philosophic theories.

Wu-yü 無欲 means "the absence of material desires." Perhaps the best characterization of the term is "objectless desire." Since neither unprincipled knowing nor nonassertive action can in the strict sense *objectify* a world or any element in it, the desiring associated with the Taoist sensibility is, in the in the strictest sense, "objectless." The "enjoyments" associated with *wu-yü* are possible without the need to define, possess, or control the occasion of one's enjoyment.

Unprincipled knowing, nonassertive action, and objectless desire have this in common: To the extent they are successful, *they leave the world as it is.*

Postmodernism Purified

I have argued that the resort to philosophical Taoism on the part of the postmodernist could provide a resource for the interpretation of self and difference grounded in a tradition of radical cosmology. Such a strategy should permit a purification of the elements that have been inadvertently imported from the old paradigm. I shall now indicate in a succinct manner precisely the advantages of having recourse to Taoism rather than attempting to "go it alone" with the resources of Western philosophic culture.

There is no easy way to avoid illegitimate concepts and methods when attempting to develop a new insight. Old habits of thought adhere to the new intuitions, cloaking them, obfuscating their meaning, muffling their thunder. This has been the case with the poststructuralist critiques of the philosophy of presence. At least the following assistance might be thought to derive from recourse to the version of "postmodernism" one finds in classical Chinese Taoism.

The Taoist method is analogical, rather than analytic or dialectical, which is to say that it is a method based upon the correlation of elements with presumed similarities of structure, character, or function without the necessity to presume holistic context. It would be a mistake, therefore, to read the Taoist no-soul doctrine as a dialectical rejection of the traditional Western conception of the psyche or self. The reason this could hardly be the case is that there is no sense of Wholeness or Oneness that defines the self or person. The "ten thousand things" do not "add up" to a Whole. There is no natural world that could be conceived as a "cosmos."

The Taoist is closer to the "many worlds" view of many of the presocratic philosophers. The Taoist no-soul doctrine is neither the result of a dialectical nor an analytic mode of argumentation, since both analysis and dialectic require a putative whole—the former in order to divide into parts, the latter in order to form the opposing parts into some synthetic whole.

The poststructuralist critique of modernity is itself dialectical, as is the shift from the philosophy of presence to the philosophy of difference. It is this that shapes the rhetoric of the postmodernist impulse. The context of the Taoist sensibility is much different, however. There is a correlativity between the Confucian and the Taoist, and though many Western interpreters have seen in the Taoist-Confucianist interactions a dialectical relation, this is a function more of their own methodological bias than of the historical realities of that relationship.

The distinction between correlation and dialectical synthesis as applied to the differences between the modern and postmodern conceptions of the soul is relevant here. Confucianism and Taoism are cultural correlatives and should not be seen, therefore, as related "parts" of a tradition that may be isolated by analyzing a some presumed cultural "whole" or seen as candidates for dialectical synthesis into such a whole.

This sort of relationship between the modern and postmodern conceptions of self is more difficult to urge upon the Anglo-European context. Ours is an agonal culture in which even the rhetorical form of the *agon* is associated with claims to comprehensiveness and wholeness. But, in point of fact, the philosophy of difference has within it no basis for dialectical modes of argumentation. Nor for that matter is the typical form of the debate, which stresses the use of emotionally persuasive rhetoric, an appropriate model for the articulation of cultural self-consciousness.

The postmodern project can be furthered significantly by recourse to the Taoist sensibility. The employment of correlativity without the necessity to posit a cosmic whole as background of one's ruminations is the essential contribution of the Taoist. From that insight follows the irrelevance of dialectical and analytic modes of discourse. From the irrelevance of the latter mode follows the implausibility of precise concepts or of univocal language. From the irrelevance of the former derives the impossibility of having objects or explanations of those objects that have any final integrity, unity, or comprehensiveness. This means that "self" cannot be one, whole, or finally inclusive.

There is an additional benefit accruing from the recourse to Taoism on the part of the postmoderns—namely, such activity cannot but increase the respectability of each mode of thinking. Taoism, more often than not understood to be a vague, arcane, mystical vision with little if any relevance to the more normal mode of life and circumstance, cannot but gain prestige from its association with a viable Western cultural movement—no matter how exotic that movement now appears.

Conversely, postmodernism will benefit from its association with a developed tradition of thought which has sustained itself in one form or another during the last two thousand years and more. For the chief criticism of postmodernism whether as philosophy, literary theory, or architectural expression, is that it is most certainly a faddish, ephemeral movement, merely parasitical upon the project of modernity. This could be so. But the fact of philosophical Taoism demonstrates the staying power of the sensibility that the postmodern is currently striving to articulate.

The Interlexical Self

The burden of my remarks, sketchy as they have been, ought to be reasonably clear. I have claimed that the postmodern interpretation of self is a legitimate response to a serious impasse in the project of modernity—an impasse that has occasioned the casual, uninformed relativism and narrow, obscurantist provincialism, as well as the more consequent forms of individual and cultural nihilism that dominate contemporary Anglo-European societies.

The embarrassment of modernity lies in the obvious failure of the creators and purveyors of intellectual culture to demonstrate the efficacy of reason in establishing a consensual basis for our social and political institutions. One of the casualties of this project has been the notion of "rational self-consciousness" upon which the free, autonomous activity of the modern self was to have been predicated.

The postmodern effort to accede to the conditions of the embarrassment of modernity has seemed to many to be a sort of tasteless and frenetic celebration of the failure of consensus that makes a virtue of necessity by saying yes to every possibility, by saying in effect: any (and every) thing goes. I have argued against this assessment on the grounds that there is indeed a criterion of evaluation operating among the postmoderns, though it is by no means a rational one.

The "principle" of postmodernism is based upon the appreciation of intensity and contrast, and the means of achieving this is the recognition of individual difference. Both the self created by recourse to this principle and the self engaged in employing this principle are functions of the creative juxtapositioning of intensely contrasting features developed from traditional modalities of self-articulation. Instead, however, of seeking a rational accommodation, the elements of the self are held together by the claims of aesthetic enjoyment.

The ages-long transmogrifications of the notion of self from Homer to the present can be told as the self's journey from the Many toward the One, from the disparate and unfocused actions, dispositions, and understandings that variously expressed the human mode of being in its world to the unity of rational self-consciousness. But the desire for wholeness and unity, already definitive of the human adventure by the close of the Hellenic period, cannot be said to have realized its goal in modernity. The modern self collapsed as soon as it was formed, its very apotheosis signaling its demise.

The human adventure seems to have turned about and has begun to retrace its path, moving now from One to Many. The postmodern self well might be the original disparate "self"—but with a remarkable difference. What is left over from the failed project of the Enlightenment, which sought in the unity of rational self-consciousness the highest expression of human sensibility, is not, of course, the unity of the self but its *self-consciousness*.

The postmodern self returns to its origins in correlativity, in aesthetic plurality, but it arrives with the gift of reflexive consciousness. In the beginning, human beings were selves, but they didn't *have* their selves. The postmodern, plural, aesthetic self has an awareness of its plurality and the insistent particularity of the elements that variously focus that plurality. This aesthetic self-consciousness rehearses the Taoist vision of no-soul, no-self (*wu-wo* 無我, *wu-chi* 無己). But beyond pointing in that direction for guidance as to the richer meaning of aesthetic self-consciousness, very little remains to be said.

One might, of course, attempt to look in other directions than the Taoist one to discover meanings of the postmodern self. There is in Nietzsche's remarkable metaphor of the *Übermensch*, and the discussions that surround that notion, just such a resource. The realization of our formation from out of incoherent, inconsistent, rationally disparate, dirempted elements is a special kind of realization—a unique form of consciousness. To rise to that new order of consciousness requires a new language, a new set of dispositions, truly novel heuristics in accordance with which to guide our thinking. If such a consciousness begins to define the form of human experience we shall have become qualitatively different—more than human. Or, at the very least, fundamentally *different*.

There is yet another resource: I refer to the poststructuralist potpourri constituted by Battaille, Foucault, Levinas, Derrida, et al. These individuals provide a myriad set of reflections upon difference and otherness, which, by seeking means of thinking difference and otherness, might permit us to think ourselves as our differences—as vague, shifting patterns of otherness.[7]

I began this essay with the metaphor of the interlexical self. I will close by indicating the two important senses in which that metaphor is applicable to our present situation. "Self" remains undefined due to the fact that its viable meanings are to be found within the chaos of interpretations associated with postmodern speculation—or alternatively, within the allusive language expressing the Taoist sensibility.

The first fact indicates that we have not yet found the language we shall use to deploy the concept of the self within the project of contemporary cultural self-consciousness. The second fact points to the conclusion that once such language is found it will be the allusive language of the Taoist who cannot in any case show us "the golden needle."

Ours is an interlexical age, and were we but able to become conscious of ourselves, we would see that we are interlexical selves. In the vectors of the plural senses open to us for self-articulation, in the interstices of the elements that denote those senses, we are to be found. I would stress that the "we" in the preceding sentence refers not merely to the multiplicity of individual human beings who own selves but also, most significantly, to the self of each being.

Each of our names is "Legion," for we are many.

NOTES

1. See "Disciplining Chaos," chap. 2 in my *Uncertain Phoenix—Adventures Toward a Postcultural Sensibility* (New York: Fordham University Press, 1982).

2. See Bruno Snell, *The Discovery of the Mind* (New York: Harper & Row, 1960); E. R. Dodds, *The Greeks and The Irrational* (Berkeley and Los Angeles: University of California Press, 1951), A.W.H. Adkins *From the Many to the One* (Ithaca: Cornell University Press, 1970), among many others, for the discussion of the development of the concept of 'integrated personality' among the Greeks.

3. See Alasdair MacIntyre's discussion in *Whose Justice? Which Rationality?* (Notre Dame: University of Notre Dame Press, 1988), 152–58.

4. See Jürgen Habermas's *Philosophical Discourse of Modernity*, and David Kolb's *The Critique of Pure Modernity* (Chicago: University of Chicago Press, 1987) for examples of this sort of analysis.

5. See the chapter entitled, "The Way Beyond 'Ways,'" in my *Uncertain Phoenix* for an elaboration of this interpretation of philosophical Taoism.

6. See Angus Graham, "Being in Western Philosophy Compared with *Shih/Fei* and *Yu/Wu* in Chinese philosophy," in *Studies in Chinese Philosophy*

and Philosophical Literature (Singapore: Institute of East Asian Philosophies, 1986), 322–59.

7. Mark Taylor has begun to develop a language from out of the various poststructuralist thinkers that would permit the speaking and thinking of otherness and self as "differences." See especially his *Altarity* (Chicago: University of Chicago Press, 1988).

10

Self and Collectivity: Socialization in Chinese Preschools

David Y. H. Wu

Introduction

Recent literature on the Chinese conceptions of self often center on the Confucian definition of personhood. Characterizing Confucian self-cultivation as a conscious process of self-development, Tu Wei-ming says: "a characteristic Confucian selfhood entails the participation of the other and that the reason for this desirable and necessary symbiosis of selfhood and otherness is the Confucian conception of the self as a dynamic process of spiritual development" (Tu 1985, 231). According to Francis L. K. Hsu's (1985) formulation of psychological homeostasis, the Chinese consciousness of self is also interactionist. In Chinese culture, the meaningful self of a Chinese person is a "smaller self" (*xiaowo* 小我), which cannot be dissociated from a "greater self (*dawo* 大我)—the collective family, society, nation. Although scholars of Confucianism emphasize the "Confucian person" as an autonomous, self-reliant, and independent social being (Tu 1985; King and Bond 1985), conscious teaching of "submitting self-interests to collective-interests" is an essential part of communist moral teaching, and "to sacrifice smaller self to accomplish greater self" (*xisheng xiaowo wancheng dawo* 犧牲小我完成大我)" is a slogan commonly found on Taiwan's primary and secondary school walls. Scholars have described, argued, and represented Confucian thought on self and collectivity in abstract terms. Now we have the chance to view these abstract thoughts put into practice in Chinese children's socialization process, with special regard to preschool education in China.

In *Preschool in Three Cultures*, which resulted from an East-West

Center project, two colleagues at the University of Hawaii and I describe the cultural meanings of preschool in China, Japan, and the United States (Tobin, Wu, and Davidson 1989). When invited to contribute an essay on the basis of our recent study, I surprised myself by rediscovering that our chapter on China's preschools presents almost nothing but discussions of the concept of 'self' and collectivity as seen by "informants" across three nations and as reflected in our own observations and interpretations.

The preschool study sprang from an early project to examine child socialization as part of broader culture and mental health issues (see Tseng and Wu 1985). In 1983 and 1984, Chinese mental health researchers invited me to Shanghai to design a joint project on child-rearing practices. Our joint concern was the lack of information on the way Chinese parents raise their young children. We were also aware of the serious concern of government authorities, educators, and mental health experts on the effects of the one-child family policy. Our research aimed to compare the single children and multiple-sibling children, boys and girls, brought up at home (from birth to five years old) and children cared for by nurseries or kindergartens, rural and urban. Surprisingly, we did not find any (statistically significant) difference in parental treatment between single children and nonsingles, or between boys and girls. In the latter two areas of comparison, however, our research yielded differential findings in the patterns of child-rearing practices and parent-child relationships (Wu 1985). This also led me to pay attention to the Chinese insistence on the ill effects of parents raising a single child at home and the believed remedial, institutional child rearing in kindergartens. I therefore began to investigate children's life in Chinese kindergartens in order to understand how Chinese adults put their assumptions about single children and the role of kindergartens into practice. Later on, when other colleagues joined me in conducting a cross-cultural and comparative study of three countries, the results provided even more insights than had my original single-country study in reviewing how Chinese conceptualize self and collectivity in training and educating young children.

In this essay, I have extracted materials mainly from our recent *Preschool in Three Cultures* and the companion videotape to present an interpretive cultural meaning of self and collectivity in the context of child socialization in Chinese preschools. I shall concentrate on research findings from this preschool project without going into lengthy background on moral teaching and preschool education, since I have dealt with these issues elsewhere (Wu 1991, 1992). It is also worth mentioning that for the purpose of comparison I am going to present comments and evaluations of American and Japanese teachers on Chinese schools, and vice versa. Two particular scenes in the companion videotape of the Komatsutani preschool in Japan and Dong-feng kindergarten (a pseudonym) in China generated many responses from viewers and warrant special mention in later discussion. One scene at Komatsutani involved a boy who disrupted the class by clowning around and punching other children without apparent and immediate intervention by the teacher, Fukui-sensei. The scene at Dong-feng Preschool throughout the day attracted negative, emotional comments from many American and Japanese viewers, but one particular scene of the entire class of children squatting on a ditch at one time in the toilet caused the most disturbing reactions, even from Chinese viewers. These scenes are mentioned here so as to sensitize readers that in our later discussion I will return to reflect on the interpretation of the concepts of groups and collectivities.

The Meaning of Preschool in the Modern World

In Japan, China, and the United States preschool is an increasingly common solution to the problem of how to care for, socialize, and educate children between infancy and the start of formal schooling. Approximately 95 percent of the four-year-olds in Tokyo, 80 percent of the four-year-olds in Beijing, and 65 percent of the four-year-olds in New York are enrolled in nursery schools, day-care centers, or group-care homes. This is indicative of the fact that more women are working outside of homes and are leaving their fewer number of children (fewer than two on average in all three countries) with group child-care institutions.

Our joint research not only provides some understanding of the three cultures' preschools, but also elucidates the three cultures as seen through their preschools. We view preschools as complex institutions serving children, parents, and, indirectly, the wider society. Embedded in communities, nations, and cultures, preschools both reflect and affect social change. For example, in China preschools are expected to provide an antidote to the spoiled child phenomenon that Chinese fear is inevitable in an era of single-child families.

The methods we used can be described as multivocal, visual, and reflective ethnography, which allows the "subjects" (policymakers, teachers, parents, and even children) of our research to become active partners in our study. They told us about the similarities and differences of these schools in the three cultures when they actually "saw" and evaluated the school activities. Video is at the heart of the method used for these studies. We taped a typical day in a typical preschool in each of the three countries. We then returned to these schools and showed the footage to teachers, administrators, professors, parents, and children. As the teachers watched themselves on our tapes, they gave us their reactions, explanations, arguments, and evaluations. We as researchers also offered outsiders' judgments, and we analyzed questionnaire responses to show cultural differences. A much fuller discussion of our work is found in the aforementioned book (Tobin, Wu, and Davidson 1989). To understand the concept of self and selfishness in contemporary China, one can begin with an examination of the meaning of spoiled Chinese single children.

On the Spoiling of Single Children

In China the single-child policy is widely viewed as a great achievement, but one that has its costs. Since the early 1980s, Chinese parents, teachers, administrators, and child-development experts have expressed a common fear that children in single-child families are spoiled by their parents and grandparents, leading to many undesirable social and economic consequences (Wu 1983, 1985, 1991). Chinese say that a child indulged by as many as six doting adults is likely to came to think of himself as "a little sun." Or, he is the little "emperor" of a home. This problem is also called the "four-two-one syndrome": four grandparents and two parents pouring their attention onto one spoiled child.

Too much attention (or love?) harms the child. They believe that a whole generation of spoiled children could undermine the values of a society based on the principles of collectivity, selflessness, and comradeship. Chinese worry about how a generation of single children can be taught to be socially responsible. How can children growing up without siblings learn to cooperate, share, and treat their fellow citizens as brothers and sisters?

What is spoiling? Some mental health researchers from China, who have participated in our conferences at the East-West Center, have offered the following defining traits:

> "Only children are usually viewed as selfish, spoiled, unsociable, maladjusted, narrow-minded, self-centered, conceited, fragile, and cowardly" (Wang 1984)

> "marked food preferences, short attention span, obstinacy, demands for immediate gratification of their wishes, disrespect

for elders, bossiness, lack of initiative, and outbursts of temper" (Tao and Chiu 1985, 158)

"overdependence on parents and adults; sluggishness in daily life;
nail sucking and biting" (Yu 1985)

When we discuss spoiling with preschool teachers or child-
development experts in China, the word *jiao* 嬌 (tenderness) is often
heard. Many preschool administrators and teachers complain that children in China have become *tai jiao* 太嬌—too delicate, too dependent,
too fussy. They are selfish, self-centered, expecting others to care, to
yield, and to serve. While traditionally children's tenderness was re-
gared as cute, in deliberately displaying helplessness to earn parents'
succor, now it is deemed undesirable (see Wu 1981, 1983 for a discussion of *sajiao* 撒嬌 in Chinese culture).

We have to be reminded that concern about spoiling in China did
not originate with the single-child family, however. Long before the
1949 revolution Chinese child-rearing texts warned of the dangers of
ni-ai 溺愛, of "drowning [a child] in love" (Solomon 1971, 65; Wu
1981, 154).

Ways to Correct Spoiling in Attending Preschool

Viewing spoiling as the most serious problem presented by the single-
child family policy, Chinese look to preschools as a solution. Preschools provide single children with the chance to interact with other
children and with teachers trained to correct the errors of single-child
parents. Some Chinese educators and social science researchers are
quite explicit about the link between the need for preschools and the
growing numbers of single children. Wang writes: "Since the inception
of the new population policy, the number [of Chinese preschools] has
been greatly increased with the aim of raising the quality of the
population while controlling the quantity" (Wang 1984, 3–4).

Regimentation

Most of the American and Japanese who have viewed our China tape
objected strongly to what they perceived to be the kindergarten's rigidity, severity, and overregimentation. These respondents have given our
typical Chinese preschool negative ratings on item such as "teachers
directed children's play too much," "teachers set limits and controlled

children's behavior too much," "the overall mood was too controlled," "children played independently too little," and "children's activity level was too passive, subdued, docile." For example, a Japanese preschool administrator said of Dong-feng:

> The children look so restricted. Nothing seems spontaneous. The feeling of the school is so cold, so joyless. The children are expected to be so, well, unchildlike. All that emphasis on sitting straight, on being perfectly quiet, on standing in straight lines. It reminds me of Japanese school in the old days. I hope the Chinese didn't get this from us!

An American preschool teacher in Honolulu reacted similarly:

> There is so much regimentation. It looks more like the army than a preschool. I guess what bothers me most is that there is such an overemphasis on order and on behaving properly at the cost of stamping out the children's creativity.

Although the kind of regimentation seen in our tape of Dong-feng is anathema to most Japanese and Americans, for many of our Chinese informants, regimentation, order, and control are essential elements of preschool pedagogy and child socialization. Many (but, by no means all) of our Chinese informants were proud of the order and regimentation that came across in the tape. When they host foreign visitors, Chinese administrators and teachers therefore take pains to have their school appear even more regimented and controlled than usual. The irony here, of course, is that the harder the Chinese work to present an impressively ordered, regimented appearance, the more many of their foreign visitors are put off.

Most of our Chinese informants told us unapologetically that they see the role of the preschool as teaching children to behave properly and instilling in them an appreciation for the values of self-control, discipline, social harmony, and responsibility. School is a place for learning, not for fun. With only one child to carry on the father's wishes—*wangzi chenglong* 望子成龍 (wishing the son to become a dragon)—parents expect the preschool to give their child a competitive edge for school competition in later days. They therefore expect their child's teacher to conduct classroom teaching responsibly. One complaint lodged against the kindergarten we chose to film, both by the more liberal-minded educators in Beijing and Shanghai and by American viewers, is that Dong-feng classrooms (for all three grades for three-to-six-year-olds) are physically arranged according to primary school settings.

Guan 管, Buguan 不管, and Chaos

One word that can be used in China to refer to teachers' control and regimentation of children is *guan* 管, literally, "to govern." One can argue that *guan* has a very positive connotation in China. It can mean "to care for" or even "to love" as well as "to govern." Chinese mothers often deal with their children's disobedience by saying to them, "*Wo bu guan ni* 我不管你!" (I am not going to interfere with your life— meaning, I don't love you, I'm not going to care for you any more).

To govern children well is hard work. Chinese believe that pre-school children are well behaved not because they are born that way but because teachers work long and hard to bring them under firm control. One secret of governing children well is to monitor and correct their behavior continuously. (See my 1981 paper for discussion on *dong shi* 懂事, "understanding things." Once one is *dong shi*, one becomes subject to punishment.)

One school principal shared with us her secret of good classroom management:

> Teachers must take charge in the classroom. Teachers must provide structure and order. That's their responsibility. That's what they are there for. . . . If things are well planned and prepared in advance, then there will not be chaos, and the teacher will find it easy to keep firm control.

Another professor of preschool education explains:

> Teachers should always make it perfectly clear to children what is expected of them and what they will not be allowed to do. . . . Control and order should come to be familiar to children, as expected, as much a part of their world, as the air they breathe or the ground they walk on.

Fear of chaos, as literally expressed by Chinese preschool teachers, perhaps reflects the Confucian psychology of self in relation to society. A high percentage of our Chinese teachers and parents viewed our American classroom as chaotic, for children were allowed to roam around in a class that supposedly was for "learning." "What are the American teachers doing?" they asked. "Why are teachers not interfering (*buguan* 不管)?"

In direct contrast to the approach taken by the staff of Komatsu-dani Hoikuen in Japan, most Chinese believe that it is important for teachers to intervene immediately in children's disputes. A Beijing teacher said of our tape of Komatsudani in which Hiroki was hitting other children while Fukui-sensei remained passive.

> I think it's terrible that the teacher just stood there while the children fought. If you let a child behave that way in preschool, he will think it is acceptable to be that way, and he will develop a bad character that may last his whole life. When children misbehave, teachers must correct their misbehavior immediately and make it clear to the children that their behavior is not acceptable.

Comparison and Competition

"Compare and appraise" is an example of the faith Chinese put in words to affect and control children's behavior. As Richard Solomon points out, "the Chinese phrase for obedience, *t'ing-hua* 聽話, [means] to 'listen to talk'" (Solomon 1971, 52).

In a class for four-to-five-year-olds at Dong-feng we observed a teacher getting her students ready for supper: "Now let's see, who is sitting properly? How about Chen Ling—is he sitting properly? Who knows what is wrong with the way he is sitting? Should he be fiddling with his hands? Look at Lin Ping. See how nicely she is sitting! See how she has her hands behind her back."

In Heilungjiang in rural Northeastern China we saw a teacher use a similar approach to get rows of children to compete for praise and avoid criticism: "I can see that the first row of little friends (*xiao-pengyou* 小朋友) is sitting very nicely, but the third row is not sitting properly. Let's see which row of little friends can be the model row for the whole class."

Chinese preschool teachers, then, see their fundamental task as controlling children's behavior calmly, consistently, and without anger. The regimentation and control Chinese preschool teachers typically exert over their classes are perceived by the teachers, the wider society, and perhaps by the children not as cold or harsh treatment but as an expression of care and concern.

Boarding Preschools

Another aspect of Chinese preschool education that Americans and Japanese find disturbing is China's "whole-care" (*quantuo* 全托) or boarding program. When the lights came back on after our screenings of the Dong-feng tape, our audiences in Japan and the United States invariably asked us, How can the Chinese do this to their children? Are Chinese parents forced to send their children away by the government?

To the Chinese, boarding preschool is the ideal child-care institution to correct the spoiled single children. Boarding school would be the norm for all kindergartens, if the government or local communities could financially afford them. About 5 to 15 percent of Chinese preschoolers are now boarding students. Some schools, like the one we filmed, have both day-care and boarding classes. Boarding programs are much more common in cities than in rural areas. Some programs keep the children at school from Monday morning to Saturday afternoon; in others the children go home for extra Wednesday nights.

People outside of China invariably ask the question, Why boarding programs for young children? Chinese explanations of the benefits of boarding programs for young children are consistent with their views on the need for order and regimentation and, more generally, with the Chinese belief that preschools, whether day care or whole care, are institutions mandated to correct the failings of the single-child family. Most Chinese, like the Chinese sociologist who offered the following comment, view their whole-care preschools less as problems than as solutions.

> After observing a boarding school program over a period of two months we drew the conclusion that though parents sometimes hit their children, teachers never do. Children in preschool learn how to behave through interaction with their peers and by imitating those children who are most praised. Children in whole-care programs, by having the chance to participate in attractive activities and games, learn to accept regulations as something natural. Chinese collectivism stresses the harmony of the individual with society and with others. It is natural to be part of a collective, anxiety-provoking to be apart. *The collective life to be enjoyed in kindergartens enables the only child to become aware not only of the existence of self but also of the existence of the collective. The Praise they receive from teachers gives them a sense of deep satisfaction and acceptance. Such a positive self-concept will lead them to have a zest for life in the future* . . . (children learn a properly prosocial attitude).

The horror Americans and Japanese feel when confronted with Chinese whole-care programs for young children have more to tell us about America than about China.

The notion held by many conservative Americans that children belong exclusively to their parents, that they belong in nuclear-family homes, and that there is something unwise, unnatural, or unhealthy about preschools are other ideas by and large not found in China. Some Chinese parents interviewed did complain about boarding preschools, but they often gave us particular and pragmatic reasons for complaining against particular schools. Chinese parents may say that in such and such a school teachers or nurses are not well trained. A possible complaint might be: "I do not like to send my daughter to that school because she may not get the best care. My daughter appeared to have lost weight after being there for three months. So, I took her home to care by myself with the help of my mother."

Instead of viewing boarding programs as a kind of punishment to be avoided, many Chinese parents "go through the backdoor" (using connections or bribes) to get their children admitted to a boarding preschool. Some young, urban parents, viewing boarding programs as a way of guaranteeing that their children will receive first-rate care and a fast academic start, complain that slots in boarding programs are parceled out to a privileged few.

At the entrance of a kindergarten, large characters of a slogan painted on the wall read: "Our [teachers'] love for children is as great as a mother's love." At Dong-feng we heard three-year-old boarding children sing, "The kindergarten is my home. My aunties [teachers] are like my mother." The idea that good teachers and nurses in the kindergartens can be better mothers than the child's own mother may sound offensive to American parents. Yet, Chinese young parents positively echo this view when interviewed. While in general Americans find a boarding kindergarten a horrifying idea, Chinese are proud to present boarding or whole-care preschools to outsiders as evidence of socialist achievement. For instance, in a model agricultural commune outside of Beijing, where a boarding kindergarten is but a few minutes' walk from some of the residences children stay away from home six days a week and are cared for by teachers and nurses. To the peasants in the commune, the existence of such boarding programs symbolizes the success of the commune in modernization and good fringe benefits for the members and is a sign of wealth. (The same can be said about the home for the elderly who have had no offspring that is supported by the same commune.)

Thinking about boarding preschools, again, we find the echoes of Confucian thinking. The ideal kindergarten teacher is not unlike the ideal Confucian father described in Tu Wei-ming's paper "Selfhood and Otherness in Confucian Thought" (1985). The ideal father must be kind and loving to earn a son's respect. Tu went further to say, "understandably, exchanging sons for formal instruction has been a common practice in [traditional] Chinese society" (Tu 1985, 244).

The Collective Good

It is apparent that in China, the social, the collective, and the group are valued over the personal, the familial, and the individual. The promotion of selflessness and collectivism lies at the core of the Chinese preschool's mission. These values are far more easily taught in preschools than at home, as a manual for teachers makes clear:

> In the kindergarten we use the classroom as a big family to teach single children that they are members of a collective. We teach children to develop the habit of treating others equally, to be friendly, considerate, concerned, to mutually give in [*qian rang* 謙讓] to others, and to obey the rules of the group. We nourish their concept of collectivism through numerous daily activites. . . . The kindergarten is the ideal place to teach children the concept of collectivity [*jiti* 集體].

In our Dong-feng videotape, the group bathroom scene, which many American and Japanese respondents found so disturbing, was seen as an unremarkable example of collectivity by most of our Chinese informants. Some Chinese educators in Beijing were embarrased with the scene only because we did not choose to film schools with "modern" bathroom facilities and thus exposed the backward part of China. They did not perceive, as Americans do, that the idea of going to toilet at one assigned time (whether the children want to or not) is horrible. Even in suburban Beijing, we observed the same practice of bathroom time, although the bathroom had two individual pits and students took turns using them.

One teacher explained the moral-education curriculum for kindergarten: "The guiding principle for moral teaching in the preschool is to emphasize the unity of the group and to cultivate a love for friendship." This emphasis on group harmony explains our Chinese informants' overwhelmingly negative reactions to little boy Hiroki's fighting and Fukui-sensei's (non)response.

To individually oriented Westerners, both China and Japan are group-oriented societies. Yet our research clearly shows that Chinese and Japanese approaches to group identity, to classroom management, and to individual transgressions such as Hiroki's are strikingly different.

Chinese notions of the group are inextricably linked to the concept of order (Wilson 1970, 1974). A disorderly collection of children is not a group. To the Japanese, in contrast, groups can be chaotic as well as orderly, spontaneous as well as structured. The tasks facing preschool teachers in Japan and China are therefore different. To prepare children to be good members of a group, Japanese teachers emphasize camaraderie and place children in situations where they can interact freely, *without adult interference. Chinese teachers emphasize order and common purpose and place children in situations where they can share the experience of discipline and control under the direction of a common leader.*

Group structure in the Chinese preschool tends to be more vertical and teacher-directed than in most Japanese preschools, where group oriented means peer-group oriented and the less involved the teacher is perceived to be, the stronger are the horizontal ties that form to bind the group together. It is no surprise that a diligent teacher in China is described to be one who is tired and has lost her voice at the end of the day, resulting from constantly interfering with (*guan* 管) the children's behavior or interaction. The other observed behavior in a Chinese classroom—whether mainland or in Taiwan—is the frequent "reporting to teacher of other mischieving children." Hence, whistle-blowers are encouraged, especially in kindergartens and lower-grade primary schools.

When the staff of Dong-feng speak of the importance of the group, the collective, and the social, they have in mind not only teaching children to play well with their classmates but also teaching them to feel a connection to something much larger—their nation. Thus, in survey responses to our question, "What are the most important reasons for a society to have preschools?" twice as many Japanese respondents as Chinese (91 versus 44 percent) answered, "to give children experience being a member of a group," whereas far more Chinese than Japanese (30 versus 18 percent) answered, "to start children on the road toward being good citizens."

Conclusion

It is a Western belief that the concept of self does not exist for young children (Johnson 1985). This belief that young children cannot comprehend the meanings of selfhood of the mature adults must be universal. Chinese share such a conviction of children's immaturity and ignorance-"*budongshi* 不懂事 (do not understand things)." *Budongshi* can also be used to refer to adults who "do not follow the proper ways of interacting with fellow human beings in the society." In my study of child abuse in Chinese culture (Wu, 1981), I discovered the advantage possessed by young children who are regarded as *budongshi*: they are excused from social sanction or adult's punishment. On the other hand, since children are *budongshi*, they must be taught to *dongshi*, to act like little adults.

Perhaps the whole issue of the Chinese apprehension about spoiled single children and preschool as a countermeasure reflects the Chinese conception of selfhood. The state, symbolizing not just the political authority but also the ideal father figure, must take over when single children's real fathers have failed their ideal role in training children to become filial, loyal, friendly, selfless, independent, and obedient members of a prosperous, modern China. One school principal put the mission of kindergarten this way:

> The works we do here is very important, more important than just caring for children while their parents work. We are not baby-sitters—we are educators. The most important lessons we teach children, in addition to numbers and reading and writing, are moral lessons. We teach children how to treat others, how to be friends, how to be citizens, concerned for others, rather than selfish. Our job here is to produce the next generation of Chinese citizens and leaders. . . . We stress to the children a love of China, a love of socialism, and a feeling of patriotism to prepare them to fulfill their responsibilities to our country when they become adults.

Summing up this principal's presentation of preschool in China, we may think of this as the official Chinese party line on civic and moral education in preschool, a point of view publicly endorsed by most Chinese. Unofficial, private beliefs are, of course, much more difficult to ascertain. But we have no reasons to doubt that far more Chinese than Japanese or Americans believe wholeheartedly in the importance of teaching children to be patriotic, civic-minded, and group oriented. Clearly, patriotism or citizenship is more widely viewed in China as something important to teach than it is in Japan and the United States.

The emphasis in Chinese preschools of "experience in a group" (which is assumed to be lacking in the home environment) and "learning to be a good citizen" are closely related. They are conceptually part of a more encompassing concern in Chinese society that young children must taught to identify with something larger than themselves and their families. Chinese have always faced concern about balancing the personal and the communal. It is important to know that, in the Chinese understanding, children belong not only to parents but also to society (thus filial piety is meant for parents and the emperor). Chinese preschools and the ongoing debate about self and collectivity summarize the search for this balance. However, as Chinese students in modern schools (of all levels) have been taught for decades (both in China and in Taiwan), one must sacrifice one's "smaller self" (*xiaowo*) for the sake of a "larger self" (*dawo*)—the collective, the society, and the nation.

I have in an earlier study (see Wu and Tseng 1985) demonstrated how Confucian thought prevailed in Chinese conceptions of education. The practices in China's kindergartens seem to indicate that Chinese authorities and educators still express the Confucian ideal of person as an insignificant self submitting to a significant larger self of collectivity. Our study leads us to view Chinese preschools as ideal agents of cultural conservation rather than change. Preschool in China functions to conserve rather than transform the value of collectivity, which is fundamental to a Chinese and communist society.

BIBLIOGRAPHY

Hsu, Francis L. K. 1985. "The Self in Cross-cultural Perspective." In *Culture and Self: Asian and Western Perspectives*, ed. A. J. Marsella, G. DeVos,and F.L.K. Hsu, 24–55. New York: Tavistock Publication.

Johnson, Frank 1985. "The Westen Concept of Self." In *Culture and Self: Asian and Western Perspective*, ed. A. J. Marsella, G. DeVos, and F.L.K. Hsu, 91–138. New York: Tavistock Publicatons.

King, Ambrose Y. C., and Michael H. Bond. 1985. "The Confucian Paradigm of Man: A Sociological View. In *Chinese Culture and Mental Health*, ed. W. S. Tseng and D.Y.H. Wu, 29–45. Orlando and London: Academic Press.

Solomon, Richard H. 1971. *Mao's Revolution and the Chinese Political Culture*. Berkeley and Los Angeles: University of California Press.

Tao, Kuotai, and Jing-hua Chiu. 1985. "The One-Child-per-Family Policy: A Psychological Perspective." In *Chinese Culture and Mental Health*, ed. W. S. Tseng and D.Y.H. Wu, 153–166. Orlando and London: Academic Press.

Tobin, Joseph J., David Y. H. Wu, and Dana Davidson. 1989. *Preschool in Three Cultures: Japan, China, and the United States*. New Haven: Yale University Press.

Tseng, Wen-shing, and David Y. H. Wu, eds. 1985. *Chinese Culture and Mental Health*. Orlando and London: Academic Press.

Tu, Wei-ming. 1985. "Selfhood and Otherness in Confucian Thought." In *Culture and Self: Asian and Western Perspectives*, ed. A. J.

Marsella, G. DeVos, and F.L.K. Hsu, 231–51. New York: Tavistock Publications.

Wang, Nianchen. 1984. "Socialization of the Only Child in China. An Investigation into Kindergarten." Paper presented at the conference "Child Socialization and Mental Health," ICC, East-West Center, Honolulu, Aug. 6–13, 1984.

Wilson, Richard W. 1970. *Learning to be Chinese: The Political Socialization of Children in Taiwan.* Cambridge: MIT Press.

———. 1974. *The Moral State: A Study of the Political Socialization of Chinese and American Children.* New York: Free Press.

Wu, David Y. H. 1981. "Child Abuse in Taiwan." In *Child Abuse and Neglect: Cross-cultural Perspectives*, ed. Jill Korbin, 139–65. Berkeley and Los Angeles: University of California Press.

———. 1983. "Child-rearing in China." Paper presented at the Annual Meeting of the American Anthropological Association, Chicago, Nov. 16–20, 1983.

———. 1985. "Child Rearing under the Single-child Family Policy in China." Paper presented at the International Symposium on China's One Per Thousand National Fertility Sample Survey, Beijing, Oct. 14–18, 1985.

———. 1989. "Explicit and Implicit Moral Teaching of Preschool Children in chinese Societies." Paper presented at the CCU-ICP International conference on Moral Values and Moral Reasoning in Chinese Societies, Taipei, May 25–27, 1989.

———. 1991. "*Zhongguo renkou zhengce yu dusheng zinu de jiaoyang*" (China's Population Policy and the Rearing of Single-child). In *Proceedings of the Second Conference on Modernization and Chinese Culture*, ed., C. Chiao et al., 277–28b. Hong Kong: Chinese University of Hong Kong.

———. 1992. "Preschool education in China." In *Early Childhood Education in the Pacific and Asia: A Sourcebook*, ed. Stephanie Feeney. New York: Garland Press.

Wu, David Y. H. with W. S. Tseng. 1985. Introduction to *Chinese Culture and Mental Health*, ed. W. S. Tseng and D.Y.H. Wu, 3–13. Orlando and London: Academic Press.

Yu, Lian. 1985. "An Epidemiological Study of Child Mental Health Problems in Nanjing District." In *Chinese Culture and Mental Health*, ed. W. S. Tseng and D.Y.H. Wu, 305–14. Orlando and London: Academic Press.

11

Beyond the Patrilineal Self: Constructing Gender in China

Margery Wolf

> ...social systems are, by definition, systems of inequality.—
> Collier and Yanagisako, *Gender and Kinship*

Most (although by no means all) feminist anthropologists agree that women and men have different views on how their shared culture works, and even of what meanings mean within its various systems (for example, Errington and Gewertz 1987; Ortner and Whitehead 1981; Weiner 1976). I certainly believe this was the case in Taiwan in the 1960s and the People's Republic of China (PRC) in the 1980s. I admit that when I first began writing about Chinese society, I did not realize that these different perspectives had theoretical significance, but then few of us did. As a novice ethnographer, I was surprised when this gendered perception of the world became apparent, but I was far more interested in women's explanations of how they coped with a social system stacked against them than I was with the implications of this for feminist or any other kind of theory. There was no doubt in my mind as to the inequalities that presented themselves to me every day.

Nonetheless, China's patrilineal kinship system seemed to me as natural and as overwhelming as a redwood tree. It was not subtle; it was unforgiving; and if necessary, it ignored biology in order to fill its needs. There was no question but that it was a "system of inequality," from the hierarchy inscribed in the lineage genealogies to the strict rules against marriage across generations to the privileging of age, sex, and economic status within domestic units.

The strength and pervasiveness of the Chinese kinship system has been written about incessantly by Chinese and by foreigners—with both awe and anger. Would-be reformers at the turn of the century blamed everything from moral failure to technological backwardness on the iron grip "The Family" had on its people. And, of course, Mao Zedong's revolutionaries were in open competition with the power of the lineages and the families in rural China. The imposition of the commune, brigade, and team system in the rural areas was presented as a model for changing economic relations, but it was also clearly an attempt to further weaken the hold of the lineages and the power of the kin groups, politically, economically, and spiritually. From the reports of ethnographers (Huang 1985; Potter & Potter 1990; Siu 1989), however, lineages and lower level kin groups managed to retain considerable power for their members within these externally imposed structures. In single surname villages, even the most ardent cadre would find it difficult to establish surname diversity within brigades let alone with the even smaller teams. And in south China where within living memory lineages had been military threats to provincial governments, the political power of the kinship organization, however deformalized, remained strong.

Nowadays, with the decollectivization of the countryside, kin relations are again a crucial factor in getting ahead, staying ahead, or in some cases simply surviving—assuming, of course, one is male (Cohen 1990). For women, the externally imposed collectives, no matter how weak or how male dominated, provided some protection and gave them some options they had not enjoyed before the 1949 revolution. However, the most successful women in the commune structure were those who avoided the traditional pattern of being married into a distant village of strangers (Diamond 1975). For reasons I cannot take the space to discuss here, the government encouraged marriages within villages, a practice frowned on in traditional society because it encouraged the woman's family to interfere in domestic disputes. Nonetheless, as I (1985) and a good many others have pointed out there has been a great improvement in the lives of most women since the revolution, and I suspect some of that improvement in the rural areas has been because even women who continue to marry out of their villages do not marry as far away as they once did. As a result, they are of somewhat more value to the kin groups of their fathers and hence can expect somewhat more help from them than in times past (Andors 1983; Croll 1981; Wolf 1985).

Even under the best of circumstances in late traditional China, women were given minimal protection by their father's lineages or domestic organizations, for once married, they belonged to someone else. Men told me this, women confirmed it, and I accepted it. I now wish I had asked more questions (what anthropologist doesn't?) and had gotten a clearer picture from women of how *they* saw themselves in relation to the lineage structure or other surname groups to which their fathers and husbands belonged. Instead, I observed closely the uterine family system they surreptitiously created for themselves (1972), and accepted as natural their defensive posture toward the kinship system. From a woman's perspective, that system was an obstacle, a barrier to be gotten around or occasionally manipulated to one's advantage. Looking back, I am troubled by this because I think it unfairly implies that the Chinese women I knew in Taiwan were passive recipients of a men's culture. It may well be that the uterine families they constructed were the extent of their thinking about kinship, but I now wonder if women who showed such creativity in their domestic kinship didn't have something other than mere defensive reactions to the patrilineal system I discuss below. Considering the degree to which women were excluded from the traditional kinship system (as agents, not as uteruses), it would not be particularly surprising to find that they ignored it as much as possible, but, alas, its influences on them could not be ignored.

In every society I have encountered or read about, the first thing asked after an infant slips from the birth canal is its sex. The construction of gender begins with the answer to that question. Biological sex is the initial cut, the information that divides one half of society from the other, and biological sex is the first building block of a system of inequality. China is no exception to this. An inequality based on sex has been maintained there for centuries and is deeply embedded in the culture's customary and codified law, social custom, and in its state philosophy.

Confucianism is sometimes assumed to be a way of life and thought from ancient China that retains a symbolic presence in Taiwan and Hong Kong but is used only as an epithet for traditional behavior in the People's Republic of China. The Confucian principles defining the propriety of hierarchical authority structures and the orderliness of the patriarchal family system seem anachronistic in this age of multinational corporations in Fujien, and young people from Shanghai acquiring Stanford MBAs. But to my surprise, books about Confucianism still sell well, and a superb Harvard scholar named Tu Wei-ming writes cogent "reinterpretations" of neo-Confucian thinking that are very close to being "guides" for modern living (Tu 1985). Tu is particularly interested in the Confucian self-realization project, and in one of his books on the subject, he said that a woman could also, "despite her structural limitation," cultivate her "self" (Tu 1985, 144).

Even after a long conversation with Tu Wei-ming at a conference, I could not seem to make him appreciate how remote the whole neo-Confucian project is for the rural people I have worked with or how crippling the so-called "structural limitations" under which he believes women must labor are. What I would consider structural difference—certainly not limitation—is a matter of different anatomical features, but Professor Tu was thinking of the cultural baggage that is usually associated with those anatomical features. As an anthropologist of contemporary society, I have gathered from rural Chinese women descriptions of proper behavior—that is, how they evaluate themselves against some ideal Chinese self—but that ideal self is a pretty local one. The major intellectual ideals in their cultural heritage, like Confucianism, have never included them either as women or as peasants. A young male peasant might conceivably rise above his muddy origins, but women, even upper class women, are usually invisible when it comes to philosophical generalizations. Nonetheless, when challenged, Chinese intellectuals grant that women are also human and that ideas about the development of the self apply to them as well, taking their "structural limitations" into account, of course.

Let me reassure those of you who are familiar with Chinese philosophy and Chinese religion that I am not about to take you on a tour of the Buddhist concept of the self and then the Taoist concept of the self. That would be a book length project and not one I am at this point prepared to even contemplate. For the thesis I want to develop here, the Confucian ideology is the appropriate source, for its influence on even the contemporary Chinese family of a socialist persuasion is enormous, no matter how remote some of its intellectual expressions may seem to the folk anthropologists usually talk with.

Tu Wei-ming describes the Confucian self as follows:

The ego that has to be protected against submersion in the waves of social demand is what the Confucians refer to as *ssu* [*sz*] (the privatized self, the small self, the self that is a closed system). The true self, on the contrary, is public-spirited, and the great self is the self that is an open system. As an open system, the self in the genuine sense of the word is expansive and always receptive to the world at large. Self-cultivation can very well be understood as the broadening of the self to embody an ever-expanding circle of human relatedness. However, it would be misleading to conclude that the Confucian self broadens horizontally only to establish meaningful social relations. The concentric circles that define the self in terms of family, community, country, and the world are undoubtedly social groups, but in the Confucian perspective, they are also realms of selfhood that symbolize the authentic human possibility for ethicoreligious growth (Tu 1985, 57–58).

So, the neo-Confucian self has three stages: the small self that seems to be a selfish little fellow, the true self that seems to be a bit more generous, and then the great self that is all embracing and toward which the Confucian aspires.

Let me contrast this trio of Chinese selves with Robert LeVine's refreshingly uncomplicated 1984 definition of a couple of selves into which I will be trying to translate my experience of the Chinese self/ selves. He says:

> . . . one of the nice things about the self is that it can be conceptualized as both an individual mental representation and a cultural or collective representation (LeVine 1984, 14).

For all humans, regardless of gender, regardless of culture, the development of a sense of one's self is apparently an arduous task. Western developmental psychologists tell us that by the age of three all children are aware of themselves as entities distinct from other entities in their social environment (Kagan 1984, 136). They assume this to be a universal experience for all normal infants. If they are correct, the construction of the *adult* self may require in some societies (Bali, for example) a denial of the total separation of the self from the other so painfully achieved by the infant (Geertz 1984).

But, *is* the achievement of a separate autonomous self part of normal human development or is it, in fact, another of those Western cultural constructions that infects the so-called objectivity of scientific research? If it is not universal but rather as malleable as any other belief, perhaps in those societies where such a concept is less valued (I cannot conceive of it ever being totally denied), the construction of an adult self is less fraught than it is in the West. For all the thinking that has been done about the self, and all the studies that have been conducted in child development, it is astonishing how much we have yet to learn.

Nancy Chodorow (1974), in a now classic essay, suggests that the process of individuation in males and females is not the same even within the same culture. According to her revision of psychoanalytic theory, the fact that infants and young children are cared for primarily by a female requires boys to replace their initial identification with their mothers in order to identify with another, less nurturing, authority figure. Girls retain a continuity of identification with their initial caretaker. Without committing to the rest of the psychoanalytic model, I find Chodorow's suggestions intriguing in what they suggest about a child's development of a concept of the self within any culture in which women do most or all of the early childhood socialization. As she states it, "The care and socialization of girls by women ensures the production of feminine personalities founded on relation and connection, with flexible rather than rigid ego boundaries, and with a comparatively secure sense of gender identity" (Chodorow 1974, 58). Little boys have a more extreme transition to accomplish—first breaking free of the mother/feminine identity and then finding a model for an "appropriate" male identity. It is during this transition that boys learn, often painfully, that they have identified through their mothers with an inferior model. As a result, boys have more anxiety over gender identity and more rigid ego boundaries. Girls learn to depend on connectedness and relations with others, and boys learn to be leery of these ties. The data from China both fit and do not fit Chodorow's theory in interesting ways.

For both boys and girls in China, as in most societies, the first sense of self comes within the context of the family. For the first month, newborns are not carried much, but their mothers are confined to the house for this period and are in constant attendance. When the month is over, and until they are six or seven months old, infants are either in someone's arms or bound to someone's back during most of the day. Unless the baby has just been fed, at the slightest whimper or dissatisfied wiggle the mother puts her nipple in the child's mouth. According to the mothers I talked with in Taiwan's villages in the 1960s and 1970s, this intimate contact made toilet training easy: after the first few weeks, the mother knew when to hold her child away from her in order to avoid getting wet. With this kind of intimate physical contact, in which all needs are met as soon as they are indicated, the consciousness that an Other is satisfying these needs may be slow in coming. But all good things come to an end, and as the infant becomes less fragile, she begins to spend more time in the care of a grandmother or an older sibling, experiences delays in feeding, and the presence of others begins to impinge forcefully on her world. By six months of age, the child is probably all too aware that there is an Other out there who must be manipulated into providing for the Self.

Weaning in Taiwan was abrupt and harsh. Unpleasant substances were put on the mother's breasts, and the child who until then slept with her mother and fed at will was given a new bed partner. This dramatic event occurred a few months earlier for a girl than for a boy. The weaned toddler was still very much pampered, but life was not the same. If she had older siblings, she spent more time in their care, and if she did not have siblings, she was handed around from adult to adult. Because boys in China are "precious bundles," adults are more conscious of their whereabouts and treatment, but both sexes are frustrated as little as possible.

Chinese parents say that until children are six years old they "do not understand"; but to the outside observer, it would appear that expectations for girl children are greater and come well before the age of reason. By the age of five, a girl usually has at least one younger sibling and may very well have two. The elder one becomes her charge. She may not "understand," but she will find herself in deep trouble if she lets her younger brother fall down or get into mischief. In Taiwan, parents were tolerant of outrageous disobedience on the part of their sons, but a daughter learned early to keep a watchful eye on her young charges as well as on her mother's moods.

According to Western psychologists, by age three children are aware of their own gender and well along toward identifying that of others (Kagan 1984, 141). In the villages of Taiwan, play groups of four- and five-year-olds reflected an awareness of the culture's rules of gender segregation, but not yet with the rigidity of school-age children. While the older children were at school, there were considerably more mixed-sex play groups, but as soon as school was out for the day, little boys tried to keep up with (and often disrupted) the group games of their older brothers and male cousins. Girls were usually excluded, both because of the sex segregation learned at school and because the small siblings they had on their backs or underfoot made them poor team members. Mothers also had other chores for girls to do, chores that kept them away from the play areas and chores that were considered inappropriate for boys.

Perhaps for the human organism qua organism, discovering that the I is not autonomous—does not have its needs met by simply signaling that they exist—is the most dramatic step in the construction of the self, but learning that the self has gender and learning the implications of that distinction is surely the most momentous step for the social organism. Discovering that there is an Other on whom one is dependent may be terrifying, but it is sudden and undeniable. Learning gender is slow, often contradictory, and often painful. In their early years, little boys in Taiwan quickly learned that their gender was an advantage they had over older and stronger siblings. Their sisters (younger and older) and even their older brothers were expected to give way to them, for they were the "precious bundles." Their fathers were amused by their outrageous demands, and their mothers were eager to encourage their dependency for their own reasons. But, learning to be male eventually brought another sharp and emotionally painful disruption. The all-giving mother was identified as a female Other, hence inferior, and the boy had to make his way into the less familiar world of his father. Moreover, after he had shifted his identity toward his male parent, his father suddenly became distant and aloof.

Taiwanese fathers believe that in order to teach their sons they must establish a social distance from them. A father who tolerates his son's disobedient or disrespectful behavior after a boy has reached the age of reason cannot hope to have a filial adult son who will accept his subordinate position in the patriarchal hierarchy, revere his ancestors, and support his father in his waning years. As a result, after the boy has submitted to the pressure of his peers, his relatives, and even of his beloved mother to emulate his father, the father becomes a cold, judgmental, punishing autocrat. Unfortunately, this transformation comes at about the same time the boy is exposed to his first experience with the harsh world of the Chinese educational system. He is suddenly expected to exercise good judgment and to behave according to a set of rules he hitherto ignored with impunity.

But what of little girls? Certainly they share with their brothers all the vicissitudes of discovering their dependency on a not always observant Other and an abrupt weaning, but when their brothers were making demands and getting them met, girl's demands were less consistently met. Moreover, they found, at a much earlier age, that *their* gender identity carried responsibilities with it, not least of which was taking care of the next younger sibling who supplanted them. When a busy Taiwanese mother told her young son to bring her a basket from another room and was ignored, she smiled and fetched it herself. A daughter was more likely to get yelled at. Little girls, because they were girls, were expected to stay closer to home, and as a result they spent more time mimicking and finally doing domestic tasks with their mothers. Also, because they were underfoot, they got more "instruction" in proper behavior. Obedience was expected earlier; aggression was punished more immediately, particularly if directed at younger children; nurturant behavior was rewarded. Little girls learned that if they wanted to play without their mother's interference, they must keep the younger child in their charge happy. They learned to bribe, cajole, distract, and coerce. Most of all they learned to keep a weather eye out for changes in mood—of adults as well as peers. Unlike little boys, their gender did not compensate for their disadvantages in strength, motor skills, and so forth. They had to depend upon their social skills.

Another difference between girls and boys was in their relationship with their primary caretakers. Mothers in Taiwan (and probably elsewhere in China) encouraged emotional dependency in their children in order to provide themselves with a loyal power base in a male-dominated family system. Boys had to overcome this dependency to some degree in order to acquire a proper male identity, a male self, if you will. Acquiring a female self does not require this break and all the psychological stress that it entails. However, this creates its own set of difficulties for the female child in that her ties with her mother discourage the development of a strong self identity. She looks to her mother for self definition throughout her childhood and adolescence and by extension defines herself primarily in terms of her relationships with others. As is often the case, it is in the exceptions to this pattern that it becomes most obvious. Some little girls in Taiwan became daddy's favorites. A man who felt he dared not risk spoiling his sons—who were the family's future and the ancestor's descendants—would shower his affection on one of his daughters, protecting her from her mother's wrath, giving her special treats, and so forth. Such a girl was often considered "fierce" by her playmates and a trouble-causer among village mothers.

Thus far, I have focused on the process of the development of the self in Chinese children, the "individual mental representation" of the self as defined by LeVine above. As I see it, gender identity is a crucial or perhaps *the* crucial variable in this development, for gender affects everything else—what we do, where we do it, how we think, and perhaps even how we think about thinking. I want now to turn to LeVine's second conceptualization of the self—as a cultural or collective representation. Again, gender is a major variable, but here I will not be concerned with the ideal male or the ideal female. Rather, what follows will be my representation of what I take to be a village woman's notion of "what the devil she is up to" (to paraphrase Geertz 1984, 125) as well as her notion of what the devil the men are up to and vice versa.

The centrality of the family in Chinese culture is one of those self-evident truths that when unpacked may no longer seem to be a truism. Establishing a definition of the family that does justice to its various constituencies is difficult enough without taking into consideration the way it is conceptualized by the outsiders who study it. This is not the place to explore these complexities. In my own research and in classroom lectures, I have found it useful to look at the family both as a physical entity—those who share a stove, as the Chinese put it—and as an abstraction whose membership is counted differently by different categories of kin. The men's family is a long line of ancestors stretching into a distant past and an equally long line of descendants waiting in an unknowable future. For women, the men's family is a reality with which they must contend as outsiders or as temporary residents. *Their* family is variously the one they create themselves out of their own flesh, that is, their children and grandchildren (I have labeled this the "uterine family" elsewhere), or their mother's family. For both men and women, in casual conversation, their *chia* is the place they take their meals, but I have heard many men living in a city with their wives and children refer to visiting their parents in a village as "going home to their *chia*."

So, The Chinese Family is not the simple concept it would appear to be. The Chinese Family in the ideology familiar to neo-Confucians is, in my terms, the men's family, revered by men and some scholars and viewed, or at least experienced, by women as a burden. Nonetheless, the men's family and the uterine family are the contexts within which the initial self is formed and the adult self is measured. Obviously, then, gender is, again, deeply implicated.

In the villages of late traditional China, a boy was born, grew up, married, became a father, a grandfather, and an ancestor in the bosom of his family. As a son, and even sometimes as a father, he was expected to respect and obey his own father, to revere and provide for his ancestors. Stereotypes aside, this was not such a difficult requirement. The authority of his father might grate as a man matured, but that authority usually yielded to discussion and eventually to the natural exigencies of the life cycle. In modern times, the rules of filial piety were clear and broad enough in interpretation at the village level to make them a light burden. More importantly, they gave a man a sense of place in history and in the future that provided dignity and position even for men of humble origin and limited opportunity. Although they might live in a poor house and struggle to scrape a meager living from miserable soil, they had a position that was recorded in the lineage genealogy and that showed their place in the long line of male relatives who preceded them. They were a link in the chain between the past and the future.

Membership in this spiritual community of ancestors long dead and descendants as yet unknown was a given, a right with some concomitant duties, to which a man was born. His sense of self was enjoined with this community, and although rupture with the community was socially possible, spiritually it was not. Sons given in adoption to people of other surnames were never told their original surnames because it was assumed that they would go in search of their true parents.

The social world into which a male child was born had a continuity similar to that of his spiritual community. From the moment of birth, he was situated in a set of kin relations that would be a part of his day-to-day world throughout his life. Even if he was not born into a single surname village, the majority of his neighbors had been residents for generations. He grew up as the son of Wang Shih-ding and the grandson of Wang Lan-fang, each of whom had a history. His playmates were the sons of his father's playmates, and the men with whom he farmed or did business were the sons of the men with whom his father and grandfather traded or farmed. Obviously, in contemporary Taiwan, there is increased migration out of villages to the cities, and if industry moves into an area, newcomers arrive; but the stability of social relationships is far greater than, for instance, in the United States. In the People's Republic, constraints imposed on change of residence for rural people perpetuated the interaction patterns of times past.

The Chinese male self, then, has a sense of historical continuity that is both limiting, in that it binds a man to a particular line of descent, and expansive, in that it links him firmly with the past and the future. Moreover, his daily life is set in a community that may be disapproving or supportive but cannot easily repudiate him. He is of them and his actions reflect upon them as do theirs upon him, for good or ill. His sense of self is defined by this continuity through time and space. I do not wish to suggest that Chinese men lack individual consciousness, and most decidedly I do not mean to suggest that they are or are expected to be selfless in relation to their various communities, but rather that their sense of themselves is as a valued part of a functioning whole.

After sorting out The Chinese Family a few pages back, I set women aside, a common practice. Now we must return women to their proper place and examine what I believe to be a very different vision of the Chinese Self. All too often it is assumed that what works for men can be applied to women as well, with some modifications for their "special circumstances"—although considering women who make up more than half of the world's population as the gender in "special circumstances" is a rather dubious proposition in itself. At any rate, in the development of the self and its relation to the Chinese community—material or spiritual—the male model doesn't fit. Little girls grow up hearing the same lessons as their brothers about filial piety and the enormous debt they owe their parents for having borne them, but those lessons are somehow provisional. Girls know they are temporary residents in their parents' home and will *never* be able to repay their debts to them. In the old days, long before a girl was old enough to even think about questioning her mother's authority, her marriage was arranged. Even now, when early marriage is discouraged in Taiwan in order to retain a girl's earning power as long as possible, and in China for that reason and because the State wants to control her fertility, girls know they must eventually leave. They are not a part of anyone's historical past and seem to be irrelevant to anyone's future but their own and, they are told, to some unknown family in some unknown place.

This knowledge has a profound effect on the development of the female self. From childhood, it stands before her like a dark cloud on the horizon. Unlike her brother, who is discovering his self to be inextricably intertwined with both the here and now as well as the past, she is warned that her scowling face will cause her trouble with some unknown mother-in-law, that her indecorous behavior will get her a bad husband, that her high spirits must be controlled if she is to be accepted by a really good family. She comes to recognize her Self as something based on other people's opinions of her. And, if she is reasonably perceptive, she recognizes something else: she can manipulate those opinions.

In the Taiwan I knew in the 1960s and the China I studied in the 1980s, rural families preferred to get their daughters-in-law from villages far enough away that the young women could not return home easily. I was told repeatedly that brides should be chosen from distant villages so they could not run back to their mothers every time they "have trouble." Brides were and are expected to transfer their loyalty and their feelings of obligation to the families of their husbands as quickly as possible. That which is for young men the basis of their identity is treated in young women as something that can be transferred, like their dowries, to a different set of people.

A woman's ties to her mother and her natal family are not totally severed at marriage. For example, in Taiwan, when a woman dies, even an old woman, her coffin cannot be nailed closed until a member of her natal family comes to inspect the corpse for evidence of an unnatural death. However, marriage brings to an end the daily reaffirmation of who she is by denying her access to those relationships that had been crucial to her self-identity. The Chinese marriage system seems designed to produce docile sources of progeny for the male family.

A young woman who *before* marriage has not learned to "watch other people's faces" discovers quickly that her well-being after marriage depends on it. The ties of kinship in her natal family turned out to mean little, for she was cast out; and in her new family she is clearly on trial. Her mother-in-law regards her with suspicion as someone who might steal away her son's affections and her sisters-in-law may be jealous of her new-bride's clothes and dowry. If she is too obvious in her attempts to find new friends in the village, her mother-in-law scolds her for not doing her work or for revealing family secrets. Besides, she is a stranger in this village and all strangers are regarded with a degree of caution, even when they are the new daughters-in-law of established village families. Her husband, usually unknown to her until her wedding day, cannot publicly reveal any affection he might feel for her without incurring ridicule.

But, for most young women, the isolation eventually eases, she makes a few friends, wins the trust of another daughter-in-law in the household, and perhaps even of her mother-in-law. But she now knows, personally and painfully, how tenuous such ties actually are. Until she provides the family with the male descendant for which they brought her in, she is there on sufferance. Only with the birth of her first son does she acquire a relationship that gives her identity and status and that cannot be severed. She has begun her *own* family.

The uterine family does not have the ritual of the men's family, the sense of history and institution, but it provides a woman with someone who has debts to *her*. I have written in detail about the uterine family elsewhere (Wolf 1972), so I will not dwell on it here, except to point out that these are subversive units within the Chinese family. A mother binds her children to her with ties of love and gratitude, subtly creating a conception of the men's family as oppressors from whom she protects them—at great personal cost. Sons of a successful woman grow up with dual loyalties—their cultural obligation to The Chinese Family of their fathers and an emotional loyalty to their mothers. Daughters may find themselves in conflict out of love for their fathers and paternal grandparents and loyalty to their mothers, but they learn at their mothers' knees that the men's family is an obstacle to be worked around, not an institution to which they owe loyalty. Village women live in a society in which The Family's best interests take precedence over individual needs and desires. They also acquire a pragmatic attitude toward many of the relationships within the men's family. Not until they are very old women does the family that is the setting for their adult lives become *their* family, by which time it is, in fact, likely to be an enlarged version of the family they have created themselves, their uterine family. Small wonder that their sense of self is dependent upon the relationships they have themselves constructed, not those that are assigned to them by the accident of marriage. When crucial relationships fail—when they are sent to a family of strangers in marriage or when as middle-aged women they see their sons transferring their affection to wives—they are bereft, and in times past a statistically disproportionate number of them completed the destruction of self by means of suicide.

*   *   *

If my argument is correct, that the male self is constructed once and permanently from a recognition of being part of a larger whole and the female self is constructed and reconstructed from relationships that require constant renewal, then as I asserted at the outset, gender is a critical variable in understanding Chinese behavior as well as the Chinese self. Not only does the world look very different through differently gendered eyes, but women and men also have been prepared to interact with that world in very different ways. However, any observer of human behavior is aware that behavioral norms are generalizations from which all individuals vary. For example, Mao's success in creating revolutionaries from the poorest levels of society may have had less to do with economics than with psychology. Many of Mao's peasant soldiers were men who by reason of poverty or other dislocation had been forced to construct selves without benefit of family or ancestors, more in the manner of women. They, like women, were less tied to tradition and less bound by traditional loyalties. Similarly, Norma Diamond pointed out that in the first few years following the revolution, the few women who attained and were successful at leadership roles at the village level were often *t'ung-yang-hsi* (Diamond 1975, 28). These were women adopted at an early age and raised to marry their adopted brothers. Like men, they married in the family in which they had grown up and, like men, they lived out their lives in the villages in which they were children. It was not necessary for them to reconstruct a self in a new setting of strangers. This is a very small sample of women, but if it is at all indicative of the psychological toll the majority of women must pay by being removed from the families in which they were raised, the cost to China as a civilization is incalculable.

Chinese, male and female, carefully attend to and evaluate the nuances of human interaction. Again, however, I think that there are significant gender differences in how social interactions are evaluated. Carol Gilligan, in an intriguing if somewhat culture-bound set of studies, has explored the differences in moral reasoning between males and females (1977, 1979, 1982, 1986; Gilligan et al. 1988). Her male informants, faced with a set of moral dilemmas to be resolved, seek justice for the protagonists. They look to rules that will establish the rightness or wrongness of a potential solution. Her female informants, faced with the same set of dilemmas, indicate that they are aware of the same cultural "rules," but search for solutions in which neither side will be hurt—even if that means disregarding the rules. This is a gross simplification of a complex and sometimes confusing body of research, but even in this skeletal form, the ideas carry meaning for the gender differences I see in Chinese approaches to social perplexities.

For example, one of the more common complaints of village men about women was that they did not understand the niceties of "human relations." At times I found this very confusing, for the examples they cited often seemed to me to indicate a very subtle understanding of human motivation and a talented manipulation of behavior. Where men would find a problem (such as severe wife beating) insoluble because of the necessity of preserving the face of the high-status perpetrator and the desirability of maintaining harmonious interfamily relations, women would send an old woman who had been the couple's go-between to scold and humiliate the man. The old woman had nothing to fear; the husband did. Where a man felt it necessary to discuss a complicated exchange of labor or water rights with the near senile head of a family, a woman would go directly to the son who actually did the farming, leaving it to him to deal with his father. Where men stated that a father had a perfect right to pull his brilliant son out of school if he needed help with the farm, women pointed out alternative solutions (some of which were not always practical) and made their suggestions known to the father, as publicly as possible.

In these and many similar situations, it seemed to me that women were well aware of the rules of propriety, filiality, and face, but felt they were simply not as important as the human suffering that resulted when they were the primary basis for decision making. Women also recognized the power they held by being outside the system. They could and did break the men's rules.

The apparent contradiction for my analysis is that in approaching the kinds of moral dilemmas Gilligan discusses, Chinese, men speak of the importance of maintaining relationships and the necessity of following traditional rules in order to preserve the harmony essential to an orderly society. Women—who *define* themselves through their relationships with others—are much more adept at manipulating those relationships because they put little faith in the traditional rules. The contradiction is only apparent, for the content of the relationships the two groups confront is not the same. One, the men's, involves relationships among statuses; the other, the women's, involves relationships among personalities with needs, frailties, and a capacity for suffering. Because the source of men's self-identity comes from a (theoretically) harmonious community maintained by traditional rules, there is an impersonal quality to the way in which men cultivate relationships. Because relationships are the *source* of their identity, women nurture and value them in their own right, rather than for their symbolic implications.

To return again to the quotation from Tu cited earlier, it is possible to associate the self I have described for women with the Confucians' *sz*, the privatized self that must "be protected against submersion in the waves of social demand." The self I have sketched out as belonging to men is closer to "the true self" that can aspire to be "the great self" of a Confucian "open system." This is not my intent for it would imply that women are content with or constrained to settle for a lower rung in a hierarchy of ethical standards. Instead, I suspect that village women, were they aware of the possibilities of self-cultivation would regard it with the same cynicism they do The Chinese Family— it is another "man's thing" that has little relevance to them and the realities of their experience. They are concerned—both by choice and by the traditional rules men hold sacred—with attending to the needs of people important to them (kin and non-kin). The more successful and happy their progeny, the more satisfaction they derive from their own lives. Village women would probably reject out of hand Tu's statement that "The ultimate purpose of life is neither regulating the family nor harmonizing the father-son relationship, but self-realization" (Tu 1985, 123). But they might take the frequently quoted Confucian idea from the *Analects*, "Wishing to establish oneself, one establishes others; wishing to enlarge oneself, one enlarges others," turn it on its head and say, with an innocent smile, "Wishing to establish others, one establishes oneself; wishing to enlarge others, one enlarges oneself."

BIBLIOGRAPHY

Andors, Phyllis. 1983. *The Unfinished Revolution of Chinese Women, 1949–1980*. Bloomington: Indiana University Press.

Chodorow, Nancy. 1974. "Family Structure and Feminist Personality." In *Woman, Culture, and Society*, ed. Michelle Rosaldo and Louise Lamphere. Stanford: Stanford University Press.

Cohen, Myron L. 1990. "Lineage Organization in North China." *Journal of Asian Studies* 49.

Collier, Jane F., and Sylvia J. Yanagisako, eds. 1987. *Gender and Kinship: Essays Toward a Unified Analysis*. Stanford: Stanford University Press.

Croll, Elisabeth. 1981. *The Politics of Marriage in Contemporary China*. Cambridge: Cambridge University Press.

Diamond, Norma. 1975. "Collectivization, Kinship, and the Status of Women in Rural China." *Bulletin of Concerned Asian Scholars*, Jan–Mar.

Errington, Frederick and Deborah Gewertz. 1987. *Cultural Alternatives and a Feminist Anthropology: An Analysis of Culturally Constructed*

Gender Interests in Papua New Guinea. Cambridge: Cambridge University Press.

Geertz, Clifford. 1984. "'From the Native's Point of View': On the Nature of Anthropological Understanding." In *Culture Theory: Essays on Mind, Self, and Emotion*, ed. Richard A. Shweder and Robert A. LeVine. Cambridge: Cambridge University Press.

Gilligan, Carol. 1977. "In Different Voice: Women's Conceptions of the Self and of Morality." *Harvard Educational Review* 47.

————. 1979. "Woman's Place in Man's Life Cycle." *Harvard Educational Review* 29.

————. 1982. *In a Different Voice: Psychological Theory and Women's Development.* Cambridge: Harvard University Press.

————. 1986. "Remapping the Moral Domain: New Images of the Self in Relationship." In *Reconstructing Individualism*, ed. T. C. Heller, M. Sosna, and D. E. Wellberry. Stanford: Stanford University Press.

Gilligan, Carol, J. V. Ward, and J. M. Taylor, eds. 1988. *Mapping the Moral Domain.* Cambridge: Harvard University Press.

Huang, Philip C. C. 1985. *The Peasant Economy and Social Change in North China.* Stanford: Stanford University Press.

Kagan, Jerome. 1984. *The Nature of the Child.* New York: Basic Books.

LeVine, Robert A. 1984. Quotation from Richard A. Shweder, "Preview: A Colloquy of Culture Theorists," in Richard A. Shweder and Robert A. LeVine, eds., *Culture Theory: Essays on Mind, Self, and Emotion.* Cambridge: Cambridge University Press.

Ortner, Sherry and Harriet Whitehead, eds. 1981. *Sexual Meanings.* Cambridge: Cambridge University Press.

Potter, Sulamith H. and Jack M. Potter. 1990. *China's Peasants: The Anthropology of a Revolution.* New York: Cambridge University Press.

Siu, Helen F. 1989. *Agents and Victims in South China: Accomplices in Rural Revolution.* New Haven: Yale University Press.

Tu Wei-ming. 1985. *Confucian Thought: Selfhood as Creative Transformation.* Albany, New York: State University of New York Press.

Weiner, Annette. 1976. *Women of Value, Men of Renown.* Austin: University of Texas Press.

Wolf, Margery. 1972. *Women and the Family in Rural Taiwan.* Stanford: Stanford University Press.

————. 1985. *Revolution Postponed: Women in Contemporary China.* Stanford, California: Stanford University Press.

Person in Indian Theory and Practice

INTRODUCTION TO PART FOUR

Wimal Dissanayake

The understanding of the concept of 'self' has largely centered on the interplay between sets of dualities: The self as fact versus construct, the self as subject versus object, the self as structure versus process, the self as unitary versus fragmented, and so forth. And scholars who have been seriously interested in the exploration of the concept of self have had to unpack these binarisms.[1]

Some thinkers have sought to theorize the self as a physical entity no different from any object found in the physical world. The primary contention of this approach is that self has substance; thinkers such as Berkley and Jung strongly favored this approach. Those who subscribe to this approach are of the opinion that this entity termed 'self' is constituted by our personal experience and can be investigated in the way that a person's material possessions could be examined. This is a theorization that is alien to traditional societies both in the East and the West. Some modern self-psychologists, too, seem to find this line of analysis productive. They prefer this approach largely due to the fact that it allows them to examine the self using methodologies borrowed from the natural sciences. However, it needs to be pointed out that this mode of theorization of the self has increasingly come to be questioned by modern scholars representing a vast array of disciplines.

A number of scholars, on the other hand, prefer to think of the self as a theoretical construct. Such an approach, it is asserted, will enable researchers say, in psychology, to predict human behavior—something vital to the objectives of the discipline. Hypothetical constructs such as "perception," "thought," "awareness," "suffering," and so forth will, it is hoped, enable them to make these predictions. But these hypothetical constructs, in point of fact, refer not to any object in the real world but to states of being labeled by psychologists. Clearly, there are advantages to regarding the self as a theoretical construct, and the propensity toward reifying concepts and attaching readily

271

observable referents is irresistibly powerful, but by doing this we run the risk of taking the hypothetical to be real.

The self as subject as opposed to the self as object is another antinomy that is commonly found in the literature. Given the fact that the ability to experience and feel is central to being a person, many would contend that the experiencing "I" is the self or subject. Those who adhere to this view regard the process of feeling and experiencing as being far more important than the object of experience. John Stuart Mill was one of the most articulate spokesmen for this view. He remarked, "the inexplicable tie . . . which connects the present consciousness with the past one of which it reminds me is as near as I think we can get to a positive concept of self.[2] Similarly, the well-known dictum "cogito ergo sum" (I think, therefore I am) in many ways laid the foundation for this line of thinking. Clearly, the accent here is on the experiencing self and the independence of the active mind.

Opposed to this, there are those who argue that all experience can be seen as experience of something; in other words, experience always contains content. Based on this assumption, it has been stated that the self should be seen not as the process of experiencing but as that which is experienced—the object of experience. To put it differently, the object of experience then assumes a far greater importance than the subject of experience. Moreover, the proponents of such an approach express the view that if self is defined in terms of the experiencing self subject, it becomes far too inclusive, bringing within its purview such diverse activities as thinking, reasoning, feeling, speculating, fantasizing, and so on, with the result that the concept of self is robbed of its heuristic value.

Another duality frequently found in the literature on self, a duality as common as that between self as subject and self as object, is that of the self as structure and self as process. The word structure has a way of conjuring up a mechanistic view of things. Here the psychological system that is associated with self is seen as a number of mechanical constituents, one acting on the other. The thrust of this approach is to invest the concept of self with a plurality of characteristics and turn it into an object that possesses a relative stability.

As against this view, we find an approach that lays stress on process. The process emphasized here is not dissimilar to that which focuses on imagination, say, as opposed to the object of imagination. Clearly, what is of importance here is not the structural elements of a mechanical whole but the actual principles of operation. If the self is taken to be basically an object of experience, we will find a structural model being upheld; if, on the other hand, the self is regarded as the subject of experience, what is being valorized is a process model.

The self as a single entity, as opposed to the self as a union of plural entities, is another binarism that is prevalent in the literature on self. Terms such as *self-image, a person's identity, self-concept, self-esteem,* and *self-worth,* which are commonly found in the works of social scientists, tend to suggest that the self is a single entity. The writings of many eminent scholars such as Mead, Fromm, and Rogers seem to support this perspective on the self. The notion of stability, which we discussed above, is central to such a viewpoint.

This approach has its share of opponents who maintain that the self is multiple in nature. The fact that an individual's behavior is highly variable from one situation to another and that it is very often characterized by a sense of inconsistency subject to internal contradictory pressures lends credence to this view. It is said that as a person moves from one social setting to another, he or she is likely to experience varying feelings about himself or herself and these feelings over time are likely to strengthen the multiple nature of the self that a person entertains. Phenomenologically oriented analyses of the self tend to move in this direction. The writings of William James, Alfred Schutz, Ervin Goffman, Peter Berger, and Thomas Luckman, to name but a few, serve to buttress this viewpoint.

These dichotomies have been in more recent times displaced by a newer one, namely, that of the sovereign and self-present self as opposed to the self that is purely a product of discourse. Clearly, this dichotomy is related to and draws on some of the earlier ones; however, it has received a more current inflection in the light of newer conceptualities in the domains of humanities and social sciences. On the one hand, there are those who, with varying degrees of emphasis, will argue that being must be seen as self-contained, self-present, self-identical, and the center of certitude and locus of truth. Here the self is accorded philosophical primacy as the center of rationality and imagination and consciousness. It is contended that such an approach posits the unity of being and the closedness and ready accessibility of reality as well as the epistemological privileging of the self that is deemed unitary. The self then becomes the site of origin of truth. This perspective on self, which thinkers like Derrida have characterized as constituting the metaphysics of the presence, has been vigorously challenged by philosophers of a poststructuralist persuasion.

On the other hand, opposed to this firmly centered and essentialized self, we have the theorizations of poststructuralists and postmodernists, who seek to decenter, deconstruct, and disperse the self into the play of language and the power of discourse. Drawing on the insights of such philosophers as Heidegger and Nietzsche, they seek to demonstrate the shaping power of language and discourse in molding subjectivity. For Heidegger, language becomes the site for the emergence of self and the disclosure of being. His statement that "language speaks not man" has had a profound impact on contemporary theorizations of the self. Similarly, Nietzsche, with his emphasis on skepticism, will to power, and the figurality of language, has contributed significantly to the newer styles of thinking on subjectivity. They oppose the concept of an autonomous and sovereign self, arguing that notions of subjectivity are created by powerful discursive formations that are vitally related to culture. This directly challenges the concept of an 'autonomous and self-present subject'. There is a pronounced tendency among theorists of a poststructuralist and postmodernist persuasion to privilege discourse over selfhood.

According to Althusser, who sees ideology not as the system of real relations that govern the existence of individuals but as the imaginary relations of these individuals to the real relation in which they live, the object of ideology is the construction of people as subjects.[3] Lacan saw language as the agent by which an unconscious is formed and the self as a nexus of linguistic relations.[4] Foucault regarded the subject as a complex and variable function of discourse. In his opinion, the modern conception of self is a hothouse product, representing a contrived unity, closely linked to social constructs of morality, law, rights, responsibilities, sexuality and sanity.[5]

This dichotomy between the autonomous and self-present subject and the notion that subjectivity is produced by discourse has given rise to much debate in recent times. Clearly, the notion of an autonomous, self-present, self-identical subject is not tenable. In our studies into Asian cultures we have realized the culturally constructed nature of the self. On the other hand, to regard self as a mere product of discourse is to disregard the whole complex question of human agency. (In fairness to Foucault, it has to be said that in his later stage of life he began to recognize the importance of this aspect of selfhood.)

In this regard, the following observation of Charles Taylor is extremely illuminating. He says, "We are selves only in that certain issues matter for us. What I am as a self, my identity, is essentially defined by the way things have significance for me. And as has been widely discussed, these things have significance for me, and the issues of my identity are worked out, only through a language of interpretation which I have come to accept as a valid articulation of these issues. To ask of a person what a person is, in abstraction from his or her self-interpretations, is to ask a fundamentally misguided question."[6] Hence, one crucial fact about a self is that it is not like an object in the way we understand that term normally. We do not possess selves in the way we possess hearts and livers. We are living beings with these organs quite independently of our self-understandings or the meanings things have for us. But we are selves only to the extent that we operate in a certain space of questions and are involved in interpretations of meaning. These observations of Taylor focus very clearly on the idea of agency, which is central to selfhood and neglected by poststructuralists.

This discussion of conceptualizing self in Western intellectual discourse foregrounds a number of complex issues that are in tension. When we turn to the Indian scene, the complexities are multiplied due to the pluralities of traditions involved and the alternative and indigenous perspectives that are called into play. The notion of self as person in India has largely been misperceived due to the stereotypes and heterologies that continue to govern our thinking. It is generally believed, in large measure due to the Western interpretations of Indian thought, that the idea of self as person and the attendant notion of agency are ignored, devalued, and marginalized. Nothing could be further from the truth. In order to understand the importance of the concept of self as person and human agency, we need to redescribe and reinterpret a number of culturally commanding concepts that have been subject to misrepresentation.

Let us, for example, consider the concept of 'karma' that is central to Indian culture in general. It clearly plays a defining role in Hinduism, Buddhism, and Jainism. Unfortunately, the concept of karma has been interpreted largely in terms of fatalism, thereby robbing it of its moral richness. In point of fact, the exact opposite is the case. As inscribed in classical texts, the law of karma is central to the ontology and epistemology of human person. It is vitally connected with issues of human agency, social order, justice, and morality. It is crucial to understanding the ontology of moral effects.

What the law of karma does is explain the complex ways in which certain consequences arise from certain moral actions performed by the agent. It not only underlines the importance of human agency but also offers a moral framework within which it could be purposefully understood. Very often the law of karma is denigrated as mere fatalism. However, a closer reading of the original texts would reinforce the point that various actions performed by human beings here and now determine the behavioral contexts as well as tendencies in the future.

The concept of karma is very closely associated with the notions of justice and social order. Human beings get what they deserve; and what they deserve is determined by the moral force of prior actions. This sense of fairness is intimately linked to questions of justice and social order. In this sense, karma is a meritorian concept of justice. This fact is made evident not only by classical texts but also by the behavior and attitudes of ordinary people. For example, in my studies of the concept of self among the Sinhalese, it was found that they frame that concept in terms of the idea of karma and that the idea of karma was seen as a mechanism that promotes social justice.

I have selected just one concept, from among many other equally commanding concepts, to point out that in order to understand properly the notion of self as person in Indian culture, we need to pay very close attention, in a way that we have not done in the past, to the defining concepts of Indian thought and to read them against the grain. In this book, which explores the question of self as person, the issue of human agency figures very prominently. The five essays, that compose this section deal with the idea of agency—sometimes directly, sometimes indirectly. By examining the concept of self as person in the Indian context, these essays serve to widen the boundaries of discourse of self and agency.

In the opening essay, Bimal Krishna Matilal starts out by stating that his suspicion is that there is an uncanny similarity between the premodern idea of the self and the postmodern ideas. He discusses the perception of self in India in three stages. In the first section of his paper he explores the discursivities of self, rebirth, and freedom as articulated in the Indian tradition, and their vital relationship to Indian soteriology. In the second section, Matilal examines the technical philosophical discourses centering around the ontological disputes between Nyāya and Buddhism pertaining to the existence of a soul-substance. In the final section of the paper, he seeks to draw out the lessons that this ancient dispute may have for us today and to see how it might illuminate the modern discussions of selfhood. The discourses related to self found in the Indian tradition are vast and heterogeneous, and their evolution over time complicates the terrain further. What Matilal attempts to do in his paper is to select two of the most prominent of these discourses and by examining them metonymically to provide us with an understanding of some of the issues related to self and agency that engaged the interest of Indian thinkers in the past.

The second essay is by Padmasiri de Silva and deals with the question of self and the emotion of pride in early Buddhist thought. The author starts out by pointing out how, in the Buddhist view, a false sense of self is the locus of negative emotions and that the emancipation from this deception is vital to the generation of positive emotions. Buddhism is generally regarded as advocating the concept of 'no-self'. However, Padmasiri de Silva rightly maintains that what the Buddha rejected was a substantialist concept of self and not the notion of a 'continuing person', who, as an agent of moral action, is capable of espousing values and expressing emotions. The author argues that the doctrine of the middle path and the awareness of contextual ambiguities associated with the notion of self offer us a useful conceptual space from which to examine the relationship between self and emotion in early Buddhism. According to him, what is especially noteworthy about the Buddhist approach to emotion is the interesting way in which the self and the roles of desire, cognition, belief, appraisal, as well as physiological and socio-cultural factors, are integrated. This essay dealing with emotion throws valuable light on the issue of self and agency from the viewpoint of early Buddhism.

In the next essay titled "Conceptualizing the Person: Hierarchical Society and Individual Autonomy in India," Mattison Mines examines the Indian notion of self as person from an anthropological standpoint. By and large, social scientists who have worked in India have emphasized the subordination of the individual to the institutions of family and caste and the overwhelming influence of hierarchy in molding human behavior. Their considered judgment has been that there is very little room for personal autonomy and individuation in Indian society. As Mines points out, if this assessment is correct, then the pursuit of personal ambition should be uncommon among Indians, and repudiation of family and caste injunctions should be rare. Mines, based on his examination of more than twenty life histories, challenges this widely held assumption. It is his contention that hierarchy has been accorded such a powerfully determining role in describing Indian society that the significance of individual choice and motivation have been downplayed. The interplay between self and culture and the idea of self as person with a distinctive sense of agency is explored cogently in this paper.

In the fourth paper in this section, Yamuna Kachru examines the notions of self, identity, and creativity in relation to women writers in India. She writes from a sociolinguistic viewpoint, and her investigation focuses on contemporary Hindi, Bengali, and English fiction. In the West, the rise of women's movements and the rapid growth of women's studies programs have brought a new dynamism to the study of the concept of self. Feminist scholars are advocating a fresh approach to the whole discourse of self. They argue that gender should be regarded as a fundamental organizing principle of human experience and thus of the self. Asian scholars, too, are increasingly paying attention to this aspect of selfhood. Kachru, in her paper, seeks to determine what a sociolinguistic approach to the analysis of women's fiction would contribute to the understanding of Indian selfhood. She shows how conflicts between tradition and modernity, inherited values and contemporary demands, are inscribed in the newer articulations of feminine selfhood in India. Kachru's essay enables us to widen the discussion of self as person in India along gender lines.

The last paper in this section on India is by Alan Roland, and it is titled "Selves in Motion: An Indian-Japanese Comparison." In comparative studies of the self, it is the customary practice to examine the notions of selfhood found in Asian countries in relation to those found in the West. In this paper, Roland has sought to adopt an inter-Asian approach by comparing the idea of self in India and Japan from a distinctly psychological perspective. Here he presses into service the psychological process of self-transformation as a way of understanding the distinct modalities of Indian and Japanese individuation. The author illustrates, among other things, how the interplay between self and family is crucial to an understanding of self as person in India and Japan.

These five essays, then, offer us an interesting and complex picture of self as person in Indian culture from different disciplinary vantage points. The first two essays have been written from a distinctly philosophical standpoint, while the other three adopt anthropological, sociolinguistic, and psychological perspectives, respectively. They encourage us to avoid the two extreme conceptualities of autonomous, sovereign self and self as product of discourse and to adopt a perspective that recognizes the cultural construction of self as well as the importance of the idea of agency. The discourses and modes of representation of self in Indian culture are varied and complex, and what this section of the book seeks to do is to give a hint of that complexity and richness.

NOTES

1. K. J. Gergen, *The Concept of Self* (New York: Holt Rinehart and Winston, 1971).

2. J. S. Mill, *Essential Works* (New York: Bantam Books, 1961), 43.

3. L. Althusser, *Lenin and Philosophy and Other Essays* (London: New Left Books, 1971).

4. J. Lacan, *The Language of the Self: The Function of Language in Psychoanalysis* (New York: Delta, 1968).

5. M. Foucault, *The Archaeology of Knowledge* (London: Tavistock Publications, 1972).

6. C. Taylor, *The Sources of Self* (Cambridge: Harvard University Press, 1989), 34.

12

The Perception of Self in Indian Tradition

Bimal Krishna Matilal

I

Holding as we do that, while knowledge of any kind is a thing to be honoured and prized, one kind of it may, either by reason of its greater exactness or of a higher dignity and greater wonderfulness in its objects, be more honourable and precious than another, on both accounts we should naturally be led to place in the front rank the study of the soul. The knowledge of the soul admittedly contributes greatly to the advance of truth in general, and above all, to our understanding of Nature, for the soul is in some sense the principle of animal life—Aristotle.

I begin with these two sentences of Aristotle's *De Anima*.[1] My purpose, however, is to talk about the perception of the self in the context of traditional or classical India. This is not directly addressed to the postmodernists. I shall instead talk about a premodern idea of 'self'. My suspicion is that there is an uncanny similarity between the premodern idea of self and postmodernist discussion of the same. The above quotation simply underlines a couple of notable phenomena. The first is the universality of concern among the philosophers in the ancient or classical (and premodern) world regarding the conception of the self. The second is the primary importance given to the knowledge of the self as well as its being the gateway to the knowledge of other things, to our understanding of Nature. In India, such pronouncements as "know thyself" or "knowledge of the self gives you the knowledge of everything" were frequently formed even in the Upaniṣads, when philosophical thinking was more poetically expressed and arguments achieved neither systematization nor sophistication. Some have claimed that the thoughts of the Upaniṣads influenced not only Buddhism but also, perhaps partly through Buddhism, the Neoplatonics, Christian mystics, and even Persian Sufis. Such a claim can hardly be substantiated, but the part about their possible influence upon Buddhism cannot be lightly dismissed. Even a late Buddhist text such as *Tattvasaṃgraha* summarizes the Upaniṣadic teaching about *ātman*, and its author, Śāntarakṣita, remarks that this teaching of *ātman* as the universal and eternal consciousness is *not totally* faulty (cf. *Alpāpardaha*), for it has some merit. Kamalaśīla, the commentator, says that if the notion of eternality of consciousness is dropped, the Upaniṣadic teaching becomes more acceptable to a Buddhist who identifies the self with the momentary consciousness-series. The importance that the Upaniṣads put upon the knowledge of the self is well known. A single quotation from *Īśa*, verse 7, suffices to demonstrate this:

He who sees unity in all diversities
He who knows the self as the Universal soul,
Is beyond all illusions and sufferings, beyond all losses and gains.

My express purpose is to talk about the perception of the self in India. I propose to do it in three parts. In the first part, I shall introduce briefly the classical Indian thinking about the trio—the self, rebirth, and ways to freedom. (The meaning of "freedom" is intriguing. It changes according to the schools and religious sects. It also changes from age to age.) There is a bewildering variety of views regarding the details of their interrelationship, but there is unanimous agreement that these three concepts constituted the building blocks of what we may very generally call "Indian soteriology." In the second part, I wish to go a bit into the technical philosophical discourse about the ontological dispute between Nyāya and Buddhism over the existence of a soul-substance. In the third part, I wish to talk briefly about what possible lesson can we derive today from this age-old dispute and what relation could it have with the modern (and postmodern) discussion of personhood.

The task, at first blush, seems to be next to impossible. There is a variety of views about the self expressed in what we tend to call "schools" and "sub-schools," or rival systems or rival philosophers in classical India. And debates and arguments surrounding the self and nonself continued for about two millennia. One illustration will do. *Tattvasaṃgraha*, a Buddhist text belonging to circa A.D. 800, mentions the views of self of six different schools, Nyāya-Vaiśeṣika, Sāṃkhya, Mīmāṃsā, Jaina, Aupaniṣada (of the Upaniṣads), and the Vātsiputrīya, as well as several individual philosophers: four of them, such as Abiddhakarṇa, belonging to the Nyāya School, and Kumārila belonging to the Mīmāṃsā School. After refuting all these views, the author presents his own (Buddhist) view, which regards perception of the self as the misattribution of a false concept to the aggregates of material forms and mental events. However this rivalry indicates that they shared a common philosophical concern. Besides, philosophical concerns can be said to be conditioned to some extent by the cultural milieu. These rival views share certain common cultural presuppositions, which could constitute our starting point for giving an impressionistic account of the perception of the self in India.

One common concern has already been noted above from the Upaniṣad: they all accord prime importance to the knowledge of the self, which is supposed to unlock the door to "freedom," or the highest good, marked by our flight from this "prison house" of *conditioned* mundane existence, which is almost universally undervalued or devalued as *duḥkha*, "suffering" or "unhappiness" or "unpreferred state." It is an "unpreferred state" because as it is *given* to us it does not have any ultimate meaning, any ultimately satisfactory value. By contrast, the attempt of all philosophers was to posit a goal possessing the ultimate value and ultimate meaning, and the claim was that only against the backdrop of such a covetable goal does this mundane existence of ours acquire any meaning.

Admittedly, the Buddha teaches how our false conception of the self has to be dissolved into the *analytic insight* (*prajñā*, literally, perfect wisdom) of the five personality aggregates or twelve bases or eighteen base-elements in order to achieve *nirvāṇa*. Here also the concern for the self is not absent. As Udayana (A.D. 1058) cleverly points out in his monumental work *Ātmatattvaviveka*, even the Buddhist has to know the true nature of the *self* or soul, so that he can comprehend fully what it is that lacks ultimate existence or ultimate essence. In Udayana's language, in acquiring knowledge of the nonself, since the counter-entity is the self, knowledge of the counter-entity is presupposed in any knowledge of its negation. In plain words, expounding of even the no-self doctrine needs a lot of stage setting, a study of many common assumptions or perceptions of the self to serve as a foil.

I would like to make two further points at the outset. Another presupposition shared among the Indian philosophers is that ways of perceiving one's self not only (unconsciously) modifies one's perception of the nonself, by which I mean here the rest of the universe of which human beings are part, but also seems to distinguish the humans from other creatures. We are thus self-perceiving, self-interpreting, meaning-seeking, and value-discovering creatures.[2] Second, the manifoldness of ways of perceiving the self—*ātman*—is almost axiomatic because *ātman* is a technical term that is, in each case, a member of a set of technical terms, all of which are interlocked and thus constitute a system that we call a "*darśana*" in India. It has thus different shades of meaning in different *darśana*s. However, a common structure is nevertheless discoverable, and this is probably because of their common cultural and social background. Each *darśana*, for example, is concerned with an outline of what I have called "the therapeutics of *nirvāṇa* or final release"—some more and some less. It is modeled after medical science. One quotation from the *Yoga-bhāṣya* will get us to the heart of the matter (under *Yogasūtra* 2.15):[3]

> Just as the medical science is a system of four items—disease, causes of disease or sickness, health (cessation of sickness) and the medicine to cure, this *śāstra* likewise is a system of four: *saṃsāra* (suffering being caught in repetitious rebirth), causes of such suffering, its cessation (freedom) and the means for achieving that state of ultimate freedom.

Obviously, this is similar to the Buddha's teaching of four great "truths": suffering, its origin, its cessation, and the Way. Even in the Nyāya, Vātsyāyana[4] (sutra 1.1.1.), while he says that knowledge of the self and the other realities eventually leads to the final goal or the "ultimate good" (*niḥśreyasa*), also mentions that the *śāstra* is concerned with the system of four "footings of reality" (*arthpada*); avoidable (i.e., future) suffering, its avoidance, means for such avoidance, and the destination or final freedom. Further documentation being unnecessary, I shall only point out that perception of the self or the nonself (cf. *nairātmya-dṛṣṭi*) occupies a central position in this so-called therapy. Hence, the sophisticated and hair-splitting argument to expose the exact nature of what it is to be a self or a person, which continued not for centuries but for a millennium in India, need not come as a surprise.

II

Recent renewed discussion in the West about the question of personal identity and the self has mainly centered around (what is now called) "reductionism" versus "nonreductionism." The reductionist holds that the fact of a person's identity over time just consists in the holding of certain particular facts that can be described without the assumption that a persistent self exists. A person's existence means occurrence of a series of interrelated physical and mental events in a brain and a body. The nonreductionist, however, holds that there are some additional facts over and above those required by the reductionists. This new reductionist view has been claimed to mandate a change in self-perception that provides additional support for the moral theory of consequentialism by rejecting the classical self-interest theory. Since the Buddhist is sort of a reductionist in respect to his conception of selfhood, some Buddhological scholars have been delighted to see this new trend in the analytical tradition. I shall refrain from making any further comment on this issue but simply point out that the problems of such comparative philosophy, while they are very suggestive on the surface, at a deeper level become extremely complicated and involved, such that each comparison ends up necessarily in noting stark contrasts; only then does it becomes philosophically fruitful or rewarding.

It is true that the Buddha was a reductionist and his soteriology was explicitly presented as deflationary. If the person's life experiences and his *saṃsāra* are by nature undervalued as suffering and pain, then the only possible way to the final and nonrecurring cessation of suffering is to perceive the person as a false, superimposed concept, which will disappear before the final liberating insight. I shall choose one particular school of Buddhism to discuss its detailed process and the argument. Among the nonreductionists, I shall present the counterargument of the Nyāya school in order to bring both arguments into sharp relief.

Almost all Indian philosophers, as well as the schools they belong to, regarded *darśana* as imparting the knowledge of the way by which one can change the existing life experience, which is, by all accounts, devalued in relation to the goal that is accorded the supreme value. Various pairs of terms are in use with the usual difference in their detailed explanation, although the basic pattern is the same due to their common cultural presuppositions (table 12–1). The general assumption was that a true perception of the self (or nonself, as the case may be) will lead one from one stage (noted in the left-hand column) to the other (the right-hand column).

Table 12–1

bondage/*bandha*	release/*mokṣa*
constraints	freedom
dahana, tapa, pīḍa	*nirvāṇa*
duḥkha, bādhanā	*vimokṣa*
preya	*śreyas, niḥśreyasa*
slavery	liberation
pain, suffering	cessation, bliss

The Buddhists, however, had a chip on their shoulder. Although it is undeniable that the Buddha rejected the notion of a persistent self that transmigrates, he accepted the transmigration process as well as the karma doctrine, which involved action, motivation, and moral responsibility. Besides, a few of his *Dialogues* contained elements that might refer to a persistent self. Further, of the early Buddhist schools, the Vātsiputrīyas and the Sāmmitīyas accepted the concept of a persistent entity called "*pudgala.*" Since this concept came very close to the Brahminical soul, these schools were viewed as being heretical.

First, consider the often mentioned *Bhāra-sutta* of the *Samyutta-nikāya* (pt. 3, pp. 25–26, sutta 22):

> Bhāra have pañcakkandhā
> Bhāraharo ca puggalo
> Bhārādānam dukkham loke
> Bhāranikkepaṇam sukham.

Here the five personality aggregates, or the psycho-physical complex, are called the "burden," whereas the "person" (*pudgala*) carries the burden. Since the passage was frequently mentioned by rival philosophers, Śāntarakṣita[5] saw fit to explain it from the "nonself" point of view. The commentator, Kamalaśīla, said that the "bundle" of the psycho-physical event was identified as the "person," such that the disciple might have recognized it as a "nominally existent" entity (*prajñapt-sat*), not a separate and eternally real entity. A "nominally existent" entity in Buddhism means a false and hence dispensable concept. Kamalaśīla also referred to a citation by Uddyotakara, the Naiyāyika, from the *Dialogues* of the Buddha, which might have had separated the self from *rūpa* ("material form"), feelings, perceptions, and so forth. Kamalaśīla explained it away by saying that such specific instructions of the Buddha were meant for those confused disciples who might have thought the bundle of feelings or the perceptions as the self.

The *pudgala* (person) of the Sāmmitīyas and the Vātsiputrīyas was not exactly the soul of the Brāhmaṇas; it was accepted, however, as a separate entity. Vasubandhu therefore elaborately refuted such a concept in the ninith chapter of his *Abhidharmakośabhāṣya.*[6] Śāntarakṣita summarized this argument in his *Tattvasaṃgraha.* He also added that the doctrine of universal flux would instantly refute any such persistent entity as the *pudgala*.

In the Yogācāra school the self was identified as the individual, but instantaneously emerging, awareness-series. It was divided into (Vasubandhu's *Triṃśikā*) eight:[7] five-sensory awareness (called *pravṛ-*

ttivijñāna, for they cause motivation to act), "mental" awareness, "ego-shrunk" mind, and *ālaya* (storehouse) awareness. This *ālaya* doctrine was posited to explain the problem of linkage between one state and the other in the same personality series. I will comment more on this later.

Udayana[8] See, in his famous book *Ātmattvaviveka*, identified four pairs of rival philosophical theses, one set of which refutes the claim that the self is something over and above the physical and psychological continuity, while the other set rejects the previous set, thereby creating the ground for our belief in a persistent self.

The first four theses, all ascribable to the Buddhists, are:

1. Everything that exists is momentary (the flux doctrine).

2. The assumed external objects are, in fact, created or given by our internal episodes. (The external object of awareness is in fact an object *in* that awareness.)

3. The attributes and their substratum are indistinguishable and hence identical.

4. No accredited means of knowledge is available to prove the existence of such an independent self.

The other set of four theses consists in the negation of these four. If everything is in a flux, the notion of a persistent self is by far refuted. If there are no external objects, we may not then cognize the self, for the self, which is distinct from internal awareness but recognizes external objects through such awareness, cannot be established. If the substratum-attribute distinction is not established, then the distinctness of the persistent self has to be sacrificed. Besides, we need evidence to prove the existence of a distinct, persistent self.

It seems in Udayana's view, we have here a package deal. The Buddhist perception of the nonself is interlocked with the above four principal philosophical theses. A Naiyāyika has to knock off all four, one by one, before he can hope to establish his belief in nonreductionism.

The "flux" doctrine is argued on the basis of an abolition of any distinction between the capability or potentiality to *do* anything (causal potency) and actually doing it. This was the essence of Dharmakīrti's argument to prove the flux doctrine in his *Hetubindu*, which was later elaborated in various ways by his followers, such as Arcaṭa, Śāntarakṣita, Jñānaśrī and Ratnakīrti.[9] If a thing's potentiality is identified with its actually doing it, and if existence is defined in terms of the potency to do something, then the flux doctrine follows as the logical outcome. But a cook does not always cook, nor a teacher always teach. Hence if either capability or potency is defined in terms of causing something to happen when and only when all accessory conditions cooperate, then as Udayana argued, persistent objects must exist, with refutes the highly counterintuitive flux doctrine.

The argument to support the Buddhist challenge to not only the persistence but also the existence of external objects was formulated in various ways,[10] but one of Dharmakīrti's arguments became the most famous and a much-debated one. An external object, say a blue thing, and our cognition of that very object, are always and invariably cognized together. Given the truth of this claim, one can draw the conclusion that what appears to be *external* is in fact indistinguishable from, and hence identical with, what is *internal* to the awareness, that is, it is the awareness itself. The Nyāya reply, which Udayana formulates, basically uses the same kind of ordinary intuition of common people as evidence. Udayana says that whenever a cognition grasps a so-called (external) object, that very cognition itself cannot at the same time conceal the distinctness of the graspable from the grasping itself. Nyāya, however, disagrees that cognition of an object and the cognition of that very cognition arise together at the same moment. But even if this so-called togetherness is conceded for the sake of the argument, Nyāya points out that such togetherness is not a strong enough evidence to prove identity beyond all reasonable doubt. Besides, "togetherness" itself implies a difference at a certain level. It takes two to tango.

The substance-attribute—or rather location-locative distinction— is so much ingrained in our ordinary experience of the structure of the reality that it would be highly counterintuitive to obliterate the distinction. From a distance we can see the substratum, for example, but because of our lack of seeing its attributes (leaves, etc., in the case of a tree, or hands and legs in the case of a person), we cannot have certainty. This shows that the substratum can be cognized as distinct from attributes. As regards the lack of any means of knowledge or evidence to establish the existence of a persistent self, Udayana claims that both perception and inference can supply the required proof of the self's existence. "I"-awareness is a sort of inner perception that all creatures universally experience. Inference of the self is based upon the evidence of what is called "recollective memory."

The main argument for reductionsim or nonreductionism turns primarily upon a proper interpretation of recollective memory and psychological connectedness, which is relevant for explaining personal identity not only over time but also, in the Indian context, over the birth, death, and rebirth process, which is perhaps misleadingly called "transmigration." The Buddhist had an additional chip on his shoulder, for he had to insist upon the said connectedness not only over some time but also from one birth to another. To explain transmigration without a transmigrating soul, one resorts, in Buddhism, to the theory of the twelve-membered "causal" chain. In this chain, the preceding member is called a *pratyaya*, a "condition" (in a very loose sense) for the arising of the succeeding member. The first two members belong to the previous birth, *avidyā* (false belief) and *saṃskara* (residual traces of karma); their being there causes the third member, *vijñāna*, to arise. This is explained by Vasubandhu as the origin of consciousness or awareness series at the time of the new life (i.e., conception in the mother's womb). Depending on this "awareness," the psycho-physical complex arises, and so on. The point to note here is that the notion of karma combined with the set of false beliefs[11] (one of which is *satkāyadṛṣṭi*, perception of the body and mind as the self) perpetuates the continuity of the false personality aggregates from one life to another. Another crucial member of the causal chain is the "thirst" or drive for pleasure or for continuing life. Life is continued because of the *hetu-pratyayas*, that is, as long as the causal conditions, such as false beliefs, karma, and the drive for becoming, perpetuate it. It is like the flame of a lamp that burns as long as it is fed with the *pratyayas*, such as the wick, and the oil and air. Just as it is not the *same* flame that goes on burning over a period of time (but each time a new flame arises), we have a false awareness of the identity of the flame of that lamp. Personal identity can be explained along the same lines.

We may at this stage take a closer look at the aggregate of awareness, which is usually the Yogācāra substitute for the self. It is interesting to note that in the Saravāstivāda school, this is divided into six types of awareness (five sensory and one "mental" or "inner"), but although "mind" (*mano-dhatu*) is mentioned, it is not considered an additional entity. Only the preceding awareness-moment is regarded as mind with respect to the succeeding awareness moment. In the Sthaviravāda school, however, the entity mind is distinguished by its three or more peculiar functions,[12] such as the adverting mind to any of the five "doors" (i.e., senses) and two classes of acceptance of "impressions." The Yogācāra, as I have already noted, speaks of not only a mind (*Kliṣṭa-manas* = mind with defilements of ego-perception, etc.) but also an *ālaya*, the locus of all "seeds."

In the Maitriya-Asaṅga-Vasubandhu school of Yogācāra the *ālaya* became an all important concept. The Sthaviravāda had a concept of 'a current of consciousness' (*bhavāṅga-vijñāna*) linking the fluctuating and transmigrating stages. It was regarded as a backdrop against which "thoughts" (*vithi-citta* in Sthaviravāda, *pravṛtti-vijñāna* in Yogācāra) arise and perish. Although this is said to be bound by birth and death, since death is a prelude to another birth, it must flow as a current from life to life. This, therefore, creates the false notion of the self that is supposed to maintain "personal identity."

The problem arises in the causal explanation of the continuity of thought-moments, where depending upon the preceding one, the succeeding one arises. For thought-moments are either good or bad, and hence a good moment cannot arise depending upon the preceding bad one. To avoid this quandry, the Sthaviras posited this "undercurrent" of awareness, which is neither good nor bad, is itself in flux (*avyākṛta*), and can intervene between a bad thought and a good one. The Sautrāntika criticized this theory and posited their concepts of 'seed' and 'maturity'. Seeds of the evil may coexist with the seeds of the good and only one of them (from either group) can obtain "maturity" at a time. Thus, good thoughts arise from good seeds, and bad ones from bad. In the context of this controversy and tension, the Yogācāra posited the *ālaya*, "the receptable," as a flow (or current) of awareness from which "thoughts" arise like waves from water (Vasubandhu).[13] All thoughts leave their residual traces in the form of seeds, which await their respective maturity to generate further thoughts. Thus, *ālaya* is called the "locus of all seeds" (they are also in a flux), and at death all other thoughts dissolve in the "mental," which in turn dissolves into the *ālaya*, retaining the seeds for maturity in the next birth. *Nirvāṇa* is achieved when this *ālaya* dissolves or "turns to itself" or "reverses itself."

The receptable (*ālaya*) awareness shares a lot of characteristics with the soul or the self of the non-Buddhists. Hence in the *Sandhisūtra* (where the doctrine was formulated as well as elaborated) the Buddha is supposed to have given the following warning:[14]

> The *ālaya* consciousness is the locus of all seeds, deep and subtle like the ocean. I have not revealed this notion (earlier) lest fools construe this as the "soul" out of confusion.

In the later Yogācāra school, the *ālaya* doctrine was not given any prominence. However, that there was a tension within Buddhism itself has been illustrated by the above brief discussion. The Naiyāyikas found that the seed theory could be faulted in various ways. There was at least an argument made against the "heaviness" of suppositions whereby at every moment millions of memory seeds and other karma seeds (residual traces) were said to continuously arise and die, for only a few seeds (or one seed) at a time could reach maturity to generate the next (particular) thought-moment or action-moment. There was no self or persistent substratum where such potentialities might reside until maturity. In fact, here the table was turned against the Buddhist, who originally blamed others for "heaviness" in suppositions (an additional self).

The main (positive) argument of Nyāya for a permanent or enduring self, which will have not only transtemporal but also transmigrational identity, is based upon an evidence of a special kind of experience, *pratisandhāna*, which I have translated as "recollective memory." Vātsyāyana used this term, but the argument was first elaborated by Uddyotakara while he gave a unique interpretation of the *Nyāya-sūtra*, namely, "For, the same object is grasped by seeing and touching." Udayana also uses this as his principal evidence. *Pratisandhāna* is not simply memory or recollection, it is not even recognition of what was already recognized (=*pratyabhijñā*), as Udayana clearly states. It is usually verbalized as, "This I (i.e., I myself) who saw the food am now eating (touching) it." Uddyotakara said that this evidence is adequate to prove not only the stability of the external objects of our perception but also the persistence of the (internal) subject who grasps the object. In other words, it cuts both ways. It seems undeniable that we have such experience where not only the transtemporal identity of the object but also the same of the subject is witnessed. If the experience is not regarded as mistaken with regard to the object at least in the majority of cases, there is no adequate reason to regard it as *always* mistaken as regards the subject.

Notice that minimal criteria are needed to reidentify something over time. The rosebush that I planted five years ago is to me still the same rosebush although probably many cells of the plant has changed, multiplied, grown, and died. For one who does not believe in the flux doctrine, it could be the same self or subject, just as it would be the same rosebush, or, for instance, the same chair that I bought five years ago.

The Buddhist, however, would have an easy answer. Being a believer in the flux doctrine, he would resort to the psychological continuity or connectedness between "cause and effect" (in the special Buddhist sense) as an adequate ground for explaining the (illusory) appearance of the subject-identity over time. This cause and effect series must belong to the same (a particular) continuum, for otherwise, as Udayana points out, when the teacher's knowledge goes on in sequence generating the body of the disciple's knowledge, the above causal criterion will misidentify the teacher's person as that of the student. The unity of the causal continuum of psychological states is, thus, to be ascertained, the Buddhist may reply, on the basis of our lack of grasping the distinctness of the bodies. But this reply would be invalid. For this may guarantee transtemporal identity of the series, but not transmigrational identity, which the Buddhist admits and where, through a different body, the awareness-series is supposed to continue. The moral responsibility implicit in the pan-Indian karma theory pervades not just one life but a series of lives with different bodies, environments, and so forth. Besides, Udayana poses a tricky question.

Suppose a boy has never seen his father; then he would have a lack of grasping the distinctness of his own body from his father's. There is causal connection as far as bodies are concerned and, therefore, the above criteria for subject identity would apply. In fact, in the case of physical objects, causal connectedness is not an adequate criterion for object-identity in all cases, even when they arise in quick succession such that we cannot grasp the distinctness of their moments of occurrence. When an earthen pot is smashed into pieces all of a sudden, we do not have even a false sense of its identity.

The problem, as Udayana sees it, is this: the causal connection between the previous experience when I *saw* the object and the present experience when I *touch* it cannot be happily explained unless some additional factor is imagined. "Belonging to the same continuum of awareness" is not an adequate explanation, because, without circularity how are we to identify the continuum? If it is done on the basis of the *ālaya*, that is not satisfactory either. For, as we have seen, the *ālaya* has to fluctuate at every moment, and this action is never registered in our awareness; what is registered there is the enduring subject-identity. It is this awareness of subject-identity over time that distinguishes one continuum from another. The theory of this being an illusion is based upon no other evidence (for we never directly experience that I am a *completely* different person at every instant) but upon such material object analogy of a river or the flame of a lamp. Even these examples can be challenged. If by "a river" we simply mean some portion of water at a particular spatiotemporal coordinate, then, of course, we cannot step twice into the same river. But if it means a continuous water flow at a particular spatial location coming from the same fountainhead of water and perhaps also being emptied in the same lake or ocean, then we can step into IT twice, thrice, and so on, for such an entity, whatever that is, will have well-known criteria for transtemporal identity. The Nyāya perception of the enduring self is similar to this: the self has both a transtemporal and a transmigrational identity, thereby taking care of the moral responsibility implicit in the karma doctrine. Short of accepting the doctrine of universal flux, it is possible to say that the universally felt common experience that I take a bath in the same *river* everyday is also veridical, unless it becomes part of the common universal illusion, which the universal flux doctrine upholds. The argument in either case seems to be evenly balanced: the idea of a multitude or "heaviness" of suppositions (the other side of the parsimony argument) works both ways. The reductionist Buddhist is shedding off only one excess baggage, that of an enduring self, while he has to accept, as we have seen, other excess baggage. The flux doctine, apart from being counterintuitive, is not by any means a simple doctrine. It is loaded with suppositions of various sorts, unsupported by common experience. Without the flux doctrine, the no-soul doctrine will lose at least one substantive argument in its favor. Then, of course, the coherence of the notion of the stability of material objects with that of an ever-fluctuating awareness-series recognizing those stable material objects, can very well be called into question.

III

Whether there is an enduring self or not, both the Buddhist and Nyāya agree that a perception of its *true* nature (which may be either a void or a substantial entity) is what adds the ultimate meaning, value, and significance to our life, which otherwise appears to be only full of suffering, absurd and devoid of any value. The moral theory would be the same or similar in both cases insofar as they accept the karma doctrine and transtemporal and transmigrational moral responsibility. The ultimate goal is, for both, and cessation of *saṁsāra* through a sort of self-realization, the ultimate knowledge of what one's own self is.

Cessation of *saṁsāra* need not ensure a blissful state. Both Nyāya and Buddhism regard it as a negative state—a value but not necessarily, as any ordinary person may imagine, a state of happiness. This falsifies the usual claim that the goal of all human begins is a sort of ultimate happiness or bliss. Both are therefore committed to answer the common question, why, then, would people be inclined to look for such a goal? A commonsense answer is that if one is carrying a heavy burden for a pretty long time, would he not be attracted to a state where he is released and relieved of his burden? It is not a happy state certainly, but something that is still a desirable goal. In the postmodern context, we may understand the implication of this underlying soteriology in a slightly different manner. We are at liberty to choose our own interpretation. The gradually dawning self-knowledge or self-realization that makes one feel the valuelessness or essencelessness of everything we tend to attach value to, will lead naturally to self-etiolation and gradually self-effacement. This, in turn, is supposed to gradually attenuate the drive for life's pleasures and pain, which would make a glimpse of something beyond possible and within reach—a truth that the original Upaniṣads initially talked about. Why is such a nirvā-nic consciousness desirable, and is it a happy or blissful state? We may reply with a comment of Udayana (twice repeated): "Why should we, small ginger-merchants, be concerned with big ocean-liners?"[15]

Buddhism, I believe, should distance itself from modern reduc-tionism, for in spite of the allure of the moral theory it seems to en-dorse (if there is much less ego, there can be successful rejection of the self-interest theory), it seems to be of one piece with modern natural-ism. Buddhism, therefore, cannot accept the whole package of Par-fitian (modern) reductionism. Besides, I have shown that in the con-text of the transmigrational subject-identity or continuum-identity, and of the action theory and moral responsibility of the karma doctrine, the Buddhist and Nyāya may endorse a similar moral theory by which the classical self-interest theory may well be defeated. What is impor-tant, it seems to me, is to move away from the scientific-materialistic picture of the universe modeled after the canons that emerged in the seventeenth-century revolution of natural science, a view that I have called "naturalism,"[16] following Charles Taylor, and that may also be called "modernism." It is true that Derek Parfit's motivation was not to argue in favor of some form of behaviorism (in fact he was probably trying to find a way out of it). But, as I have noted, the dispute in clas-sical India had some common presuppositions about one's understand-ing of the self. This type of understanding had features that added real significance to human beings and their agency, their actions and their self-understanding. It may be necessary to revive, within the modern Western analytical philosophy circle, the old classical Indian or the eighteenth-century Western (anti-scientist) "premodern" concern for the dignity of human nature. To me, only in such a context would analysis and understanding of the different perceptions of the self in different non-Western traditions have true significance.

Our Indian poet Rabindranath Tagore once said that there is a "Surplus in Man." In his nonphilosophical language, he said, "How-ever crude all this may be, it proves that Man has a feeling that he is truly represented in something which exceeds himself. He is aware that he is not *imperfect*, but *incomplete*. He knows that in himself some meaning has yet to be realized."[17] This may be regarded by some as the premodern view that has long been shattered by science. But has it been totally shattered? And where have science and technology brought us?

Albert Einstein in his conversation with Tagore once said: "There are two different conceptions about nature; (i) the whole world as a unity dependent on humanity; (ii) the world as a reality independent of human factor." He added, however, that although the second was necessarily presupposed by natural science, no one had been able to prove it to be the true doctrine *scientifically*. Thus, while we need not attempt to undermine (or devalue), like some eighteenth-century thinkers, the value of natural science and the progress of modern technology, it may now be the right time to do some rethinking about what direction our serious philosophical activity should take. It may be that we badly need reconsideration of the old-fashioned and classical ways of perceiving the self as, to some extent at least, free agents invested with some self-conscious moral sensitivity. In view of the world situation today and some of the serious crises that modern science and technology have brought along with its blessings, it is this "Surplus in Man," his own self-understanding and rational self-wisdom, that can save us from disasters. As the poet Tagore said a long time ago, "In spite of the present gloom we should not lose faith in humankind. For if that goes, we lose everything."[18] Recent research in cognitive psychology takes into account the indeterminacy of the mental, but it treats a human being more as a computing machine. Why not reverse the metaphor and treat machines as simple models of human beings, thereby preserving the proper dignity of humankind and making the "Surplus in Man" more visible to us in our perception of the self. Thus, perhaps, a new humanistic science can develop. If this still sounds old-fashioned, I might conclude with a comment, a rhetorical question, from Sir Isaiah Berlin:

> Yet what solution have we found, with all our new technological and pscyhological knowledge and great new powers, save the ancient prescription advocated by the creators of humanism—Erasmus and Spinoza, Locke and Montesquieu, Lessing and Diderot—reason, education, self-knowledge, responsibility—above all, self-knowledge? What other hope is there for men, or has there ever been?[19]

The reason may also be given by another quotation from him:

> It is neither rational thought, nor domination over nature, but freedom to choose and to experiment that distinguishes men from the rest of nature.[20]

I conclude with the comment that I started with. There is an uncanny similarity between premodern and postmodern self. Analysis of some premodern (traditional) cultures, such as those of India and China, might help us to better understand the postmodern self.

NOTES

1. R. McKeon, ed., *The Basic Works of Aristotle* (New York: Random House, 1941), 535.

2. This comment, in spite of its Sartrean overtone, can, with confidence, be ascribed to the premodern thought.

3. See Svāmī Brahmalīna Muni, *Yogadarśana*, Kashi Sanskrit Series, no. 201 (Varanasi: Chowkhambha, 1970).

4. See A. Thakur, ed., *Nyāyadarśana* (Mithila, 1967); *Bhāṣya* under sutra 1.1.1.

5. See Dwarikadas Sastri, ed., *Tattvasaṃgraha* (Varanasi: Bauddha Bharati, 1968), chap. on *Ātmaparīkṣā*.

6. See Dwarikadas Sastri, ed., *Abhidharmakośabhāṣya* (Varanasi: Bauddha Bharati, 1970–72). See also J. Deurlinger, "Vasubandu's 'Refutation of the Theory of Selfhood' (*Ātmavādapratisedha*)" in *Journal of Indian Philosophy* 17, no. 2 1989, 129–87, for a new annotated translation and comments.

7. See S. Levi, ed., *Vijñaptimātratāsiddhi* (Paris, 1925).

8. See Pandit Dhundhiraja Sastri, ed., *Ātmatottvaviveka* (Varanasi: Chwokhamba, 1940), 5.

9. See also B. K. Matilal, *Logic, Language and Reality* (New Dehli: Motilal Banarsidass, 1985), 276–77.

10. See B. K. Matilal, *Perception* (Oxford: Clarendon Press, 1986), 229–40.

11. See Matilal, *Logic, Language and Reality*, 319–32.

12. See Aniruddha, *Abhidhammatthasamgaho*, ed. R. Sastri (Varanasi, 1965).

13. See *Trimśikà*, in *Vijñaptimātratāsiddhi*.

14. See Matilal, *Logic, Language and Reality*, 346.

15. See Sastri, *Ātmatattvaviveka*, 223.

16. See Charles Taylor, *Philosophical Papers*, 2 vols. (New York: Cambridge University Press, 1985).

17. See the appendix to R. N. Tagore, *The Religion of Man* (Oxford: Oxford University Press 1920).

18. R. N. Tagore, *Sabhyatār Saṃkaṭ*; see his *Collected Works* in Bengali.

19. See I. Berlin, *Four Essays on Liberty* (Oxford: Oxford University Press 1969), 198–99.

20. Ibid., 208.

13

Emotion Profiles: The Self and the Emotion of Pride

Padmasiri de Silva

Emotions and the "Self"

Robert Solomon, who wrote the first comprehensive, well-known study of emotions in recent times,[1] maintains that a central feature of emotions is that they are "self-involved."[2] He also says that in many emotions the judgment of the self is implicit or in the shadows, implying that the self casts a shadow on emotions like admiration, indignation, anger, and envy. "Anger, which always involves a judgment that one's self has been offended or violated, may nonetheless focus its fervor strictly outwards toward the other person. Resentment, although clearly self-involved and based upon a personal stance of defensiveness, protects its self with a projected armor of objectivity . . ."[3] He says that in every case the self is an essential pole of emotional judgment. Solomon even seems to suggest that the nature of emotions will remain incomprehensible without a theory of the self.[4] But ultimately for him the self in emotions is a point of reference implying subjectivity, and self-involved does not indicate being selfish, nor does it entail self-indulgence.

Though Solomon does not pursue these questions, the interesting question is whether the fact that emotions are self-involved may imply that they are selfish, whether emotions are bad because they emerge out of self-centered attitudes, and whether emotions can be grouped under "egoistic" and "nonegoistic" emotions. Even in the recent literature that refers to the problematic relationship between the self and the emotions, sometimes there is an unwillingness to probe deeply into the question of the *reality of the self*, as well the moral criticism of emotions.

To cite another study, where there is a reference to the self in an extremely interesting study of jealousy, Leila Tov-Ruach makes the following observations: jealousy is one of those emotions that perceive a danger to the self at its center, and all the varieties of jealousy depends on a "contextually determined state of the person's ego."[5] But having presented a very stimulating analysis of jealousy in relation to the self, there is a reluctance to take this analysis further and examine the status of the "self" concept: "Whether the sense of the unity of the self and protection that sense evokes is an illusion, is a question we must leave for another occasion."[6]

Another work by Gabriele Taylor, deals with the emotions of self-assessment, pride, shame, and guilt, and it makes the linkage between emotions and the conception of the self very central. But here again the notion of the self does not receive sufficient critical analysis.[7] Taylor says, as a passing remark, that there is no unchanging object of consciousness, which may be referred to as the "self" but that the concept of a moral agent requires a degree of connectedness between states of consciousness.[8] But here again, apart from these clarificatory passing comments, the issue is not integrated into the main texture of the work. Specially as the Humean notion of pride is one of the main concerns of this study, a more focused discussion of the issues pertaining to the reality of the self and the consequent implications for emotions would have been very rewarding. The Buddhist point of view is that a false sense of the self is the foci for negative emotions and the liberation from this deception is the path toward the generation of the positive emotions. And since Hume did consider the self as a "fiction," the discussion of the self and the emotion of pride deserves more sustained examination. Taylor's analysis is concerned with the reflexive nature of certain emotions like pride, shame, and guilt and with beliefs related to the emergence of these emotions, but the issue about the *reality* of the self, which is a Humean concern, is not pursued. Taylor does raise the issue about the Humean comment that excessive pride is vicious and examines possible grounds for it, like a person's pride being disproportionate, badly grounded, and excessive. She also says that excessive pride being vicious may be due to an "undue degree of self-preoccupation." But the link between the Humean position about the unreality of the self and its relation to morally negative emotions is not discussed. This is of course a central concern of Buddhism, as the cognitive distortion about the nature of the self has an impact on the psychological and the ethical in Buddhism. There have been objections against the use of such strong generalities (like the self or ego) as a conceptual aid to tidy our attempt to study the emotion taxonomies. But yet it appears that emotions can be understood at various *levels of generality* and that levels of generality need not be isolated from each other. In fact if one follows the Sartrean orientation, one could say that emotions involve a whole mode of orientation toward the world.[9] While it may be futile to search for absolute patterns of order or some fixed foci for classifying emotions, there are some recurring residual strains of some emotions, casting a longer shadow and pointing toward a relatively larger and unifying focus. In understanding emotions, we move in two directions, we look for the specific features of different emotion profiles, as well as the more general features and the larger frames for obtaining a more integral perspective. Not merely for *understanding* emotions but sometimes for *assessing* them, according to their place in the good life, we need a large frame to chart them and see them according to some principle of organization. Thus in spite of the very high degree of generality of the venture of looking at the relationship between the emotions and the "self," it can turn out to be a useful venture. The fact that it is not merely a concern of ancient ethical or religious beliefs is seen by a glance at the recent literature on emotions in the West, where the ego-emotion relationship as a problematic concern has emerged.

Terrence Penulhum's paper "Self-identity and Self-regard" raises certain significant issues about the *idea of the self in our emotional lives*.[10] He says that though he is raising the question in relation to Humean exegesis, he is also interested in the more general implications of the issue—"the role that the idea of the self plays in our thinking about some of the areas of the emotional life that Hume considers."[11] Toward the end of the paper, he remarks: "There is an interesting historical contrast to Hume's procedure, one which would have surprised Hume if he had been aware of it . . . Buddha is said to have argued that the Hindu view of the self as identical with the cosmic soul is false, somewhat as Hume rejects the substantial analysis of the self."[12]

Thus Penulhum presents us with some significant issues: what is the place of the self in our emotional lives? If the self is a fiction as Hume says, does it have any role in our emotional lives? Finally, if there are parallelisms between Buddhism and Hume, how does Buddhism deal with this problem? Penulhum also feels that in Hume's attempt to link up the emotion of pride to the sense of the self creates a problem, as there is a great deal of ambiguity in the use of words like *pride* and *humility*: "Pride is often discussed in theological contexts as though it included all forms of inordinate self-concern or self-absorption, not only those that involve a high estimate of oneself. One very common form of such *self-absorption* (my emphasis) is obsession with one's own inadequacies, so that one can find oneself speaking of some apparent forms of humility as examples of pride in this sense."[13]

Apart from these critical comments on pride and its linkage with the Humean notion of the self, Penulhum also points out a kind of tension (if not an inconsistency) between the analysis of the self of thought and imagination in book 1 and the self and the passions in book 11. Thus there are three points that emerge in the discussion: the issue about pride and humility, the self and the passions, and the parallelisms between Hume and Buddhism. While appreciating the fact that Penulhum has focused interest on some key issues, I shall attempt a critical response to these comments. What is valuable in his analysis is that he puts his hands into the central issue—if as Hume says, the self is a fiction (specially as laid out in his book 1 of the *Treatise*), then are we to say that the passions are also fictions, and are we deluded when pride and humility emerge within us?

The Humean Position on Self and Pride

David Hume, a British philosopher, is associated with the celebrated view that what is called the "self" is but a bundle of perceptions. Hume basically associated the self with the "mind," and the mind for him was a theater where you will see emerging and passing photographic impressions. But yet Hume was perplexed, as people had certain habits that appeared to be paradoxical; this is the practice of talking about people as single and unitary beings, though they are constantly subject to change. In the words of Hume, "What then gives us so great a propension to ascribe an identity to these successive perceptions, and to suppose ourselves possest of an invariable and uninterrupted existence thro' the whole course of our lives?"[14] Here Hume rejects the metaphysical view that accepts a self with perfect identity and simplicity. But yet Hume feels that the spell of this illusion is so strong among men that the only thing to do is to consider "carelessness and inattention" to the spell of such a fiction as the only remedy. This is the general outlook of the book 1 of *A Treatise of Human Nature*, whereas in book 2 there is a slight change of focus. The first book deals with the notion of the self in terms of "thought and imagination," but the second book deals with it in terms of the emotions.[15] In the words of Hume, "We must distinguish betwixt personal identity, as it regards our thought or imagination, and as it regards our passions or the concern we take in ourselves."[16]

In the second book, Hume makes an analysis of the passions, of which the most important are the passions of *pride and humility* as they are related to our idea of the self. Hume divides what he calls the "perceptions of the mind" into impressions and ideas, and the impressions admit another division into original and secondary. Original impressions, or impressions of sensation, arise from "the constitution of the body" or "from the application of ideas to external objects." "Secondary or reflective impressions" proceed from original ones, either immediately or by the interposition of its idea: (1) of the first kind are impressions of the senses, and all bodily pains and pleasures; (2) of the second kind are the passions and the other emotions resembling them. He says bodily pleasures and pains can be a cause for certain types of passions, for instance, when a fit of gout produces fear and grief. But his focus is on the reflective impressions, which are again divided into calm and violent passions, the former are basically those with an aesthetic flavor, as the raptures of poetry or music (beauty in action, composition, and external objects). The passions proper are those of love and hatred, grief and joy, pride and humility. Of these, pride and humility are a central concern in the Humean analysis of the passions. Also in general, the study of the passions provides a new and stimulating entry to the notion of the fictional self. As Amélie Rorty remarks, "the passions provide the distinctive elements that compose the fictional idea of the self . . ."[17]

It would be useful to look at the emotion of pride in greater detail. Hume makes these observations about pride and humility: "The passions of PRIDE and HUMILITY being simple and uniform impressions, 'tis impossible we can ever, by a multitude of words, give a just definition of them . . . the utmost we can pretend to do is a description of them."[18] Thus in an attempt to describe the emotions, he says that though pride and humility appear as contraries, they have the *same object*, and the object is the self. Thus we get elated by pride or dejected by humility. When self does not enter into consideration, there is no room for pride or humility. There is also the cause of pride. If a main is vain of a beautiful house that belongs to him or which he has built, here the *object* of the passion is the self and the *cause* is the beautiful house. The cause itself has two aspects, the quality that operates upon the passion (beauty) and the subject in which the quality inheres (house). These qualities generate the feelings of pleasure and pain, and the subject on which these qualities are placed (the house) is related to the self. The initial pleasure about the beautiful house is independent of pride. A minimum condition for the experience of pride is that the beautiful house is considered as "mine." The self features also in the analysis as the object of pride, that toward which pride is directed. Thus it may be summed up in this manner: "So pride on this account can be summed up as consisting of a self-directed pleasure based on a distinctive pleasure derived from something that is also mine."[19] Does this mean that everything related to us that produces pleasure also produces pride? Hume raised this question, as there is a difference between the logic of "joy" and the logic of "pride." The agent may continue to feel joy in a self-related agreeable object but *not* make the transition to pride. Thus Hume laid certain restrictions or limiting principles about the emergence of pride: first, in pride and vainglory, the connection between the self and the agreeable object is a close one; second, it involves comparison with others, rather than the intrinsic worth of the object; third, the object of pride must be relatively enduring; fourth, it is said that "We fancy ourselves more happy, as well as more virtuous or beautiful, when we appear so to others . . ."; fifth, there is the impact of customs, conventions, and rules that influence the direction of passions.[20]

The Critical Examination of the Humean Position

It is clear that the idea of the self that plays a key role in the genesis of passions like pride is not the one he finds in the metaphysicians whom Hume attacks in book 1 but is perhaps a kind of personal continuity, rather than any sense of strict personal identity. As Amélie Rorty points out, in discussing the relationship between passions and the self, "Hume's project does not require that he show the strict identity of a person's motivational structure. All that the common sense idea of the self requires is that such changes form a continuous narrative."[21] I tend to agree with Rorty's interpretation, and perhaps this provides a satisfactory response to Penulhum's fears about a possible inconsistency between perspectives on the notion of the self in books 1 and 2.[22] Rorty in fact observes in an additional note to the cited reference, "It is not surprising that Derek Parfit saw Hume as a predecessor who defended a theory of personal continuity, rather than strict personal identity, and who connected the criteria for person's identity with the characterisation of that person's interests and motives."[23] Though Hume does not make a comprehensive analysis of the way in which this concept of continuity provides a background for his analysis of passions, the material is available.[24]

Book 2 does offer an important stage in the Humean analysis of the self. In book 1 he makes the following observation: "Pain and pleasure, grief and joy, passions and sensations succeed each other, and never all exist at the same time. It cannot therefore be from any of these impressions, or from any other, that the idea of self is derived;

and consequently there is no such idea."[25] In book 2 he has found how the idea is derived, though it is a fiction, and yet a powerful and persistent fiction. This fiction emerges on certain passions, and the passions in turn are fed by the fiction. This means that people act as if there is a "self" (within double quotes). Pride and humility are the passions par excellence bound to the false sense of the self in this manner. Hume of course does not make this change of direction neatly; it is riddled with some ambiguities. But the link between the passions and the fictional self is very strong, and the passions account for the strength and persistence of the fiction. In fact Amélie Rorty emphasizes this point very well: "It should not therefore be surprising that the passions provide the distinctive elements that compose the fictional idea of the self as distinguishable from a reorganization of the impressions and ideas that compose external objects."[26] Hume of course would allow causal stories other than passions to generate the irresistible notion of the self, but we are in this analysis concerned with emotions and the self. I have now drawn the general picture about the emotions and the self as clearly as possible, so that it is possible to examine Penulhum's critique of Hume regarding passions and the self, but more important, the moral criticism of the emotions.

Apart from issues about the fictional nature of the self in books 1 and 2, the issue of moral criticism has been raised by Penulhum. The question whether pride and humility are to be considered morally evil or bad is a hard question in the context of the Humean scheme, as Hume considers pride as something morally neutral at times, yet makes a distinction between pride and overweaning conceit. This is an issue that will show some significant differences in our approach in Hume and Buddhism. Buddhism makes a clear distinction between negative and positive emotions, as well as emphasizes the fact that negative emotions are being fed by a deluded notion of an unchanging ego. The linkage between the fictional nature of the self and emotions is quite strongly worked out in Buddhism.

How do we critically decide about the soundness of certain emotions, whether they are appropriate, well grounded, fitting, and so forth?

We can say that a person's pride is excessive, that his achievements are not as high as he imagines them to be; decisions can be made on a wrong appraisal of the facts, for instance, high assessment of wealth and a low estimate of scholarship; we can question the facticity of the claim and say that it was not X who did it; we can also say that the supposed connection between one self and the aroused emotion does not exist.[27]

Penulhum feels that the last claim is the most important and can emerge on three grounds: it may be said, for instance, the affluence of my children is a matter about which my pride is possible but not that of my neighbor, thus it ought not lead to pride; if my pride is based on a false report of my son's success, then again the connection does not exist; if the very notion of the self which generates pride does not exist, then it rests on a false supposition of personal identity. Penulhum says, "This would not preclude pride and humility from occurring, but it would make them ineluctably groundless, for they would presuppose that the object of the high or low estimate that the subject made incorporated stretches of personal history that it could not incorporate."[28]

A Buddhist Perspective on the "Self" and Pride

Penulhum sees the Buddhist position as an "interesting contrast to Hume's procedure" and says that Hume would have been surprised if he heard of it. He sees some parallels between the Humean rejection of the substantialist view of the self and the Buddhist analysis of the metaphysical conceptions of the self current in India at the time. But when Penulhum says that the Buddha went beyond the rejection of the eternalist conception of the self to the "denial of the conventional belief in the persisting identity of the individual,"[29] he does not take into consideration the Buddhist meaningful but cautious use of the 'person' concept, use that is aware of its conceptual pitfalls. It is true, as he says, that whereas Hume advocates carelessness and inattention as the only panacea for the spell of the illusion of the self, the Buddha advocates a path to eradicate the illusion.

But the Buddha also uses a meaningful and cautious logic and vocabulary to talk about the emotions, as well as a very critical use of the notion of 'personal continuity' rather than strict identity. While not accepting the substantialist concept of the self based on permanence and pleasure, the Buddha left room for the meaningful use of a concept of 'qualified continuity'. In rejecting the existence of a permanent soul, the Buddha is also not rejecting the critical use of the notion of 'a continuing person' as an agent of moral action, one capable of generating values and having purposes of his own, having memories and thoughts as well being capable of emotional expression. It is basically a psychophysical process in flux but maintains a relative individuality within the cosmic scheme. Though there is no substratum, one serial process may be distinguished from the other. In very specific terms, the doctrine of egolessness implies that living beings have no eternal souls and also that there is no cosmic Self.

The richness of the Buddha's analysis lies in the diversity of directions through which the Buddha traversed to convey the nature of the doctrine of egolessness.

One very crucial point is that the Buddha pointed out that his description of the universe, the moral order, and the law of dependent origination lies within two extremes: eternalism and annihilationism. The Buddha has pointed out that the deepest source of human suffering and all the negative emotions rest on the futile attempt to preserve a false conception of the self. The fivefold identification emerging from corporeality, feeling, perception, dispositions, and consciousness generates different aspects of wrong personality beliefs, of which there are twenty forms. These all get linked up with negative desires and emotions.

But these identity manifestations all stem from the basic illusion of seeing a "self" where is no such thing. The fact that the Buddha rejects eternalism does not mean that one has to embrace any doctrine of annihilationism, of chance or chaos. There are certain regularities and patterns that help us to talk in terms of interim and critical unities. The doctrine of no-self does not mean that person is just a bundle of chaos or a protoplasm without any sense of direction. There is a basic ambiguity and a lack of essence in humans, yet there are certain causal patterns through which discourse about human beings become possible. There is a kind of paradox that more and more we realize the false sense of the "self" into which we fall from time to time, the more vibrant and robust is the sense of directionality that guides us. I have described the situation in another context: "the dissolution of the ego does not imply a dimunition of one's co-ordinating powers. Somewhere within the narrow ridge between the paths of chaos and nihilism and the traps of identity illusions, one has to penetrate through a razor's edge, a realm of interim and critical identities, dissolving as we cross them, transcending them as we cut across their inner dialectic."[30] There is a friction between what may be called the "illusionist" and the "integrative" perspectives on identity, and once we accept the reality and yet the conditioned nature of the causal patterns that generate both negative and positive emotions, Penulhum's dilemma need not disturb the Buddhist. If a person projects a wrong conception of self into the causal order in the universe, including the modified types of patterns and dispositions (*sankhāra*), which are true of the interim unities we call "human beings," the wrong conceptions generate negative emotions, for instance, self-conceit. An emotion like conceit in this context arises dependently, and with effort and training it may be eliminated. In the puzzle that Penulhum has raised, one has to be careful that the words *true* and *false* are contextually rooted in Buddhist usage.

The "false" sense of the self that people betray has a kind of phenomenological reality, as this has (to use Hume's terminology) the "persistence and power" to generate negative emotions, and it can be eradicated by the path to liberation in different stages. The spell of the wrong view of self (*sakkāyadiṭṭhi*) and expressions of it in different forms of craving will be eliminated at an early stage on the path to liberation, but its manifestation as conceit (*māna*) will remain till the final stage of perfection is attained. As one matures on the path to liberation, though one is struck by the causal connections and continuities that we refer to as "individuals," it will be realized that relative unity is a matter of degree (more or less), and it is not, in the language of Parfit, "an all or nothing affair." The person who does not see the true state of affairs (*puthujjana*) implicitly or explicitly holds on to a *belief* in the self (*atta-vāda-upādāna*, holding on to a belief in the self). But he cannot do so as there is no such self to be found. Thus it is the *belief* about the nonexistent self, rather than the nonexistent self as such, that has the psychological and the phenomenological power and persistence to generate negative emotions.

At this stage we can move from the approach of the middle path to a more contextually oriented approach. Thus though in actuality there is no self, a "self" (within quotation marks) is created by the ignorant worldling (*puthujjana*). Thus something is considered as self and this false self that is created may be referred to as "self." This self should not be considered as the continuities and connections that go to make the interim identities, which we refer to as "individuals." The continuities or the relative endurance we see has nothing to do with the self, and the self has to do with the subjective feeling of "I" and "mine." In fact the self indicates even a more "blown-up subjectivity" than 'I' does, a more voluntary or deliberate activity."[31] On the other hand, the "I" conceit is a more subtler component. "The 'self' is a coarse layer that stands over the more subtle conceit 'I'."[32] Thus as Wettimuny puts it, "'self' is something necessarily ambiguous to the *puthujjana*. It makes him think that for him there is really and truly a self; but if he tries to make certain what precisely it is, he fails. The deer thinks there is water when the sun shines upon the sand and produces the mirage 'water' before his eyes; but whenever the deer runs after the 'water', it fails to find water."[33] Now if the deer is told, there is water, it will say that it cannot find the water; but if it is told, there is no water, it will say that it sees water. Thus the two statements "There is a self" and "There is no self" can in a context of this sort be rooted in a fundamental ambiguity. Thus we can understand why, in the celebrated dialogue with Vacchagota, for the questions, Is there a self? and Is there no-self? the Buddha was silent. The statement "there is no self for me" can mislead him to thinking that he is devoid of both self and "self," for that would take his attention out of the real fact that there is a "self" for him, which belief has to be eradicated.[34]

Wettimuny in fact comments on this passage from Hume: "Pain and pleasure, grief and joy, passions and sensations succeed each other, and never all exist at the same time. It cannot, therefore, be from any of these impressions, or from any other, that the idea of self is derived; and consequently there is no such idea."[35] He says that here Hume has failed to see the strength and origin of the false sense of "self": "There is indeed no doubt whatsoever that Hume does not know the source of the idea of self; but for this reason, to say that there is no such idea or to dismiss it saying that it is a false idea is only to close the stable door after the horse has escaped."[36] But if one examines book 2 of Hume's *A Treatise of Human Nature* and its discussion of the self and the passions, one gets a picture of the role of the passions in generating the fictional self and one gets a phenomenological feel for the persistence and power of this fiction.

These two approaches to the *anatta* doctrine, the doctrine of the middle path and the awareness of the contextual ambiguites embedded in the notion of the fictional self, give us a useful perspective to develop a framework for understanding the link between emotions and the self in Buddhism. If we understand the human being, not as an enduring psychic entity or as a substance, but as a patterned flow of change through time, we have a basis for understanding the positive emotions as well as the negative emotions, the negative emotions emerging out of a wrong conception of the self. Human characters and their emotional lives are not states of fixed identity but "patterns of configuration without a core."[37] Derek Parfit has shown that this perspective opens up the horizons for the positive emotions of compassion, as there is a homology between earlier and later "selves" constituted by one's sense of continuity, and the "selves" of other people. Thus there need not be a conflict between compassion toward one self and others. In the words of Steven Collins, "the rationale for action which acceptance of Buddhism furnishes provides neither for simple self-interest nor for self-denying altruism. The attitude to all 'individualities', whether past and future 'selves', past, future or contemporary 'others' is the same loving kindness, compassion sympathetic joy, and equanimity."[38] This is another dimension of the linkage between positive emotions and the Buddhist perspective of the self. As was hinted at earlier in my discussion of this issue, the stronger the realization of the fictional nature of the self, the more vibrant and robust are the positive emotions of compassion and kindness. It is this paradoxical nature of the emergence of the positive emotions that provides an answer to Penulhum's question, how can passions emerge on a fictional self? Negative emotions have their negative nature as they are related to a wrong notion of the self, but their "strength and persistence" (to use the words of Hume) cannot be denied.

Now I have sufficiently clarified the Buddhist perspectives on the nature of the self, insofar as they are related to the nature of emotions. The next point is the nature of pride and humility in Buddhism. Penulhum says that pride is used in theological contexts to cover all cases of self-concern or self-absorption, not only those that involve a high estimate of one self, and that it is even used as a kind of blanket term to cover sensuality. The Buddha makes a special attempt to define the nature of what may be called "conceit," which is completely different from humility and distinct from sexual impulses or aggressive impulses. Now I shall describe in detail perspectives on pride and humility.

Pride, Conceit, and Humility in Buddhism

What is conceived as a negative emotion in Buddhism is conveyed by the Pali term *māna*. I shall consistently render this as "conceit," rather than by the more general translation of "pride," which in English usage and cross-cultural contexts may have a more healthy and positive meaning. As the Humean analysis of pride is not consistently anchored on a moral point of view, and since Hume slips from the usage of pride as vicious to a more neutral usage, the strong moral flavor in the Buddhist usage of the reference to conceit may be noted. Second, the Buddha does not use the term *conceit* as a blanket term to cover all kinds of self-concerns, and its specific distinctive features in terms of its origin, nature, persistence, and possible elimination will be shown in the descriptions of it that follow. In fact the Buddha has clearly shown that the basic egocentricity of man finds expression in three forms: as craving, as wrong conception of the self, and as conceit. Thus Penulhum's criticism of the loose usage of pride as a blanket term may not apply to Buddhism. Third, in Buddhism humility is considered as a virtue and is clearly distinguished from feelings of inferiority.

Māna (conceit) is metaphorically described as "flaunting a flag," implying a desire to advertise one self.[39] Etymologically, the term is derived from *māneti* (to honor) or *mināti* (to measure). In usage, however, it is associated with the terms *maññati* and *maññanā*, giving us the connotation, to conceive false notions.[40]

There is in man what may be called a "bias towards egocentricity" (rooted in a wrong belief in an abiding entity) that manifests at various levels, linguistic, emotional, intellectual, ethical, and so on. The acquisitive and the possessive personality structure of the egocentric person has threefold expression in craving (*taṇhā*), conceit (*māna*), and false views (*diṭṭhi*). Craving is expressed in the linguistic form "This is mine," conceit manifests in the form, "This I am," and false views in the form, "This is my self."

From one aspect, the notion of "I" with its related concomitant notions of "my" and "mine" develops toward craving; another aspect is seen in the comparison with another, a not-I, and here there is a measurement of one's standing with another, which is the basis for conceit; finally there is an adherance to the notion of an ego, which is a wrong view. This triune nature of the egocentric predicament is described in the Pali canon as *mamatta, asmīmāna*, and *sakkāyadiṭṭhi*.

Thus self-conceit (*māna*) has to be distinguished from ego belief (*sakkāya-diṭṭhi*), which implies a definite view regarding the assumption of an ego. This is the first of the ten fetters and disappears when one becomes a stream winner, whereas the conceit, which is the eighth fetter and can vary from a crude feeling of conceit to a more subtle feeling of distinctiveness, prevails until the attainment of arahatship. These are two levels, the *self-view* and the *I-sense*, the first indicating the lower or the immediate fetter of view and the latter the higher or the more remote fetter of conceit. Thus it is seen that *māna* as conceit is not used as a blanket term to cover all forms of self-concern.

Self-conceit takes three forms: it can take the form of a feeling of superiority with the thought "I am superior to the other" (*seyya māna*); it can be a conceit based on the feeling of an equality with another, "I am equal to the other" (*sadisa māna*); there can be a feeling of inferiority with the thought "I am inferior to the other" (*hīna māna*). The roots of conceit can exist at a deeper level, as dormant proclivity (*anusaya*). We are subject to the latent proclivity described in the form "I am the doer" and "this is my doing" (*ahamkāramamam-kāra mānānusaya*). This insidious tendency to vain conceits can take the form of certain vain imaginings in relation to all five aspects of personality. Superiority and inferiority conceits are a dual manifestation of the same root, an inflated sense of vanity (*māna-mada*).

Buddhism considers conceit (whether superiority or inferiority conceit) as unwholesome and of a negative nature. While inferiority conceits express a sense of inadequacy, in the Buddhist context, due humility is a virtue. Thus in contrast with the Humean position, humility is a virtue, and is not on the same level as conceit. Humility is based on self-confidence and not on feelings of inadequacy. Due humility plays a significant role in the ethics of the reciprocal relations found in Buddhist ethics. Hume uses the term *humility* in a very negative sense:

"Accordingly we find, that a beautiful house belonging to ourselves, produces pride; and that the same house, still belonging to ourselves, produces humility, when by any accident its beauty is changed into deformity, and thereby the sensation of pleasure, which corresponded to pride is transformed into pain, which is related to humility."[41]

According to Hume, we are elated by pride and dejected by humility. The Buddhist position is different. *Hīna-māna* inferiority conceits are unwholesome, but due humility is a virtue: "Buddhism as a religion of self-control and contentment will naturally regard humility highly. This is another important Buddhist virtue. When a monk is spoken of as walking, turning his eyes to the ground and being fully possessed of decent deportment, it is not merely his outward appearance, but also his mental condition, that is in view. The outward appearance is merely a visible manifestation of the inner psychology; and decent deportment implies a humble restrained mind."[42] It is said that such a person will never regard himself more highly than he deserves. The Buddhist position has its distinctive way of charting out the nature of humility, and sometimes these different ways of looking at humility may be due to difference in cultural outlook.

In the same way that the Buddha admonishes the monks to live with a sense of humility, he has placed humility at the center of the reciprocal human relations true to a Buddhist society, which has been given paradigmatic expression in the homily to Sigāla.[43] It is a charming code of relations where respect, reverence, tender concern, compassion, gratitude, and humility are blended in the most refined way. The relationships among parents and children, husband and wife, student and teachers, friends, masters and servants, recluses and laymen are all outlined here. Thus both for the monk and the layman humility is placed as a central character trait and an emotion to be cultivated.

But conceit in the most subtle way can stay even at some of the higher reaches, before perfection is attained; this emphasizes in an important way that confidence in one's powers and a feeling of satisfaction with one's spiritual standing should not be converted into a conceit by comparing oneself with other:

1. Because of honors, gains, and fame he can be satisfied, and say, "I am famous," but not the other recluse.

2. Because of success in moral habbit he is satisfied and says, "I am good."

3. Because of success in concentration he is satisfied and exalts himself, "I am composed."

4. Because of success in knowledge and vision, he says, "It is I who dwell knowing and seeing, but these other monks dwell not knowing and seeing."[44]

Thus the venerable Sariputta says that in the attainment of the second *jhāna*, he was free from the thought, "It is I who am attaining second *jhāna*." Thus it is maintained that the leaning to I-making and mine-making was rooted out from him.

Emotions and the Self: A Perspectival Transformation

The examination of Hume's analysis of the relationship between the self and the passions, with a focus on pride and humility, has opened up in an interesting way—the possibility of developing another theoretical orientation of looking at emotions, using the issues about the self, as a point of anchorage. Though the discussion in book 2 of Hume's *Treatise* is very rewarding in this context, Hume does not consistently use his analysis for a viable moral criticism of the emotions. While this kind of purpose colors the whole tenor of the Buddhist analysis, I have found in the work of Spinoza a more holistic way of looking at the moral standing of emotions. As interpreted by Stuart Hampshire, Spinoza's position is that "The passions and negative emotions of men rest, intellectually, upon an error of egocentricity and of short-sightedness. One sees the universe as revolving around oneself and one's own interest as central in it . . . Like the geocentric perceiver of the sun, one ordinarily has a false perspective and a false scale, and one's emotions betray this."[45]

What Spinoza says is that, the more one gets away from the egocentric predicament, and gets out of the spell of the negative emotions, the greater is the transformation: "The enlightenment entails a change of standpoint and therefore a change of perspective; this is the parallel with the correction of perceptual judgments. A self-centered standpoint, determining a particular limited point of view, is to be succeeded by an attempt to understand one's own beliefs, sentiments and attitudes from a more objective, less confined, point of view—ideally from the standpoint of impersonal reason."[46]

During recent times, Iris Murdoch has maintained that self-centeredness interferes with obtaining moral objectivity: "By opening our eyes we do not necessarily see what confronts us. We are anxiety-ridden animals. Our minds are continually active, fabricating an anxious, usually self-preoccupied, often falsifying *veil* that partially conceals the world."[47] Murdoch says that a change in the direction of unselfishness, objectivity, and realism is connected with virtue. She maintains that it is difficult to find someone who is not under the avaricious tentacles of the self: "Humility is a rare virtue and an unfashionable one and one which is often hard to discern. Only rarely does one meet somebody in whom it positively shines, in whom one apprehends with amazement the absence of the avaricious tentacles of the self . . . The humble man, because he sees himself as nothing, can see other things as they are."[48]

Thus following these points of view put across by Spinoza and more graphically voiced by Iris Murdoch, one can refer to the possibility of a *perspectival change* in the way one looks at the negative emotions.

The issue of moral objectivity in relation to the distortions of self-centeredness and fantasy has also been discussed by John Kekes, who agrees with the general standpoint of Murdoch, although not with the implications of Murdoch's notion of "unselfing." Kekes says that Murdoch's notion of accepting our own "nothingness" may not leave room for vigorous moral action. Kekes, of couse, qualifies his comments by saying that unselfing may be just a metaphor and that perhaps what Murdoch means by unselfing is the "process of getting into the habit of not allowing selfishness to distort what we see."[49] He also feels that before we can heed the call to unselfing, we need the building of a "robust self" or a strong self.

My own reaction to Kekes's comments is that, while agreeing with him very much on the linkage between moral objectivity and not letting selfishness to distort our moral perception, the paradox about unselfing may be integrated against a Buddhist background. According to my understanding, as was mentioned earlier in this text, the more penetrating our insight into the no-self doctrine is, the more vibrant becomes the self-transcending emotions of compassion and kindness.[50] Instead of talking about a self, we may say that there is a more robust directionality toward *nibbāna*. Thus in the words of Spinoza, by understanding the true nature of negative emotions we move from egocentricity to detachment. While Spinoza offers a strong cognitive orientation to throw off the shackles of bondage to the egocentric predicament (a point that I have discussed elsewhere concerning the therapeutic orientations of Buddhism),[51] Buddhism also has a cognitive orientation in its own distinctive way but is blended with the role of a number of other factors that generate emotions, such as making evaluations, having desires, experiencing physiological needs, and so forth.

This shift from egocentricity to detachment, the moving away from the negative emotions of lust, hatred, envy, conceit, and jealousy to those like compassion, kindness, humility, and sympathetic joy and, in general, the breaking away from "the avaricious tentacles of the self" (to use a phrase of Murdoch)—all these involve a radical change of viewpoint, *a perspectival change.*

Thus in the understanding of emotions, the moral assessment of emotions, and the therapeutic process of the handling of negative emotions and the generation of positive emotions, in all these tasks, the relationship between the emotions and the self becomes quite central. I wish to use the phrase, the "perspectival theory of emotions" to summarily refer this way of looking at emotions. What is interesting about the Buddhist analysis of emotions is that, while giving a central place to the role of the self in emotions, Buddhism very clearly, integrates the role of desires with cognitive factors such as beliefs and appraisals, and physiological and sociocultural factors.

NOTES

This essay first appeared as chapter 4 in Padmasiri de Silva, *Twin Peaks: Compassion & Insight* (Singapore: Buddhist Research Society, 1991).

1. Robert C. Solomon, *The Passions* (New York: Doubleday Anchor, 1977).

2. Ibid., 187.

3. Ibid., 188.

4. Ibid, see chap. 4.

5. Leila Tov-Ruach, "Jealousy, Attention and Loss," in *Explaining Emotions*, ed., Amélie Oksenberg Rorty (Berkeley and Los Angeles: University of California Press, 1987), 477.

6. Ibid., 480.

7. Gabrieli Taylor, *Pride, Shame and Guilt* (Oxford: Clarendon Press, 1985).

8. Ibid., 108.

9. Jean-Paul Sartre, *The Emotions: A Sketch of a Theory*, trans. B. Frechtman (New York: Philosophical Library, 1948).

10. Terrence Penulhum, "Self-identity and Self-regard," in *The Identities of Persons*, ed. Amélie Oksenberg Rorty (Berkeley and Los Angeles: University of California Press, 1969), 253–80.

11. Ibid., 253.

12. Ibid., 277.

13. Ibid., 275.

14. David Hume, *A Treatise of Human Nature* edited by L. A. Selby-Bigge (London: Oxford University Press, 1888 rep. 1989), 253.

15. Ibid., bk. 2, 275–454.

16. Ibid., 253.

17. Amélie Oksenberg Rorty, "Pride Produces the Idea of Self: Hume On Moral Agency," in *The Australasian Journal of Philosophy* 68, no. 3 (1990): 255–69; see 257.

18. David Hume, *A Treatise of Human Nature*, 277.

19. Ibid.

20. David Hume, *A Treatise of Human Nature*, 292.

21. Rorty, "Pride Produces the Idea of Self," 264.

22. Penulhum, "Self-identity and Self-regard."

23. Rorty, "Pride Produces the Idea of Self," 264 n. 11.

24. During recent times, there have been some interesting discussion about Parfit's analysis of "self" and the Buddhist notion: see Steven Collins, *Selfless Persons* (Cambridge: Cambridge University Press, 1982); Matthew Kapstein, "Collins, Parfit, and the Problem of Personal Identity in Two Philosophical Traditions," a review of *Selfless Persons*, by Steven Collins and a review of *Reasons and Persons* by Derek Parfit, *Philosophy East and West* 36, no. 3 (1986).

25. David Hume, *A Treatise of Human Nature*, 251–52.

26. Rorty, "Pride Produces the Idea of Self," 257.

27. Penulhum, "Self-identity and Self-regard."

28. Ibid., 277.

29. Ibid.

30. Padmasiri de Silva, "The Logic of Identity Profiles and the Ethic of Communal Violence," in *Ethnic Conflict in Buddhist Societies*, ed., K. M. de Silva, et al., 17.

31. R. G. de S. Wettimuny, *The Buddha's Teaching and the Ambiguity of Existence* (Colombo: M.D. Gunasena, 1978), 116.

32. Ibid., 117.

33. Ibid.

34. *Saṁyutta Nikāya* IV, Sutta 10.

35. Hume, *A Treatise of Human Nature*, 252.

36. Wettimuny, *Buddha's Teaching*, 127.

37. Rorty, *The Identities of Persons*, 305.

38. Collins, *Selfless Persons*, 19.

39. *Anguttara Nikāya* I, 340.

40. See Nanananda, *Concept and Reality* (Kandy: Buddhist Publication Society, 1971), 10.

41. Hume, *Treatise of Human Nature*, 289.

42. S.Tachibana, *The Ethics of Buddhism* (Colombo: Baudha Sahitya Sabha, 1943), 124.

43. Dîgha Nikāya III, Sutta 31.

44. *Majjhima Nikāya* I, Sutta 30.

45. Stuart Hampshire, *Morality and Conflict* (Cambridge: Harvard University Press, 1983) "Two Theories of Morality," 50.

46. Ibid., 50.

47. Iris Murdoch, *The Sovereignty of Good* (London: Routledge & Kegan Paul, 1970), 84.

48. Ibid., 45, 47, 106.

49. John Kekes, "Purity and Judgment in Morality," *Philosophy* 63 (1988): 460.

50. See chap. 8 for the development of this theme.

51. Padmasiri de Silva, *Emotions and Therapy: Three Paradigmatic Zones*, in *Buddhist and Western Psychology*, ed. Nathan Katz (Boulder: Shambala Publishers, 1983).

BIBLIOGRAPHY

Collins, Stephen. 1982. *Selfless Persons*. Cambridge: Cambridge University Press.

de Silva, Padmasiri. 1981. *Emotions and Therapy: Three Paradigmatic Zones*. Inaugural Lecture for the Chair of Philosophy, University of Peradeniya, published by Lake House Investments 1981. Also published in *Buddhist and Western Psychology*, ed. Nathan Katz. Boulder: Shambala Publishers, 1983.

Hume David. 1989. *A Treatise of Human Nature*. London: Oxford University Press. Ed. L. A. Selby-Bigge.

Kekes, John, 1984. "Moral Sensitivity" *Philosophy* 59.

Murdoch, Iris, 1970. *The Sovereignty of Good*. London: Routledge & Kegan Paul.

Ñānananda Bhikkhu. 1971. *Concept and Reality*. Kandy: Buddhist Publication Society.

Parfit, Derek. 1984. *Persons and Reasons*. Oxford: Clarendon Press.

Penulhum, Terrence. 1969. "Self-identity and Self-regard." In *The Identity of Persons*, ed., Amélie Oksenberg Rorty. Berkeley and Los Angeles: University of California Press.

Rorty, Amélie Oksenberg. 1980. *Explaining Emotions*. Berkeley and Los Angeles: University of California Press

————. 1990. "Pride Produces the Idea of the Self." *The Australasian Journal of Philosophy* 68, no. 3:255–69.

Sartre, Jean-Paul. 1962. *Sketch for a Theory of Emotions*. London: Methuen.

Solomon, Robert C. 1977. *The Passions*. New York: Doubleday Anchor.

Taylor, Gabrieli. 1985. *Pride, Shame and Guilt*. Oxford: Clarendon Press.

14

Conceptualizing the Person: Hierarchical Society and Individual Autonomy in India

Mattison Mines

In all viable systems there must be an area where the individual is free to make choices so as to manipulate the system to his own advantage.—Edmund Leach, "On Certain Unconsidered Aspects of Double Descent Systems"

The individual is a social being, but we must never forget that he is an individual social being, with a biography not the same as that of anyone else.—Marshall Sahlins, "Individual Experience and Cultural Order"

Does individualism, or more particularly a concern for individual autonomy, have a place in the understanding of Indian behavior? It is commonly accepted that individualism is devalued in India (Dumont 1970, 8–9; Marriott and Inden 1977, 232; Kakar 1981, 37; Erikson 1979, 25; Ramanujam 1979, 54), that personal autonomy is subordinated to familism (e.g., Opler 1968; Kakar 1981), and that explanations of motivation for behavior are expressed in the logic of caste rules and kinship ideologies, or in terms of extrinsic factors such as astrological considerations or beliefs about the actions of demons, deities, and supernatural forces (*drishtis*) (Barnett 1976, 149; Marriott 1976). These explanations are consistent with the view that in India the individual is subordinated to caste and family interests (Dumont 1970, 8–9; Kakar 1981). In contrast to egalitarian societies, in India hierarchy structures all relationships and proscribes autonomy (Dumont 1970, 8–9; Barnett 1976;149; Barnett, Fruzzetti, and Ostor 1976; Ostor, Fruzzetti, and Barnett 1982; Kakar 1981, 117).

Yet, despite the consensus among scholars, when Indians talk

317

privately about their lives they frequently depict themselves as active agents, pursuing private goals and making personal decisions that affect the outcome of their lives (Singer 1972; Mines 1981). Some describe struggling to find ways to express their personal interests and to control decisions that affect their lives. In 1978–79, I collected twenty-three life histories of Indians, ranging in age from twenty-three to eighty-three, in the South Indian state of Tamil Nadu. These histories reveal that, as Indians age, their explanations of their life courses increasingly emphasize their own actions or failures, rather than cultural explanations, as a feature of their growing awareness of personal responsibility for their lives. Instead of becoming increasingly conservative as they advance in age and life station, individuals find that opportunities to pursue personal interests increase. These findings contradict the hierarchical-collectivist view of the Indian person and indicate that such a view better characterizes the younger ages and stages of life and is more ideological than behavioral in orientation.

What is the source and meaning of this conflict between the way the Indian person is described by social scientists and the person's self-assessment? Is the conflict a matter of levels of explanation that people offer a variety of explanations for the same behavior? Or is it a matter of methodology and analytic focus, for example, that personal explanations are discarded in favor of textual and normative explanations that are thought to have greater cultural validity? Or might it be a theoretical preference for recreating "the structure of Indian civilization as embodied in its traditional religious code," and ignoring contemporary behavior seen as idiosyncratic or uninteresting because it is judged mundane or non-Indian (see Allen's comment on Béteille [1986, 128–129] and Béteille's reply [1986, 32–33])? These questions have an importance that extends beyond the realm of Indian ethnography, because they challenge the descriptive goals of anthropologists who study other cultures, and they point up the limitations of cultural depictions of the concept of person and cultural explanations of motivation generated primarily by ideological interpretations.[1] Surely a goal of anthropology is to limit the discrepancy between what we see in the field and what we describe. We seek to improve our methods and means of understanding another culture so as to limit distortions (Béteille 1986, 121).

Before examining case material, a brief review of the literature is necessary in order to characterize the hierarchical-collectivist view of the Indian person and to demonstrate how an analytic emphasis on hierarchy has generated it. This is followed by an analysis of life-history case materials that contradict this view and require its reconsideration.

Explanations of the Indian devaluation of individualism take two forms: the ethnosociological approach and the social-psychological approach. Both approaches are founded more on ideology than on behavior. Both are ahistorical, presenting timeless characterizations of the person.

The Ethnosociological Approach to Individualism and Autonomy

Ethnosociological approaches are concerned with explaining Indian culture as a system and with examining the configuration of ideas surrounding the conceptual person. Among ethnosociologists there are two main viewpoints. One is espoused by Dumont and his followers. Dumont argues that "individualism, as a virtue, expressed by such values as equality and liberty" is disapproved of in India because the person is submerged in the social whole. Each "particular man in his place must contribute to the global order" (Dumont 1970, 9). Individual happiness and the autonomy that produces it are irrelevant; the emphasis is on the collective whole, on collective man. Liberty is surrendered to the interests of castes and families. And equality is displaced by hierarchy as the principle structuring social relationships within groups and among groups.

The other ethnosociological viewpoint takes as its inspiration Schneider's (1968) ideas opposing consanguinity to affinity, defining them as relationships by nature (substance) versus relationships by law (code). Also of this kind are Marriott and Inden's (1977) concept of the Indian as embodying "coded-substance," and Steve Barnett's (1976) description of caste purity as symbolically embodied in blood, which is perceived as a product of heredity (substance) and of behavior (code).

Marriott and Inden's view of the South Asian person contrasts with Dumont's in emphasizing the indigenous logic of what constitutes a person, rather than holism. Individualism is nonexistent, not so much because the person is encompassed by social groups as because the person is a composite of transferable particles that form personal substance. Since the person's substance is divisible and transferable, the person is more aptly described as a "dividual" rather than as an individual. This ancient South Asian conceptualization of the dividual embodies a logic of motivation: the person can maintain or improve personal substance and thus rank by regulating exchanges or transactions that involve a transmission of substance particles. This logic underpins and maintains hierarchy and family and caste codes for behavior and the logic of personhood, depicted as coded-substance.[2]

The Social-Psychological Approach to Individualism and Autonomy

The second approach offered by social science to explain the Indian devaluation of individualism and autonomy is social-psychological. Explanations of this sort stress that the ideology and values that accompany India's hierarchical social system rewards compliance and punishes autonomy. Adult identity is seen as an identity of adjustment rather than as one of self-choice (Erikson 1979, 25), in contrast to the way identity formation is perceived as occurring in the West.

> The [Indian] social structure does not permit the emergence of a cogent adult role as perceived in Western societies. Subordinating one's individual needs to the interests of the group, be it a family, a kinship group, a clan or a class is upheld as a virtue. . . . Thus self-assertion becomes selfishness, independent decision making is perceived as disobedience. The response from the in-group is tacit disapproval if not outright condemnation. Under such circumstances it is easier to play safe. The only way this can be accomplished is by passive aggressive behavior or regression into total passivity. (Ramanujam 1979, 54)

According to this characterization, the social norms of Indian social groups exact a heavy psychological price. The self is confronted either with conforming and giving up individuation or with rebelling and receiving condemnation.

Although the emphasis of this depiction of the person is on compliance and passive subordination to the group, the description implies that persons perceive themselves as having interests distinct from those of their social groups. A choice is present: to comply or not to comply.

This perception of distinctive personal interests is psychologically important. One social psychologist, Sudhir Kakar, recognizes this awareness of self versus group interests as a fundamental aspect of Hindu psychology (Kakar 1981, 34). Like others, Kakar believes that caste and kinship are encompassing features of Indian society that demand the rejection of autonomy and of the everyday process of individuation, fostering instead a personal identity dependently fused with group identity. Normative culture stresses the fusion of the individual first with the hierarchical family, next with the caste, and ultimately with the universal spirit through the attainment of salvation, *moksha.* However, Kakar recognizes that fusion within groups, let alone with the universal spirit, is feared by the person because it means a loss of identity and the obliteration of the ego. Fusion is a kind of death as a distinctive being. Balancing this fear of social suffocation is the possibility of separation. Kakar believes all humans experience themselves as separate from others. But separation is also problematic and socially unacceptable as a corrective to obliteration because it ultimately means isolation and social annihilation if carried beyond cultural limits. The person is left with an unresolved psychological polarity.

Kakar believes Hinduism offers a solution to this frightening polarity in the *asramadharma*, a four-stage model of life. According to this model, an individual can approach the feared goal of fusion and *moksha* gradually through a life of *dharma*. The greater part of life is taken up with education and householding, involving the childhood tasks of learning and the adult tasks of work, marriage, and parenting. Essentially, the ultimate dreaded fusion and loss of identity can be put off until late in life. Indeed, the person can live out his life according to his status and obligations and leave salvation for another existence.

Note that Kakar's analysis is more ideological and normative than it is behavioral. Kakar believes the *asramadharma* model "is deeply etched in the Hindu psyche" (Kakar 1981, 43). It tempers the Hindu male's perception of adulthood and guides his sense of what life is about. Fusion, therefore, is the Hindu solution to the polarity, but it is a solution allowing one to achieve the ultimate goal indirectly by leading a social life very much involved with the here and now.

Thus Indians do imagine the possibility of autonomy and independence, just as they also recognize fusion. However, ethnosociological and social-psychological conceptualizations of the Indian person have failed to give attention to how this polarity affects motivation and personal, rather than textual, explanations of personhood. Instead interpretations have favored the normative and have discounted the possibility of a need for separation and autonomous self-interest as an important motivation.

Personal Histories: Memories of the Self

It is striking that explanations of the Indian person focus on hierarchy and rank almost to the exclusion of any other feature of identity and motivation. If the descriptions of Dumont, the ethnosociologists, and the social psychologists are correct, personal goals should be rare among Hindus, rebellion against family elders or the joint family and caste should be unusual, and deviation from the etiquette of hierarchy should be infrequent. Therefore, these assumptions prompt several questions. Do Hindu individuals develop personal goals separate from the goals of their encompassing social groups? If Indians have such goals, do they ever rebel against the etiquette of hierarchy and pursue their personal goals against the dictates of elders and the demands of their social groups? If they do rebel, at what periods in life are these rebellions most likely to occur? What place do choices or goals have in the perception people have of their lives and of their motivations?

In 1978–79, I collected twenty-three life histories of Indians, ranging from twenty-three to eighty-three years in age, in the South Indian state of Tamil Nadu. The interviewees were selected from a wide range of educational, economic, and social backgrounds, incorporating members of ten castes. An effort was made to include both Brahman and non-Brahman subjects, since some Indianists see Brahmans as traditionally espousing the hegemonic Brahmanical ideology that has served as the basis of many interpretations of Indian society and culture. Seven of the interviewees were members of Brahman castes. Eight were Kaikkoolaars, a middle-ranked weaver caste. One Christian and one Muslim were interviewed. Thirteen had college education; eight had elementary education; one had the equivalent of high school education; and one had obtained a vocational degree. Fifteen came from working-class or peasant backgrounds, and eight came from white-collar or professional backgrounds. Five of the interviewees were women.

All interviews took place in Tamil Nadu State. Interview locations included the state capital, Madras City, the hinterland cities of Salem, Erode, and Trichengode, and Akkamapettai, a small village. Although the interviewees were not randomly selected, an effort was made to achieve representativeness. The expectation was that if patterns emerged out of social diversity—caste, class, or education alone would not explain them.

Analysis of these histories reveals that, after the transition from childhood into adulthood, the interviewees experienced three age-related stages, each of which followed a period of transition in their lives.[3] The first stage characterizes the informants in their twenties, and is a period of dependence on elders and of conformity to cultural and social-structural dictates. During this period, informants are engaged in beginning the adult tasks of marriage, work, and parenting. In their late twenties to early thirties, informants enter a period of transition, in part characterized by descriptions of motivation and action that question or reject acceptance of dependency and compliance with the wishes of family and seniors. Many described rebellions that forced splits with their families. Others described trying to take control of aspects of their lives. Those who sought autonomy in the stage of life that followed described pursuing the goals their choices opened for them.

The next transition occurs between thirty-seven and forty-five years of age. Informants described entering a period when they felt the dictates or work, marriage, and parenting were no longer as pressing. For a few there was a growing sense of disappointment in life associated with repressed desires. But most described being able to turn their attention to meaningful, personally motivated interests they had previously had to put aside. Autonomy, defined as control over decision making affecting one's life, was characteristic. There was also a strong and growing sense of responsibility for oneself. The decisions informants described indicate they felt some dictates of social conformity to be less compelling. It might be expected that as a person ages, senior status would dictate conservatism and conventionalism and would limit a person's options. The case material suggests the opposite is true. Young adults perceived themselves as having fewer options, while older adults pursued goals that they had to put aside at younger ages.

Do Hindu Individuals Develop Personal Goals Separate from the Goals of Their Encompassing Social Groups?

When asked to describe their first goals in life, the interviewees responded by recounting their earliest memories of things they wanted to do. The age at which informants were first aware of these early goals or wishes was usually between fourteen and seventeen. The goals described were personal and covered a range of possibilities. Some were vague, some specific, some were long-term, and some short-term in nature. Among the goals sought were getting an education, going to a particular college, leaving agriculture, becoming a doctor, becoming an army officer, traveling abroad, going into business, outperforming others in school, getting into the police service, becoming an Indian Administrative Service officer, getting married, becoming a professional musician, and finding employment in order to eat. Some accomplished their early goals. Other goals were outgrown or were discouraged by elders. But most informants went on to describe their lives in terms of later goals and what they did or failed to do to accomplish them. By no means was everyone successful in achieving his or her life goals, but all twenty-three persons from whom life histories were taken described themselves as having had goals at some points in their lives.

Of the twenty-three interviewees, seven described their early goals as being opposed by family expectations and put them aside for the time, conforming to family or social dictates. The goals of all seven were related to selection of life work or preferences for what to study in school. For example, one man wished to study history in college, but his father insisted on math and science. Another wanted to study Tamil literature, but his father decreed that he become a shopkeeper, an occupation he never liked. One man wanted to follow a career in the army, but his family chose accounting for him. Two others sought government service, but their families disallowed this because it would have meant that they would live away from their families. The presence of opposition reflects the perception of choices available to individuals. Some who were very poor did not perceive themselves as having choices. Their goals arose from necessity and, as some stated, flowed from circumstances. They saw themselves less as makers of their circumstances than as responders to them. Nonetheless, they felt themselves responsible for how they responded to their situations. Choice was narrowed by their efforts to survive.

The fact that Indians readily describe a wide range of personal goals as well as family opposition may seem so obvious a truth that it hardly warrants the mention it is given here simply because few Indians would deny it. Yet ideological conceptions of hierarchy, holism, and coded-substance, and the social norms of social psychologists seem to deny them. If Indianists acknowledge the manifest truth of personal goals, then why do they disregard what is so obvious? Indianists have discounted the private voices of individuals because what they say seems banal. But what these voices say in important, because it refutes India's supposed denial of individuation and autonomy. Further, it shows that by giving esoteric ideology an arbitrary precedence over individual explanation, Indianists have hierarchized Indian knowledge in such a way that they deny the Indian person the right of representing himself or herself (Inden 1986, 440).

Do Indians Rebel against the Etiquette of Hierarchy and the Dictates of Family and Caste?

By "rebel" I mean oppose conformity but without wanting to change the social system that conformity supports. Of the twenty-three interviewees, nine performed twelve acts of rebellion that went contrary to norms of caste, family, or hierarchy. Five of the twelve acts precipitated splits with the family, resulting in eight partitionings or estrangements. Three rebellions involved quitting jobs that the persons disliked, resulting in hardship for their families. Three involved love marriages, a form of marriage considered at best to be a social embarrassment in a society that places great stock in arranged marriages. At worst, love marriages may be considered grounds for becoming outcaste. One of these marriages, which was intercaste, led to the man being disowned by his family, and this is counted among the five cases of family splits noted above. One act involved a son traveling abroad against his mother's wishes, and one involved a married woman taking a lover.

Reflection on the character of these rebellions indicates that all challenge family codes and most challenge hierarchical etiquette, since they involve opposing the wishes and interests of families or elders. Only three can be seen as personal acts that potentially rebel against caste codes. All of these involve sex and so are regulated by codes of purity. These instances include two intercaste love marriages and the taking of a lover. One of these marriages involved a crippled man of *deevi daasi* (female temple dancer, courtesan) descent who married a Christian and was unopposed by his family and caste. A third revolutionary act against caste codes is not listed above because the man entered into it with his family's support. This act, his marriage in 1932 to a woman of his caste but not of his endogamous unit, divided his kin network into opposing camps; he was threatened with being outcaste but never was.

At What Periods in Life Do Rebellions Occur?

Most interviewees saw their lives reflectively in terms of major events, goals, and decisions. These took place at predictable periods in life, marking transition points in the respondents' perception of their adult life course. The youngest age of rebellion was that of a village woman who ran away from her in-laws shortly after marriage at the age of eighteen. She never returned and enticed her husband to join her, thereby separating him from his family also. Of nine rebels out of twenty-three interviewees perpetrating twelve acts of rebellion (not counting the family that married their son outside their endogamous unit in 1932), five rebelled during the twenty-seven to thirty-three age period. Six acts of rebellion occurred during the thirty-seven to forty-five age period; three of the six were second acts of rebellion. One act was conducted at the age of twenty-five. The youngest informant reporting rebellion was thirty-eight years old at the time of the interviews, so that, of informants thirty-eight years or older, more than half (nine out of sixteen) reported at least one act of rebellion.

The clustering of rebellions into two age periods, twenty-seven to thirty-three and thirty-seven to forty-five, is indicative of several factors involving perception of personal interests as distinct from those of family and caste. Although they may have had strongly felt dreams for autonomy before this age, twenty-seven to thirty-three is a period of life when most Indians first feel capable of leading a life separate from their parents' control. A sense of self-sufficiency or knowledge of alternatives to family support is needed, because rebellion may precipitate total estrangement lasting for years, if not for a lifetime. This first period of adult transition tends to be precipitated by a combination of personality and social-structural constraints. Families that are too controlling create psychological crises in their dependent adult children. These children perceive themselves as having to rebel. For example, one male informant described attempting to escape the control of his mother by taking work in a different city. When this man's father died, his mother asked him to quit work and return to take care of her. He contemplated disobeying her, stalling while he sought work in his mother's city. When he found work, he felt forced by social norms to return to her. This man described his disappointment in life at a later age and said that by moving back to his mother he lost his friends, the work he liked, and the possibility of marriage. His behavior fits well with the previously mentioned analysis of social psychologists such as Kakar and Ramanujam.

By contrast, successful rebels, despite hardships, are vitalized by their actions. They speak of their lives in terms of decisions they have made and of their sense of responsibility for their lives. As one woman informant said, "Each must learn to stick up for himself. Don't blame others for our troubles; we're at fault for letting ourselves be cheated." Similarly, nonrebels who found themselves in circumstances that allowed them to make their own decisions described their lives in terms that revealed their sense of responsibility. Critical here is a sense of being able to make decisions that determine one's life course in ways that the individual sees as important. All informants over the age of thirty-eight described either making decisions that they felt had a significant influence on their lives or reaching the point of making such decisions but failing to follow through, usually because they felt unable to challenge social norms. These later tended to blame others for the way their lives turned out.

The second period of rebellion, from age thirty-seven to age forty-five, also involves a number of factors. This is the period by which the individual should have attained the primary socially dictated goals that constitute adult life, including marriage, work, and children, and begun to experience the growing desire to fulfill some internally generated needs. However, most Indians by this point in life are entering the senior world within their households. If their parents are still living, they will have relinquished control to their sons, or partitioning of the joint household will have occurred. The result is that informants during this age period have less to lose by making decisions based on their own self-interest and often are expected to act in ways unacceptable for the young. For example, men and women who have not married before this may select their own spouses. Consequently, unusual marriages are much easier. One informant selected his own wife at the age of forty-one. His wife was thirty-seven. They agreed to three conditions before marrying (1) no dowry, (2) his wife could continue to work, and (3) since his wife was past thirty-five, they would have no children, for fear of birth defects. All are unusual conditions for South Indians.

Older informants also perceived this age period as their last chance to make major changes in the kind of work they did. From among sixteen interviewers aged thirty-eight or older, twelve experienced what they felt were major changes in their work. Some quit their jobs to pursue their work. Some lost their employment. Many tried to make what they did more meaningful to themselves. For example, while retaining his ticket-vending job at a theater, one man began to work part-time as an apprentice auto mechanic because he had always thought he would like the work. Another quit work to begin his own business because, as he said, service palled for him even though he had been successful at what he had been doing. Another began studying Tamil literature, his first interest, which he had been prevented from doing at an earlier age. At fifty-five this man retired to become a full-time Tamil folk scholar. Changes of this sort are made because family and financial constraints are reduced by death of elders, partitioning, and the fulfillment of social expectations regarding marriage, child rearing, and work, or by a relaxing of normative pressures governing the behavior of persons over forty. In other words, they feel less constrained by society and family obligations and expectations and freer to pursue their internally generated interests. They have became their own decision makers. It should be apparent, therefore that rebellion is only one way autonomy is achieved.

What Place Do Choices or Goals Have in the Perception People Have of their Lives and of Their Motivations?

For some interviewees major life events were fortuitous, while for others they were the result of conscious decisions. For example, one informant described age forty-five as the point when he made a major change in his personal goals. This man, a villager who ran a small textile shop, went bankrupt because his desire to be seen as generous resulted in his selling too much on credit. From age thirty-three, when he was elected to the town *panchayat* (council), until age forty-five his main goal in life was public service and maintaining a reputation for generosity that he felt was the low point in his life. He changed his goals. He decided not to run for the *panchayat* again. He decided that public service was less important than building up his business so that, when he died, his sons would have an established enterprise. Moreover, he changed his goals regarding his sons. Before bankruptcy he wanted his children well educated and well married. After bankruptcy he wanted to leave them with a good business and came to regard costly education and the large expenses of fancy weddings as misguided. This man, I believe, blamed bankruptcy on his former conviction that being generous would result in positive returns only: to the generous honor is returned. He was greatly shaken by his misfortune and failure to look out for his own economic interests. But like others his age, he still believed that action generates its own rewards. This belief underlies the acceptance of responsibility expressed by many of this group for how their lives have turned out. Age fifty-five at the time of the interview, this man felt his bankruptcy was his own responsibility, a result of failing to see life's unexpected dangers. He had thought life would always be good, and he was caught off guard. At fifty-five he is trying to control his future.

This sense of responsibility and of making conscious decisions points to the central place of self-conscious motivation. Interviewees act to achieve or to avoid particular consequences; they also recognize or attribute to themselves their life's failures and successes. Interviewees self-assess what they believe to have been the best time of their lives and what they believe to have been the worst. They describe what in later life they see as self-destructive behavior and what they see as constructive. The sense of responsibility for actions and for how one responds to adversity is clear.

The interviewees describe what has happened to them in their lives as the outcome of their own actions. The interviewees describe this sense of responsibility for how their lives have turned out in the second and third periods of adulthood. In the first period of adulthood they see seniors as responsible. One woman described how, as a young bride, she had attempted to be a dutiful daughter-in-law. However, this resulted in denial of her own needs: she had no time for herself and experienced severe depression. For her it was difficult to accept the realization that no one else could help her overcome her troubles. When she did realize this, she began acting in ways to change her circumstances, ultimately encouraging her husband to wrest control from her dictatorial father-in-law. Her actions led to family partitioning, her husband's prolonged estrangement from his father, and the establishment of an independent household, which she ran. Her life improved as her sense of control increased. When her first grandson was born she began what she describes as the happiest time of her life.

Even those who do not see their life course as their own making nonetheless express a sense of responsibility for how they lead their lives. They describe their lack of awareness of this viewpoint in young adulthood, but see it as something they learned from experience. Some hope that this awareness can be taught. Others feel it must be learned from experience. At age fifty-four, one interviewee described his early adulthood as self-destructive. He came from a non-Brahman musician family that was well known but poor and of low social status. This lack of status was compounded by childhood polio, which had left him crippled. In South India the burden of physical disability is exacerbated by social attitudes. The disabled are discouraged from going into public places, and they find marriage and employment hard to arrange. At twenty-four, full of his sense of musical ability and despite his bad leg, he had tried to become a professional *mrdungam* (a tuned, doubled-headed drum) player, but he was blocked, he thought, by the music establishment. He became discouraged and gave up drumming. From twenty-four to thirty-one, he said, he had a very low opinion of himself. He could not get a decent job or marry. Throughout this period he engaged in what he now sees as self-destructive behavior. Then at thirty-one he took a job at an orphanage and realized for the first time that he could do something useful in life. This marked a great change in his behavior and life. He began to perform again and at thirty-six joined his sister, a dancer, as her accompanying drummer. He became a drum teacher and at forty-two married a woman who had come to study dance with his sister. At fifty-four, with sons and a teaching job, this man feels his life is very good. He does not feel that his life course is the outcome of goals, for his early dream of becoming a professional drummer was thwarted. But he feels responsible for how he has acted in life. As a teacher his goal is to teach children to work hard and not to harm themselves by self-hate as he did because of his crippled leg.

All twenty-three interviewees described having at least one goal in life (sometimes expressed as having a dream for something, for example, marriage, maintaining a joint household, or hoping one day to become a historian) that they have attempted to achieve by their own actions (for example, agreeing to marriage, or studying hard in order to get an education and escape the village). Goals are closely associated with the sense of responsibility for the actions taken in life, and this sense of responsibility for one's life increases with age. At age eighty-three, my eldest informant said, "Ignorance is the cause of all misery. Remove ignorance and the man is all right. No one can inflict harm on me. It depends on the mind. If wrong is done to us, it is because of ourselves. We place ourselves in positions to be harmed."

Conclusions

The above discussion reveals that the twenty-three interviewees conceptualized their lives and motivations in ways that contrast strongly with the expectations of the ethnosociologists and the social psychologists. What is the source and meaning of this contrast between the way the Indian person is described by social scientists and the interviewees' self-assessments? The social scientists' view of the Indian person derives from conceptualizing Indian culture and society primarily from the point of view of hierarchy. The logic of hierarchy requires compliance so there can be no room for autonomy. If this view of the Indian person were correct, personal goals would be rare among Hindus, rebellion against family and caste would be unusual, and deviation from the etiquette of hierarchy would be infrequent. By contrast, the life histories reveal that perception of self-interest and control over decisions affecting one's life (autonomy) play central roles in defining the goals and events that people describe as key features of their lives. Achieving a degree of autonomy is an important theme in adult life and is closely associated with rebellion against hierarchy and with personal perception of responsibility for how one's life turns out.

Hierarchy has been given such a dominant role in describing Indian society that it blinds social scientists to the significance of behavior that is not hierarchical, including how Indians describe their motivations and explain their sense of responsibility for their lives. The hierarchical-collectivist view sees the concept of person only within the context of ideology in relationship to an abstracted, nondevelopmental social structure. The concept's relationship to behavior is consequently removed and abstracted.

Like all ideal model explanations, the hierarchical-collectivist view generates a distorted picture of the person and of motivation, because the person is depicted as passively trapped within the frame the model describes without any mechanism for generating change. Further, these hierarchical-collectivist explanations are confined to motivation related to the social structures they describe, particularly caste and kinship. What of motivation oriented toward goals that lie in part outside the hierarchical frame of caste and kinship, such as personal interests and gain-oriented economic behavior?

The hierarchical-collectivist approach fails to deduce actively voiced patterns of motivation from the changing ways that Hindus at different ages explain their lives. To do so requires placing the progressively changing personal explanations of self in relationship to structure and its corresponding ideology. What we discover is that persons are very much interested in explaining their personal lives in terms of how they have been able to affect them. And what they reveal are dimensions of life that they actively attempt to create for themselves and an awareness of the events that they consider central to their personal histories. Their concern with caste and kinship relates to how these have impinged on their ability to achieve goals and control decision making and to what they have done or left undone to overcome these constraints. Since kinship and caste do impinge on some self-generated motivations, their structures dictate the kinds of rebellion that occur, such as rebellion against the etiquette of hierarchy (e.g., partitioning) and rebellion against caste codes regarding sexuality (e.g., taking a lover). These rebellions occur nonrandomly in the adult life cycle. When they occur is dictated by social structural factors and the length of time it takes to marry, have children, establish secure work, and establish one's own supportive kin network. Only then can a person pursue goals in opposition to elders.

But the person is faced with cultural norms that call for compliance. Life histories reveal that Hindus question these when they begin to feel responsible for what happens to them in life. This can only occur when they have reached a point in adulthood where they are in charge of decision making, when they head their own households, and usually after they have accomplished the major social dictates of marriage, work, and having children. At that point continued compliance means giving up the chance of affecting the events of one's life. If a person is unhappy with aspects of his life or is still a dependent by his thirties, in his late thirties or early forties he finds himself progressing in age to a point where he is forced by circumstance to take charge of his life. He can arrange his own marriage, quit work, and pursue goals of interest to himself. These circumstances are brought about by the diminished role of elders in his life.

Aging propels the person through a series of stages in the social framework, each of which impinges on the individual in different ways. However, the focus of social demands and cultural interpretations is not equal at each stage. Instead, these are most elaborate at the earlier states of adulthood. The older the Indian gets, the less compellingly specific are the cultural guides to tasks for his or her stage of life. As a result, the person increasingly finds room for the pursuit of his or her own interests.

NOTES

Acknowledgments. I wish to thank Donald E. Brown, David Brokensha, Morris E. Opler, and A. F. Robertson for their helpful readings of this article in manuscript. I also wish to thank the American Institute of Indian Studies, which sponsored the fieldwork upon which this article is based.

1. Concept of person analysis has became increasingly popular. Among recent publications are Shweder, Bourne, and Geertz in *Culture Theory: Essays on Mind, Self, and Emotion* (Shweder and LeVine 1984), *Culture and Self: Asian and Western Perspectives* (Marsella, DeVos, and Hsu 1985), and *Fluid Signs: Being a Person the Tamil Way* (Daniel 1984).

2. It should be noted in this context that both Dumont's and the coded-substance conceptualizations of the Indian person, culture, and society have had their critics. Thus, Dumont is critical of coded-substance interpretations espoused by scholars of what he labels the Chicagoan school because he thinks them Western in origin (Dumont 1983, 154–55). From a different perspective, Fox (1985, 4) accuses Marriott and Inden of ahistoricism and of perpetuating Orientalism.

More recently, Béteille (1986) has raised criticisms about how the Indian person and society have been characterized. Particularly, he is critical of Dumont's linking of hierarchy with inequality and individualism with equality. He notes that equality of opportunity based on merit is a widely accepted value of some antiquity in India. However, Béteille does concede that individualism is subordinated to collective identity in the contexts of caste and kinship. His point is that Dumont's ratio (individualism : equality :: collective identity or holism : hierarchy) incorrectly characterizes both contemporary Western and Indian cultures and societies, exaggerating and misrepresenting their differences.

Béteille (1986) is also critical of the ahistoricism characterizing ideological approaches that allow the generation of distorted images of non-Western societies in general and India in particular. He admonishes that studies that emphasize norms and values must place them in the context of behavior and social structure. If in our emphasis on India as hierarchial we argue that spheres of equality in present-day Indian society are to be discounted because they represent Western influences that are somehow contaminating or uninteresting, we are guilty of trying to create a pristine Indian world, a world without cross-cultural influences, that has never existed. To see textual sources or the past as more worthy of consideration or as more representative of truly indigenous custom than the present simply distorts our research and creates an ahistoric portrayal of India.

3. In India it appears that males and females experience similar life states, but my sample of females is small. See my earlier paper (Mines 1981) for a more detailed analysis of the transitions of Indian adulthood and their comparison with Western adult life states and transitions as these have been

presented by social psychologists such as Erikson (1978), Gould (1978), and Levinson et al. (1978). While there are timetable differences, especially in the transition into adulthood, I conclude that the pattern of adult development is remarkably similar in the United States and India.

BIBLIOGRAPHY

Allen, N. J. 1986. "Comments on Individualism and Equality by Andre Beteille." *Current Anthropology* 27:128–29.

Barnett, Steve. 1976. "Coconuts and Gold: Relational Identity in a South Indian Caste." *Contributions to Indian Sociology* 10:133–56.

Barnett, Steve, L. Fruzzetti, and A. Ostor. 1976. "Hierarchy Purified." *Journal of Asian Studies* 35:627–46.

Béteille, Andre. 1986. "Individualism and Equality." *Current Anthropology* 27:121–34.

Daniel, E. Valentine. 1984. *Fluid Signs: Being a Person the Tamil Way*. Berkeley and Los Angeles: University of California Press.

Dumont, Louis. 1970. *Homo Hierarchicus: The Caste System and Its Implications*. Chicago: University of Chicago Press.

———. 1983. *Affinity as a Value*. Chicago: University of Chicago Press.

Erikson, Erik, ed. 1978. *Adulthood*. New York: Norton.

Erikson, Erik. 1979. "Report to Vikram: Further Perspectives on the Life Cycle." In *Identity and Adulthood*, ed. Sudhir Kakar, 13–34. Delhi: Oxford University Press.

Fox, Richard G. 1985. *Lions of the Punjab: Culture in the Making*. Berkeley and Los Angeles: University of California Press.

Geertz, Clifford. 1984. "'From the Native's Point of View': On the Nature of Anthropological Understanding." In *Culture Theory: Essays on Mind, Self, and Emotion*, ed. R. A. Shweder and R. A. LeVine, 123–36. Cambridge: Cambridge University Press.

Gould, Roger L. 1978. *Transformations: Growth and Change in Adult Life*. New York: Simon & Schuster.

Inden, Ronald. 1986. "Orientalist Constructions of India." *Modern Asian Studies* 20(3):401–46.

Kakar, Sudhir. 1981. *The Inner World: A Psycho-analytic Study of Childhood and Society in India*. 2nd ed. Delhi: Oxford University Press.

Leach, Edmund. 1962. "On Certain Unconsidered Aspects of Double Descent Systems." *Man* 62:130–34.

Levinson, Daniel J., with Charlotte N. Darrow, Edward B. Klein,

Maria H. Levinson, and Braxton McKee. 1978. *The Seasons of a Man's Life*. New York: Knopf.

Marriott, McKim. 1976. "Hindu Transactions: Diversity without Dualism." In *Transaction and Meaning: Directions in the Anthropology of Exchange and Symbolic Behavior*, ed. Bruce Kapferer, 109–42. Philadelphia: Ishi Press.

Marriott, McKim, and Ronald Inden. 1977. "Toward an Ethnosociology of South Asian Caste Systems." In *The New Wind: Changing Identities in South Asia*, Kenneth David, ed. 227–38. The Hague: Mouton.

Marsella, Anthony J., George DeVos, and Francis L. K. Hsu, eds. 1985. *Culture and Self: Asian and Western Perspectives*. New York: Tavistock Publications.

Mines, Mattison. 1981. "Indian Transitions: A Comparative Analysis of Adult Stages of Development." *Ethos* 9:95–121.

Opler, Morris E. 1968. "The Themal Approach in Cultural Anthropology and Its Application to North Indian Data." *Southwestern Journal of Anthropology* 24:215–27.

Ostor, A., L. Fruzzetti, and S. Barnett, eds. 1982. *Concepts of Person: Kinship, Caste, and Marriage in India*. Cambridge: Harvard University Press.

Ramanujam, B. K. 1979. "Toward Maturity: Problems of Identity Seen in the Indian Clinical Setting." In *Identity and Adulthood*, ed. Sudhir Kakar, 37–55. Delhi: Oxford University Press.

Sahlins, Marshall. 1982. "Individual Experience and Cultural Order." In *The Social Sciences: Their Nature and Uses*, ed. William Kruskal, 35–48. Chicago: University of Chicago Press.

Schneider, David M. 1968. *American Kinship: A Cultural Account*. Englewood Cliffs, N.J.: Prentice-Hall.

Shweder, R. A., and E. J. Bourne. 1984. "Does the Concept of Person Vary Cross-culturally?" In *Culture Theory: Essays on Mind, Self, and Emotion*, ed. R. A. Shweder and R. A. LeVine, 158–99. Cambridge: Cambridge University Press.

Shweder, R. A., and R. A. LeVine, eds. 1984. *Culture Theory: Essays on Mind, Self, and Emotion*. Cambridge: Cambridge University Press.

Singer, Milton. 1972. "Industrial Leadership, the Hindu Ethic, and the Spirit of Socialism." In *When a Great Tradition Modernizes: An Anthropological Approach to Indian Civilization*, ed. Milton Singer, 272–380. New York: Praeger.

—————————————— *15* ——————

Self, Identity, and Creativity: Women Writers in India

Yamuna Kachru

Introduction

In the post-1950 period an important aspect of sociolinguistic research has been the development of paradigms that focus on a speaker of a language as a member of a family, class, caste, community, or some other type of social group, the idea being to view him/her as learning and using a language in its social context. The contributions of M.A.K. Halliday, Dell Hymes, William Labov, and Kenneth L. Pike have led to the emergence of several "socially realistic" paradigms of linguistic research (B. Kachru 1981).[1] The work of these linguists is deeply rooted in the tradition of earlier linguists, Edward Sapir and J. R. Firth, and the anthropologist Bronislaw Malinowski. If the Chomskyan approach stresses the affinity of linguistics to psychology (Chomsky 1986), the approach by sociolinguists presents the alternative of viewing linguistics as related to sociology (Halliday 1978).

The purpose of this presentation is not to look at the multifaceted concept of self and identity (i.e., social, ethnic, and individual) that emerges from such an approach to the investigation of language and its use. Rather, my aim here is a modest one: to determine what an approach based on sociolinguistics to the analysis of creative writing could contribute to the understanding of self and identity in a limited domain. I am mainly interested in looking at contemporary fiction in Hindi to see how the sense of self, identity, and individuality is projected by women writers in the context of postcolonial India. I will draw some parallels with writing in Bengali and Indian English, wherever relevant, although, in the case of English, there may be some concern that creativity in a second language—especially a foreign one—has its own characteristics. My justification for using Indian English writing is based on two facts: first, English has been "nativized" and "institutionalized" in India (B. Kachru 1983); second, English and Hindi are the two languages of wider communication in India, and creativity in either of these two languages is not restricted to any particular state of the Indian Union. It is my belief that a methodology based on sociolinguistics is a legitimate approach to the study of self and identity, since "Language as Art" is a recognized perspective on language, and language, after all, is the major means of preserving and transmitting the beliefs and values of a culture and civilization (Halliday 1978, 11).

Since the sociological-ethnographic approach considers the overall context of any verbal behavior crucial, at the outset I shall briefly discuss the concept of self in the Indian tradition. The contemporary context of India necessarily involves issues of Westernization and modernization. Therefore, an overview of the interaction of tradition and modernity in postcolonial India is provided next. Subsequently, the issue of self and identity in the context of Indian women is discussed briefly. An analysis of selected works by particular women writers in the context of Indian, especially Hindi, literary tradition follows. Finally, conclusions are drawn with regard to the contribution such studies make to the cross-cultural understanding of the concept of self and identity.

Self in Indian Tradition

It has widely been recognized by commentators on ancient Sanskrit texts, Indologists, philosophers, psychologists, and linguists that there is no one-to-one correspondence between Sanskrit items such as *ātman, puruṣa, jīva, ahaṃkāra, abhimāna, antaḥkaraṇa, manas, buddhi, citta* and English words such as *self, soul, spirit, person, individuality, ego, identity, mind, intellect,* and *heart.*[2] One just has to look at Sanskrit dictionaries such as Monier-Williams 1976 to be convinced of this (see also the discussion on the etymology and meaning of *brahman* and *ātman* in Winternitz [1927] 1977). The Indian tradition, unlike the Western tradition, does not make a sharp distinction between spirit and matter, sacred and secular, phenomenological self and transcendental God (Singer 1972; Roland 1988). While it recognizes the experiential duality of the phenomenological self (*jīva*), particularly the everyday consciousness of I-ness (*ahaṃkāra*), it also emphasizes the fact that various aspects of the phenomenological world, including the phenomenological self, are essentially manifestations of the nonphenomenological spirit or the Absolute (*brahman*). Both the Great and Little traditions of India have reinforced this belief in monism over the millennia.[3] Whatever the philosophical and legendary (i.e., puranic) distinctions between them, in everyday life, Indians use *brahman*, *īśvara*, *hari*, *narāyaṇa*, *viṣṇu*, *rāma*, *kṛṣṇa*, and *śiva* interchangeably to name the Absolute.[4] They believe that the individual soul (*ātman*) is a part of the Absolute (*brahman*) and, upon the attainment of *mokṣa*, *mukti*, *kaivalya*, or *nirvāṇa*, merges with the Absolute. In most New Indo-Aryan (NIA) languages, *ātmā* (the NIA form of *ātman*) and *ātmajñāna* (self-realization) have positive connotations, *ahaṃkāra* (egotism, the consciousness of separate existence of I), on the other hand, has negative connotations, and the term *abhimāna* (self-awareness or egoity) has both positive and negative connotations, depending upon the context.[5]

In Modern Standard Hindi (Hindi, henceforth), the following words are used in approximately the following senses: *ātmā*, "soul," "self" (hence, *ātmīya*, "belonging to one's self, related intimately to one's self"; *ātmābhimān*, "pride in oneself or self-respect"; etc.); *sva*, "one's own" (hence, *svajāti*, "one's own *jāti*"; *svajan*, "one's own people"; *svatva*, "self existence," "personal identity," "personal property"; *svadeś*, "one's own land," i.e., country; *svabhāv*, "inherent qualities," "dispositions"; *svadharm*, "one's duty," "one's own personality"; etc.); *asmitā*, "egoism"; *nij*, "innate," "one's own"; *apnā*, "one's own"; *ahaṃkār*, "egotism," "pride"; *abhimān*, "pride"; *astitva*, "state of being," "existence"; *paricay*, "identity"; and *vyakti*, "individual" or "person."[6] The items *apnā* (Bengali *āpan*, Marathi *āpaṇ*), *nij*, and *sva* are antonymous to *par* "distant," "other" (hence, Hindi *pardeś*, "distant lands"; *parāyā*, "other people," i.e., not one's own; etc.). Some of these items are useful in analyzing the literary works under focus in this study; I have noted which ones are attested in the writing under focus with what connotations.

Tradition, Modernity, and Self

Concepts of self and identity do not develop in a vacuum. Nor is it clear that self-concept is "a fixed entity, a stable quality possessed by each individual" (Miller 1979, 244; see also Hoy 1986 for Foucault's discussion of how the conception of self changed from Greco-Romans to Christians in Europe). During the first three to five years of life, a child develops his/her motor skills and learns a language. All this learning takes place in the context of interaction with the child's care-givers. The child learns not only the language of his/her surroundings but also how to express his/her intended meanings in order to become a social being. A social identity develops as a result of this socialization process. Subsequently, within this social identity, an individual identity develops as the child continues to undergo the socialization process while progressing toward adulthood. Language, patterns of literacy, and conventions of language use play a major role in the emergence of a social and an individual identity. According to Halliday, "In the de-velopment of a child as a social being, language has the central role. Language is the main channel through which patterns of living are transmitted to him, through which he learns to act as a member of a 'society'—in and through the various social groups, the family, the neighbourhood, and so on—and to adopt its 'culture', its modes of thought and action, its beliefs and its values" (Halliday 1978, 9). In the case of Indians, the English language is increasingly becoming a sig-nificant factor in the development of a sense of self and identity.[7]

This brings us to the two contextual factors relevant to the discus-sion of the Indian self and identity: tradition and modernity, especially what impact modernization has had on the four thousand-year-old con-cept of Indian self and identity in the twentieth century. By "tradi-tion," I refer to the long cultural continuity that India has enjoyed: Vedic hymns composed three thousand years ago are still part of daily observances, rites, and ceremonies of most Hindus; the rites of passage are still based on the *grhyasūtras* (composed between the sixth and second centuries B.C.); and the characters of the epics *Ramayana* and *Mahabharata* (predating the Christian era) are still a living presence in most Indians' consciousness. By "modernity," I am referring to the impact of English education and Western science and technology on Indian society.

While many social scientists have taken it for granted that tradi-tional Indian self had necessarily to dissolve before a more modern, progressive self could emerge, others have seen modernization in the context of India in quite a different perspective.[8] A few facts have to be remembered while talking about modernization of India: The first is the colonial experience of the past two centuries; the second is the emergence from the colonial past four decades ago; the last, but not the least important, relates to the experience of colonization and Western education by only a selective set of Indians.

It is worth noting that a majority of Indians remained untouched by the attitudes and behavior of the colonial masters and by Western education; only a handful of Indians came in contact with the British during the Raj. Hence, "Outside the small section of Indians who were once exposed to the full thrust of colonialism and are now heirs to the colonial memory, the ordinary Indian has no reason to see himself as a counterplayer or an antithesis of the Western man" (Nandy 1983, 73). This is crucial as far as Indian women are concerned; a large majority of women, including those from the middle and upper classes, escaped any direct contact with the colonial masters. As such, the impact of colonialism on the psyche of Indian women was relatively less than men. This, of course, is not to claim that India in general and Indian women in particular have remained unchanged throughout the last three centuries of increasing contact with the West. These facts are mentioned here only to put the contact with the West and its impact in a balanced perspective.

It is obvious that the Western impact has resulted in India modernizing itself through modern science and technology. This, however, does not necessarily mean that modernization (Singer 1972) is to be equated with Westernization (Srinivas 1966).[9] As Singer (1972) points out, Western technology and values have been traditionalized in many contexts. Nevertheless, it may be said that, to some extent, one can hyphenate Westernization/modernization as Roland does (Roland 1988, xxi–xxii). Westernization/modernization, then, "connotes that there are always varying degrees of Western values, life styles, technology, and other cultural contributions in modernization in India, even when Western innovations are totally assimilated into Indian society and traditionalized. Westernization and modernization are thus intertwined in highly varying complex ways and cannot be easily or readily separated" (Roland 1988, xxii; see also Gould 1987).

The same could be said about traditional Indian values, lifestyles, and cultural contributions; one cannot easily separate them from some apparently modernized phenomena. As Singer observes, the dichotomy between "traditional" and "modern" is of limited use in understanding India. There are too many cases of coexistence and interaction between the "traditional" and the "modern." "The more important and interesting task is to find out more about the processes and mechanisms of cultural change involved in these coexistences and interactions" and to find out "how Indians are becoming more modern without becoming less Indian" (Singer 1972, 247).

The label "traditional" has to be understood in its proper sense in the case of India. According to Singer,

> Traditional India is not a monolithic and immovable accumulation of immemorial customs and beliefs blocking the road to progress. India's traditionalism is rather a built-in adaptive mechanism for making changes . . . Essentially, it is a series of

processes for incorporating innovations into the culture and validating them. The process includes enclavement, neutralization, compartmentalization, vicarious ritualization, typological stylization, reinterpretation, archaization, and undoubtedly, others. The validation culminates when a change can be related to the traditional layer of the culture. (Singer 1972, 404)

Similarly, it would be misleading to assume that before the impact of the West, there was little, if any, change in India. As Basham points out,

In fact India has always been steadily changing. . . . The religious life of India, for all her "ancient wisdom," has changed greatly over the centuries. Between the time of the early Greek philosophers and that of St. Thomas Aquinas, Buddhism developed into a great religious movement in India, changed its outlook, almost completely declined, and finally sank back into the Hinduism from which it had emerged, but only after Buddhist missionaries had spread their message throughout half of Asia. The Athenian Acropolis was at least 500 years old before the first surviving stone Hindu temple was built. Some of the most popular gods of Hinduism, for instance, Ganesa and Hanuman, are not attested until well after the time of Christ. Certain other features of Hinduism also, for instance the cult of divine Rama and the complex and difficult system of physical training known as hatha yoga, are centuries later than Christianity. (Basham 1975, 1)

In spite of the steady change, there is also continuity. To quote Basham again,

No land on earth has such a long cultural continuity as India, since, though there were more ancient civilizations, notably in Egypt and Iraq, these were virtually forgotten by the inhabitants of those lands. . . . On the other hand in India the Brahman still repeats in his daily worship Vedic hymns composed over 3,000 years ago, and tradition recalls heroic chieftains and the great battles fought by them at about the same time. In respect of the length of continuous tradition China comes second to India and Greece makes a poor third. (Basham 1975, 2)

It is obvious that no civilization and culture could have had such a long continuity without strength and vitality. In Norman Brown's words, what gives Indian civilization its distinct character and vitality has to be found in the field of values and attitudes (Brown 1966). Part of the vitalizing principle of Indian civilization must be in the concept of self, since, as the *Bṛhadāraṇyaka Upaniṣada* says:

> Verily, a husband is not dear, that you may love the husband; but that you may love the Self, therefore a husband is dear.
> Verily, a wife is not dear, that you may love the wife; but that you may love the Self, therefore the wife is dear.
> Verily, the sons are not dear, that you may love the sons; but that you may love the Self, therefore the sons are dear.
> Verily the Devas are not dear, that you may love the Devas; but that you may love the Self, therefore the Devas are dear.
> Verily, creatures are not dear, that you may love the creatures; but that you may love the Self, therefore creatures are dear.
> Verily, everything is not dear that you may love everything; but that you may love the Self, therefore everything is dear.
> Verily, the Self is to be seen, to be heard, to be perceived, to be marked, O Maitreyi! When we see, hear, perceive and know the Self, then all this is known. (*Bṛhadāraṇyaka Upaniṣada*, 2.4, quoted in Winternitz 1927, 256)[10]

In order to understand the nature of self in India, it is useful to view the self through the philosophical categories of *jīva* (finite) and *ātman* (infinite) as well as the more contemporary concepts denoted by the linguistic labels of *sva* (I), *svatva* (personal identity), *astitva* (being), *vyakti* (person), and *paricay* (identity). It is also useful to utilize the psychoanalytical notion of the "three overarching or supraordinate organizations of the self: the familial self, the individualized self, and the spiritual self, as well as an expanding self" (Roland 1988, 6). According to Roland, the familial self is "a basic inner psychological organization that enables men and women to function well within the hierarchical intimacy relationships of the extended family, community, and other groups" (Roland 1988, 7). It is characterized by several properties: intensely emotional intimacy relationships where there is a constant affective exchange through permeable outer ego boundaries, where the experiential sense of self is a "we-self," but where a highly private self is maintained in spite of the intimacy relationships. The individualized self is characterized by inner representational organizations that emphasize an individualistic "I-ness," competitive individualism and self-actualization, and strong orientation toward rationalism, self-reflection, efficiency, mobility, and adaptability to extra-familial relationships. The spiritual self is the inner spiritual reality that is within everyone and is realized and experienced to varying extents by a very limited number of persons through a variety of spiritual disciplines. The spiritual self is psychologically deeply engraved in the preconscious of all Indians, even if they make no particular effort to realize it. It is usually confined to a highly private self (Roland 1988, 7–9). These three psychoanalytical concepts of self are useful for cross-cultural comparison.[11] The expanding self is posited specifically to represent "a growing individuation of the self. Its attendant conflicts derive primarily from the experience of inter-civilizational contacts and the social change that is generated in the process" (Roland 1988, 6). The concepts of social and individual identity that are of interest to sociolinguistics are equally relevant for our discussion. These depend on the socialization process and are intimately connected with one's language and membership in various social groupings—family, caste, class, educational group, profession, and so forth. All the writers and the characters they create in the works discussed below manifest the Indian identity fashioned by the factors discussed above.

Indian Women and Self

It is difficult to make any universally applicable statement about India; it is equally difficult to make a statement that would be valid for all women in India. Sociologically speaking, there are at least four categories of women in India: the poor, subject to exploitation, with little, if any, political consciousness; the lower middle class, moderately educated, working to supplement family income, to some extent politically conscious; the upper middle class, well educated, occupying mid-level positions in government, industry, and so forth, with a great deal of political consciousness; and the rich, either highly educated and occupying powerful political, bureaucratic or managerial positions, and politically conscious, or, irrespective of education, managing wealthy households and either somewhat involved or neutral to sociopolitical concerns. Members of the upper middle and rich classes usually occupy the leadership positions in the Western style feminist movement, although the purpose of the struggle is social justice for the lower middle class and social and economic justice for the poor.[12]

Three factors have resulted, to some extent, in two types of major social changes that have affected women deeply: the breakup of the joint family system, and a weakening of adherence to the norms of one's own caste (*jāti*), mostly in the urban centers, but increasingly radiating toward small towns as well. The three factors are: (1) Western education and the resultant potential for career outside the traditional structure of family-owned land or business; (2) the reform movements of Brahmo Samaj (1828), Arya Samaj (1875), the Theosophical Society (1875), Ramakrishna Mission (1897) and others; and, most important, (3) the Gandhian movement for independence and sociopolitical justice.[13] In urban India, there are nuclear families, women are educated and find employment outside the home, and there is less concern for caste norms in everyday life. Nevertheless, the hold of extended family and, to some extent, the caste norms still continue to be powerful in social as well as psychological terms (Mehta 1970, 1976; Nanda 1976; and Roland 1988). India lives in many ages simultaneously; so do Indian women. The educated Indian women do not see modernization necessarily as Westernization; in fact, it is clear that neither Western values in the domestic realm, nor the Western concept of 'individualism' is felt to be worth emulating (Mehta 1970, 207). In the case of the poor, rural women, the motivation for seeking an independent identity is basically economic; the driving force is family responsibility—whether as a daughter, wife, or mother (see the interviews reported in Jung 1987).

This is not hard to understand if one looks at the traditional role of women in Indian society. As Roland (1988) observes, the overt hierarchical structure of Indian family is completely male oriented, all important decisions seem to be made by the male elders, and women are subordinate and deferential to the men. In more covert structures, the women do most of the work in arranging rites and ceremonies that strengthen family relationships and status. For instance, they play a decisive role in arranging marriages, thereby working out new family alliances that have enormous significance for the social position of the family. They manage the internal family affairs and give definition to and preserve family hierarchical structures through ritual practices such as participating in family festivals, and so on (Wadley 1980). They are the main conveyers of the multiple myths, legends, and folk wisdom to the children and keepers of the culture. As mothers they have enormous power over their sons. They are perceived as agents of the supernatural or aspects of the divine, aspiring to powers of the goddess to further the growth and process of development of the family. Family honor depends a great deal on women's sexuality, particularly the daughter's chasteness before marriage and her behavior in the in-law's family. "Overall, the overt hierarchical structure of male dominance . . . is balanced by the enormous, covert structural power of the women" (Roland 1988, 217).[14]

As far as tradition is concerned, an Indian woman's identity is wholly defined by her relationship to others: first, she is a daughter to her parents; second, she is a daughter-in-law to her husband's parents and a wife to him; and third, she is a mother to her sons and daughters. The preference for a son as an offspring is as old as the Indian culture and civilization itself. There is, however, no evidence for heightened female hostility toward males, or a pronounced antagonism between the sexes in the inner world of Indian women according to the available psychoanalytical research findings. On the whole, two circumstances prevent any pathological condition developing as a result of the manifest sexism of Indian society: (1) the special maternal affection reserved for a daughter who is perceived as a mere "guest" in her natal family and (2) the presence in the extended family of at least one adult who gives a little girl the kind of admiration and sense of being singled out as special that every child needs to develop a sense of self-worth (Kakar 1978, 56–61). In addition, the brother, more than the father, plays an extremely important role in a girl's life.[15] Once a woman becomes a mother—especially, the mother of a son—her status rises enormously. According to *manusmṛti* (second or third century A.D.), "The teacher is ten times more venerable than the sub-teacher, the father a hundred times more than the teacher, but the mother is a thousand times more than the father."[16] In addition to these psychosociological factors, one must also mention the philosophical-religious dimension in which God and creation are feminine. Even those systems of belief that conceptualize God as male recognize the feminine principle, for example, the concept of '*ardhanāriśvara*' (Male-and-Female God), an aspect of *śiva*.[17]

An Indian woman's sense of self and identity is thus largely determined by patterns of socialization in infancy, especially the close affective relationship with her mother and others in the extended family, and in the context of the institution of caste. Both the family and the caste shape attitudes and beliefs and provide norms of behavior (see Das 1979 for an account of the raising of girls in Punjab, which exemplifies most of these statements).

Literary Tradition in Hindi

Literature of protest advocating social change is not new to the Hindi belt:[18] since the beginnings of literary tradition in Hindi, there have been various figures who have flouted traditional norms, medieval saint poets like Nanak (1469–1539), Kabir (1440–1518) and Mirabai (1503–73) prominent among them. Both Nanak and Kabir were opposed to rigid caste hierarchy and to the trivial ritualistic practices that separated the two great religions of Hinduism and Islam. Mirabai was a Rajput princess who was widowed at an early age. She left the court and devoted herself to the worship of Krishna. Her relationship to Krishna was a personal one, that of a spiritual marriage. Her poetry is full of a deep pathos; her songs of separation project her sorrow and pining for Krishna onto all nature around her. She broke all the family and *jāti* norms, but it was for the realization of her spiritual self, hence her individualism was acceptable to the larger society.[19]

Medieval devotional (*bhakti*) poetry in almost all Indian languages contains elements of social protest, especially rebellion against religious persecution, rigid caste hierarchy, stifling hold of family, and so on. But all this is in the context of devotion and hence receives wide acceptance. The next phase of protest literature begins soon after the consolidation of British power over India. The concerns in this period are more social: the benefits of women's education, the desirability of instituting widow remarriage, the undesirability of segregation of women in *purdah*, and the evils of *sati* ("suttee" in British English).

In the third decade of the twentieth century, the literature of realism gained momentum under the Marxist movement. A large part of this literature dealt with various economic, political, and social ills. The themes of exploitation of women (e.g., the literature devoted to prostitution), ill-treatment of young women by in-laws, the curse of dowry, early marriage, and marriage of young women with older men, the terrible consequences of illiteracy and *purdah* among women, all were taken up. But most of these themes were dealt with by men; very few women wrote literature of any consequence. One of the most prominent writers of this era is Premchand (1880–1936), whose novels and short stories deal with all the above themes.

There were a few exceptions, of course. In Hindi, Mahadevi Verma (1907–87) was one of the four major poets of the romantic-mystic school (1918–35). Her prose, however, portrayed the outcast, the poor of the village as well as small towns. Her word portraits of these characters, some of them women—illiterate but possessing remarkable personalities—are exquisite. Her essays on women's position in Indian society, *Śrnkhalā kī kariyā* (*Links in the chain*, published in 1942), boldly exposed the myth of wife and motherhood—one devoid of any respect, the other of any glory. She rejected both these roles for herself and continued to write and speak on women's issues till her death (see the collections in Sharad 1969 and Pandey 1983). In Mahadevi Verma's writings, there is a clear-eyed perception of the social construction of womanhood in India, particularly in the post *manusmṛti* period, but there is no bitterness or militancy. There are references to the position of women in the Vedic period, when they were free to be *brahmavādins* (pursuers of the knowledge of the *brahman*) and there was no social pressure for them to be married, and there are impassioned pleas as well as rational arguments for the kind of equality that would enable women to realize their full potential.

In contemporary Hindi fiction, the number of women novelists and short story writers is much greater than in any previous period, and a large number of these writers have received critical acclaim. The themes that recur are: women's sexuality and sensuality (e.g., short stories by Usha Priyamvada, the novel *Mitro marjānī* [*Mitro the Dead*] by Krishna Sobti); the heightened imagination, high intelligence and extraordinary sensitivity to inner and outer environment in women (e.g., short stories by Mrinal Pandey); the institutions of divorce and remarriage and their impact on the woman and the child (e.g., the novels *Āpkā banṭī* [*Yours Banti*] by Mannu Bhandari, *Śeṣ yātrā* [*The Last Journey*] by Usha Priyamvada); rape and its effect on a young woman's sexuality (e.g., the novel *Sūrajmukhī andhere ke* [*Sunflowers of the Dark*] by Krishna Sobti); economic power of the working woman (the novel *Anāro* by Manjul Bhagat); and search for identity, or realization of individual potential through work outside the home (e.g., the novel *Uske hisse kī dhūp* [*The Sun Due to Her*] by Mridula Garg [translated into English by the author herself with the title *A Touch of Sun*]).

What is remarkable about this literature is that there is little reflection of Mahadevi Verma's *Śrnkhalā ki kaṛiyā* in these writings; instead, there is a total absence of denial of traditional roles of daughter, daughter-in-law, mother, and so on in most short stories and novels. There is a realization of the woman's sorry plight in contemporary society but none of the bitterness that is associated with a great deal of feminist rhetoric, at least in journalistic writing.[20] This becomes clear if one analyzes some of these works in some detail.

Analysis of Contemporary Fiction

It is impossible to survey the entire range of the themes and trends in Hindi fiction by women writers here. I will concentrate on a few works by some of the prominenent contemporary novelists and short story writers.

In the novel *Anāro* by Manjul Bhagat, the protagonist is a woman of the same name who earns her living by washing dishes and cleaning several homes in a big city. Her work situates her on the bottom rung of the social ladder. Her husband is a trained auto mechanic, but he is an alcoholic who cannot hold a steady job and who loves to run off to Bombay and have extramarital relationships whenever possi-

ble. He stays only long enough for Anaro to have two children by
him—a girl and, much later, a boy. Even when he is with Anaro, he
gets involved with another, younger woman and has a son by her, too.
Anaro knows all this; the language she uses when she is thinking about
him provides enough clues to what she really thinks of him.[21] But she
is a loyal wife and clings to the family structure by never publicly humi-
liating him or leaving him. She is not willing to tolerate the other
woman in her home, but once the other woman has a son, she is
realistic enough to know that two sons are better than one, so she suggests her husband bring his illegitimate son home for her to raise. She
is a typical Indian wife and mother; she wants her hut to have a proper
(*pakkā*) roof and her home to have affordable gadgets like a radio, her
children to be educated, and her daughter to be married to a respectable man. And she manages all this alone, driven by two forces: her
pride (*abhimān*) in herself (p. 73) and her love for her own family
(*apnā khāndān*, p. 96). Ultimately, she earns the individual identity
and recognition that she struggled for. As the friends and relatives enjoy the feast following her daughter's wedding, her husband declares:
"Today I have realized [*āj . . . mān gayā*] what my wife is. She is not
my wife, friends, she is my older brother—do you understand, my older brother! Like a brother, she gave me her support. She raised my
standing [*nāk ūcī kar dī*] in everyone's eyes" (p. 95). Anaro turns red
with pride (*garva*); "What prestige [*mān*]? . . . May she always have
prestige, respect [*kadar*] in her man's eyes!" (p. 96). Anaro's identity
and self-worth are inextricably intertwined with her roles as wife and
mother and as a member of her community, and even the laudatory
words of a half-drunk husband are enough to give her the sense of
fulfillment that she dared not expect.

Another novel that deals with a woman struggling to realize her
sense of self is *Uske hisse kī dhūp* by Mridula Garg. It deals with the
age-old triangle, but with a different twist for India, that of husband-
wife-other man. The heroine, Manisha, was married to the workaholic
Jiten, who gave her a luxurious life but, in her perception, little of
himself. She got a job teaching in a college to keep herself occupied,
but that did not fill the gap in her life. Enter the charismatic Madhukar, a colleague temporarily on loan from an institution in Delhi, and
she is swept off her feet. She leaves Jiten and her job for Madhukar,
but as the novelty of her remarried life wears off and Madhukar becomes more and more engrossed in his work and political activities,
her professed occupation of writing becomes less and less satisfying.
She tries to have a child, but the pregnancy ends in a miscarriage. In a
chance encounter with Jiten, she ends up in Jiten's bed, but Jiten has

to leave suddenly to solve a crisis at work. Manisha comes back to Madhukar, realizes the futility of her attempt "to fill her life with the love of a man" (p. 164), and suddenly recalls the joy she feels when she writes something. And then she decides that she will write: "I will write all that has been churning inside me all these days. I will write about this individual [*vyakti*, "person"] inherent in me, which I cannot keep inside me without expressing through writing" (p. 171).

This, however, is not a proclamation of an individuality free from traditional roles; she still wants to be a wife and a mother. "And the child, that too will happen. . . the birth of a child in itself cannot be the aim of one's life. But that. . . is a sweet responsibility, a fulfillment that she cannot give up for no reason. . . . [Madhukar] wants this fulfillment as much as she does, maybe even more. It is as essential for a man's ego [*aham*] as it is for a woman's" (p. 171). And she decides, "I will write, with the child in my womb, I will write a novel" (p. 172). At the end of the novel, when Madhukar announces his college has declared a strike to protest against corruption and exploitation, she doubts that the strike will achieve anything. Madhukar taunts her, saying that sitting at home and writing will not achieve anything either. There are several exchanges that make it very clear that Madhukar does not have much respect for her writing. At the end of several exchanges, finally, Madhukar insists, whatever the outcome, at least he will be satisfied that he did whatever he could. And Manisha bursts out with full realization. "That's it, Madhukar, that's it. That's the doing, a human being's real achievement!" (p. 176). As Madhukar leaves her to join his striking colleagues, she finds "the sun of loneliness [*akelāpan*, "the state of being alone"] does not frighten her anymore, it caresses her with love" (p. 176). Illiterate, destitute Anaro found solace in work and fulfillment in her roles as wife and mother; her more educated, middle-class sister, Manisha, finds her salvation in work and fulfillment in the same roles, but with one difference: for Anaro, her man's approval is worth a great deal; for Manisha, it does not matter whether Madhukar understands what she does or not—she will do it to establish her own identity. Of course, neither one of them expects material rewards for herself; what they are looking for is a sense of self-worth through karma in the sense of the *Bhagvad gītā*. The karma they chose, of course, reflects the difference in terms of social class and tradition vs. modernity. Anaro can only wash dishes and do housecleaning; Manisha has available to her an opportunity that is denied to Anaro, and, just a few decades ago, was denied even to women of her own social class.

The same is true of the female protagonist of Manjul Bhagat's

Tirchī bauchār. Vismita (Visu for short) is happily married, but she is dissatisfied with her life, which revolves around taking care of her aged mother-in-law, her husband struggling to become successful, and her daughter engrossed in her own career. She toys with the idea of falling into a Platonic relationship with a rich and successful patron of her husband, but he does not respond in the way that she would have liked. Ultimately, as her health suffers, she looks for a job in an advertising agency, where her creativity leads to her success. She then realizes that "A human being may not have wealth, may not have a lock and key, s/he must have a state of free being [*mukt-sā*, "free-like"; *astitva*, "being," "existence"], an eternal one [*kabhī na mar miṭnevālā*, then s/he is fortunate" (Bhagat 1984, 108–9).

The picture that emerges when one considers Indian English novels such as *Cry, the Peacock* and *Voices in the City* by Anita Desai is quite different. In *Cry, the Peacock*, the imagination, intelligence, and sensitivity of the protagonist, Maya, ultimately leads to a psychotic state. In *Voices in the City*, Monisha, unable to adjust to the stifling role of a traditional daughter-in-law, with no hope of gaining a change in status by becoming a mother, commits suicide. In neither novel does the mother appear as a compassionate, nurturing figure. In fact, in *Fire on the Mountain*, the debunking of wifehood and motherhood is complete. The same is true of the Bengali short story "Standāyinī" ("the Breast Giver") by Mahashveta Devi; it is a story of the ruthless exploitation of motherhood. Written with wry humor, this twenty-eight-page story chronicles the life of a simple, poor Brahmin woman who is taken advantage of, not only by her husband and sons but also the women of her village. Jashoda, the protagonist, the "professional mother," is a healthy, buxom woman who is appointed the nursing mother of more than thirty babies, produced by the sons of a wealthy family in the village, to provide for her family when her husband loses his legs in a car accident. The mistress of the household and her daughters-in-law going in and out of the maternity room treat her as they treat their milch cows. In order to keep the milk flowing, at her husband's suggestion, she delivers and nurses twenty babies of her own: "Does it hurt a tree to bear fruit?" Toward the end of her life, when the flow of milk stops and she is of no use to either her husband or her patrons, she develops breast cancer, dies in a hospital, and is cremated by the low-caste functionaries of the burning *ghat*. The last lines of the story are "Jashoda was God manifest, others do and did whatever she thought. Jashoda's death was also the death of God. When a mortal masquerades as God here below, s/he is forsaken by all and s/he must always die alone."[22] The voice of Mahadevi Verma finds an echo in the writings of Anita Desai and Mahashveta Devi! And, to some extent, in the short stories by Mrinal Pandey.

One thing that emerges very clearly from this discussion is that the traditional ideal of a chaste woman (*pativratā*, "ever loyal to one's husband") is no longer as important as it used to be for the woman writer; there is no guilt in Manisha when she enters into a relationship with Madhukar while married to Jiten or goes to bed with Jiten while married to Madhukar. In the first case, she wants to be honest with Jiten and hence seeks a divorce; in the latter case, she simply wants to avoid a confrontation with Madhukar and does not tell him about her chance encounter with Jiten or its temporary consequences. The same is true of the heroines of *Śeṣ yātrā* and *Āpkā Baṇṭī*; in the latter, Banti's mother has no feelings of guilt about her remarriage, only about its effect on her son, Banti.

The reasons for this attitude are transparent. The notion of loyalty exemplified by Sita and Savitri are no longer practical; it is incompatible with divorce, remarriage, and widow remarriage—all sanctioned by religious and legal codes of conduct.[23] Also, though the ideal of *ek-patnīvrat* (loyalty to one wife), as exemplified by Rama, has also been familiar, men have not found it necessary to adhere to it. Thus, the inequality inherent in the insistence on women's loyalty and the ambiguity apparent in the context of divorce and remarriage have made it impossible to extol the virtues of *pātivratya* (eternal loyalty to one's husband). Besides, the requirement that a woman be forever loyal to her one and only husband was restricted to the twice-born castes; others were free to divorce and remarry.

The attitudes toward wifehood and motherhood, on the other hand, are ambivalent. While there is more deglamorization of wifehood and motherhood in Bengali and Indian English fiction, and the tension between the norms of traditional womanhood versus the more modern sense of individual identity either remains unresolved or leads to pathology in the Indian English fiction, the women in Hindi fiction face the reality of their position and work out their individual selves and identity within the context of family and society. One wonders if this has something to do with the difference in the sensibility determined by the respective media—Bengali versus English versus Hindi. This, of course, needs further investigation.

Conclusion

Does this mean that the traditional values are crumbling, at least to some extent, in Indian society? The answer has to be both yes and no.

The ideal of a *pativratā* woman may no longer be relevant, but the value of the extended family, respect for elders, consciousness of a woman's role in maintaining family and sociocultural traditions, and so forth are still relevant for the majority of women. In *Tirchī bauchār*, the mother-in-law is always complaining, and though Vasu gets irritated occasionally, she does not think of her as a burden. Whether the protagonist is a Hindu woman, as in the cases discussed above, or a Christian, as in the novel *Uskā ghar* (*Her House*) by Mehrunissa Parvez, the familial as well as the spiritual self is as prominent as ever. The expanding self has made it possible for women to assert their individuality, their personal existence in addition to, not in lieu of, the familial self.[24] In a culture and civilization that has a long tradition of reconciling different religions, philosophies, and norms of behavior, this is not surprising. It is crucial to remember this for cross-cultural comparisons.

The methodology of sociolinguistic analysis of a part of Indian literature illustrated in this study could be extended to other parts of Indian literature or other literatures. For instance, the investigation of women fiction writers reveals the fact that "her [a woman's] soul is no longer asleep: she has learnt to be a person [*vyakti*] before a woman [*nārī*]" (Ray 1963, introduction). Although the women's movement in India is strong, in Mahadevi Verma's words, "We [i.e., the women] do not want to conquer, or to be defeated by anyone, we do not want any power over anyone, nor do we want any authority over us. We want only that place, those identities [*svatva*] which are of no use to men but without which we cannot be a useful part of the society" (Sharad 1969, 379).

This analysis has been restricted to one facet of Indian self only—that of Indian women. It would be instructive to see what other facets of the complex Indian self are revealed in Indian literature. It would also be interesting to determine if the differential cultural change that the sociological survey of Chu 1989 reveals in literary works written in Taiwan and in The People's Republic of China is apparent in various literatures in India, too. Since the Japanese and the Indians share some organizations of self, investigations of contemporary Japanese writing may confirm or disconfirm the theory of overwhelming global trend toward Westernization of traditional cultures. Oral folk literature, myths, texts of the Great tradition and cultural performances (in the sense of Singer 1972), and so forth have all been utilized to gain insight into important aspects of self and identity in a culture. Contemporary creative literature could be an additional source for such research.

NOTES

An earlier version of this paper was presented at the "Conference on Perception of Self" organized by the Insitute of Culture and Communication at the East-West Center, Honolulu, on August 14–19, 1989.

1. See, e.g., Halliday 1978; Hymes 1974; Pike 1967; Labov 1972; Le Page and Tabouret-Keller 1987. Studies collected in Gumperz 1982 exemplify the application of the sociolinguistic-ethnographic approach to the study of cross-cultural verbal interaction.

2. See Monier-Williams 1976; Potter 1970, 1977, 1981; and Larson and Bhattacharya 1987. I have followed the usual conventions of transliteration from Sanskrit, Hindi, and other Indo-Aryan languages.

3. See Singer 1972 for a discussion of the interaction between the Great and Little traditions in traditional as well as contemporary India.

4. Kabir uses, in addition, *allāh* and *xudā*.

5. The Indo-Aryan languages of India are genetically related to the Indo-European family of languages. The history of the Indo-Aryan is usually described in terms of Old Indo-Aryan (1500–600 B.C.), Middle Indo-Aryan (600 B.C.–A.D. 1000) and New Indo-Aryan (A.D. 1000).

6. The last is an interesting development: the word did not have this sense in Sanskrit. It meant "acquaintance," "familiarity," "intimacy with," or "knowledge of" in Sanskrit. The word has these senses in NIA languages also.

7. In most psychoanalytical literature, Indian thinking is said to be representational and affective, based on the primary process perception of posture, vibration, rhythm, tempo, resonance, and other nonverbal expressions and unlike the secondary process thinking expressed in language in the West (Kakar 1978; Roland 1988). However, socialization through language too is important in India. Concepts of *kul*, *vaṃś*, or *xāndān* (family), *kul maryādā* or *xāndān kī izzat* (family prestige), and *lajjā* or *śarm* (shame) are important linguistically formulated concepts. The English language has added certain other concepts such as the independence of the individual (*vyakti svātantrya*) and modernity (*ādhuniktā*) to these. According to B. Kachru (1986), at least 4 percent of India's population is competent in English, which means a population of approximately thirty-two million. Also, English has had tremendous impact on Indian languages in terms of inspiring new genres (e.g., most genres in prose) and in expanding the register range so topics related to science and technology could be discussed through the medium of these langauges.

8. E.g., Weber 1958; Shils 1961; Myrdal 1968 subscribe to the first view, whereas Srinivas 1966; Rudolph and Rudolph 1967; Singer 1972; and Roland 1988 hold very different opinions.

9. For a definition of Westernization, see Srinivas 1966, and for a definition of modernization, see Singer 1972.

10. For the original text, see *Upaniṣad Bhāṣya* (Gorakhpur: Gita Press, 1968), vol. 4. *Bṛhadāraṇyakopaniṣad* (with *Śankar Bhāṣya*), 548–49.

11. For a comparison of American, Chinese, Indian, and Japanese concepts of self, see Roland 1988.

12. See Garg 1988 for a slightly different view. According to her, "There are, broadly speaking, three kinds of women in India"; the first are the "women of the third world, who are no better than beasts of burden," the second the "middle class with a certain degree of education. . . being pushed to work outside the home. . . out of economic necessity. . . . They have a certain degree of political and social awareness" and the third "highly educated, well placed, holding important and socially powerful jobs, articulate and adventurous. . . These, along with those women who are merely objects of decoration. . . compose the first world within the third world country of India."

13. Brahmo Samaj was founded in 1828 by Raja Ram Mohan Roy (1772–1833) in Bengal; Arya Samaj was founded in 1875 by Swami Dayanand Saraswati (1824–1883) in the Punjab; the Theosophical Society was founded in 1875 by H. P. Blavatsky, becoming prominent under the leadership of Annie Besant (1847–1933) in Madras; and the Ramakrishna Mission was founded by Narendranath Datta, later known as Swami Vivekananda (1863–1902), under the inspiration of Swami Ramakrishna Paramahamsa (1834–1886). See Jordens 1975; and Owen 1975 for a brief account of these and other reform movements in different parts of India.

14. This paragraph draws on Roland 1988 to a great extent.

15. Hence the festivals devoted to brother-and-sister relationships, e.g., *rakṣā-bandhan*, celebrated on the full moon day of the fifth month of the Hindu lunar calendar (which corresponds to July–August) and *bhrātṛ dvitīyā*, celebrated on the second day of the dark fortnight in the eighth month of the Hindu calendar (which corresponds to October–November). There are several legends about the brother rushing to a sister's rescue at enormous cost to himself, and the historical incident involving the Mughal Emperor Humayun (1530–42, 1555–56) and the Rajput queen Karmavati of Chittor makes it clear that the special brother-sister relationship in India is not restricted to the Hindus. Emperor Humayun responded to the letter and the *rakṣā* (*rākhī* in Hindi) sent by Queen Karmavati and rushed back to Rajasthan to assist Chittor to fight Bahadurshah, leaving his troops to fight Shershah in Bihar, and thus lost his kingdom, which explains the break in his reign.

16. Quoted in Kakar 1978, 77.

17. See Kramrisch 1981 for details.

18. In fact, it is not new to the Indian literature in general. The Buddhist collections in Theragatha and Therigatha as well as a large body of Sufi literature exemplify literature of protest in the Indian tradition.

19. Instances of flouting of social norms are attestable in the Buddhist *therī gāthā* compilation (collection of poems by Buddhist nuns in the pre-Christian era) and the poetry of the medieval saint poets in practically all Indian languages.

20. There are some exceptions to this generalization, e.g., Mrinal Pandey's short stories. These, however, are not discussed here in detail since the remarks on women and their plight come as asides in these stories (e.g., in the collection *Ek nīc ṭrejeḍī* [*A low tragedy*] published in 1981).

21. "The Runaway! Here I went to my natal family with Ganji in my womb, and there he brought a rival to sit on my chest" (p. 5). All the quotations from Hindi are in my translation of the original.

22. The quotes are from Spivak 1987, which contains a translation of the short story discussed here. I have taken the liberty of changing the instances of *she* in the last line to *s/he* as I felt that since Bengali does not make a distinction between *he* and *she*, and neither does the verb agree in gender with the gender of the subject or any other noun in the sentence, this may better reflect the original. It is, of course, impossible to translate the speech of the characters in the story; each character uses the regional rural dialect typical of the eastern part of the Bengali-speaking region of the subcontinent.

23. See Kakar 1978 for Sita as the ideal Hindu woman. The Hindu Code Bill has provisions for all these; traditionally also, in certain specific circumstances, all these were permissible as discussed in the "bible" of the Arya Samaj, Dayanand Saraswati's *Satyārth prakāś* (first published in 1875).

24. One manifestation of this is the institutionalization of new "goddesses" in village India. Jung 1987 mentions a temple in a village in Karnataka where Akkamahadevi (a Kannada medieval saint poet, a woman) has been installed as an income-generating goddess and goddess Kalyaneshwari has been installed to inspire women to have smaller families. The temple is wholly owned and operated by women.

BIBLIOGRAPHY

Basham, A. L. (ed.) 1975. *A Cultural History of India.* Oxford: Clarendon Press.
Bhagat, Manjul. 1977. *Anaro.* Delhi: Parag Prakashan.
———. 1984. *Tirchi bauchar.* New Delhi: National Publishing House.

Brown, Norman. 1966. *Man in the Universe: Cultural Continuities in India*. Berkeley and Los Angeles: University of California Press.

Chomsky, Noam. 1986 *Knowledge of Language: Its Nature, Origin and Use*. New York: Praeger.

Chu, Godwin C. 1989. "Empirical studies of cultural change in Asia." Discussion working paper presented at East-West Center, Honolulu.

Das, V. 1979. "Reflections on the Social Construction of Adulthood. In *Identity and Adulthood*, ed. Sudhir Kakar, 89–104 Delhi: Oxford University Press.

Devi, Mahashveta. 1983. *Mahashveta Devīr shreṣṭha galpa*. Calcutta: Prema Prakashani.

Firth, J. R. 1957. *Papers in Linguistics 1935–1954*. London: Oxford University Press.

Garg, Mridula. 1988. "The Reality and the Metaphor of Womanhood in Indian Literature: With Special Reference to Writing by Women in Hindi." Paper presented at the International Conference on Feminist Critique and Writing, Dubrovnik, Yugoslavia. [A short version appeared in *Times of India*, Dec. 4, 1988]

———. 1975. *Uske hisse kī dhūp*. Delhi: Akshar Prakashan.

Gould, Harold A. 1987. *Caste Adaptation in Modernizing Indian Society*. Delhi: Chanakya Publications.

Gumperz, John J. 1982. *Language and Social Identity*. Cambridge: Cambridge University Press.

Halliday, M.A.K. 1978. *Language as Social Semiotics: The Social Interpretation of Language and Meaning*. London: Edward Arnold [U.S. edition published by University Park Press, Baltimore.]

Hoy, David C., ed. 1986. *Foucault: A Critical Reader*. Oxford: Basil Blackwell.

Hymes, Dell. 1974. *Foundations in Sociolinguistics: An Ethnographic Approach*. Philadelphia: University of Pennsylvania Press.

Jordens, J.T.F. 1975. "Hindu Religious and Social Reform in British India." In *A Cultural History of India*, ed. A. L. Basham, 365–82. Oxford Clarendon Press.

Jung, Anees. 1987. *Unveiling India: A Woman's Journey*. New Delhi: Penguin Books (India).

Kachru, Braj B. 1981. "Socially Realistic Linguistics: The Firthian Tradition." *International Journal of the Sociology of Language* 31:65–89.

———. 1983. *The Indianization of English: The English Language in India*. Delhi: Oxford University Press.

———. 1986. *The Alchemy of English: The Spread, Functions and Models of Non-native Englishes*. Oxford: Pergamon Press.

―――. 1987. "The Bilingual's Creativity: Discoursal and Stylistic Strategies in Contact Literatures." In *Discourse Across Cultures*, ed. Larry E. Smith 125–40. Oxford: Pergamon Press.

Kakar, Sudhir. 1978. *The Inner World: A Psychoanalytical Study of Childhood and Society in India*. Delhi: Oxford University Press.

Kakar, Sudhir, ed. 1979. *Identity and Adulthood*. Delhi: Oxford University Press.

Kramrisch, Stella. 1981. *The Presence of Śiva*. Princeton: Princeton University Press.

Labov, William. 1972. *Sociolinguistic Patterns*. Philadelphia: University of Pennsylvania Press.

Larson, Gerald J., and R. S. Bhattacharya, eds. 1987. *Encyclopedia of Indian Philosophies*. New Delhi: Motilal Banarsidass.

Le Page, Robert B., and A. Tabouret-Keller. 1987. *Acts of Identity: Creole-based Approaches to Language and Ethnicity*. Cambridge: Cambridge University Press.

Mehta, Rama. 1970. *The Western Educated Hindu Woman*. Bombay, India: Asia Publishing House.

―――. 1976. "From Purdah to Modernity." In *Indian Women: From Purdah to Modernity*, ed. B. R. Nanda, 113–28. New Delhi: Vikas Publishing House.

Miller, Peggy J. 1979. "Sex of Subject and Self Concept Variables." Chap. 5 in *The Self-concept*, vol. 2, ed. Ruth C Wylie in collaboration with P. J. Miller, S. S. Cowles, and A. W. Wilson, 241–352. Lincoln: University of Nebraska Press.

Monier-Williams, Monier. 1976. *Sanskrit-English Dictionary: etymologically and philosophically arranged with special reference to cognate Indo-European languages*. New Indian ed. New Delhi: Munishiram Manoharlal.

Myrdal, G. 1968. *Asian Drama*. New York. Pantheon.

Nanda, B. R. 1976. *Indian women: from Purdah to Modernity*. New Delhi: Vikas.

Nandy, Ashish. 1983. *The Intimate Enemy: Loss and Recovery of Self under Colonialism*. Delhi: Oxford University Press.

Owen, Hugh. 1975. "The Nationalist Movement." In *A Cultural History of India*, ed. A. L. Basham, 391–405. Oxford: Clarendon Press.

Pandey, Ramji. 1983. *Mahādevī: pratinidhi gadya racnāen*. New Delhi: Bharatiya Gyanpith Prakashan.

Parvez, Mehrunissa. 1972. *Uskā ghar*. New Delhi: National Publishing House.

Pike, Kenneth L. 1967. *Language in Relation to a Unified Theory of the Structure of Human Behavior*. 2nd ed. The Hague: Mouton.

Potter, Karl H. 1970. *Encyclopedia of Indian Philosophy*. Vol. 1. Delhi: Motilal Barnasidass.

―――. 1977. *Encyclopedia of Indian Philosophy*. Vol. 2. Delhi: Motilal Barnasidass.

―――. 1981. *Encyclopedia of Indian Philosophy*, Vol. 3. Princeton: Princeton University Press.

Ray, Bina, ed. 1963. *Lekhikā Man*. Calcutta: Sahityayan.

Roland, Alan. 1988. *In Search of Self in India and Japan: Toward a Cross-cultural Psychology*. Princeton: Princeton University Press.

Rudolph, L., and S. Rudolph. 1967. *The Modernity of Tradition* Chicago: University of Chicago Press.

Sharad, Onkar, ed. 1969. *Mahadevī sāhitya*. Jhansi: Setu Prakashan.

Shils, E. 1961. *The Intellectual between Tradition and Modernity: The Indian Situation*. Comparative Studies in Society and History, supp. 1. The Hague: Mouton.

Singer, Milton. 1972. *When a Great Tradition Modernizes: An Anthropological Approach to Indian Civilization*. New York: Praeger.

Sobti, Krishna. 1967. *Mitro marjān*. Delhi: Rajkamal Prakashan.

―――. 1972. *Sūrajmukhī andhere ke*. Delhi: Rajkamal Prakashan.

Spivak, Gayatri C. 1987. *In Other Worlds: Essays in Cultural Politics*. New York, Methuen.

Srinivas, M. N. 1966. *Social Change in Modern India*. Berkeley and Los Angeles: University of California Press.

Wadley, Susan. 1980. "Hindu Women's Family and Household Rites in a North Indian Village." In *Unspoken Worlds: Women's Religious Lives in Non-Western Cultures*, ed. R. Gross and N. Falk, 94–109. New York: Harper & Row.

Weber, M. 1958. *The Religion of India: The Sociology of Hinduism and Buddhism*. Glencoe, Ill.: Free Press.

Whitehead, Tony L., and M. E. Conaway, eds. 1986. *Self, sex and gender in cross-cultural fieldwork*. Urbana, University of Illinois Press.

Winternitz, M. [1927] 1977. *History of Indian literature*. 2nd ed. Reprint. New Delhi: Oriental Books Reprint Corporation.

16

Selves in Motion: An Indian-Japanese Comparison

Vantage Points and Perceptions of the Self

The vantage point upon which one is perched determines a great deal of one's perceptions of the self. A view from one part of the road, or discipline, can be dramatically different from just around the bend. I am sure that a Japanese psychoanalyst, or for that matter an Indian one, would emphasize very different aspects of an Indian-Japanese comparison of the self than I do as a New York City Jewish psychoanalyst. As an outsider from these Asian cultures, I may perhaps more easily see certain things in common structurally in the nature of the Indian and Japanese selves and in the subtle dimensions of hierarchical relationships with which these selves are so intimately related—which on the surface can seem wholly different. Whereas not being an insider of either culture, I can be certain of missing a great variety of subtle matters. Our vantage points thus determine much of what we perceive.

But the question of vantage points and perceptions is still more complex in making an Indian-Japanese comparison of the self. Unless one is wedded to making universal statements about the nature of the self, which is exactly what psychoanalysts tend to do, a whole other issue of perceptions arises once one begins to particularize the nature of the Indian or Japanese self. A cross-cultural perspective is immediately involved. I would submit that it is extremely difficult if not impossible to have a workable vantage point within one's own culture to comment meaningfully and comprehensively on the nature of a particular cultural self—at least from a psychoanalytic standpoint. An implicit comparison almost always has to be made with others, or at very minimum with another historical period within one's own culture.

Thus, most of the psychoanalytic and psychological work on the Indian and Japanese selves comes from just those analysts who have trained in the West or who are extremely knowledgeable in Western psychological paradigms. In India for instance, there is the psychoanalytic work of Sudhir Kakar (1978, 1979, 1982), who worked with Erik Erikson in Boston and trained psychoanalytically in Germany; and of B. K. Ramanujam (1979, 1980a, 1980b, 1981a, 1981b, 1986), who trained at the Menninger Foundation in America, and also in England. While in Japan, Heisaku Kosawa, who trained in Vienna and became the dean of Japanese psychoanalysis, wrote about the greater relevance of the Ajase complex to the Japanese self than the Oedipus complex (Okonogi 1978, 1979). Certainly, the seminal work of Takeo Doi (1973) on *amae* relationships stems from this cross-cultural perspective from his training at the Menninger Foundation.

On one hand, the particular cross-cultural vantage point of being Western trained enabled these analysts to sharpen their perceptions and elucidate their indigenous selves. On the other hand, it resulted in all of the implicit and explicit comparative perceptions of Indians and Japanese to be with Westerners. The contrasts are immediate and dramatic. The sense of uniqueness is intensely heightened. But there is much to be gained as well from the vantage point of an inter-Asian comparison of the self: it would more truly show what is indeed unique to either the Indian or Japanese self and what these selves have in common—though it may be in different measure or balance.

There is still another vantage point with its particular perceptions and insights that is central to this paper, that of psychoanalysis. As I have discussed at length in my book, *In Search of Self in India and Japan: Toward a Cross-Cultural Psychology*, a whole set of issues arises once psychoanalysis is used to elucidate the Indian and Japanese selves, since psychoanalysis is a Western healing paradigm and theory. Yet, psychoanalysis has also been practiced and adapted in India for some seven decades and in Japan for almost five. Clearly, it has relevance in both cultures for an understanding of the self.

I found that to use the vantage point of psychoanalysis for understanding the Indian and Japanese selves, I could easily employ the various categories of psychoanalysis—for example, conscience (superego and ego-ideal), unconscious conflict, psychic structures, narcissism or self-esteem, and so forth; but I have had to change the content of these categories from how they are elaborated upon in current-day psychoanalysis to be relevant to the Indian and Japanese selves. That is, I had to decontextualize the content from Western personality and recontextualize it on the basis of clinical data with Indians and Japanese. Certainly, conscience, for instance, can be significantly different. Moreover, I have had to formulate new categories for certain dimensions of the Indian and Japanese selves, since these dimensions may only be minimally present in Westerners and have not been conceptualized in psychoanalysis—for example, the intense dependency and interdependency relationships, or kinds of cognition related to the magic-cosmic world of astrology, palmistry, the spirits, and such. The alternative to this kind of revamping of psychoanalysis is Takeo Doi's ingenious solution: to elaborate on Japanese linguistic terms psychologically as in *Anatomy of Dependence.*

Then there are the issues of what I have come to term the "spiritual self," which is an assumed ground of being in Indians and is also relevant in Japanese. But, with rare exceptions, it is missing or denigrated as regressive or psychopathological in psychoanalytic thinking. I have thus used Indian formulations of a phenomenological self (*jīva ātman*) and a spiritual self (*ātman*). In this sense, psychoanalytic studies are of the phenomenological self; but with occasional patients, one gets into issues of a spiritual self. I have posited the psychological process of self-transformation as central to Indian and Japanese individuation; whereas the self-creation of identity is more the crux of the contemporary Western self.

I have also had to rethink the organization of the self from a cross-cultural perspective, positing a familial self that varies among Asians, an individualized self that varies among those of the northern European-North American culture belt, and a spiritual self. I have used different psychoanalytic perspectives on the self, including: theories of organization; an object-relations approach involving the internalization of early relationships and culture, and the true and false self or issues of authenticity; and self-psychology, which so prominently focuses on issues of self-esteem and the development of a cohesive self.

Even with a cross-cultural and a modified psychoanalytic perspectives, the perceptions they allow of the Indian and Japanese selves can still be seriously limited unless another important vantage point is taken into account. The problem is that cross-cultural and psychoanalytic viewpoints are essentially static, ahistorical ones. They rarely involve the historical process as it manifests psychologically in what I have come to term an "expanding self."

This vantage point for perceiving the self is of importance in any culture area, but it is particularly so in India and Japan. For not only on a cultural level but also on a psychological one are the effects of prolonged contact with the West profound. And in any cross-cultural comparison of the Indian and Japanese selves, it is essential to take into account the differing nature of the engagements with the West, as well as the differing resulting effects. What I am obviously emphasizing is that the historical process is as much a part of the self as cultural symbol systems and social patterns. They are not simply out there, but are deeply embedded within the self.

It is from this often ignored historical vantage point that I have entitled this paper "Selves in Motion." Since psychoanalysis has been an ahistorical discipline with but few exceptions (e.g., Erikson 1946, 1958, 1969; Rank 1932; Menaker and Menaker 1965), it becomes necessary to erect a scaffolding that will adequately support the psychological manifestations of the historical process. One such approach is that of the Japanese psychoanalyst, Masahisa Nishizono (unpublished), who formulates a layering of the selves in an identity that may well be beset with conflict. On the uppermost level of the self is the encounter with Western values and its incorporation, usually in later stages of childhood and adolescence; whereas on the more basic level of the self is indigenous culture, more firmly emotionally anchored from earlier childhood relationships. This same paradigm is quite applicable to Indians, but it is manifested very differently, as I shall indicate below, because of prolonged contact with British colonial attitudes.

Another necessary part of the scaffolding to contain the historical process is a conceptualization of different psychological processes of the self that are related to the modernization that has occurred in both India and Japan. Here, there must be a more complex psychological schema that shows how the Indian and Japanese familial selves are congruent with the modernization process, what broad changes in the familial self are brought about by modernization, and what psychological conflicts are engendered. The historical experience of modernization in both countries belies the viewpoint of certain psychologists and psychologically oriented social scientists that to modernize successfully the indigenous self must become transformed into a Western, individualized self.

A final vantage point of the historical perspective encompasses how Indians and Japanese react and adapt to American culture. The encounter with a totally different life-style highlights aspects of the Indian and Japanese selves that are quite adaptive and other aspects that are thrown into emotional conflict and anguish, while showing how the self is partially changed by slowly incorporating certain American values and ways of relating. If the person stays long enough in America, he or she gradually has an expanding or bicultural self. I have had psychoanalytic experience with both Indians and Japanese in New York City, which I shall comment upon below in this framework.

Selves in Motion

The issue of identity as related to historical change is a major one in any Indian-Japanese comparison; but it is manifested entirely different-ly in the psychological makeup of each, since Indians and Japanese en-countered the West in entirely different ways. In the Indian context, identity conflicts and resolutions were profoundly colored by the colonial experience with the British. The British not only introduced Western institutions, technology, legal and economic systems, life-styles, and ideologies but also pervasively denigrated Indians and Indian culture. Thus, Indians did not have the luxury of freely assim-ilating or rejecting Western imports, as was the case with Japan until the American occupation.

Indian identity resolutions took basically three different direc-tions in response to the colonial presence (which I describe in greater detail elsewhere [Roland 1988, 22–25]); these, in any particular person, might well have been mixed. The first was identification with the raj and rejection of everything Indian. The second was its opposite: iden-tification with indigenous culture and complete rejection of everything Western. The third was a selective incorporation of the West in the framework of a more basic identification with Indian culture, with efforts to reform the latter.

Identity conflicts were particularly acute in sons whose fathers had good positions with the British colonial administration and who often closely identified themselves with colonial attitudes, therefore depreciating Indian culture. Their sons, with normal expectations of the Indian familial self, identified with their fathers' values and tried to gain their fathers' respect and reflect well on their fathers. This fre-quently resulted in their depreciating Indian culture and, therefore, their more core self, which was closely associated with indigenous cul-ture through the earlier maternal relationships. A study of biographies and autobiographies of some of these sons reveals that many of these men suffered from psychological paralysis (Walsh 1982). In the case study of Ashis (Roland 1988, 25–47), whose father had a highly re-sponsible position in the Indian civil service, I describe at length the enormous identity conflicts engendered by his father's Westernized attitudes as well as his psychic paralysis when he first saw me for psychoanalytic therapy in New York City. To this day, I have found that most Western-educated Indian men still must make conscious decisions between how much they are Indian or Western in identity. Indian women, on the other hand, seem much more comfortably rooted in indigenous culture, even when they are college educated and pursue careers.

These painful kinds of identity struggles are not really present in Japanese because there has been no pervasive denigration of their culture by a colonial presence. Since the Meiji Restoration, there have indeed been oscillations between acceptance and rejection of Western ideologies, institutions, and technology, with at times historically some depreciation of indigenous values; but it is certainly not on a scope compared to India. Japan's genius of modernizing has been to assimilate foreign imports while maintaining totally Japanese modes of group hierarchical relationships and values.

Major identity conflicts have arisen only with the American occupation, when a totally different value system was introduced and fostered in a climate of profound disillusionment with traditional values of the male hierarchy. Western values of egalitarianism, individual rights, and individualism (such as individual autonomy and independence, self-determination on major life decisions such as marriage and career, equality, rationality in the social sphere, and self-reflection) were stressed through education. To the extent that these values are imbibed, and they certainly seem to be to varying extents by youth, identity conflicts easily occur. Western values around individualism and egalitarianism are a profound antithesis to traditional Japanese values of *on* and *giri* in hierarchical relationships and, therefore, to a more traditionally oriented ego-ideal. By report, Japanese psychoanalysts who have trained abroad have had a decidedly more difficult time reconnecting to the indirection and innuendo of Japanese ways as well as to the rigorous social etiquette of hierarchical relationships than Indian analysts who have returned home. On an emotional level, a Western life-style and modes of relating contrast more for Japanese than for Indians.

As related to the modernization process, it is by now apparent that many facets of the familial self of both Indians and Japanese lend themselves well to it, but in somewhat different ways. The Indian inclination for psychological contextualization of every situation has enabled Indians to work well in modern, industrialized settings in a lifestyle that may be very different from that at home without any inner conflict (Roland 1988, 94–97; Singer 1972). New situations are constantly being contextualized by Indians, not infrequently through the use of traditional myths.

Whereas in Japan, the extension of familialistic hierarchical principles of relating in the work group from the original, that is, occupational household, has resulted in the familial self being able to function extremely well in the modernization process. In both India and Japan, the motivation to achieve is an integral part of the familial self to reflect well on family and group, in contrast to a Western individualized self with its emphasis on independence, mastery, and the self-creation of its own identity. Japanese achievement motivation and the Japanese ego-ideal for standards of skill and performance are, in general, much higher than in most Indians. I have encountered in Japanese in therapy a much greater fear of failure and a constant inner tension to perform everything extremely well than is present in Indian patients—though some of the Indians I have worked with are unusually creative. One hypothesis is that these extremely high standards are related to aesthetic ideals of perfection (Yasuhiko Taketomo, personal communication). In any case, it seems clear that they result from the incorporation of maternal expectations: in one case it was a man's mother, in another a woman's grandmother who ruled the family roost.

The modernization process in Japan with its extremely high inner standards in the Japanese self has not been without its price. The development of the *shinkeishitsu*-personality syndrome characterized by perfectionistic ideals, compulsive rituals, and social withdrawal—first described and treated by Professor Morita, a Japanese psychiatrist— was due to a clash of value systems and ego-ideals between the older values of harmony and cooperation in the work group, and newer values fostered by the Meiji Restoration and implemented in the educational system for competitive achievement (Takeo Doi, Akihisa Kondo, and Masahisa Nishizono, personal communication). More recently, another form of psychopathology idiosyncratic to the Japanese has arisen: parent abuse, where teenage boys may beat up their mothers. This, too, is related to the high maternal expectations for performance in a traditional relationship of dependency, but in the context of the boy usually doing poorly or failing in school. In India, too, the clash between more traditional ideals of group harmony and cooperation and modernizing educational ideals of competitive achievement has also generated considerable inner conflict at times; but it is without the symptomotology of Japanese, since Indians do not have perfectionistic ideals.

Westernization and modernization in both India and Japan have also brought about definite psychological changes in the self, what I have come to term "individualization." With individualization, there is greater choice in marriage, schooling, and career, with somewhat greater scope for personal identity in family and group relationships. The wishes and inclinations of adolescents are given more recognition.

While this is, on the whole, a benign process that is being gradually integrated into the functioning of a familial self, emotional conflicts not infrequently occur between the increasing individualization and traditional expectations. They may take many forms such as a wish for greater self-determination at a point when expectations from superiors start taking over or simply a partial ignoring of the social etiquette of traditional hierarchical relationships.

My definite impression is that Indians have decidedly less conflict in the area of individualization than do Japanese. The historical exposure to two centuries of British influence and the greater overt individuality that Hindu culture fosters have made it easier for Indians to individualize. Moreover, their postindependence experience has been one where there is a large emigration of the urban educated elite to various Western countries. This group is constantly returning to visit every year or two, while having family members visit them, thus furthering the individualization process.

Whereas individualization did not really occur in Japan until the occupation, when abrupt changes were implemented from above: a legal undermining of the male hierarchy, a breaking up of the *ie* stem family, guaranteeing various rights for women, including marital choice and democratization and universal suffrage. Even now, the more individualized time of a man's life tends to occur in college, where there is a partial moratorium between the stresses of the high school examination system and engrossment in the hierarchical relationships of the work group. It is furthermore clear that affluence contributes not to greater individualization but rather to the incorporation of Western values. It will be interesting to see the eventual psychological effects on many Japanese who are now working in business in Western countries once they return home.

Individualization has significantly occurred in the women's sphere in both India and Japan. In India, women gained considerably more rights with the national movement and independence, whereas in Japan this occurred with the American occupation. In both societies, an increasingly large number of urban women in particular are being college educated, with some going on to graduate and professional schools, especially in India. There is now more of a choice of marital partner than in the traditional forms of arranged marriage that was common to both; in Japan, since the occupation, there is even greater emphasis on individual choice.

There is, however, a significant difference between educated Indian and Japanese women in the actualities of combining a family with a career—differences stemming not only from their social patterns but also from cultural values internalized into the self. A number of educated Indian women from the middle and upper-middle classes, usually upper caste, both at home and abroad combine career and motherhood. Whereas very few Japanese educated women combine family with career, although this is changing somewhat, the overwhelming majority opting for family with a few for career—reminiscent of America before the women's movement. What accounts for this considerable difference when educational levels are similar and there are at least some positions in the workplace for a highly educated, well-trained woman?

To have a career, an Indian woman depends overwhelmingly on her family culture and in part on *jati* (caste) norms, where the family determines whether daughters as well as sons will have an advanced education and a career. In these cases from my psychoanalytic experience, there will be as high expectations for daughters as for sons. In one instance, a father was sorely disappointed that his daughter just missed by two points attaining distinction on the Cambridge Examination—which would have put her in the top two students in her state that year—even though she did considerably better than her older brothers. Another Indian woman I know socially has recently won a very major literary award. She comes from a family where her father was just below Nobel prize consideration as a scientist and clearly wanted his daughter to fulfill his own ambitions. If the family does not have expectations for a career for their daughters, it is extremely difficult for an Indian woman to have one—in some contrast to American women today.

When a family has these expectations for its daughters, it will usually arrange a marriage where it is clearly understood by the prospective husband and in-laws that she will have a career. One young woman requested her parents to find a prospective bridegroom from their general caste background who was a physician trained in the United States: a physician so he would be quite occupied and wouldn't mind her having her own career, and trained in America so he would be used to American women and could accept her as a more openly assertive and outspoken wife than is characteristic of most Indian women. Three suitable prospects were found.

Assuming adequate child care is present through either extended family members or servants, she can then have a high-level career and raise her children with far less emotional conflict than many American women who combine career and motherhood. For an Indian woman pursuing a career and having children are both essentially family endeavors, where earnings and status clearly reflect on family reputation, however much satisfaction she may personally gain from her work. Moreover, she can easily contextualize her work setting from family without having to have the inner consistency of an integrated self that Westerners tend to have. Career and family thus pose little internal conflict for these Indian women I have seen in therapy. It is noteworthy that one group of women in Rajput went in one generation from purdah to having advanced degrees and careers when their community needed it after independence (Mehta 1976). On the other hand, if child care is not available, an Indian woman will be under considerable duress, as hierarchical expectations of most Indian husbands are that the wife will take care of home and children.

My impression is that one key factor in educated Japanese women not combining careers with family is the Japanese cultural ideal internalized into the self that one should be thoroughly involved in and committed to one group only. Since family is considered a career, to have a high-level job as well would mean having two careers. And indeed those couples where the wives do have a work career are termed "four-career family." Otherwise, the typical educated Japanese middle-class woman works for a few years after college in a lower-level job and then marries and becomes totally involved in the raising of her children and running her household, participating in various voluntary organizations as the children get older. Only in the last several years have some of these women combined career and family or considered careers when their children reached college age.

However much individualization has occurred in India and Japan, the encounter with the American life-style by Indians and Japanese who are settling in the United States is of a whole other order. Working with both Japanese and Indian patients as well as having discussions with others sheds considerable light on their adaptation here and the nature of their selves as they interact with American culture and society. There is much in the Indian and Japanese selves that enables the person to adapt successfully in the United States; but differences in modes of relatedness and overall values may make the experience extremely distressful at times.

Since emotional conflict and duress are usually more readily apparent and discussed, I would first like to stress the adaptive nature of the self. Both Indians and Japanese are extremely sensitive to group norms and quickly pick up the cues in a nonverbal way. Thus, upon entering an American university or working on a job, Indians and Japanese rather quickly learn what is expected of them. Indians, moreover, easily contextualize one setting from another so the dissonance between American ways of doing things and Indian ways is reduced. Japanese, on the other hand, with very high standards of performance, are usually greatly appreciated.

Problems arise when the values and modes of relating are drastically different. The Indian and Japanese values of modesty, self-effacement, and deference to hierarchical superiors are often experienced by Americans as passivity and ineffectuality. A much more openly assertive and competitive stance is the norm in current American society. Thus, an Indian woman, Veena, running for president of a large graduate school student body on Gandhian principles of service and self-effacement was appalled by her opponent's (an American woman) aggressive, self-serving campaign. The latter was elected, as the American student body perceived Veena's stance as being ineffectual.

In the same vein, a Japanese woman, Yoshiko, working in an American firm found it extremely difficult to bargain with clients in the openly aggressive manner that was called for. It went completely against the grain of the politeness, modesty, and communication by innuendo with which she was raised and in keeping with which she ordinarily functioned. Paradoxically, it is of note to mention that Yoshiko had purposefully chosen to work for an American firm rather than a Japanese one in New York City because she had already become too individualized in an American graduate school setting and marriage to be able to comply with the normal deferential requirements for a woman in Japanese group hierarchical relationships. At the point in therapy that I saw Yoshiko, she was caught between two cultures in her work functioning: too individualized to work easily in a Japanese hierarchical setting and too traditionally Japanese to function without emotional distress in American competitive business ways.

Yoshiko's Japanese makeup also engendered other problems at work that caused her considerable mental anguish. On one hand, her high standards of performance made her a particularly valuable employee. Both Yoshiko and a male Japanese patient have commented more than once that Americans tend to be quite inefficient compared to Japanese. On the other hand, at a point when she made an inevitable mistake—far fewer by report than her coworkers—she was reprimanded in such an explicit way that she suffered for the next couple of days. Her inner standards were so strict that only a casual indication that a mistake was made would be more than enough for her never to commit such an error again. The boss's criticism that easily rolled off of her coworkers like water off of a duck's back stung her to the quick.

In the classroom, American values call for much more discussion and expression of individual views, even when the person may not know the subject matter well, in order that the person be able to think for himself or herself. This contrasts sharply with Indians and Japanese, who remain far more deferential of the teacher as a hierarchical superior and seem mainly interested in imbibing the subject matter. This deference may then be taken by Americans as passivity.

Further tensions may occur both in a university or work setting when Indians and Japanese expect a greater involvement and nurturance on the professor's or boss's part than is usually characteristic in American-style hierarchical relationships.

It is not only in the workplace and classroom that drastic clashes between American values and modes of relating and Indian and Japanese ones occur. It is frequently in intimacy relationships as well. Japanese seem to suffer even more than Indians in the lack of group intimacy relationships characteristic of American life. One Japanese filmmaker expressed the intense emotional void one faces upon settling in America—though it offers her far more opportunity for individualistic, creative expression; while a Japanese graduate student commented on the general lack of sympathetic understanding (*omoiyari*) in American relationships that is characteristic of Japanese ones.

Indians I have had in therapy or interviewed also comment on the lack of closeness, involvement, and empathic resonance in American-style relationships. They have by now, however, a relatively large Indian community in the United States with whom they can socialize and fall back on, as well as being able to easily visit India or having family or friends visit them in America. Japanese, on the other hand, who choose to settle in America can feel quite isolated as they are not accepted by the increasingly large Japanese business community; nor are they easily able to shuttle back and forth home as Indians can. One still tends to be either in or out of Japanese society.

There is still another facet of the self that is of great import in the way Indians and Japanese adapt to American social life: their notions and social patterns of insider and outsider relationships. While both cultures have insider and outsider social patterns, the ways they are implemented, especially outsider ones, are considerably different. Japanese are much more restrained both in verbal communication and in dependency requests in outsider relationships than are Indians. Japanese will not ask much of another until the relationship becomes an insider one. This can make friendships somewhat more difficult to attain in America, where the social pattern is of an easy surface friendliness with much less of an insider dependency relationship. However, it is also clear that Americans greatly respect Japanese emotional restraint in these outsider relationships.

Indians, on the other hand, are constantly reaching out in their outsider relationships to transform them as quickly as possible to more intimate, insider ones. Outsiders are incorporated into the extended family in a way that is not characteristic of Japanese. I have found that if one is on the same wavelength, it can literally take minutes to begin talking on an intimate level; whereas with Japanese, it usually takes several meetings. This probing for intimacy that Indians do is a double-edged sword in an American setting. On one hand, it facilitates encounters with Americans and the possibility of friendships. On the other hand, Americans usually experience the requests that are part of Indian intimacy strivings as an affront to their autonomy and can become quite annoyed at it.

I had once introduced a well-qualified Indian young man, Sunil, who had recently come to the United States and was looking for a job, to a friend, Carl, who had a high position in an American corporation. Carl reported to me soon after they met that he really liked Sunil and was on the lookout for him for a suitable position; but a couple of months later, he was quite annoyed because Sunil kept calling him every several days. For Sunil, this was proper intimacy behavior because I was a good friend of the family and had introduced him to one of my friends; for Carl it gradually became an annoying imposition. Japanese who also encounter this totally different outsider pattern in Indians have expressed to me their not knowing how to handle it as well as some irritation. Japanese are also bothered by Indians being far less restrained in talking in these outsider relationships.

Hierarchical Relationships and the Indian-Japanese Familial Self

Since there are such apparent differences in Indians and Japanese in their behavior in outsider relationships, and since the difference in inner standards of performance are also so obvious, the tendency is to perceive each to be remarkably different from the other. Indeed, Japanese see themselves as being unique, and certainly Indians also perceive themselves as being considerably different from others.

Some years ago before I worked in Japan, when I presented various facets of the Indian familial self before a couple of Japanese psychoanalysts, Masahisa Nishizono and Mikihachiro Tatara, they remarked on the close similarities to the Japanese self. There are indeed remarkable similarities in various facets of the familial self of both and in the related psychosocial dimensions of their family and group hierarchical relationships—although these are often in different measure and balance. Since the familial self can be understood only by the nature of these hierarchical relationships, I shall briefly discuss the latter first.

As I have discussed at greater length (Roland 1988, 212–23), there are three common psychosocial dimensions of hierarchical relationships in both India and Japan—and, I certainly suspect, in China as well. The first, which I term "structural hierarchy," is the one most studied by social scientists. It has its own formal social etiquette with

reciprocal obligations, attitudes of deference and loyalty by the subordinate or junior, and nurturance and responsibility by the superior
or senior. This kind of hierarchy, patterned by neo-Confucian codes in
Japan and those of Manu in India, goes more by seniority, male-sibling
order, and gender differences, with females being subordinate to
males. There is little question that Japanese observe the social etiquette
of the structural hierarchy in a more disciplined, rigorous way than
Indians.

The second psychosocial dimension encompasses intimacy relationships, what I have termed the "qualitative mode." It is integrally
related to Francis L. K. Hsu's (1963, 1971) quality of hierarchical intimacy relationships, Takeo Doi's (1973) exposition of *amae*, and
Sudhir Kakar's (1978) dependency relationships in India. In both India
and Japan, persons will constantly sense the degree of intimacy they
have with the other, the nature of the formal hierarchy, and the kinds
of balances between them. Family and group relationships are always
governed by a highly complex interaction between structure and
intimacy in hierarchical relationships. Thus, a young wife in both
societies will in her early years of marriage be governed mainly by formal hierarchical considerations with her mother-in-law; but after the
younger woman has children, the degree of intimacy that develops between these two women usually becomes quite strong. Communication is often governed by these different hierarchical considerations:
the verbal communication often fulfilling formal social etiquette, the
nonverbal with its exchange of affect often fulfilling the intimacy
relationship.

The third psychosocial dimension Indians and Japanese have in
common is hierarchy by the quality of the person; that is, the distinction they make between who is truly a superior person versus who is
superior in the structural hierarchy, the two either coinciding or being
different. Thus, a wife or servant is lower in the formal hierarchy but
might well be looked up to as being the superior person. Where attitudes of deference or respect are central in the structural hierarchy,
veneration is present in hierarchy by quality.

The familial selves of Indians and Japanese are integrally related
to these three dimensions of their family and group hierarchical relationships (Roland 1988, 223–87). Closely related to structural hierarchical considerations is the conscience, or ego-ideal and superego, of
Indians and Japanese. They differ in nature from that of Westerners
and tend to have much in common structurally with each other. In
each, there is a strong inculcation of reciprocal obligations and responsibilities between subordinate and superior, with the nature of the re-
ciprocities varying considerably from one hierarchical relationship to

another, from one situation to another. The ego-ideal for proper behavior is far more contextual or situational than is present in Westerners, even in Western women (Gilligan 1980). The great difference between the Indian and Japanese conscience is that the latter is far stricter, has higher standards of performance, and emphasizes the will more in values of endurance, persistence, and restraint. It is this difference in conscience that so accounts for the differing modes of outsider relationships.

Another major facet of the familial self related to all three kinds of hierarchical relationships is that of narcissism or self-esteem, what is now termed in psychoanalysis, "selfobject relationships." Idealizations of superiors are culturally emphasized in both India and Japan in the structural hierarchy, but especially so in hierarchy by quality. In India, the superior person is one of spiritual endowments or godlike qualities; in Japan, it is more the mature or natural man. By idealizing and identifying with such persons, the esteem of the subordinate is thus enhanced and the self becomes partially transformed. Moreover, there is emphasis in both societies on constant empathic resonance between superior and subordinate, each enhancing the other's esteem and being sensitive not to hurt it. Preserving face is the more popular notion related to this.

Related to hierarchical intimacy relationships are various facets of the familial self that I have termed "symbiosis-reciprocity," in contrast to the Western stress on separation-individuation. The experiential sense of self in both Indians and Japanese is much more of a we-self than the individualistic I-self of Westerners, a we-self that varies more with relationships. That is, persons are always experiencing their close relationships in their own sense of who they are, the we-self being integrally related to the reputation of both family and group as well as specific others in hierarchical relationships.

Outer ego boundaries between self and other are much more permeable than in Westerners, with some tendency to partially merge with others; whereas each has a kind of inner ego boundary to preserve a private self of feelings, thoughts, and fantasies that form a reservoir of individuality that is not to be intruded upon, and which is quite different from that of most Westerners. The measure of these two boundaries does differ between Indians and Japanese: the latter tend more toward merger in the group in their outer boundary, while preserving a more secretive, private self that is usually only communicated by innuendo. With regard to an innermost ego boundary that is in contact with fantasies, wishes, feelings, and impulses, Indians tend to be much more in touch with these than Japanese and even, I sense, than most Westerners. Again this is related to issues of conscience, the stricter conscience of Japanese making it more difficult to be in touch with themselves.

Another facet of the familial self related to intimacy relationships is the tremendous dependency and interdependence in insider relationships in both India and Japan. Frequently this is subtly tied in with issues of esteem where the dependency requests of the subordinate is actually a giving to the superior, as it enhances the latter's self-esteem by acknowledging the latter's superior position and reinforces the superior's ego-ideal as the one who can give (Moses Burg and B. K. Ramanujam, personal communication).

Individuality in both Indians and Japanese is maintained not only in the private world of the private self; it also surfaces in subtle personal styles of fulfilling the formal social etiquette. Culturally, individuality is cultivated and enhanced by the notions of the particularization of a person's intrinsic self—in India by philosophical concepts recognizing a person's inclinations from past births and having different qualities, or *gunas*, in Japan by the concept of '*hare*', or the inborn inclinations of the self. There is a careful balance maintained in both cultures between the observance of social etiquette and the cultivation of individuality. Indians have a greater scope for a more overt expression of individuality, being quite free to have whatever thought or opinion they want; whereas in Japan, adherence to the ideology and opinions of the group leader is more operative. The libidinal wishing, wanting self is also given more scope in Indians, who are freer to maneuver for what they want than are Japanese; on the other hand, there is the Townsman tradition in Japan that gives men time off from their rigorous responsibilities in the group hierarchies.

Developmental aspects of the familial self also have much in common in both societies. There is a strong emphasis on more symbiotic modes of mothering in both, cultivating the intense dependency-interdependency relationships with a nonverbal empathic sensing of others' moods, wishes, and esteem—but not particularly inclinations for autonomy. Sleeping arrangements are also relatively similar, with infants sleeping next to their mother until the next sibling is born, and then usually with another in the family—in marked contrast to current American norms. Around the ages of four or five there is a crackdown for proper behavior in formal hierarchical relationships. There is little of the *Sturm und Drang* of American adolescent rebellion in either society, the teenager remaining an integral member of the family and school group. Considerable anxiety is engendered if anger is to be expressed toward any superior—an integral part of the superego in both societies—fearing that the nurturing side of the relationship will be jeopardized.

The major difference in the development of the conscience is that Japanese mothers inculcate high standards of performance from an early age, children feeling guilty if they let their mother down, since she is so self-sacrificing (DeVos 1973). But there can also be intense feelings of resentment and entitlement if things should go awry and the child is not doing well: mother is out of touch with him and has let him down.

The nature of the Oedipus complex is also relatively similar, at least as compared to Westerners. There is little intergenerational conflict between son and father, as the son has a close relationship with the mother throughout life. Instead, sons have a profound need for the father—who usually remains overtly distant as a restrained authority figure—to rescue the son from a maternal symbiosis (Kakar 1980) and a fear that the father will be jealous of the lifelong mother-son relationship. Indeed, in Indian mythology it is the father who frequently harms the son out of jealousy, not vice versa. This is a complete turnaround from the Oedipus myth where the father's jealousy is a subsidiary theme.

There is also much in common in psychopathology where there is considerable somatization of unacceptable feelings, particularly ambivalent ones. Since angry feelings must be contained in the close-knit family and group hierarchical relationships from which there is no exit, if relationships are too stressful, then a variety of psychological symptoms may result. Again, there can be a different flavor to the problems in the Japanese because of the strict conscience.

The Spiritual Self in Indians and Japanese

Without touching upon issues of the spiritual self, no paper would even begin to do justice to Indians and Japanese. Longstanding cultural traditions give meaning to everyday relationships in the transformation of the self to a spiritual being—in contrast to the dominant psychology of the West as the self-creation of one's identity. There are a number of different modes toward this transformation in Indian and Japanese society, some overlapping, some being differently oriented.

In both cultures, transformation takes place as one tries to associate as closely as possible and identify with a superior person in a hierarchy by quality. Transformation into more refined qualities is also given meaning through the numerous exchanges and gifts. There are some similarities, too, in both societies in the use of myths, the myth orienting the person not only to complex everyday relationships but also to the interlinking of the transcendent with the mundane. Rituals, too, are used for purposes of self-transformation as well as for attaining mundane ends. Still another cultural area that links the spiritual with the everyday in the sense of personal destiny is the magic-cosmic world of astrology, palmistry, the spirits, divination, and such. For the Japanese, the meaning in which work is performed can also be viewed in terms of self-transformation.

Then there are various specific spiritual disciplines in both India and Japan, some of which, such as various forms of meditation, devotional practices, and prayer, clearly overlap. My impression is that the Japanese with a Taoist tradition from China rely much more on being in nature and on using various aesthetic disciplines such as tea ceremony, flower arranging, and calligraphy. Counterpointing this are some of the martial arts, which can also be used for cultivating the spiritual self.

Indians, on the other hand, tend to particularize the specific spiritual discipline somewhat more to the person, where members of the same household may be worshiping different gods and goddesses or using different mantras in their meditation. They also seem to have a greater variety of different meditative and devotional practices and perhaps to have the spiritual dimension as a more central part of their culture and psychology.

BIBLIOGRAPHY

DeVos, G. 1973. *Socialization for Achievement*. Berkeley and Los Angeles: University of California Press.

Doi, T. 1973. *The Anatomy of Dependence*. Tokyo: Kodansha.

Erikson, E. [1946] 1959. "Ego Development and Historical change." In *Identity and the Life Cycle*. Reprint. New York: International Universities Press.

———. 1958. *Young Man Luther*. New York: Norton.

———. 1969. *Gandhi's truth*. New York: Norton.

Gilligan, C. 1980. *In a Different Voice*. Cambridge: Harvard University Press.

Hsu, F.L.K. 1963. *Clan, Caste and Club*. Princeton: Van Nostrand.

———. 1971. "Psychological Homeostasis and *Jen*: Conceptual Tools for Advancing Psychological Anthropology." *American Anthropologist* 73:23–44.

Kakar, S. 1978. *The Inner World: A Psychoanalytic Study of Childhood and Society in India*. Delhi: Oxford University Press.

Kakar, S., ed. 1979. *Identity and Adulthood*. Delhi: Oxford University Press.

Mehta, R. 1970. *The Western Educated Hindu Woman*. Bombay: Asia Publishing House.

Mehta, R. 1976. "From Purdah to Modernity." In *Indian Women: From Purdah to Modernity*, ed. B. R. Nanda, 113–28. New Delhi: Vikas.

Menaker, E., and W. Menaker. 1965. *Ego in Evolution*. New York: Grove Press.

Nishizono, M. "Problems Imposed on Psychotherapeutic Intervention in Traditional Milieux—Acculturation in Japan and Psychotherapy." Unpublished paper.

Okonogi, K. 1978. "The *Ajase* Complex of the Japanese (1): the Depth Psychology of the Moratorium People." *Japan Echo* 5:17–39.

———. 1979. "The *Ajase* Complex of the Japanese (2)." *Japan Echo*. 6:104–18.

Ramanujam, B. K. 1979. "Toward Maturity: Problems of Identity Seen in the Indian Clinical Setting." In *Identity and Adulthood*, ed. S. Kakar, 37–55, Delhi: Oxford University Press.

———. 1980a. "Technical Factors in Psychotherapy in India." Unpublished paper.

———. 1980b. "Odyssey of an Indian Villager: Mythic Orientations in Psychotherapy." Unpublished paper.

———. 1981a. "The Importance of Fathers: An Overview of Indian Cases." Unpublished paper.

———. 1981b. "Response to Change: Adaptive and Pathological Seen in a Clinical Set-up in India." Unpublished paper.

———. 1986. "Social Change and Personal Crisis: A View from an Indian Practice." In *The Cultural Transitions, Human Experience and Social Transformation in the Third World and Japan*, ed. M. White and S. Pollak. London: Routledge & Kegan Paul.

Rank, O. 1932. *Art and the Artist*. New York: Knopf.

Roland, A. 1988. *In Search of Self in India and Japan: Toward a Cross-cultural Psychology*. Princeton: Princeton University Press.

Singer Milton. 1972. *When a Great Tradition Modernizes: An Anthropological Approach to Indian Civilization*. New York: Praeger.

Walsh, J. 1982. *Growing up in British India*. New York: Holmes and Meier.

ROGER T. AMES received his Ph.D. in classical Chinese philosophical texts from the University of London. He is Professor of Philosophy at the University of Hawaii, and is Director of the Center for Chinese Studies. He is Editor of the journal of comparative philosophy, *Philosophy East & West*, and Executive Editor of *China Review International*. Professor Ames has published many books and articles in Chinese and comparative philosophy, including *The Art of Rulership* (1983), *Thinking Through Confucius* (with David Hall) (1987), and most recently, a new translation of *Sun-tzu: The Art of Warfare* (1993).

PADMASIRI DE SILVA has been a Senior Teaching Fellow in the Philosophy Department at the National University of Singapore. He was formerly Professor and Head of the Philosophy and Psychology Department at the University of Peradeniya in Sri Lanka. He is author of *An Introduction to Buddhist Psychology, Buddhist and Freudian Psychology, Tangles and Webs, Value Orientations and Nation Building*, and *Twin Peaks*, and editor of *Suicide in Sri Lanka* and *Environmental Ethics in Buddhism*.

WIMAL DISSANAYAKE is a Senior Fellow at the East-West Center in Honolulu, and in this capacity, was responsible for organizing and hosting the conferences which produced the trilogy of SUNY Press books on "the self": *Self as Body in Asian Theory and Practice* (1993), *Self as Person in Asian Theory and Practice* (1994), and *Self as Image in Asian Theory and Practice* (forthcoming). He is the author of several books on literature, cinema, and communication, six books of poetry, and is the Editor of *East-West Film Journal*. His most recent work (with Stephen Alter) is the *Penguin Book of Modern Indian Short Stories*.

DAVID L. HALL is Professor of Philosophy at the University of Texas at El Paso. He received a Bachelor of Divinity degree *summa cum laude* from the Chicago Theological Seminary and a Ph.D. in philosophy from Yale University. Professor Hall has written several books in the philosophy of culture and culture studies. He is the author (with Roger Ames) of *Thinking Through Confucius*. His most recent publications include a philosophical novel (*The Arimaspian Eye*), and a book on the philosophy of Richard Rorty. Professor Hall is the Managing Review Editor of *Philosophy East & West*.

YAMUNA KACHRU is Professor of Linguistics and of English as an International Language at the University of Illinois at Urbana-Champaign. Her research interests include syntax, semantics, and pragmatics of South Asian languages, especially Hindi; world varieties of English; cross-cultural pragmatics; constrastive analysis; second language acquisition; translation; interface of language and literature; and bilingual lexicography. Professor Kachru has authored five books, edited or co-edited six volumes, and published more that seventy chapters and papers in these areas.

THOMAS P. KASULIS is Professor of Comparative Studies in the Humanities at The Ohio State University. He has been a Numata Visiting Professor in Buddhism at the University of Chicago, a Japan Foundation Fellow at Osaka University, and Mellon Faculty Fellow at Harvard. He is the author of *Zen Action/Zen Person*, and the editor and co-translator of *The Body: Toward an Eastern Mind-Body Theory*.

TAKIE SUGIYAMA LEBRA, a native Japanese and naturalized American, received her Ph.D. from the University of Pittsburgh. Since 1978 she has been Professor of Anthropology at the University of Hawaii. Professor Lebra has published several books including *Japanese Patterns of Behavior* (1976), *Japanese Women: Constraint and Fulfillment* (1984), and edited *Japanese Social Organization* (1992), all from the University of Hawaii Press. Most recently she authored *Above the Clouds: Status Culture of the Modern Japanese Nobility* (University of California Press, 1993).

JOHN C. MARALDO is Professor of Philosophy and Religion, University of North Florida, and has been Guest Professor, Kyoto University 1987–88. He authored *Der hermeneutische Zirkel: Untersuchungen zu Schleiermacher, Dilthey, Heidegger*, co-authored *The Piety of Thinking: Essays of Martin Heidegger*, co-edited *Buddhism in the Modern World*, and has published extensively on contemporary Japanese philosophy, Nishida, Zen Buddhism, and the theory of religion in journals, anthologies, and encyclopedias. Professor Maraldo has also published translations of works on Zen and Buddhist-Christian dialogue.

BIMAL KRISHNA MATILAL held the Spalding Chair of Eastern Religion and Ethics at All Souls College, Oxford, where he taught until his untimely death in 1991. He was the author of many books in Indian philosophy, including *The Navya-Nyāya Doctrine of Negation*, *Perception*, *The Word and the World*, and many scholarly articles spanning a broad field of interests: Buddhist logic, Bhartṛhari's philosophy of grammar, Jainism, ancient skepticism, and mysticism. He was also the Editor of the *Journal of Indian Philosophy*, and held teaching positions around the world.

MATTISON MINES is Professor of Anthropology at the University of California, Santa Barbara. He has conducted field research in several locations in Tamil Nadu, India, and is the author of *Muslim Merchants: The Economic Behaviour of an Indian Muslim Community* (Shri Ram Centre for Industrial Relations and Human Resources, New Delhi: 1972), *The Warrior Merchants: Textiles, Trade, and Territory in South India* (Cambridge: 1994), and *Public Faces—Private Voices: Community and Individuality in South India* (California: forthcoming).

DIANE B. OBENCHAIN is a Teaching Fellow in the Department of Philosophy, National University of Singapore, where she teaches courses on Chinese philosophy. She is on leave from her position as Associate Professor in the Department of Religion, Kenyon College. Having attended Drew University and Stanford, she received her Ph.D. in Comparative Religion from Harvard. Professor Obenchain has taught at Waseda and Peking Universities, and was a Research Fellow at the Institute of East Asian Philosophies in Singapore.

ALAN ROLAND, Ph.D. is a practicing psychoanalyst in New York City. He spent ten months in India on grants from the American Institute of Indian Studies doing clinical psychoanalytic research, and two months in Japan on the same project. He has published this research in a book, *In Search of Self in Indian and Japan: Toward a Cross-Cultural Psychology* (Princeton University Press), as well as in fifteen articles in journals and books. He is also editor and contributor to *Psychoanalysis, Creativity, and Literature: A French-American Dialogue* (Columbia, 1978), and (with Barbara Harris) *Career and Motherhood: Struggles for a New Identity* (Human Sciences 1978).

AMÉLIE OKSENBERG RORTY is Professor of Philosophy at Mt. Holyoke, presently visiting at the Harvard Graduate School of Education. She is the author of *Mind in Action* (Beacon, 1988) and numerous essays on the history of moral psychology and the philosophy of mind. She also edited *The Identities of Persons* (University of California, 1976), *Explaining Emotions* (University of California, 1980) and (with Owen Flanagan), *Identity, Character and Morality* (MIT, 1990). She is preparing *Essays on Aristotle's Rhetoric* for the University of California.

ROBERT C. SOLOMON is Quincy Lee Centennial Professor at the University of Texas at Austin. He is the author of *From Rationalism to Existentialism, The Passions, In the Spirit of Hegel, From Hegel to Existentialism, About Love* and *A Passion for Justice*. He is also editor (with Kathleen M. Higgins) of *From Africa to Zen: An Invitation to World Philosophy*.

TU WEI-MING is professor of Chinese History and Philosophy at Harvard University, and a fellow of the American Academy of Arts and Sciences. He is the author of *Humanity and Self-Cultivation: Essays in Confucian Thought, Confucian Thought: Self as Creative Transformation* (SUNY 1985), *Way, Learning, and Politics* (SUNY 1993), and scores of articles on Confucian philosophy in both English and Chinese.

MARGERY WOLF is Professor of Anthropology and of Women's Studies at the University of Iowa. She is the author of *The House of Lim, Women and the Family in Rural Taiwan, Revolution Postponed,* and *A Thrice Told Tale: Feminism, Postmodernism, and Ethnographic Responsibility*. She is currently working on a historical ethnography of an area in northern California and a cross-cultural study of violence against women.

DAVID YEN-HO WU holds his Ph.D. in Anthropology from Australian National University, and is a Senior Fellow at the East-West Center in Honolulu. He has written, co-authored, or edited books on *Preschool in Three Cultures: Japan, China, and the U.S.* (with J. Tobin and D. Davidson) (Yale 1989), *Chinese Culture and Mental Health* (with W. S. Tseng) (Academic Press, 1985), *Ethnicity and Interpersonal Interaction* (Maruzen Asia, 1982), and *The Chinese in Papua New Guinea: 1880–1980* (Chinese University, 1982).

Index